Assessing Impact

Assessing Impact

Handbook of EIA and SEA Follow-up

Edited by
Angus Morrison-Saunders
and
Jos Arts

EARTHSCAN

London • Sterling, VA

First published by Earthscan in the UK and USA in 2004 and in paperback in 2006

ISBN-10: 1-84407-139-1 (hardback)
1-84407-337-8 (paperback)
ISBN-13: 978-1-84407-139-5 (hardback)
978-1-84407-337-5 (hardback)

Typesetting by JS Typesetting Ltd, Porthcawl, Mid Glamorgan
Printed and bound in the UK by Cromwell Press, Trowbridge
Cover design by Danny Gillespie

For a full list of publications please contact:

Earthscan
8–12 Camden High Street
London, NW1 0JH, UK
Tel: +44 (0)20 7387 8558
Fax: +44 (0)20 7387 8998
Email: earthinfo@earthscan.co.uk
Web: **www.earthscan.co.uk**

22883 Quicksilver Drive, Sterling, VA 20166-2012, USA

Earthscan publishes in association with WWF-UK and the International Institute for
Environment and Development

A catalogue record for this book is available from the British Library

Library of Congress Cataloging-in-Publication Data

Assessing impact : handbook of EIA and SEA follow-up / edited by Angus Morrison-
Saunders and Jos Arts.
        p. cm.
    Includes bibliographical references and index.
    ISBN-13: 978-1-84407-337-5 (pbk.)
    ISBN-10: 1-84407-337-8 (pbk.)
    1. Environmental impact analysis. I. Morrison-Saunders, Angus, 1966- II. Arts,
Jos.
    TD194.6.A875 2006
    333.71'4–dc

                                                                2006002664

Printed on elemental chlorine-free paper

Contents

List of Figures, Tables and Boxes

Figures

Tables

Boxes

List of Acronyms and Abbreviations

ACE	Advisory Council on the Environment (Hong Kong)
AEMP	Aquatic Effects Monitoring Programme (Canada)
BACI	before-after-control-impact study design
BDIV	Policy Plan on Drinking Water Supply (The Netherlands)
BHP	Broken Hill Pty Ltd
BHPB	BHP Billiton Diamonds Inc
BOD	biological oxygen demand
CBP	Columbia Basin Project (US)
CEA	cumulative effects assessment
CEAA	Canadian Environmental Assessment Agency or Act
CEARC	Canadian Environmental Assessment Research Council
CEC	Commission of the European Community
CEE	control of environmental effects (document)
CEQ	Council on Environmental Quality (US)
CHP	combined heat and power (plant)
CSIR	Council for Scientific and Industrial Research (South Africa)
CSO	Adviesbureau voor milieuonderzoek (The Netherlands)
DB	design and build
DCE	Department of Conservation and Environment (Western Australia)
DEP	Department of Environmental Protection (Western Australia)
DETR	Department of the Environment, Transports and the Regions (UK)
DMB	decision-making bodies (UK)
EA	environmental assessment
EARP	environmental assessment and review process (Canada)
EC	European Commission
ECW	Evaluation Committee *Environmental Management Act* (The Netherlands)
EEC	European Economic Commission
EIS	Environmental Impact Statement
EIA	Environmental Impact Assessment
EIAO	Environmental Impact Assessment Ordinance (Hong Kong)
EM&A	Environmental Monitoring and Audit (Hong Kong)

EMA	*Environmental Management Act* (The Netherlands)
EMP	environmental management programme or plan
EMS	Environmental Management System
ENPO	Environmental Project Office (Hong Kong)
EPA	Environmental Protection Authority (Western Australia)
EPD	Environmental Protection Department (Hong Kong)
ERM	Environmental Resources Management
ERMP	Environmental Review and Management Programme (Western Australia)
ESA	*Endangered Species Act* (US)
ESA	environmental sustainability assurance
ET	Environmental Team (Hong Kong)
EU	European Union
FMD	foot-and-mouth disease
GCD	Grand Coulee Dam (US)
GCFMP	Grand Coulee Fish Maintenance Programme (US)
GDP	gross domestic product
GIS	geographical information system
GNWT	Government of the Northwest Territories (Canada)
ha	hectares
HK	Hong Kong
HTML	hypertext markup language
IAIA	International Association for Impact Assessment
IEA	Institute of Environmental Assessment (UK)
IEC	Independent Environment Checker (Hong Kong)
IEMA	Independent Environmental Monitoring Agency (Canada)
IPPC	Integrated Pollution Prevention and Control Directive (EU, 1996)
ISO 14001	International Standards Organization series 14001
kV	kilovolts
LUA	Landesumweltamt (Land Environment Protection Agency, Germany)
MW	megawatts
NEPA	*National Environmental Policy Act* 1969 (US)
NFH	National Fish Hatchery (US)
NIMBY	'not in my back yard'
NMFS	National Marine Fisheries Services (US)
NPPC	Northwest Power Planning Council (US)
NRC	National Resource Council (US)
NWT	Northwest Territories (Canada)
OECD/DAC	Organization for Economic Cooperation and Development/ Development Cooperation Directorate
PDF	portable document format
PDO	Pacific decadal oscillation
PROAV	Provincial Waste Disposal Company South Holland (The Netherlands)

PZH	Province of South Holland (The Netherlands)
RIVM	National Institute for Public Health and the Environment (The Netherlands)
RAC	Regulatory Advisory Committee (Canada)
ROD	record of decision (US)
RPG	Regional Planning Guidance (UK)
RWS	Public Works Council (The Netherlands)
SEA	strategic environmental assessment
SIA	social impact assessment
SVVII	Second Transport Structure Plan (The Netherlands)
TMC	Transportation/EIA Centre (The Netherlands)
μg/litre	micrograms per litre
UK	United Kingdom
UN	United Nations
UNECE	United Nations Economic Commission for Europe
UNEP	United Nations Environment Programme
US	United States of America
USACE	United States Army Corp of Engineers
USBR	United States Bureau of Reclamation
USDOE	United States Department of Energy
V&W	Ministry of Transport, Public Works and Water Management (The Netherlands)
VROM	Ministry of Housing, Physical Planning and Environment (The Netherlands)
WSSD	World Summit on Sustainable Development

List of Contributors

Jos Arts
is Manager of the EIA/Transportation Centre of the Dutch Ministry of Transport, Public Works and Water Management. He is also part-time lecturer in environment and infrastructure planning at the University of Groningen, The Netherlands. Since completing a PhD on EIA follow-up at the University of Groningen in 1997, he has conducted international workshops and published in the field of EIA and infrastructure planning.

Elvis Au
is the Assistant Director of Hong Kong Environmental Protection Department, Hong Kong Special Administrative Region Government, in charge of the EIA and environmental monitoring and audit policy and legislation in Hong Kong. He is a former President of the International Association for Impact Assessment.

John Bailey
is an Associate Professor in the School of Environmental Science, Murdoch University, Western Australia. He is a former member of the Western Australian Environmental Protection Authority and is the current Chairman of the Conservation Commission of Western Australia.

Jill Baker
is an Environmental Assessment Officer with the Environmental Assessment Branch of Environment Canada. She is a member of the Board of Directors of the International Association of Impact Assessment (2004–2007) and has conducted workshops on EIA follow-up at IAIA and other conferences.

Thomas B. Fischer
is Senior Lecturer in the Department of Civic Design at University of Liverpool, UK. After working as a consultant and public servant on EIA in Germany from 1990 to 1995, he did a PhD in SEA in the UK. Since then, he has researched, trained and published extensively on SEA. Thomas is also chair of the SEA section of the International Association for Impact Assessment.

Simon Hui
is the Principal Environmental Protection Officer of Hong Kong Environmental Protection Department, Hong Kong Special Administrative Region Government, in charge of the EIA and environmental monitoring and audit policy and legislation in Hong Kong.

Bryan Jenkins
is Chief Executive of Environment, Canterbury, New Zealand. He was formerly the Chief Executive Officer of the Department of Environmental Protection, Western Australia.

Ross Marshall
is EIA Manager of the National Environmental Assessment Service of the Environment Agency of England and Wales, and a visiting Fellow in EIA and SEA at the University of Strathclyde, Scotland. He was formerly the Environment and Planning Manager for ScottishPower's Transmission and Distribution utility businesses. He has a PhD in EIA follow-up with an emphasis on the role of mitigation and self-regulation.

Christine L. May
is an Associate at Philip Williams and Associates, Consultants in Hydrology, in San Francisco, California. She has a PhD in Environmental Fluid Mechanics from the Department of Civil and Environmental Enginnering at Stanford University, California.

Johan Meijer
is Manager in charge of the implementation of the Water and Environment Policy Plan, Province of South Holland, The Netherlands. Formerly he was the provincial EIA Coordinator in the Province of South Holland, and responsible for the implementation of EIA and monitoring and evaluation (EIA follow-up).

Angus Morrison-Saunders
is Senior Lecturer in Environmental Assessment in the School of Environmental Science at Murdoch University, Western Australia. He has a PhD in EIA follow-up and has published extensively in this field. Other research interests include industry self-regulation and sustainability assessment.

Leonard Ortolano
is the UPS Foundation Professor of Civil Engineering at Stanford University in Stanford, California. Currently, he is also serving as the Peter E. Haas Director of Stanford's Haas Center for Public Service. He has researched and published extensively on EIA.

Maria Rosário Partidário
is Assistant Professor at the Department of Sciences and Environmental Engineering, New University of Lisbon, Portugal and also works as an international consultant in SEA, sustainable policy and planning. She has a PhD in SEA and is a former President of the International Association for Impact Assessment.

William A. Ross
is Professor of Environmental Science in the Faculty of Environmental Design, University of Calgary, Canada. His area of study is the professional practice of Environmental Impact Assessment with a focus on follow-up, cumulative effects and scoping. Bill has served on five environmental assessment panels in Canada, chairing one and has been a member of the Independent Environmental Monitoring Agency (the subject of his chapter) since its inception; he is now the chair of the Agency.

Barry Sadler
has been involved with EIA review and follow-up since 1972. He was editor of the first international review of this field in 1987 and directed the multi-country international study of the effectiveness of environmental assessment in 1996. Based in Victoria, BC, Canada, he is an adviser on EIA to a number of international organizations.

Preface

Citizens are increasingly concerned about the health of their environment. They expect their governments to protect the public good and look to them to set high standards for environmental protection. This is not to preclude allowing for economic development to improve standards of living but to approve developments in the context of avoiding or minimizing environmental degradation.

Environmental Impact Assessment (EIA) is a powerful tool that has been remarkably successful in allowing for the consideration of social, economic and environmental effects in the review of major project developments. Now into its fourth decade of application, EIA has evolved into an essential environmental management and decision-making instrument that is used throughout the world. Having grown steadily in use since early applications in the 1970s, the recognition of EIA at the Earth Summit in Rio de Janeiro in 1992 saw an explosion of EIA application worldwide. Today, EIA is used in over 100 countries, and many other types of impact assessment have evolved.

At the World Summit on Sustainable Development in Johannesburg in 2002 the key focus continued to be on sustainability. It is recognized that Strategic Environmental Assessment (SEA) is the next evolution in EIA, as we have seen a growing recognition that to move towards a truly sustainable society, environmental assessment has to be applied earlier than in the project planning phase. Even though EIA is an important instrument towards the goal of social and economic development in a sustainable fashion, it has one systemic weakness. To achieve sustainable outcomes the consequences of decisions taken must also be investigated, communicated and acted upon as necessary. This is where the weakness lies. The vital role of follow-up in EIA has not been systematically required or fully implemented.

Follow-up provides the missing link between EIA decision-making and continued project implementation. It is a key mechanism for feedback, learning from experience and adaptive management. Specifically, without some form of follow-up, the usefulness of EIA and the environmental outcomes of development activities will remain unknown.

To date the greatest emphasis in EIA texts has been placed on procedures, activities and techniques undertaken during EIA in the lead up to the principal decision to proceed with a proposal. Given that the actual environmental impacts and changes to the existing environment occur after the approval decision when proposals are actually implemented, it is surprising that few books have investigated this stage of EIA. Without examination of EIA follow-up, it is not possible to determine how successful the process is at protecting the environment or to demonstrate accountability for the process.

Recognition of the importance of the role of EIA follow-up was well established in Canada in the 1980s with a major conference in Banff. As part of the International Study on the Effectiveness of Environmental Assessment, practitioners from Hong Kong and Australia contributed further to development of the field in the 1990s. More recently, Environment Canada has sponsored seminars in Canada as well as a series of EIA follow-up workshops at the annual conferences of the International Association for Impact Assessment (IAIA). Having contributed to the start of these workshops and participated in them, it is wonderful for me to see that these workshops have attracted presenters from all over the world representing developed and developing countries alike. Currently, EIA follow-up is given special attention at international conferences and a network of practitioners is evolving. This book is a result of the collaboration and sharing of ideas through this emerging network.

The recent growing interest internationally in EIA follow-up has been accompanied by the development of new follow-up procedures and regulations in many countries and jurisdictions. Although follow-up has long been a focus of EIA practice, Canada formalized its commitment to EIA follow-up in 2002 with amendments to the *Canadian Environmental Assessment Act*, which makes follow-up a mandatory component of EIA practice. We will continue to participate and support the international exchange of knowledge and experiences with EIA follow-up.

This book is unique in bringing together an overview of the theory of EIA follow-up and practical insights into how it can be undertaken. It does this by showcasing examples of best practice EIA follow-up from leading countries around the world. Theoretical and legislative perspectives are examined in light of detailed case studies. Besides explaining the steps involved in EIA follow-up including various technical issues, the volume also discusses the roles of EIA regulators, private and governmental proponents and the affected public. In addition to undertaking a close examination of EIA follow-up practice at the project level, this book is the first to address how follow-up can be undertaken for SEA.

It also considers follow-up at different scales of application that extend beyond the individual project, plan or policy level. Through learning from experience, EIA practice within a particular country can be improved. At the next level up again, the collective knowledge and understanding gained from follow-up programmes can be used to evaluate the utility of fundamental EIA concepts and practices worldwide.

The final chapters deal with the future evolution of EIA and SEA follow-up. Three issues seem to be relevant for making the next steps:

- The further development of an international network to enhance a body of knowledge
- The formulation of guiding principles on EIA follow-up, which could be adopted by an international organization such as IAIA
- The further development of EIA and SEA follow-up into sustainability assurance.

I know this book will prove to be an invaluable reference and guide for EIA practitioners in industry, consultancies and regulatory agencies, as well as in the education and training sector. I sincerely hope this international handbook provides a solid foundation for the advancement of EIA follow-up theory and practice in the future.

Paula Caldwell
Director General, Environmental Protection Service
Environment Canada
July 2004

1

Introduction to EIA Follow-up

Angus Morrison-Saunders and Jos Arts

Introduction

Environmental Impact Assessment (EIA) is a process for taking account of
the potential environmental consequences of a proposed action during the
planning, design, decision-making and implementation stages of that action.
Follow-up should be an integral part of this process. From its origins under
the *National Environmental Policy Act* 1969 in the US, EIA procedures have
been widely adopted throughout the world. EIA can be undertaken at many
different jurisdictional levels including:

- local level (e.g. local government procedures)
- state or provincial level (e.g. state governments in the US, Canada and
  Australia have implemented their own EIA procedures)
- national or federal level (e.g. countrywide procedures)
- supranational or international level involving more than one country
  (e.g. European Community Directives for impact assessment that apply
  throughout the European Union).

As might be expected, EIA procedures vary considerably between jurisdictions
(a comparative review of various systems can be found in Wood, 2003).
However, a generic EIA process can be identified which consists of a series of
iterative steps (Box 1.1). Despite these generic steps indicating an established
role for follow-up, it remains the weakest stage in most jurisdictions where
EIA is practised.

Much of the considerable body of literature on how to conduct EIA
focuses on the lead up to the project consent decision by the appropriate
(usually government) EIA decision-making authority. EIA follow-up is more
concerned with events once approved actions are actually implemented. In

Box 1.1 Generic Steps in the EIA Process

The following generic steps in EIA can be distinguished (after Sadler, 1996).

Preliminary assessment

- *Screening* to establish whether EIA is required and the likely extent of process application
- *Scoping* to identify the key issues and impacts that need to be addressed and prepare terms of reference for EIA and proponent's Environmental Impact Statement (EIS).

Detailed assessment

- *Impact analysis* to identify, predict and evaluate the potential significance of risks, effects and consequences
- *Mitigation* to specify measures to prevent, minimize and offset or otherwise compensate for environmental loss and damage
- *Reporting* to document the results of EIA in an EIS, including recommended terms and conditions
- *EIS review* to ensure the report meets terms of reference and standards of good practice
- *Decision-making* to approve (or not) a proposal and establish terms and conditions (i.e. the consent decision).

Follow-up

- *Monitoring* to check that actions are in compliance with terms and conditions, and impacts are within the ranges predicted
- *Audit/evaluation* to compare the monitoring results with standards, predictions and expectations, to appraise and document the results, to learn from experience, and to improve EIA and project planning
- *Management* activities to address unforeseen events or unanticipated impacts.

a sense the term can be taken to mean 'follow-up to the consent decision'. The ultimate success of EIA is determined by the outcomes of proposals. In its simplest conception EIA follow-up seeks to understand EIA outcomes. Implicit in this process are activities such as checking, feedback, learning and communication.

In order to understand EIA outcomes, follow-up might address questions such as:

- How did the actual impacts of a project compare with the predictions made in the EIS?

- Were impacts mitigated and managed in accordance with approval conditions set by decision-makers?
- Is some additional action needed to prevent unacceptable environmental impacts?
- How effective was the EIA process itself?

To address questions such as these, EIA follow-up draws upon monitoring and auditing data. However, it involves more than just an analysis of such data and includes tasks such as evaluation, mitigation and management, and communication (reporting) of environmental outcomes. Clearly it is not enough to simply identify and investigate environmental protection options before decisions are made; it is equally important to monitor and evaluate what happens afterwards and to take corrective action when needed. This is the role of EIA follow-up. Without some form of follow-up, the consequences of EIA and the environmental outcomes of development activities will remain unknown.

Having introduced the concept of EIA follow-up, this chapter clarifies some important terminology, including a definition of follow-up and consideration of the different levels at which follow-up can be undertaken. The need for and importance of EIA follow-up are examined and a brief account of the historical evolution of EIA follow-up is provided. The contextual setting for follow-up, which determines the scope and effectiveness of EIA outcomes, is then explored. The chapter ends with some challenges for EIA follow-up and the overall book structure is explained.

What is EIA follow-up?

The term 'follow-up' has been in use for some time (e.g. Caldwell et al, 1982; McCallum, 1985, 1987) and is used here as an umbrella term for various EIA activities, including: monitoring, auditing, ex-post evaluation, post-decision analysis and post-decision management. These words are used quite loosely and overlap considerably, and so it is convenient to group them under the generic term of EIA follow-up.

When discussing follow-up, it is useful to divide the EIA process into two stages based around the principal consent decision for a proposal. The *pre-decision stage* incorporates the early components of EIA prior to proposal implementation (e.g. project planning, screening, scoping, impact prediction and mitigation design, extending through to the decision itself). Planning for EIA follow-up programmes is important when these pre-decision activities are being undertaken. For example, identifying significant impacts during the screening and scoping stages of EIA can provide a focus for subsequent impact monitoring and follow-up evaluation.

Generally though, EIA follow-up is concerned mainly with the *post-decision stage* of a proposal. It relates to the various components of the plan or project life cycle after the consent decision has been taken (e.g. final detailed design; construction, operation and decommissioning phases; project and environmental management). A definition of EIA follow-up is provided in Box 1.2.

Box 1.2 A Definition of EIA Follow-up

Building upon earlier work (e.g. Munro et al, 1986; Sadler, 1996; Au and Sanvicens, 1995; Arts and Nooteboom, 1999; IAIA, 1999) and various workshops during recent International Association for Impact Assessment conferences, EIA follow-up at the proposal level can be simply defined as:

> *The monitoring and evaluation of the impacts of a project or plan (that has been subject to EIA) for management of, and communication about, the environmental performance of that project or plan.*

Thus, EIA follow-up comprises four elements (Arts et al, 2001):

1 *Monitoring* – the collection of data and comparison with standards, predictions or expectations. *Base-line monitoring* measures the initial state of environmental indicators during the pre-decision stages and provides the basis for prediction and evaluation in the EIS. In the post-decision stages, monitoring may relate to both *compliance* with and *effects* of that decision. *Area-wide monitoring* is the monitoring of the general state of the environment in an area, which may incorporate multiple projects (e.g. cumulative effects). Closely related to the continual activity of monitoring is *auditing*, the periodical objective examination of observations by comparing them with pre-defined criteria (e.g. standards, predictions or expectations).

2 *Evaluation* – the appraisal of the conformance with standards, predictions or expectations as well as the environmental performance of the activity. It often relates to subjective policy-oriented judgements in addition to purely scientific and technical analysis, and consequently may require *value-judgements* to be made. *Ex-ante evaluation* is 'forward looking' and predictive in nature. It focuses on the pre-decision activities (e.g. EIS preparation). *Ex-post evaluation* has a 'backward looking' nature. It concerns the appraisal of a policy, plan or project that has been or is currently being implemented. It especially involves an evaluation of the activities and situations that followed a particular decision.

3 *Management* – making decisions and taking appropriate action in response to issues arising from monitoring and evaluation activities. Ongoing management decisions may be made by both proponents (e.g. responding to unexpected impacts) and EIA regulators (e.g. reviewing consent conditions and management requirements) alike. An *environmental management*

system (EMS) is a voluntary system of compliance that operationalizes the implementation of environmental protection and management measures.

4 *Communication* – informing the stakeholders as well as the general public about the results of EIA follow-up (in order to provide feedback on project/plan implementation as well as feedback on EIA processes). Both proponents and EIA regulators may engage in communication programmes. Some follow-up programmes extend beyond simple communication to specifically include direct stakeholder participation in the monitoring, evaluation and management steps as well.

EIA follow-up and SEA follow-up

Environmental assessment can be carried out at different *planning levels*. Correspondingly it has become common to use the term Environmental Impact Assessment (EIA) for project assessments and the term Strategic Environmental Assessment (SEA) for the assessment of policies, plans and programmes. Follow-up can be applied to both EIA and SEA situations. This book focuses mainly on EIA follow-up, as greatest emphasis has been on the follow-up of projects, although SEA follow-up is becoming more evident (Chapter 10 focuses on SEA follow-up). In this book (especially in Chapters 1 and 2) the term 'EIA follow-up' is used as a generic term referring to both EIA and SEA follow-up. If a distinction is needed, the more specific term SEA follow-up is used.

Meta, macro and micro scale follow-up

EIA follow-up can be conceptualized at three different *abstraction levels*:

• the individual proposal level (micro scale)
• the EIA jurisdiction/system level (macro scale)
• the conceptual and/or multi-jurisdictional level (meta scale).

These are defined in greater detail in Box 1.3. It should be noted that EIA follow-up, as discussed in this book, relates mainly to the follow-up of individual plans or projects that have been subject to environmental assessment (i.e. micro scale).

The book generally does not extend to the macro scale evaluation of EIA systems (e.g. analysis of EIA regulations, EIA system performance or EIS quality in a particular jurisdiction). This is often a key interest of EIA regulators who may engage in periodic evaluations of their own EIA systems through activities such as judicial review of EIA legislation as well as learning from experience provided by micro scale follow-up activities. One example of a macro scale follow-up study, involving evaluation of a series of EIA systems around the world in a comparative step-by-step review of international procedures and practices, can be found in Wood (2003) and it is not intended to duplicate this work here. Further discussion about macro scale evaluation of EIA practice is provided in Chapter 11.

Discussion about meta scale EIA follow-up is also presented in Chapter 11. This is based upon the collective results of follow-up for individual EIA projects and EIA systems and builds upon the previous work of Sadler (1996) in this area.

Box 1.3 Approaches to EIA Follow-up

Three conceptually different approaches to EIA follow-up can be distinguished based on the level of analysis.

Monitoring and evaluation of EIA activities (micro scale)

Conducted on a project-by-project basis, this relates directly to specific components of EIA (or SEA) such as impact prediction, impact monitoring, compliance auditing and implementation of mitigation and environmental management actions. A key question is: was the project and the impacted environment managed in an acceptable way?

Evaluation of EIA systems (macro scale)

This examines the effectiveness of an EIA (or SEA) system as a whole in a certain jurisdiction (e.g. the influence of the EIA process on decision-making, efficiency of EIA procedures and utility of EIA products). A key question is: how efficient and effective is the EIA system as a whole?

Evaluation of the utility of EIA (meta scale)

This is closely related to the previous level, but going a step further to determine whether EIA (or SEA) is a worthwhile process and concept overall. A key question is: does EIA work?

Chapter 11 provides further elaboration of these three approaches to EIA follow-up.

Need for EIA follow-up

The fundamental need for EIA follow-up has been articulated earlier in terms of understanding EIA outcomes: without some form of follow-up, the consequences of pre-decision EIA activities will not be known. By incorporating feedback into the EIA process, follow-up assesses the impact of impact assessment and thereby enables *learning from experience* to occur. At the micro scale, learning about the impacts of a proposal and the effectiveness of mitigation measures to control or contain impacts is especially important. Feedback from follow-up programmes can also facilitate learning about pre-decision EIA activities (e.g. the accuracy of impact prediction methods). This knowledge can be utilized by regulators and proponents alike to improve future EIAs. At the macro and meta scales, learning about the outcomes of EIA enables the effectiveness and utility of EIA procedures and concepts to be evaluated; again with the aim of improving future EIA practice.

A key feature of EIA is that it deals with the future and consequently is intrinsically *uncertain*. Follow-up addresses the uncertainties in EIA. Consent decisions are based on an evaluation of predicted impacts and proposals for mitigation for an activity that does not yet exist. Additionally, all environments are dynamic and subject to ongoing change, generating another layer of uncertainty. Through activities such as monitoring and auditing, EIA follow-up provides concrete evidence of environmental outcomes. It thereby enables EIA practitioners and stakeholders to move from a mainly theoretical perspective on a proposal (i.e. based on predictions and expectations) to actual understanding and knowing of the real situation. To do this, EIA follow-up itself cannot be static. Rather, an adaptive and flexible approach is needed, which is capable of responding to unanticipated events or outcomes (Holling, 1978; see also Chapter 2).

Follow-up links the pre- and post-decision stages of EIA (Figure 1.1), thereby overcoming the gap that arises when there is a considerable difference

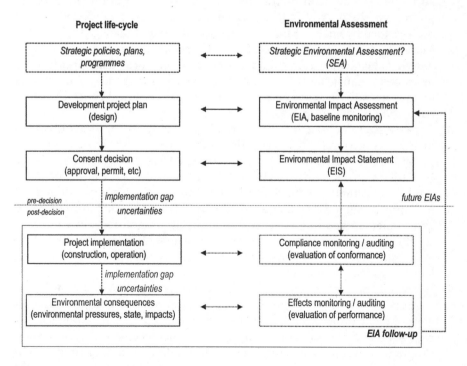

Source: Arts et al, 2001

Figure 1.1 *EIA Follow-up as a Link Between EIA and Project Implementation*

between project plans (and their related EISs) and their implementation. Ultimately it is not the predicted impacts, but rather the real effects that are relevant for protecting the environment. Follow-up not only provides information about the consequences of an activity as they occur, but it also gives proponents and/or EIA regulators the opportunity to implement measures to mitigate or prevent negative effects on the environment.

Objectives of EIA follow-up

EIA follow-up can serve many purposes ranging from the technical and scientific to socio-political and management aspects. All share the common goal of improving EIA knowledge and practice. Arts and Nooteboom (1999), IAIA (1999) and Arts et al (2001) identify various objectives of EIA follow-up:

1 *Control of projects and their environmental impacts* EIA follow-up provides both verifying and controlling functions for implemented projects. For example, compliance audits can verify that projects have been correctly implemented and are being operated in accordance with approval conditions and relevant environmental standards. Environmental monitoring programmes may provide feedback on the actual impacts that arise from a project, thereby enabling these to be understood and managed.
2 *Maintain decision-making flexibility and promote an adaptive management approach* Feedback from follow-up programmes provides opportunities for project managers and regulatory agencies to respond when changes in an activity, in the environment or in the socio-political context warrant adaptation of current practices.
3 *Improve scientific and technical knowledge* Many of the tasks involved in EIA are grounded in scientific method (e.g. base-line and impact monitoring, impact prediction, engineering design and mitigation). Some EIA follow-up activities evaluate the utility and effectiveness of these tasks. For example, feedback from prediction accuracy audits can be used to improve methods, techniques and EIA predictions for future projects, and implementation of ecological monitoring programmes can improve scientists' understanding of environmental cause–effect relationships. This may result in improving the quality of mitigation measures or construction techniques used in projects.
4 *Improve public awareness and acceptance* Ongoing EIA follow-up pro- grammes may improve public awareness about the actual effects of development projects on the environment and thereby allay public con- cerns about these, leading to improved public acceptance of proposals. Programme results may legitimize the EIA decision-making process and enhance public acceptance and support of the activity if it is evident that the environment is being protected adequately. Thus EIA follow-up provides socio-political benefits.

5 *Integration with other information* EIA follow-up programmes may dovetail with other existing environmental information programmes such as state of the environment reports and EMSs. Hence they may contribute to greater understanding of both area-wide effects and issues as well as detailed project operations. This will produce benefits for resource managers, environmental regulatory agencies and proponents alike.

These objectives emphasize the benefits of follow-up for individual projects that have undergone EIA. Other wider benefits of EIA follow-up – in terms of providing feedback on overall EIA systems and on evaluating the overarching utility and effectiveness of EIA itself (Box 1.3) – often emerge from the lessons learnt at the project level.

Historical overview

The concept of EIA follow-up is not new and there have been attempts to engage in follow-up of EIA activities for almost as long as the process has been in operation. An early attempt to bring EIA practitioners together to discuss EIA follow-up techniques and outcomes took place in Canada in 1985 (Sadler, 1987a, b). There have been numerous EIA follow-up studies since then, many of which are discussed in subsequent chapters. However, this is the first time that a volume has been produced that is specifically dedicated to EIA follow-up theory and practice for an international audience.

The historical development of EIA follow-up is reflected in the literature on the topic (Box 1.4). The issues in EIA follow-up have shifted from mainly technical and scientific to management aspects. Key issues in the early literature concern the accuracy of impact predictions and the quality of EISs. These documents were expected to contain testable hypotheses, and monitoring and follow-up focused on predictive accuracy and compliance issues. Later, attention has been paid to plan and project implementation including mitigation and project management. More recently, focus has widened to include communication issues and the roles and stakes of the various parties involved as well as resources and capacity building.

There are many different institutional requirements for EIA follow-up in practice around the world and it is not possible to review them all here. Practices vary from voluntary commitments for monitoring and reporting on EIA outcomes, through to specific command and control approaches, some of which provide for specialist independent follow-up review bodies. Generally, jurisdictions with a long history of EIA tend to be more advanced in their requirements for follow-up. In many jurisdictions, EIA regulations are in their third or fourth generation of evolution (e.g. in Canada and Hong Kong) and there is a trend for increasing requirements for EIA follow-up to occur. One objective of this book is to showcase some of the innovative and successful approaches to EIA follow-up that have been implemented around the world (principally at the micro scale). Subsequent chapters provide examples and case studies from a variety of jurisdictions and perspectives.

Box 1.4 Literature on EIA Follow-up

There is a considerable body of international literature on EIA follow-up. This focuses on a range of issues such as:

*   *definition of terms* (e.g. Munro et al, 1986; Tomlinson and Atkinson, 1987a, b; Thompson and Wilson, 1994; Arts and Nooteboom, 1999)
*   *relevance and rationale* (e.g. Holling, 1978; Bisset, 1980; Sadler, 1988; Arts, 1994; Dipper et al, 1998)
*   proposed *methodologies* for EIA follow-up (e.g. Marcus, 1979; Bailey and Hobbs, 1990; Davies and Sadler, 1990; UNECE, 1990; Bailey et al, 1992; Serafin et al, 1992; Bass and Herson, 1994; EPD, 1996; Sippe, 1997; World Bank, 1997; Arts, 1998; Shepherd, 1998; Wilson, 1998; Baker, 2002)
*   evaluating *technical aspects* of the EIA process such as accuracy of predictions and quality of EISs (e.g. Beanlands and Duinker, 1984; Bisset, 1984; Canter, 1985; Culhane et al, 1987; Sadler, 1987a, b; Bisset and Tomlinson, 1988; Elkin and Smith, 1988; Buckley, 1991; Lee et al, 1994; Barker and Wood, 1999)
*   relationships with monitoring and *environmental management* (e.g. Canter, 1993; Glasson, 1994; Petts and Eduljee, 1994; Au and Sanvicens, 1995; Brew and Lee, 1996; Sanvicens and Baldwin, 1996; Morrison-Saunders and Bailey, 1999; Marshall, 2001)
*   *approaches and case studies* in follow-up (e.g. Ross, 2000; Arts et al, 2001; Morrison-Saunders et al, 2001, 2003; Ross et al, 2001; Hulett and Diab, 2002; Marshall, 2002; Storey and Jones, 2003; Noble 2003, 2004; Gallardo and Sanchez, 2004; *Impact Assessment and Project Appraisal* journal Special Issue on EIA Follow-up, vol 23, no 3, September 2005).

Contextual setting for EIA follow-up

There are a number of important contextual factors (*what?*) in which follow-up takes place and three important stakeholder groups (*who?*) that have a role to play in answering the question: *how* do you make EIA follow-up successful? These are addressed in turn and their relationships are summarized in Figure 1.2.

Contextual factors

The context in which EIA follow-up occurs is a function of the interplay of four factors:

*   regulations and institutional arrangements that have been put in place
*   approaches and techniques utilized in follow-up practice
*   resources and capacity to undertake follow-up
*   type of activity that is being followed up.

It is important to realize that no two follow-up programmes will be identical, even if undertaken in the same jurisdiction, owing to variation in these contextual factors. Naturally, EIA follow-up in different jurisdictions can be expected to vary considerably, as subsequent case study chapters in this book demonstrate.

Regulations and institutional arrangements

The regulatory and institutional arrangements include the legal requirements and administrative framework for conducting EIA follow-up. It is determined in part by wider societal norms (e.g. processes in a democratic country will take a different approach to those in places controlled by centralized governments). As EIA systems mature and the importance of follow-up is recognized, the integration of follow-up requirements in EIA regulations is increasingly occurring. Generally, the existence of some formal requirements for follow-up are an important prerequisite for follow-up practice. Subsequent chapters highlight some of the regulatory arrangements for EIA follow-up in various jurisdictions around the world. The spectrum of follow-up approaches includes:

*   self-regulation by proponents (e.g. EMS)
*   command and control by government regulators (e.g. permits, standards, surveillance, enforcement and prosecution of offences for non-compliance)
*   public pressure by community stakeholders (e.g. public concern, media attention and lobbying by interest groups).

Approaches and techniques

The approaches and techniques available for the collection of data and the development of skills and expertise in EIA follow-up methods vary considerably. They can range from rigorous scientific studies to more informal and pragmatic approaches involving simple checks and use of existing management systems and data sources. The approaches and techniques will differ because of the objectives EIA follow-up has to serve. For improving understanding of cause–effect relationships (learning), more extensive and precise measurements are needed than for controlling whether the proponent complies with the consent decision. The approaches will also vary with the party who is doing follow-up (e.g. a local public interest group in a developing country versus a national government in a Western country). Overall, the approaches and techniques encapsulate the monitoring, evaluation and management activities identified in Box 1.2.

Resources and capacity

EIA follow-up can easily extend over long periods of time, become complex and require considerable effort in money, time and staff resources. However, follow-up does not need to be complex and expensive. Effective outcomes can be achieved by a pragmatic approach using common sense. EIA follow-up necessitates some investment in both staff and financial resources by all stakeholders involved in the process – especially proponents and regulatory agencies. To be worthwhile, the benefits of follow-up need to outweigh the costs in terms of time, capacity and money. Careful scoping of follow-up programmes plays an important role here.

Project type

The characteristics of the activity that has been subject to EIA are important for determining how to conduct EIA follow-up. Two important characteristics relate to the size of the project (e.g. small versus big investments) and initiator of the project (private versus government proponents). Generally speaking, major projects can be expected to cause greater environmental impact, but also have a greater budget for follow-up activities. Expectations for the types of follow-up activities engaged in by government proponents may be different to those of the private sector, as the former has a particular responsibility to manage public resources for the greatest common good.

A third consideration concerns the planning level at which the activity occurs. Generally two types of environmental assessments are distinguished: operational EIA involving specific projects and SEA for policies, plans or programmes (Therivel et al, 1992; Therivel and Partidário, 1996; Sadler, 1996). However, between these two extremes of operational and strategic environmental assessments lies a grey area involving route or location choices (Arts, 1998; Ten Holder and Verheem, 1996).

Consequently, three levels of environmental assessment follow-up can be distinguished, which are associated with three levels of abstraction, three levels of scale, three tiers of alternatives, and three different issues in planning and decision-making:

1   *strategic level* SEA activities about the adoption of objectives and constraints in strategic policy plans, with an emphasis on 'what'. This tends to operate at the political level – for example a plan for a national transport policy. The main focus of SEA follow-up is on subsequent decision-making about locations or operational projects. Hence SEA impacts on other 'paperwork', not necessarily on the environment directly.
2   *spatial level* EIA activities involving choices about routes or locations for developments with major spatial implications (e.g. infrastructure project plans, development of roads or urban expansion), with an emphasis on 'where' and for which cumulative effects are relevant.
3   *operational level* EIA activities involving specific projects for which environmental permits (or other consent decisions) are needed, with an emphasis on 'how' and a focus on technical issues (e.g. engineering design aspects for particular activities such as the provision and operation of power plants or landfills).

Stakeholders

Generally, three principal groups of stakeholders (parties) are involved in EIA follow-up as initiator, conductor or participant:

1 *Proponent* Proponents are the private companies or governmental organizations that develop a project. Just as project management and mitigation of impacts are normally the responsibility of proponents in EIA, proponents are often expected to perform most follow-up activities. It is useful to realize that voluntary, self-regulatory or industry-led initiatives such as EMS (e.g. the ISO 14000 series) may also incorporate some EIA follow-up functions. Self-regulatory initiatives of proponents may fill the gap in EIA regulations in some jurisdictions (Morrison-Saunders et al, 2003). Follow-up initiated and carried out by proponents may be considered as *first party follow-up*.
2 *EIA regulator* The second group consists of the EIA regulator, a competent authority or other government agency. Here, the emphasis is typically on ensuring that proponents comply with EIA approval conditions as well as on learning from experience to improve EIA processes in the future, and hence EIA regulators have an important role to play. General state of the environment monitoring and policy monitoring activities conducted by government agencies may be relevant to EIA follow-up in addition to project feedback provided by proponents. Follow-up carried out by regulators may be called *second party follow-up*.
3 *Community* The third stakeholder group is the community – a body involving the public or other independent persons. The public may have special knowledge of local areas and, being independent of both proponents and regulators, they may have interest in evaluating the performance of both of these stakeholders in the EIA process. Additionally, pressure arising from public scrutiny of development projects is often a driving force for proponents and regulators alike to implement EIA follow-up programmes. The extent of public involvement may range from direct community involvement in follow-up programmes to simply being kept informed of follow-up activities and outcomes. Follow-up activities carried out or initiated by the community can be considered as *third party follow-up*.

In addition to initiating or implementing EIA follow-up, other parties may have specialist knowledge that may contribute to follow-up activities. One could think of, for instance: (non)governmental agencies, academics and the wider scientific community, consultants, contractors etc.

The stakeholders involved in EIA follow-up are likely to be affected by the *scale of projects* too. This can be generalized as follows:

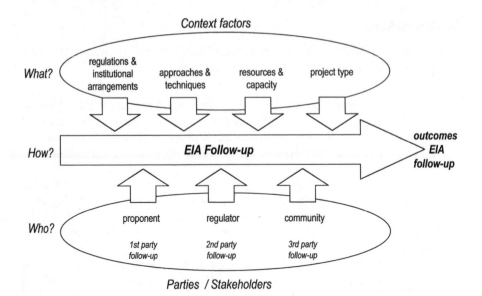

Source: Morrison-Saunders et al, 2003

Figure 1.2 *Contextual Factors and Stakeholder Groups for Successful
EIA Follow-up*

- operational level – proponent, regulator and local community (project focus)
- spatial level – as for the operational level plus other agencies and other proponents (multiple projects and cumulative effects in an area)
- strategic level – government level mainly and national or international interest groups (policy issues).

Towards successful EIA follow-up

Interaction between stakeholder groups and the contextual factors determines the nature of EIA follow-up that emerges and, consequently, whether it is successful or not. There is no single recipe for success. This book explores different approaches to EIA follow-up in various jurisdictions around the world to highlight some of the possibilities. Concluding comments on what makes EIA follow-up successful, including best practice principles, are presented in Chapter 12.

Outcomes of follow-up

It was previously noted that each of the three main stakeholder groups can be drivers for follow-up programmes. Similarly, each stakeholder group can benefit from EIA follow-up (Figure 1.3).

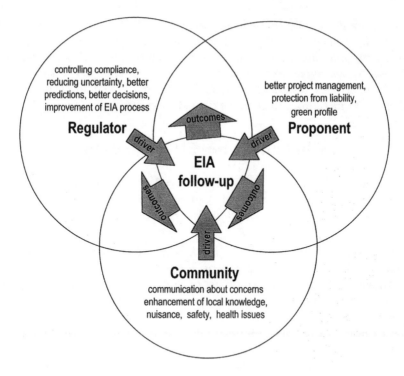

Source: Morrison-Saunders et al, 2001

Figure 1.3 *Outcomes of EIA Follow-up for Different Stakeholders*

Benefits for *proponents* range from protection from liability, maintaining community acceptance, maintaining EMS certificates, better project management and establishing a 'green profile' or image.

For *EIA regulators*, follow-up provides linkage between pre- and post-decision stages. In addition to providing a mitigation linkage (Chapter 6), follow-up activities such as monitoring and auditing can provide an account of EIA performance, regulatory compliance, mitigation performance evaluation, verification of residual effects and linkages into contractual, permitting, licensing and other management systems. Many of these functions overlap and interlink with the intentions of EMS and environmental permitting.

For *communities* EIA follow-up can provide enhanced knowledge about real impacts occurring in their neighbourhood, reduction of uncertainties about (cumulative) impacts, and generate adequate management responses to complaints and concerns about nuisances, safety or health issues. Ross et al (2001) argue that (cumulative) health issues provide the most important justification for carrying out EIA and follow-up in urban areas.

A key question in this book is how to improve EIA follow-up and enhance its utility for stakeholders. It is important to acknowledge that the relevance of follow-up outcomes may be different for each of the parties and that some tension of competing interests may arise. Subsequent chapters seek to focus on the division of roles, tasks and responsibilities of the stakeholders involved and to identify opportunities to enhance the value of EIA follow-up for them.

Challenges for EIA follow-up

Many of the challenges for EIA follow-up reflect similar problems with the implementation of EIA. These have been well articulated elsewhere and were summarized by Arts and Nooteboom (1999) as five key problems:

1 *Uncertainty and limited information* Uncertainty during the pre-decision stages of EIA is a principal reason for initiating EIA follow-up studies. However, these uncertainties do not necessarily go away, and may continue to pose difficulties during follow-up investigations (discussed further in Chapter 2).
2 *Deficiencies in EISs* As with uncertainty, deficiencies in EISs may provide a key reason for conducting EIA follow-up. Inadequacies in EISs have been well documented in the past and include problems with vague and qualitative impact predictions, extrapolation from little or no base-line monitoring or simply an absence in rigour with which projects are described and arguments constructed. The focus on impact monitoring and mitigation during EIA follow-up highlights the extent of these deficiencies but also enables actual environmental outcomes to be determined.
3 *Lack of guidance* While there is a wealth of available information on how to conduct EIA (particularly during the pre-decision stages of the process), there is little guidance currently on how to conduct EIA follow-up studies. This book is intended to redress this. Additionally there is a need for training and capacity building for EIA follow-up, especially in countries with little experience.
4 *Legislative deficiencies* Part of the reason why there is minimal guidance available on EIA follow-up is because there are relatively few jurisdictions with a formal legislative requirement for follow-up in place. This book showcases a number of jurisdictions where formal procedures for EIA follow-up have been implemented.
5 *Demands on financial and staff resources* EIA follow-up requires considerable resources in terms of time, money and staffing in both proponent and regulatory agencies. Until the benefits of EIA follow-up are more widely recognized in terms of long-term cost savings and improved environmental management, the demands on financial and staff resources are likely to impede progress in this area. For example, environmental effects monitoring is generally costly, especially over the time and scale boundaries that are often needed to determine the extent and level of environmental

change caused by a project. Additionally, when multiple projects with similar impacts occur together, it can be problematic determining which proponent(s) should be held financially responsible for area-wide and cumulative effects monitoring. Staffing continuity is another important issue. Personnel changes in both proponent and regulatory agencies may disrupt follow-up programmes and impede learning from experience.

Overview of the book

This chapter has presented an introduction to the theory of EIA follow-up and clarified terminology and the context in which follow-up occurs. The remaining chapters in this book fall into three parts:

*   theory of EIA follow-up (continued in Chapters 2 and 3)
*   case study chapters of EIA follow-up in project-based and SEA applications (Chapters 4–10)
*   concluding chapters (11–12).

Chapter 2 extends the theory of EIA follow-up further and explores the relationship between planning, decision-making and follow-up. A generic framework for conducting EIA follow-up is presented in Chapter 3. Important steps and issues introduced in this framework are explored in greater depth in subsequent chapters.

The remainder of the book roughly mirrors the historical development of follow-up and EIA more generally. The case study chapters focus on project-based EIA follow-up initially, but broaden out to include SEA practice (i.e. micro level follow-up initiatives). Each case study chapter explores specific aspects of EIA follow-up, as well as providing an account of the follow-up regulations and practices in the jurisdiction of focus (i.e. institutional arrangements for micro level follow-up).

Chapter 4 examines the need for EIA follow-up and discusses the role of screening and scoping in EIA follow-up with an emphasis on experience in The Netherlands. Chapter 5 showcases a long-term scientific monitoring and analysis programme from the US. Chapter 6 focuses on proponent-initiated and self-regulatory approaches to follow-up by ScottishPower in the UK. It also explores the role of mitigation, environmental management programmes (EMPs) and EMS in follow-up. Chapter 7 continues the focus on management aspects of EIA follow-up by discussing the role of adaptive management, using examples from Western Australia. The role of the community is examined in Chapter 8 using a Canadian case study involving an independent monitoring agency. The strong regulatory focus of EIA follow-up in Hong Kong is presented in Chapter 9, along with the role of the public and an overview of recent SEA follow-up interest. Chapter 10 provides a detailed theoretical and practical examination of SEA follow-up, drawing upon a number of recent examples for policies, plans and programmes in several countries.

Chapter 11 explores the role of follow-up in evaluating the overall success of EIA. In doing so, it draws upon the findings of both project-based follow-up studies as well as other evaluations to provide a micro scale through to macro and meta scale evaluation of EIA and SEA practice. Finally, in concluding the book, Chapter 12 summarizes best practices in EIA follow-up, identifies international follow-up principles and considers some future directions and challenges for development of the field. Overall, through assessing the impact of EIA and SEA at all levels, this book seeks the advancement of follow-up theory and practice.

References

Arts, J (1994) 'Environmental Impact Assessment: From Ex Ante to Ex Post Evaluation', in Voogd, H (ed) *Issues in Environmental Planning*, London, Pion Limited, pp145–163

Arts, J (1998) *EIA Follow-up – On the Role of Ex Post Evaluation in Environmental Impact Assessment*, Groningen, Geo Press

Arts, J and Nooteboom, S (1999) 'Environmental Impact Assessment Monitoring and Auditing', in Petts, J (ed) *Handbook of Environmental Impact Assessment Volume 1. Environmental Impact Assessment: Process, Methods and Potential*, Oxford, Blackwell Science, pp229–251

Arts, J, Caldwell, P and Morrison-Saunders, A (2001) 'EIA Follow-up: Good practice and future directions: Findings from a workshop at the IAIA 2000 Conference', *Impact Assessment and Project Appraisal*, vol 19, pp175–185

Au, E and Sanvicens, G (1995) 'EIA Follow-up Monitoring and Management', in Environment Protection Agency (ed) *International Study of the Effectiveness of Environmental Assessment: Report of the EIA Process Strengthening Workshop*, Canberra, 4–7 April 1995, Environment Protection Agency, available at www.deh.gov.au/assessments/eianet/eastudy/aprilworkshop/paper5.html

Bailey, J and Hobbs, V (1990) 'A proposed framework and database for EIA auditing', *Journal of Environmental Management*, vol 31, pp163–172

Bailey, J, Hobbs, V and Saunders, A (1992) 'Environmental auditing: Artificial waterway developments in Western Australia', *Journal of Environmental Management*, vol 34, pp1–13

Baker, J (2002) 'A Framework for Environmental Assessment Follow-up', presented at *Assessing the Impact of Impact Assessment: Impact Assessment for Informed Decision Making, 22nd Annual Meeting of the International Association for Impact Assessment*, 15–21 June 2002, The Hague, The Netherlands, published on CD ROM: *IA Follow-up Workshop*, Hull, Quebec, Environment Canada

Barker, A and Wood, C (1999) 'An evaluation of EIA system performance in eight EU countries', *Environmental Impact Assessment Review*, vol 19, pp387–404

Bass, R and Herson, A (1994) *CEQA Compliance: A Step-by-step Approach*, Point Area, California, Solano Press Books

Beanlands, G and Duinker, P (1984) 'An ecological framework for EIA', *Journal of Environmental Management*, vol 18, pp267–277

Bisset, R (1980) 'Problems and issues in the implementation of EIA audits', *Environmental Impact Assessment Review*, vol 1, pp379–396

Bisset, R (1984) 'Post-development audits to investigate the accuracy of environmental impact predictions', *Umweltpolitik*, vol 4, pp463–484

Bisset, R and Tomlinson, P (1988) 'Monitoring and Auditing of Impacts', in Wathern, P (ed) *Environmental Impact Assessment, Theory and Practice*, London, Unwin Hyman, pp117–128

Brew, D and Lee, N (1996) 'Monitoring, environmental management plans and post-project analysis', *EIA Newsletter*, vol 12, pp10–11

Buckley, R (1991) 'Auditing the precision and accuracy of environmental impact predictions in Australia', *Environmental Monitoring and Assessment*, vol 18, pp1–23

Caldwell, L, Bartlett, D, Parker, D and Keys, D (1982) *A Study of Ways to Improve the Scientific Content and Methodology of Environmental Impact Analysis*, Advanced Studies in Science, Technology and Public Affairs, School of Public and Environmental Affairs, Bloomington, US, Indiana University

Canter, L (1985) 'Impact prediction auditing', *The Environmental Professional*, vol 7, pp255–264

Canter, L (1993) 'The role of environmental monitoring in responsible project management', *The Environmental Professional*, vol 15, pp76–87

Culhane, P, Friesema, H and Beecher, J (1987) *Forecasts and Environmental Decision-Making, The Content and Predictive Accuracy of Environmental Impact Statements*, Boulder, Colorado, Westview Press

Davies, M and Sadler, B (1990) *Post-project Analysis and the Improvement of Guidelines for Environmental Monitoring and Audit*, Environmental Protection Series EPS 6/FA/1, Ottawa, Beauregard Printers Ltd

Dipper, C, Jones, C and Wood, C (1998) 'Monitoring and post-auditing in environmental impact assessment: A review', *Journal of Environmental Planning and Management*, vol 41, pp731–748

Elkin, T and Smith, G (1988) 'What is a good environmental impact statement? Reviewing screening reports from Canada's national parks' *Journal of Environmental Management*, vol 26, pp71–89

EPD, Environmental Protection Department (1996) *Generic Environmental Monitoring and Audit Manual*, Hong Kong, Hong Kong Government

Gallardo, A and Sanchez, L (2004) 'Follow-up of a road-building scheme in a fragile environment', *Environmental Impact Assessment Review*, vol 24, pp47–58

Glasson, J (1994) 'Life after the decision: The importance of monitoring in EIA', *Built Environment*, vol 20, pp309–320

Holling, C (ed) (1978) *Adaptive Environmental Assessment and Management*, Chichester, UK, John Wiley

Hulett, J and Diab, R (2002) 'EIA follow-up in South Africa: Current status and recommendations', *Journal of Environmental Assessment Policy and Management*, vol 4, pp297–309

International Association for Impact Assessment and Institute of Environmental Assessment, UK (1999), *Principles of Environmental Impact Assessment Best Practice*, available at www.iaia.org/publications.htm

Lee, N, Walsh, F and Reeder, G (1994) 'Assessing the performance of the EA process', *Project Appraisal*, vol 9, pp161–172

Marcus, L (1979) *A Methodology for Post-EIS (Environmental Impact Statement) Monitoring*, US Geological Survey Circular 782, Washington, DC, US Geological Survey

Marshall, R (2001) 'Application of mitigation and its resolution within Environmental Impact Assessment: an industrial perspective', *Impact Assessment and Project Appraisal*, vol 19, pp195–204

Marshall, R (2002) 'Developing environmental management systems to deliver mitigation and protect the EIA process during follow-up', *Impact Assessment and Project Appraisal*, vol 20, pp286–292

McCallum, D (1985) 'Planned Follow-up, A Basis for Acting on EIAs', presented at *Annual Meeting of the International Association for Impact Assessment, Utrecht, The Netherlands*, 27–28 June 1985

McCallum, D (1987) 'Environmental Follow-Up to Federal Projects, a National Review', in Sadler, B (ed) *Audit and Evaluation in Environmental Assessment and Management. Canadian and International Experience Volume II. Supporting Studies* Ottawa, Beauregard Press Ltd, pp731–749

Morrison-Saunders, A and Bailey, J (1999) 'Exploring the EIA/environmental management relationship', *Environmental Management*, vol 24, pp281–295

Morrison-Saunders, A, Arts, J, Baker, J and Caldwell, P (2001) 'Roles and stakes in environmental impact assessment follow-up', *Impact Assessment and Project Appraisal*, vol 19, pp289–296

Morrison-Saunders, A, Baker, J and Arts, J (2003) 'Lessons from practice: Towards successful follow-up', *Impact Assessment and Project Appraisal*, vol 21, pp43–56

Munro, D, Bryant, T and Matte-Baker, A (1986) *Learning From Experience, A State-of-the-Art Review and Evaluation of Environmental Impact Assessment Audits*, Canadian Environmental Assessment and Research Council (CEARC), Minister of Supply and Services, Canada

Noble, B (2003) 'Auditing strategic environmental assessment practice in Canada', *Journal of Environmental Assessment Policy and Management*, vol 5, pp127–147

Noble, B (2004) 'A state-of-practice survey of policy, plan, and program assessment in Canadian provinces' *Environmental Impact Assessment Review*, vol 24, pp351–361

Petts, J and Eduljee, G (1994) 'Integration of monitoring, auditing and environmental assessment: Waste facility issues', *Project Appraisal*, vol 9, pp231–241

Ross, W (2000) 'Reflections on an environmental assessment panel member', *Impact Assessment and Project Appraisal*, vol 18, pp91–98

Ross, W, Green, J and Croal, P (2001) 'Follow-up Studies in Cumulative Effects: Management Implications in Developing Nations', presented at *Impact Assessment in the Urban Context, 21st Annual Meeting of the International Association for Impact Assessment*, Cartagena, Colombia, 26 May–1 June 2001, published on CD ROM: *IA Follow-up Workshop*, Hull, Quebec, Environment Canada

Sadler, B (ed) (1987a) *Audit and Evaluation in Environmental Assessment and Management, Canadian and International Experience Volume I. Commissioned Research*, Ottawa, Beauregard Press Ltd

Sadler, B (ed) (1987b) *Audit and Evaluation in Environmental Assessment and Management. Canadian and International Experience Volume II. Supporting Studies*, Ottawa, Beauregard Press Ltd

Sadler, B (1988) 'Evaluation of Assessment: Post-EIS Research and Process Development', in Wathern, P (ed) *Environmental Impact Assessment, Theory and Practice*, London, Unwin Hyman, pp129–142

Sadler, B (1996) *International Study of the Effectiveness of Environmental Assessment, Final Report, Environmental Assessment in a Changing World: Evaluating Practice to Improve Performance*, Canadian Environmental Assessment Agency and the International Association for Impact Assessment, Minister of Supply and Services, Canada

Sanvicens, G and Baldwin, P (1996) 'Environmental monitoring and audit in Hong Kong', *Journal of Environmental Planning and Management*, vol 39, pp429–441

Serafin, R, Nelson, G and Butler, R (1992) 'Post hoc assessment in resource management and environmental planning: A typology and three case studies', *Environmental Impact Assessment Review*, vol 12, pp271–294

Shepherd, A (1998) 'Post-project Impact Assessment and Monitoring', in Porter, A and Fittipaldi, J (eds), *Environmental Methods Review: Retooling Impact Assessment for the New Century*, Fargo, ND, Army Environmental Policy Institute (AEPI), The Press Club, pp164–170

Sippe, R (1997) 'Establishing rules for environmental acceptability for reviewing EAs: The Western Australian experience', *Environmental Assessment*, vol 5, pp17–20

Storey, K and Jones P (2003) 'Social impact assessment, impact management and follow-up: A case study of the construction of the Hibernia offshore platform', *Impact Assessment and Project Appraisal*, vol 21, pp99–107

Ten Holder, V and Verheem, R (1996) 'Strategic EIA in The Netherlands', in EIA Commission (ed) *Environmental Impact Assessment in the Netherlands, Experiences and Views Presented by and to the Commission for EIA*, Utrecht, EIA Commission, pp17–31

Therivel, R, Wilson, E, Thompson, S, Heaney, D and Pritchard, D (1992) *Strategic Environmental Assessment*, London, Earthscan

Therivel, R and Partidário, M R (1996) *The Practice of Strategic Environmental Assessment*, London, Earthscan

Thompson, D and Wilson, M (1994) 'Environmental auditing: Theory and applications', *Environmental Management*, vol 18, pp605–615

Tomlinson, P and Atkinson, S (1987a) 'Environmental audits, proposed terminology', *Environmental Monitoring and Assessment*, vol 8, pp187–198

Tomlinson, P and Atkinson, S (1987b) 'Environmental audits, a literature review', *Environmental Monitoring and Assessment*, vol 8, pp239–261

UNECE, United Nations Economic Commission for Europe (1990) *Post-project Analysis in Environmental Impact Assessment*, Environmental Series no 3, Geneva, United Nations

Wilson, L (1998) 'A practical method for environmental impact assessment audits', *Environmental Impact Assessment Review*, vol 18, pp59–71

Wood, C (2003) *Environmental Impact Assessment – A Comparative Review*, 2nd edition, Harlow, Pearson Education Ltd

World Bank (1997) *Environmental Performance Monitoring and Supervision*, *Environmental Assessment Sourcebook*, Washington, DC, World Bank

Theoretical Perspectives on EIA and Follow-up

Jos Arts and Angus Morrison-Saunders

Introduction

This chapter provides a theoretical background for EIA follow-up. It elaborates on concepts introduced in Chapter 1 and builds upon the work of Arts (1998) to examine the relationships between EIA and planning and decision-making in some detail. Box 2.1 defines some important terms used. The chapter first considers the origins of the concepts of EIA and follow-up in terms of seeking to rationalize decision-making and planning. Subsequent discussion explores the tension between the theoretical concepts and complex practice of planning, decision-making and project management, thereby highlighting the limitations of rational planning (i.e. EIA). The chapter ends with an examination of the role of EIA follow-up for fitting EIA better in decision-making and the plan/project life cycle including implementation and management (Figure 1.1). Key theoretical issues raised in this chapter are consolidated in a practical framework for EIA follow-up in Chapter 3 and in the various case study chapters thereafter.

Origins of the concept of EIA and follow-up

Several important theoretical foundations of EIA and follow-up warrant more detailed examination than given in Chapter 1.

Reasons for pre-decision analysis: The start of EIA

Because planning and policy-making are prospective activities, uncertainty is intrinsic to their nature. Consequently, planning failures are hard to

Box 2.1 Decision-making, Policy, Planning and Adaptive Management

The terms 'planning', 'decision-making' and 'policy-making' are closely related (Friend and Jessop, 1969; Lichfield et al, 1975) and in practice are often mixed up or used as synonyms. Some general definitions of these notions follow. 'Adaptive management' is also defined as it has many uses and is relevant here for providing the means to operationalize policy and planning decisions.

'Decision-making' can be defined very broadly as 'the process of choice which leads to action' (Simon, 1957). Here, the term is mainly used to refer to the consent decision made by EIA regulators. However, during the planning process and the project life cycle many other decisions made by regulators, proponents and other parties can be relevant to EIA outcomes (e.g. determining project objectives, screening and scoping, detailed design and activity operation and management). In democratic society decision-making by government is expected to meet specific requirements, especially as it might affect other parties. Governments are expected to consider both (political) interests and (environmental) impacts and to choose the best of various alternatives in a well-considered way. Consequently, public decision-making is strongly related to the concepts of policy and planning.

The term 'policy' can be simply described as a course of action, or more elaborately as: 'a goal or a set of goals ("what ought to be") to govern the course of action and decision-making ("what is")' (Mayda, 1996, p91). Policy consists not only of setting objectives, means and time choices, but it is also an answer to a problem or situation (Healey, 1983). In this respect, not acting (e.g. not making a decision) can also be seen as an element of policy-making.

'Planning' is defined by Dror (1963, p330) as: 'the process of preparing a set of decisions for action in the future, directed at achieving goals by preferable means'. The results of the planning process can be laid down in policy, programmes, plans or other decisions such as environmental permits for projects. Planning involves analysing the past and the present, anticipating the future, designing alternative programmes, implementing a chosen programme and evaluating the results of this process. It represents an attempt to apply scientific method to policy-making (Faludi, 1973).

'Adaptive environmental assessment and management' refers to the process pioneered by Holling (1978) and his colleagues in which assessment takes place through a series of workshops and model building. Throughout this book, the term 'adaptive management' is used more generally to refer to a flexible approach to EIA and especially to follow-up activities in which changes are made to impact mitigation and project management strategies in response to the findings of monitoring studies (Morrison-Saunders and Bailey, 1999). EIA activities should be an ongoing investigation and management of impacts rather than a one-time prediction during the pre-decision stages. It is through adaptive management that policy, planning and decision-making goals are attained in practice. There is also a feedback loop (often implicit) for future goal setting.

prevent. In the 1960s, planners became increasingly aware of this problem as negative effects of policies occurred more often. To address this, an effort was made to give planning proposals a sound, more rational scientific basis in which information played a pivotal role. The assumption is that making more information available about the impacts of a decision and subjecting that information to systematic analysis will improve the quality of decisions and planning proposals by reducing uncertainty and preventing unexpected consequences. Consequently, planners have devoted much attention to the *ex-ante evaluation* of plans, projects and decisions. To support this effort in pre-decision analysis, numerous methods have been developed including cost–benefit analysis, overview methods, multicriteria analysis (e.g. Voogd, 1983; Nijkamp et al, 1990; Petts, 1999) and, more recently, the so-called 'communicative methods' (Guba and Lincoln, 1989; Woltjer, 2000; Voogd, 2001).

The US *National Environmental Policy Act* (NEPA) of 1969, which made EIA mandatory, is essentially the brainchild of this rationalist decision reform movement (Caldwell, 1982; Taylor, 1984; Bartlett, 1986). EIA is a typical example of an ex-ante evaluation instrument in environmental planning. Its main activities are the gathering of information about effects, developing alternatives and appraising these alternatives (Partidário, 2001; Sadler, 1996). This approach has great appeal, and EIA has become a standard procedure in the (environmental) planners' toolbox around the world. EIA – and its younger derivative strategic environmental assessment (SEA) – is applied to a variety of plans and projects of both government and private proponents. Its main objective could be described as 'to take full account of the environmental interest at stake in the decision-making process on a particular project or plan' (ECW, 1990).

Rationale for post-decision analysis: The need for follow-up

As noted in Chapter 1, a major weakness of EIA is the general lack of *follow-up* after the consent decision. In practice, EIA all too often appears to be no more than a pre-decision analysis (i.e. an ex-ante evaluation, resulting in an EIS) and little effort is made to follow up (i.e. to evaluate ex-post) the actual effects of projects and plans that have been subject to EIA (or SEA). There has been limited interest in 'life after the decision' (Glasson, 1994).

The rationale for EIA follow-up is similar to that of EIA itself: *getting a grip on uncertainties* intrinsic to a prospective activity. Although a thorough pre-decision analysis such as EIA (or SEA) is a necessary prerequisite for informed decision-making, it is not sufficient for sustainable planning, decision-making and management of projects. There will always be uncertainties and gaps in knowledge. EIA and decision-making are performed in a complex and dynamic environmental context: an area and its sensitivity to environmental impacts change over time when new developments occur or political priorities change.

As Holling (1978, p7) states: 'The challenge... is to cope with the uncertain and the unexpected. How, in short, to plan in the face of the unknown'. Consequently, an adaptive, flexible approach is often recommended; one which allows for adequate reactions to unanticipated decision outcomes and for the adjustment of imperfect knowledge sets concerning society and environment. To provide for this flexibility, feedback of information about the real effects is vital. This is an important reason for conducting follow-up. While it is impossible to know beforehand which unexpected intervening developments will take place, 'we do know that we can expect the unexpected' (Holling, 1978, p136). Follow-up tries to minimize uncertainty by putting in place planned but adaptable strategies to trace the cause and event consequences of projects or plans. Without some form of follow-up the outcomes of EIA decisions and actions cannot be determined and *learning from experience* cannot occur.

Using the consent decision as a 'watershed', ex-ante and ex-post evaluation can be distinguished. Both types play specific but complementing roles in the planning process (Figure 2.1). Ex-ante evaluation (pre-decision EIA) is simply the process of moving from project conceptualization to consent decision-making. Ex-post evaluation of EIA activities (i.e. follow-up) can contribute both to:

- the adaptation of an existing project or plan for its management – i.e. micro scale follow-up based on day-to-day, 'single loop' learning at the project level
- the starting of a new round in the planning cycle for developing a new plan or project – i.e. macro scale follow-up based on a deeper, 'double loop' learning process (Schön, 1983), particularly when learning from multiple projects occurs.

Follow-up may address EIA activities that have been or are currently being implemented. It can be seen as the 'missing link' between project preparation and implementation which bridges the 'implementation gap'. EIA follow-up may help in closing the project management cycle. In that sense it is closely related to the concepts of risk management and quality control in which learning and feedback are essential to deal with uncertainties and risks (e.g. Deming's (1986) quality control cycle of plan-do-check-act).

As EIA concerns activities that could have harmful effects on the environment, it is important to evaluate performance once the decision is made and the activity commences. Ultimately, it is not the predicted effects but the real effects that are important. Without a post-decision analysis, EIA is actually open ended. Thus, follow-up is a critical aspect of EIA. Not only does it provide information about the consequences of an activity as they occur, but it also gives the responsible proponents and/or authorities the opportunity to take adequate measures to mitigate or prevent negative effects on the environment.

Although the rationale for performing EIA follow-up is clear, the directions for doing this in practice are not. However, clues for this can be found in the sometimes problematic relationship between EIA (and follow-up) and planning practice.

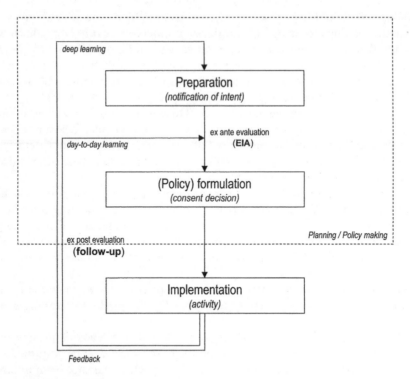

Source: after Voogd, 1996

Figure 2.1 *The Role of EIA and Follow-up – Ex-ante and Ex-post Evaluation – In the Planning Process*

Relationship between planning and EIA

The process of EIA as implemented in most jurisdictions is characterized by a rational, almost scientific, approach to planning and decision-making. This is known as the *rational-comprehensive approach*, which comprises a rather linear process in which:

- the problem and objectives of a project (or plan) are defined
- several alternatives are developed
- the environmental impacts are assessed
- it is determined how (negative) impacts can be avoided or mitigated by taking appropriate management action
- through comparison of their (positive and negative) impacts the preferred alternative is chosen
- the results of this analysis are reported in an EIS which is communicated and reviewed
- a (motivated) decision is taken about giving consent to the project.

These generic steps in the EIA process (Box 1.1) correspond well with Etzioni's (1967, p217) description of rational planning as the process whereby: 'an actor becomes aware of a problem, posits a goal, carefully weighs alternative means, and chooses among them according to his estimates of their respective merit, with reference to the state of affairs he prefers'.

In practice, planning and decision-making is much more complex than this rather simplistic, linear account of rational planning. The 'classical' rational-comprehensive approach has been criticized on at least four major grounds (Faludi, 1973; Breheny and Hooper, 1985), which are briefly summarized in turn.

First, the ability to be *comprehensive* is questionable as the exacting demands on the scope and quality of the information necessary for a rational-comprehensive approach cannot be met in practice. Given that planners are unlikely to have a totally comprehensive understanding of a policy problem, it is not possible to be certain that a chosen alternative is optimal in an absolute sense. In such circumstances of 'bounded rationality' decision-makers often show 'satisficing behaviour' instead of 'optimizing behaviour' (Simon, 1957). A *disjointed-incremental approach* emerges in which planning is described as a step-by-step approach; but in the face of incomplete knowledge or understanding by the participants, it becomes the 'science of muddling through' (Lindblom, 1959). Subsequently, Etzioni (1967) articulated a *mixed-scanning approach* in which planners comprehensively examine some (important) parts of a system, while the rest is only roughly or incompletely reviewed. This approach comes down to 'zooming in' on particular issues. It is particularly relevant to scoping in EIA and follow-up (Chapter 4).

Second, as with the lack of comprehensive information, the *quality of the information* gathered in an EIA study will always leave something to be desired. There will always be insufficient data to treat the problem at hand adequately as there will always be some gaps in knowledge and some uncertainty (Friend and Jessop, 1969). One reason for this is that our knowledge about *causal relationships* is too limited.

The third failing of the rational-comprehensive model is that it ignores the *influence of different parties* in the planning process by implying that decision-makers are the only player. In practice, the result of the planning process is determined by many different actors (e.g. responsible authorities, proponents, the community or special interest groups) who have different roles and stakes in the planning and decision-making process as well as in EIA follow-up (Figure 1.3). To some extent, all parties have *power for making decisions* relevant to a project or plan development, which will influence outcomes. This is mainly the power to obstruct decisions and developments, since individual parties usually have little or insufficient power to enforce these decisions (Teisman, 1992). The descriptions of EIA given so far tend to oversimplify the decision-making process. In practice, there is usually no single determinant decision; for example:

- EIA regulators are responsible for the consent decision.
- Proponents make investment decisions with respect to their projects. It is not uncommon for a project to receive EIA regulator approval, but for the proponent to subsequently decide not to proceed with the action.

- Affected community members and special interest groups may lodge appeals or generate media publicity for or against a proposed development, which may result in political intervention in their favour.

Similarly, each party may also have *specific knowledge* relevant to their particular role in the process; for example, regulators may know about other policy proposals, proponents may have specialist technical knowledge of their projects, and community members may have special knowledge of local areas. Not only does planning and decision-making need to accommodate the various 'networks of actors' in the process, but the importance that is attached to plans or projects (and the related SEA or EIA studies) depends on the many parties to the subsequent decision-making processes after the adoption of such plans (Faludi and Van der Valk, 1994). For instance, planning proposals specified today that are to be decided upon at some time in the future may no longer appear appropriate when that decision point arrives. Recognition of the relevance of multiple parties and the conceived gap between governments, proponents and citizens has led to the *communicative planning approach* (Healey, 1996), in which attention is devoted to consensus building, coordination and communication and the role of government in promoting this, as a way to deal with the conflicting interests of different parties and to come to collaborative action (Healey, 1997; Woltjer, 2000). This approach has recently received attention in EIA practice (e.g. De Bruijn and Ten Heuvelhof, 2002; Stolp et al, 2002; Deelstra et al, 2003).

The fourth failing of the rational-comprehensive model is that the influence of governmental policy, planning and decision-making is also limited by *implementation failures*. Although advanced planning techniques (including EIA) were applied during the 1960s and 1970s, many plans and policies were not adequately implemented, and planning failures often occurred (Hall, 1982; Hoogerwerf, 1983) leading to what Dunsire (1978) has called the *implementation gap*. As stated before, the context in which planning and decision-making are done is complex and dynamic. Where a rational-comprehensive approach may view planning as a linear process in which plans are formed as an unambiguous guide (or blueprint) for action, planning and policy can be seen as a direction, not a directive (Mayda, 1996). Ultimately, the implementation and effectiveness of plans are subject to many disturbing factors and limitations (Bressers, 1989): thus planning failures, unanticipated situations and unanticipated decisions are inevitable.

These limitations further highlight the need for EIA follow-up. They also provide clues for how to better adapt EIA and follow-up to planning and decision-making.

The tension between theory and practice

It is clear from the previous discussion that there will always be a tension between the theoretical concept of 'classical' rational planning (and thus EIA) and the complex practices of planning, decision-making and project management (Figure 2.2). This tension is relevant to EIA follow-up in two main ways. On the one hand, because of such tension, EIA follow-up is a useful way to deal with the problems related to the linear nature of EIA – building in feedback loops in the EIA process and making EIA more flexible and adaptive to complex daily practice. On the other hand, the same tension applies to EIA follow-up itself, making such follow-up a difficult exercise. However, by analysing this tension, clues can be found for implementing EIA follow-up and overcoming these issues in day-to-day practice.

EIA is commonly depicted in the classical rational planning approach as a linear process of clearly defined steps (Box 1.1) that is followed by experts. Objectifying, quantitative data, structured analysis and scientific methods are central to the process as well as minimizing negative impacts and optimizing the development proposal in order to come to a well-considered decision. In practice, however, the picture is much more blurred. EIA (and planning generally) is seen as a dynamic process in which information flows create feedback and allow for adjustment (Friend and Jessop, 1969; Holling, 1978). A plan or project is developed in a cyclic, iterative process in which discussions with a variety of parties about normative, subjective arguments (non-scientific, non-rational considerations and information) play an important role, and in which development of alternatives and assessing impacts alternate with each other. Plans and projects are developed and decided on by many parties, and often 'informal' decisions are crucial to them. Moreover,

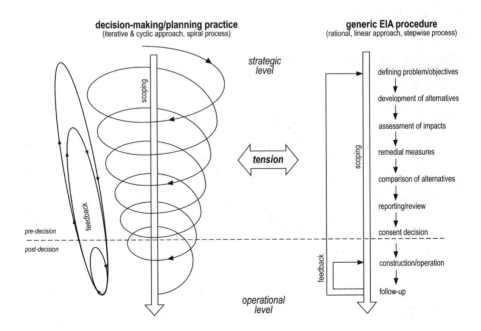

Figure 2.2 *Cyclic, Iterative Practice of Planning Versus the Linear, Classic Planning Approach of EIA*

in this cyclic process solutions may well precede problems and operational issues may precede strategic ones. The dynamic context in which planning and decision-making occurs may also be characterized by changes in, for example, the physical environment of the area, political priorities, regulations or policies, societal views and scientific knowledge. During this process the scope of the project will become more clearly defined in order to come to a satisfactory outcome for most or preferably all parties involved (a consensus). Understood in this way, planning is not only a process of (joint) fact-finding and learning, but also a process of bargaining and negotiations ('negotiated knowledge') as well as a process of persuasion and will-shaping (Woltjer, 2000; Voogd, 2001; Deelstra et al, 2003).

Much of the criticism of EIA practice relates to this tension between the linear approach assumed by EIA principles and the dynamic, complex nature of planning and decision-making practice. For example EIAs are often viewed as (World Bank, 1995; Sadler, 1996; IAIA, 2002):

- costly
- time-consuming
- requiring much capacity
- suffering from information-overload and too much detail
- having a limited scope (important issues are decided on before or afterwards, sustainability considerations are missing)
- having limited usefulness for decision-making (e.g. just pro-forma exercise, or 'paperwork')
- focusing on gaining consent rather than the practicalities of implementation.

Barriers for implementing EIA follow-up in practice

Additionally, this tension also relates to five key *barriers* that hinder the implementation of EIA follow-up in practice (Au and Sanvicens, 1996; Arts and Nooteboom, 1999):

1   *Limitations of EISs*   EISs are often descriptive rather than analytic, containing vague and qualitative predictive statements that fail to make a clear reference to time periods, thereby rendering them untestable (Beanlands and Duinker, 1984; Bisset, 1984; Culhane et al, 1987). Other limitations include information gaps and assumptions about future developments that soon become outdated because of intervening developments, especially in areas with a dynamic land use and inadequate monitoring and mitigation proposals. However, these weaknesses can be explained by the argument that EISs have been prepared for an ex-ante evaluation that seeks to assess the political acceptability of worst-case impacts. In this regard, inexact information may often be sufficient for an adequate comparison of alternatives in order to make a consent decision. However, the lack of scientific rigour hampers comparison with post-decision monitoring data necessary to gauge the actual effects of a project or plan.

2 *Less-developed techniques for follow-up* Methods and techniques for follow-up are less developed than other components of EIA. Most methods can be considered only minor variations on the standard research design (see Arts, 1998 for more detailed discussion). In physical and environmental planning, ex-ante evaluation methods are widely applied and many methods have been developed; for example, cost–benefit analysis, multicriteria analysis, overview methods and EIA itself (Voogd, 1983; Nijkamp et al, 1990). Ex-post evaluation and follow-up have been especially applied in the social sciences, mainly in psychology and sociology, and in sectors such as education and public health (Buit, 1985; Rossi and Freeman, 1989). Although it is theoretically possible to use many of the existing methods for EIA follow-up, many practical problems arise, such as:

- limited knowledge about dose–effect relationships
- difficulty in establishing cause–effect relationships between a given activity and observed environmental changes
- inadequacy of base-line and impact monitoring data (e.g. monitoring techniques may not be accurate enough, indicators may not be fully representative) or difficulty in appraising the data.

3 *Organizational and resource limitations* Monitoring environmental changes and linking them to a source (a project or plan) may require considerable time, money, staff, expertise and the involvement of many parties. The division of tasks, responsibilities and costs may be unclear. During the long time period the EIA follow-up may cover, the project may be handed over to others or there may be changes in personnel. The task of organizing EIA follow-up may be complex while little guidance and training exist.

4 *Limited support for conducting EIA follow-up* In general, authorities and proponents alike seem to give EIA follow-up a low priority. In many jurisdictions, EIA follow-up is not part of the EIA framework or it is a mandatory requirement, not implemented in practice. Reasons for this lack of support include:

- expected benefits of EIA follow-up and its added value in relation to the costs are unclear – or at least, many practitioners are not convinced of its value
- EIA follow-up may overlap with other evaluative instruments and activities (depending on the type of EIA project or plan and on the legal and administrative context)
- the extent to which EIA follow-up can perform its potential functions may be less than expected (e.g. it may not perform optimally because of a limited potential to take remedial measures, because the knowledge gained is not fully applicable to other cases, or because the information proves to be unsuitable for justification or communication about the activity)
- EIA follow-up may be considered threatening and a burden on both the proponent of the activity and the consenting authority (Box 2.2); as a consequence, only limited resources may be made available
- external pressure may be lacking with community and environmental groups focusing on (opposing) new development proposals rather than ongoing management of existing activities.

5   *Uncertainties about EIA follow-up benefits and cost-effectiveness* Currently the benefits of EIA follow-up are not always clear to practitioners, and there is little insight into how to undertake follow-up in a cost-effective way relative to other elements of EIA. There seems to be an imbalance between the various 'stick' and 'carrot' factors (enforcement versus incentives). The stick is usually perceptible to practitioners, unlike the carrot, which may be less obvious. The latter relates to the objectives and functions that EIA follow-up may serve, as well as to the ways in which EIA follow-up can be undertaken. This imbalance, in turn, is related to a discrepancy between short-term and long-term interests; a dilemma which lies at the root of many environmental issues in general.

These five barriers to implementing EIA follow-up have to be taken carefully into account in order to fit follow-up well in the planning process. Identification of these barriers provides insight for the development of useful approaches to EIA follow-up, which are discussed in the next section.

Box 2.2 Potential Barriers to EIA Follow-up Implementation

Fear of opening Pandora's Box?

Most of the resistance against planning proposals – such as a road project or waste management facility – arises from the so-called 'NIMBY effect' (not in my back yard). People may be generally supportive of providing public services or infrastructure, but oppose solutions that directly intervene in their own living area (e.g. losing ownership of property or experiencing noise, air pollution or other nuisance). In a democracy, the objections of local community members have to be taken into account by decision-makers. However, the final decision may be in favour of the wider interest and against the local interest of one or more individual citizens. To protect the latter as much as possible, mitigation and compensation measures are usually proposed in an EIA study.

Based on their experience with road projects, Van Lamoen and Arts (2002) found that regulators can also experience a kind of NIMBY syndrome when it comes to follow-up. The outcome of follow-up studies mostly concerns local problems and local measures to remedy these. Out of fear of creating a precedent and of 'opening Pandora's Box', proponents (especially government agencies involved in widespread or multiple developments of a similar kind) may be reluctant to implement small-scale mitigation measures. While the cost of one mitigation measure may be acceptable, the possibility that such measures would subsequently be expected or required for all other similar projects under their control would be prohibitive. Consequently, proponents may avoid engaging in follow-up in the first place.

A post-decision impasse?

There are important differences between the pre- and post-decision stages of EIA. In the first stage the reward is clear for the proponent. They are prepared to 'jump through the hoop' of pre-decision EIA in order to get an approval decision. For the EIA regulator and the public, matters are relatively clear in the pre-decision stages: a proponent's proposal is subject to a formal EIA process in which the various parties may negotiate and bargain about changing the proposed development to suit their own needs or interests.

However, after the consent decision the situation may change dramatically, with follow-up viewed as being threatening or redundant. For proponents, EIA follow-up may be perceived as a costly exercise which they may avoid unless the law requires otherwise. Similarly, the public tends to lose interest as its attention cycle moves on to other new projects and issues in the pre-decision stage (i.e. the opportunity to halt or minimize the potential damage of a new development proposal might be considered of greater interest than an existing project for which the major 'damage' has already occurred). If the follow-up study reveals that the project's environmental performance is within the boundaries of the consent decision and the pre-decision EIA appraisal, the follow-up seems to be redundant. Such information would be interesting for the proponent and regulators, but they might question whether their limited staff and financial resources might better be used for alternative purposes. If the follow-up study shows that environmental performance is lacking, then it shows the proponent in a negative light. And if it is revealed that the pre-decision EIA evaluation was wildly inaccurate (e.g. significant unpredicted impacts actually occurred), then it casts a negative light on the pre-decision process itself (i.e. proponents would have to admit that their EIS investigations were inadequate and EIA regulators would have to acknowledge that their consent decision had been based on insufficient information). Finally, the public is confronted with a project and a consent decision that proved to be subject to failures and they may subsequently become (even more) suspicious of proponents and regulators or disenchanted with EIA at large.

In general there is a real risk that follow-up will reveal error, which most people do not readily embrace. These potential barriers highlight the need for an adaptive and cooperative approach to EIA follow-up. The case study chapters in this book showcase practical examples of the benefits that EIA follow-up can bring and the way that these potential barriers can be effectively overcome. It is important to realize that, providing it is done well, EIA follow-up is a positive and beneficial process.

Positioning EIA follow-up in the planning process

Having established the theoretical foundation and limitations of rational planning and decision-making, this section examines the role of EIA follow-up in the planning process.

The role of EIA follow-up for enhancing rationality in planning

From the previous discussion, it should be clear that, in practice, planning and decision-making are not carried out in a fully rational way. However, this does not imply that EIA that adopts the classic rational planning approach should be abandoned straight away. Rationality can be considered as a methodological principle. As Faludi (1985) noted, the rationality principle does not refer to how decisions *are made* in reality but to how they *ought to be made*. Popper's (1972) ideas of 'critical rationality' and the notion of a 'communicative rationality' (Habermas, 1981), which emphasize the importance of open discussion, freedom of opinion and learning, are relevant here.

Understood in this way, a *rational-analytical approach* to planning and decision-making can still be useful as an ideal and an objective for planning. It may work in an iconic manner, in the sense of preventing governmental consent decisions from being made on the basis of habit and intuition only, while enhancing the structured application of knowledge and methodology (i.e. evaluation techniques) in order to stimulate more explicit and open argumentation based on credible information. Democratic decision-making based on transparency and accountability and which pays due attention to vulnerable interests such as the environment may then result (Faludi, 1985; Guba and Lincoln, 1989; Nijkamp et al, 1990). Indeed, it can be argued that the instrument of EIA has been developed for these reasons and with this ideal in mind.

It can also be argued for the same reasons, that a follow-up to pre-decision EIA is necessary. Both EIA and EIA follow-up are meant to rationalize the cyclic, iterative, complex and dynamic processes of planning, project development and decision-making in practice. While the complex and dynamic nature of planning and decision-making may make EIA follow-up a fairly difficult task, it may nevertheless provide a useful instrument to overcome the limitations of EIA and to adapt EIA better to the non-linear nature of planning and decision-making. Some tension will always remain between EIA principles (including follow-up principles) and their practical application. But it can be argued that criticism of EIA follow-up in practice is a sign that it works (i.e. good advice needs to chafe a little, like sandpaper, in order to get a more polished and clear outcome).

Better fitting of EIA follow-up into planning practice

Within the field of EIA, various answers have been developed to resolve this tension and to better fit EIA in the process of planning. Examples include: careful screening and scoping, paying more attention to the early stages of planning through the development of SEA, addressing cumulative effects, enhancing public participation, and increasing awareness that EIA follow-up is essential for EIA to deliver its objectives. In the end, what matters is the environmental performance of an implemented EIA project in day-to-day life.

It is important to avoid the weaknesses and pitfalls of EIA when doing EIA follow-up. From the previous discussion, various clues for better fitting EIA follow-up in the planning process in practice can be derived. These clues are ordered in terms of some overarching principles followed by key points relating to the four elements of EIA follow-up (Box 1.2) as well as cost and timing practicalities:

Overarching principles

1 EIA follow-up should rationalize the process of decision-making, planning and project management in practice through an approach consisting of clearly defined steps that provide a structured process. A practical framework for project level EIA follow-up is presented in Chapter 3.

2 In this process the four central elements of follow-up (monitoring, evaluation, management and communication; Box 1.2) should be carefully given their place. These elements mesh with the concept of rational planning and its related criticisms. *Monitoring* is related to objectifying; i.e. the systematic collection, measurement and structuring of information (Suchman, 1967; Rossi and Freeman, 1989). It should be separated from the normative, subjective elements of follow-up, i.e. the appraisal and *evaluation* of monitoring data. The outcomes of EIA follow-up should lead to *management* actions and *communication* (if not also participation) with stakeholders. In this way the major pitfalls of the classical rational approach can be overcome.

Monitoring

3 Comprehensiveness is neither feasible nor relevant in practice; therefore it is important to have careful and early screening and scoping for EIA follow-up which begins in the pre-decision stages of EIA. What are the important uncertainties and gaps in knowledge that remain after the pre-decision EIA stage and how can they be dealt with via EIA follow-up? Rather than gathering more information in the EIA before taking a consent decision – i.e. a *content-oriented approach* – EIA follow-up encourages a *process-oriented approach* by addressing uncertainties in the follow-up stage in order to allow for remedial management responses through monitoring and adaptive management (Box 2.3).

4 The quality of the information gathered will always have its limits. Deficiencies in EISs, less-developed techniques for follow-up and lack of knowledge about causal relationships need to be taken into account when determining a useful and pragmatic EIA follow-up programme. Problems of causality may be avoided and practical usefulness for project management may be enhanced by choosing, for example, indicators that focus on protective facilities and provisions of the project and activity emissions, instead of on measuring impacts on flora, fauna and humans. It might be useful to combine this with state of the environment monitoring, which overcomes the intrinsic weakness of EIA of considering individual

projects in isolation. Synergistic or cumulative impacts are difficult to take into account in traditional EIA impact monitoring. Changes in the state of the environment (as opposed to impacts!) are quite straightforward to measure. Although it will often not be easy to link changes in the environment unambiguously to the management of a specific EIA activity, such a 'two-track strategy' – monitoring of the activity as well as monitoring of the environment – may help to safeguard the general environmental quality in an area.

Evaluation

5   Many different parties have influence in the process of planning, decision-making and project management and each will bring different values to it. At the extreme ends of the values spectrum, conservation groups such as Greenpeace will tend to be environment-centred, whereas proponents will generally be development-oriented. When establishing EIA follow-up processes for a proposal, it is important to take into account the decision-making power, roles and stakes of the various parties and to seek to enhance the potential for useful outcomes of EIA follow-up for them. Additionally, EIA follow-up should exploit the information already available within the various parties as they may usefully contribute to the follow-up process and outcomes.

Management

6   The planning process for plans or projects takes place in a specific and dynamic context, and implementation failures will always exist. Consequently, it is important to use a flexible, adaptive approach to EIA follow-up that allows for adequate management reactions to unanticipated situations and for the adjustment of our imperfect knowledge about our actions, society and environment (Box 2.3). Additionally, it is important to be aware of the interplay of the contextual factors introduced in Chapter 1 (regulations and institutional arrangements, approaches and techniques, resources and capacity, and activity type) as EIA follow-up is *contingent* upon these.

Communication

7   Just as open communication with stakeholders is a hallmark of effective pre-decision EIA practice, it is equally important during follow-up. Well-structured open processes, effective communication and active participation will enhance cooperation of the various parties and contribute to better outcomes for all involved. This is especially important as many of the parties involved have considerable power to obstruct decision-making and project development but little or insufficient power to enforce approval decisions once they have been made.

Costs

8   Because of organizational and resource limitations combined with the limited support for conducting follow-up, EIA follow-up programmes should be cost-effective and pragmatic, especially as they may operate over long time frames. It is important to determine at an early stage the objectives of EIA follow-up in order to focus the effort invested in follow-up and to clarify its relevance to the various stakeholders. It is also important to link up with other evaluative instruments and activities rather than overlap or duplicate them. The legal and administrative context in which follow-up is undertaken will determine resource requirements to a large extent. It is important to ensure that there is a clear division of tasks, responsibilities and costs of EIA follow-up for the key players involved.

Timing

9   To account for the tension between EIA follow-up principles and the nature of planning practice, the stepwise approach of EIA follow-up has to be carefully dovetailed with the cycles in existing planning, decision-making and project management activities. Notwithstanding the continuous nature of the planning process, 'evaluative moments' can be distinguished when a decision is made on important aspects and an assessment of impacts may be relevant. The point at which the consent decision is made is an example of an evaluative moment which has a specific place in the regulatory framework and therefore requires an EIA. Other important decision points may arise after the consent decision and may provide 'windows of opportunity' for useful follow-up (Deelstra et al, 2003) such as: detailed activity design, issuing of contracts for construction, manner of operation, extension or change to the activity and decommissioning.

From theory to practice

In this chapter, the rationale as well as the problems and pitfalls of EIA follow-up have been discussed from a theoretical perspective of planning and decision-making. This provides a good foundation for the subsequent chapter in which a practical framework for EIA follow-up is presented. The case study chapters that follow also address further the issues raised here.

EIA follow-up provides a positive and practical way to overcome the theoretical limitations of classical rational planning and decision-making (and thus EIA). Follow-up builds feedback loops into the EIA process making it more flexible and adaptive to complex practice. It provides a useful approach to deal with uncertainty that is intrinsic to project planning and decision-making. Through its learning-by-experience approach, EIA follow-up also gives clues on how to improve EIA practice. Finally, through follow-up the environmental performance of an EIA project or plan can be established to

Box 2.3 Hedging and Flexing

Two main complementary principles for dealing with uncertainties may be distinguished. One tries to 'box' them in by gathering as much information as possible and taking measures for the containment of risks (*hedging*). The other tries to master risks by using an early warning system and an adaptable design (*flexing*) so that if problems do occur, reparation is possible and the focus is on adaptive management (Holling, 1978). If hedging of uncertainties is not possible, flexing may be a way to overcome this (and vice versa). Ideally, both principles should be in balance in order to deal well with uncertainty (Collingridge, 1983).

The EIA-process up to the consent decision can be seen as a form of hedging – the motto can be described as 'think before you act'. EIA follow-up is based on the principle of flexing and lends itself towards an adaptive management approach. Scoping in follow-up involves a quick scan for the most important environmental aspects, based on available information. This general scan acts as an early warning system for likely 'trouble spots'. When problems arise, project managers are already tuned in to them. An in-depth assessment can then be carried out and an appropriate management response implemented. This flexing approach to EIA follow-up corresponds well to the 'mixed-scanning approach' of Etzioni (1967).

answer the question: have the interests of the environment been safeguarded? (the original rationale of the instrument of EIA). To this end, both the pre- and post-decision components of the EIA process are vital. Therefore, post-decision monitoring, evaluation and adaptive management actions (i.e. follow-up) are an integral part of a fully fledged EIA process.

References

Arts, J (1998) *EIA Follow-up – On the Role of Ex Post Evaluation in Environmental Impact Assessment*, Groningen, Geo Press

Arts, J and Nooteboom, S (1999) 'Environmental Impact Assessment Monitoring and Auditing', in Petts, J (ed) *Handbook of Environmental Impact Assessment Volume 1. Environmental Impact Assessment: Process, Methods and Potential*, Oxford, Blackwell Science, pp229–251

Au, E and Sanvicens, G (1996) 'EIA Follow-up Monitoring and Management', in *EIA Process Strengthening*, Canberra, Australian Environmental Protection Agency

Bartlett, R V (1986) 'Rationality and the logic of the National Environmental Policy Act', *Environmental Professional*, vol 8, pp105–111

Beanlands, G and Duinker, P (1984) 'An ecological framework for EIA', *Journal of Environmental Management*, vol 18, pp267–277

Bisset, R (1984) 'Post-development audits to investigate the accuracy of environmental impact predictions', *Umweltpolitik*, vol 4, pp463–484

Breheny, M and Hooper, A (eds) (1985) *Rationality in Planning, Critical Essays on the Role of Rationality in Urban and Regional Planning*, London, Pion

Bressers, J (1989) *Naar een nieuwe cybernetica in de beleidswetenschap (Towards new cybernetics in policy sciences)*, Enschede, Universiteit Twenthe

Buit, J (1985) 'Explicit Evaluation in a Period of Decline and Scarcity', in Faludi, A and Voogd, H (eds) *Evaluation of Complex Policy Problems*, Delft, Delftsche Uitgeversmij, pp67–77

Caldwell, L (1982) *Science and the National Environmental Policy Act: Redirecting Policy through Procedural Reform*, Alabama, University of Alabama Press

Collingridge, D (1983) 'Hedging and flexing, two ways of choosing under ignorance', *Technological Forecasting and Social Change*, vol 23, pp161–172

Culhane, P, Friesema, H and Beecher, J (1987*) Forecasts and Environmental Decision-Making, the Content and Predictive Accuracy of Environmental Impact Statements*, Boulder, Colorado, Westview Press

De Bruijn, H and Ten Heuvelhof, E (2002) 'Policy analysis and decision making in a network: how to improve the quality of analysis and the impact on decision making', *Impact Assessment and Project Appraisal*, vol 20, pp232–242

Deelstra, Y, Nooteboom, S, Kohlmann, H, Van den Berg, J and Innanen, I (2003) 'Using knowledge for decision-making purposes in the context of large projects in the Netherlands', *Environmental Impact Assessment Review*, vol 23, pp517–541

Deming, W (1986) *Out of crisis*, Massachusetts Institute of Technology, Cambridge, MA, MIT Press

Dror, Y (1963) 'Planning Process: A Facet Design', reprinted in Faludi, A (ed) (1973) *A Reader in Planning Theory*, Oxford, Pergamon Press, pp323–344

Dunsire, A (1978), *Implementation in a Bureaucracy*, Oxford, Pergamon Press

ECW, Evaluation Committee Environmental Management Act (1990) *Naar een volwaardige plaats: advies over de regeling m.e.r. uit de Wabm (Advisory report on the performance of the EIA regulations)*, Advies no3, Leidschendam, Ministerie VROM

Etzioni, A (1967) 'Mixed Scanning: A 'Third' Approach to Decision-making', reprinted in Faludi, A (ed) (1973) *A Reader in Planning Theory*, Oxford, Pergamon Press, pp217–229

Faludi, A (ed) (1973) *A Reader in Planning Theory*, Oxford, Pergamon Press

Faludi, A (1985) 'Return of Rationality', in Breheny, M and Hooper, A (eds) (1985) *Rationality in Planning, Critical essays on the role of rationality in urban and regional planning*, London, Pion, pp27–47

Faludi, A and Van der Valk, A (1994) *Rule and Order, Dutch Planning Doctrine in the Twentieth Century*, Dordrecht, Kluwer Academic Publishers

Friend, J K and Jessop, W N (1969) *Local Government and Strategic Choice*, 2nd edition (1977), Oxford, Pergamon Press

Glasson J (1994) 'Life after the decision: The importance of monitoring in EIA', *Built Environment*, vol 20, pp309–320

Guba, E and Lincoln, Y (1989) *Fourth Generation Evaluation*, Newbury Park, California, Sage Publications

Habermas, J (1981) *Theorie des kommunikativen Handelns (Theory of Communicative Action)*, Parts 1 and 2, Frankfurt am Main, Suhrkamp

Hall, P (1982) *Great Planning Disasters*, California Series in Urban Development no1, Berkeley, University of California Press

Healey, P (1983) *Local Plans in British Land-Use Planning*, Oxford, Pergamon Press

Healey, P (1996) 'The communicative turn in planning theory and its implications for spatial strategy formation', *Environment and Planning B, Planning and Design*, vol 23, pp217–234

Healey, P (1997) *Collaborative Planning, Shaping Places in Fragmented Societies*, London, Macmillan Press

Holling, C (ed) (1978) *Adaptive Environmental Assessment and Management*, Chichester, UK, John Wiley

Hoogerwerf, A (ed) (1983) *Succes en falen van overheidsbeleid (Success and Failure of Governmental Policy-making)*, Alphen a/d Rijn, Samsom

IAIA, International Association for Impact Assessment (2002) *The Linkages between Impact Assessment and the Sustainable Development Agenda, and Recommendations for Agenda*, Statements and Policy Briefing for the World Summit on Sustainable Developments in Johannesburg August 2002, Fargo, ND, IAIA International Headquarters

Lichfield, N, Kettle, P and Whitbread, M (1975) *Evaluation in the Planning Process*, Urban and Regional Planning Series vol 10, Oxford, Pergamon Press

Lindblom, C (1959) 'Science of Muddling Through', in Faludi, A (ed) (1973), *A Reader in Planning Theory*, Oxford, Pergamon Press

Mayda, J (1996) 'Reforming impact assessment: Issues, premises, and elements', *Impact Assessment*, vol 14, pp87–96

Morrison-Saunders, A and Bailey, J (1999) 'Exploring the EIA/environmental management relationship', *Environmental Management*, vol 24, pp281–295

Nijkamp, P, Rietveld, P and Voogd, H (eds) (1990) *Multicriteria Evaluation in Physical Planning*, Amsterdam, North-Holland

Partidário, M R (2001) 'Environmental and Sustainability Assessment – New Challenges in Evaluation in Planning', in Voogd, H (ed) *Recent Developments in Evaluation in Spatial, Infrastructure and Environmental Planning*, Groningen, Geo Press

Petts, J (ed) (1999) *Handbook of Environmental Impact Assessment*, vol 1 and 2, Oxford, Blackwell Science

Popper, K R (1972) *The Logic of Scientific Discovery*, 2nd edition, London, Hutchinson

Rossi, P and Freeman, H (1989) *Evaluation, A Systematic Approach*, 4th edition, Newbury Park, California, Sage Publications

Sadler, B (1996) *International Study of the Effectiveness of Environmental Assessment, Final Report, Environmental Assessment in a Changing World: Evaluating Practice to Improve Performance*, Canadian Environmental Assessment Agency and the International Association for Impact Assessment, Minister of Supply and Services, Canada

Schön, D (1983) *The Reflective Practitioner, How Professionals Think in Action*, New York, Basic Books

Simon, H (1957) *Administrative Behavior*, New York, Macmillan

Stolp, A, Groen, W, Van Vliet, J and Vanclay, F (2002) 'Citizens' values assessment: Incorporating citizens' value judgements in environmental impact assessment', *Impact Assessment and Project Appraisal*, vol 20, pp11–23

Suchman, E (1967) *Evaluative Research, Principles and Practice in Public Service and Social Action Programs*, New York, Russell Sage Foundation

Taylor, S (1984) *Making Bureaucracies Think, Environmental Impact Assessment Strategy of Administrative Reform*, California, Stanford University Press

Teisman, G (1992) *Complexe besluitvorming (Complex Decision-making)*, The Hague, Vuga

Van Lamoen, F and Arts, J (2002) 'EIA Follow-up for Road Projects: What Do We Want and Need to Know?', presented at *Assessing the Impact of Impact Assessment: Impact*

Assessment for Informed Decision Making, 22nd Annual Meeting of the International Association for Impact Assessment, 15–21 June 2002, The Hague, published on CD ROM: *IA Follow-up Workshop*, Hull, Quebec, Environment Canada

Voogd, H (1983) *Multicriteria Evaluation for Urban Regional Planning*, London, Pion

Voogd, H (1996) *Facetten van de Planologie (Aspects of Planning)*, 3rd edition, Alphen a/d Rijn, Samsom H.D. Tjeenk Willink

Voogd, H (2001) 'Social dilemmas and the communicative planning paradox', *Town Planning Review*, vol 72, pp77–95

Woltjer, J (2000) *Consensus Planning – The Relevance of Communicative Planning Theory in Dutch Infrastructure Development*, Aldershot, Ashgate

World Bank (1995) *The Impact of Impact Assessment*, draft report, Washington, DC, World Bank Environment Department

3

A Practical Framework for EIA Follow-up

Jill Baker

Introduction

This chapter consolidates the key elements of EIA follow-up into a practical framework in order to develop guidance for the design and implementation of more specific follow-up programmes and strategies. This guidance is flexible enough that it may be applicable in many EIA regimes around the globe. It is not meant to be prescriptive, but rather presents common elements that can be used by practitioners in their own development of more defined and focused follow-up programmes.

The framework's application is aimed at project EIAs. It has been suggested that a project approach to follow-up may not be the most effective, and that a more holistic approach to follow-up is warranted, such as approaching it from a regional perspective (Arts et al, 2001). Such an approach would be best if the associated EIA is also undertaken in this manner; however, the reality still exists that most assessment work continues to be conducted at the project level, and therefore the follow-up component will likely also remain at the project level for now.

Background

The concept of EIA follow-up is commonly referred to as monitoring, auditing, ex-post evaluation, post-decision analysis and post-decision management (Chapter 1). In association with the various terms used to describe this concept, several definitions of follow-up are also found in the scientific and professional literature. One definition of follow-up proposed by the International Association for Impact Assessment (IAIA, 1999) states that:

The EIA process should provide for follow up – to ensure that the terms and conditions of approval are met; to monitor the impacts of development and the effectiveness of mitigation measures; to strengthen future EIA applications and mitigation measures; and, where required, to undertake environmental audit and process evaluation to optimize environmental management.

The last point is particularly important; given that one of the key goals of follow-up is to ensure that unacceptable environmental impacts are corrected, this goal must be attained either through proposed mitigation measures or through follow-up management actions. Such management is important not only for regulators and the affected public, but for the proponents as well. As noted by Marshall et al (2001), the private sector often needs to prove its competence with respect to environmental affairs, in the eyes of all stakeholders. Additionally, proponents need to understand that there may be important potential financial savings realized through environmental management via environmental follow-up.

Various purposes of EIA follow-up are provided in Chapter 1, in addition to the context in which follow-up takes place. However, it is noted here that the rationale for conducting follow-up can be summarized as follows (Sadler, 1988):

Unless there is a minimum follow-up capability, EIA operates as a linear rather than iterative process and lacks continuity. Even worse, the process risks becoming a pro-forma exercise rather than a meaningful exercise in environmental management.

Methodology

Development of the EIA follow-up framework is based on a review of existing policies, papers and projects on EIA follow-up. Previous attempts at developing a framework and at developing a standardized methodological approach are evident in the literature (Sadler, 1987a, b, 1988; Au and Sanvicens, 1996). The framework reported on here is largely based upon previous work conducted for Environment Canada (Baker and Dobos, 2001). A draft of this framework was presented at the IAIA annual conference in 2002; comments and recommendations received at the conference were utilized in the final development of the framework.

A practical follow-up framework

Existing follow-up requirements in EIA legislation can be found in several countries such as: Portugal, Australia, The Netherlands, China (Hong Kong), Canada and the US. The proposed framework incorporates components from some of these jurisdictions, as well the findings of other countries as expressed by participants at three recent international workshops on follow-up (Arts et al, 2001; Morrison-Saunders et al, 2001, 2003) This section first defines each of the key elements, and then discusses how they relate to one another within the context of the entire framework. It ends with a brief discussion of the elements of the framework in relation to the generic EIA and project development processes, with a focus on when to conduct follow-up.

Basic issues

There are a number of issues that should be taken into consideration before and during the development of any follow-up programme (Box 3.1). These are the underlying assumptions that should be considered carefully during design of the follow-up programme. By striving to encompass these principles, the practitioner will likely optimize the probability of achieving success for the follow-up programme.

Box 3.1 Basic Issues for EIA Follow-up

Many of the following issues for EIA follow-up are also basic principles of EIA, as described by IAIA (1999). Follow-up should strive to be:

- goal-oriented and focused
- practical and relevant
- cost-effective and efficient
- adaptive and flexible, with orientation towards continuous improvement
- participative (inclusive of all stakeholders)
- interdisciplinary
- transparent and credible.

Firstly, like EIA itself, the associated follow-up programme should be goal-oriented and focused. It needs to be practical and relevant to the most important issues. This will maximize cost-effectiveness and efficiency.

Given that EIA work is predictive, based on the best available knowledge at the time of the assessment, it should be expected that the EIA may not be completely accurate in its predictions. Therefore, the follow-up work that will be required to correct errors will need to be set in an environment that is adaptable. Rigid mitigation measures and plans associated with a follow-up programme may not allow for corrective actions to be taken when and where they are needed. Similarly, there may be a need for flexibility on the part of the regulatory agencies to allow for innovation in corrective actions to be taken by the proponent.

Like the EIA process itself, the follow-up programme should attempt to include all stakeholders at many different points in the process. It may also benefit from taking an interdisciplinary approach, whereby the various specialists and professionals involved in the follow-up programme work together from the beginning. This approach may create opportunities for efficiencies to be gained through cooperative efforts.

Finally, the follow-up programme, as with the EIA itself, should be transparent. The objectives, approaches, findings and conclusions of the programme should be presented in a manner that makes them easy to understand by all stakeholders, not just the experts involved. In other words, it is important to keep the follow-up programme simple and focused.

Key elements

The key elements of the proposed framework include (Figure 3.1):

1 determination of the need for follow-up
2 determination of the roles and responsibilities, the scope of issues to be addressed and the selection of methodology and tools that may be incorporated into the programme
3 follow-up implementation
4 evaluation of results and outcomes
5 issue management
6 stakeholder communication.

In Figure 3.1, the framework itself is presented alongside a simple diagram of the pre-decision stages of EIA, the project development process and the consent decision itself (column 1). Stakeholder communication (column 3) represents the final key element of the framework. Communication with stakeholders should be included in many of the steps of the framework, and thus needs to be separated out and uniquely identified within the context of the rest of the framework. A detailed discussion of these elements and their relationships to one another and to the EIA and project development processes follows.

Many practitioners associate EIA follow-up primarily with the post-decision stages of a project (Arts et al, 2001). This largely holds true for the implementation aspects of follow-up programmes. However, the framework proposed here deviates from this perception in that several aspects of follow-up need to be considered before a consent decision is made. The first two components of the framework – determining the need for follow-up and designing the follow-up programme – should ideally be completed during the pre-decision EIA process. By doing so, information provided in the follow-up programme may be provided to decision-makers prior to a final decision. In turn, decision-makers may use the consent decision itself to influence the final form of the follow-up programme.

Determination of need (step I)

The follow-up framework begins with the question: why do follow-up? The need for follow-up may be strictly related to a legal obligation; however, it

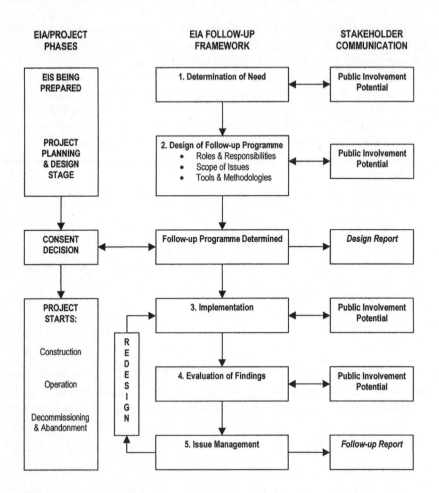

Figure 3.1 *Environmental Impact Assessment Follow-up Framework*

appears that few countries have legislated a follow-up requirement into their EIA regimes. Au and Sanvicens (1996) suggest that project surveillance and auditing for compliance, as conditions of approval, should be regarded as the minimum requirements in any situation. If the need for follow-up relates to reasons other than legal requirements then there must be a clear indication of the added value of conducting the follow-up. Added value can be demonstrated by taking into consideration all of the objectives outlined in the previous chapters.

The question of why conduct a follow-up programme can be answered with a multitude of different solutions. The approach used in The Netherlands (Chapter 4) clearly identifies the added value of follow-up and focuses on three core purposes of follow-up: control, information and communication (Arts and Nooteboom, 1999; Meijer and Van Vliet, 2000). Although formally required for every EIA under the Dutch system, Meijer and Van Vliet (2000) suggest that the regulators may decide against follow-up if it is defined as unproductive for any of these purposes. In contrast, the Canadian follow-up regulatory requirements focus the purpose of follow-up on determining effectiveness of mitigation measures and accuracy of EIA predictions. Similarly, the Portuguese follow-up regulations are focused on compliance monitoring of the detailed project design with the EIA decision, and monitoring and auditing for all other issues (Jesus, 2000).

A second component to the question of need must also be considered: if a need is identified, is there a mechanism that will allow for a response (such as taking extra mitigation measures)? That is, if or when an issue is identified through a follow-up mechanism, is there some means of addressing it? If the answer is clearly no, then there is likely no point in engaging in follow-up.

More often than not the need for follow-up will be determined by the regulatory agency, but may also be identified by any of the other stakeholders involved. For example, Marshall (2001) explains the need for follow-up as being crucial for proponents as a means of issue resolution and ensuring that mitigation measure promises are integrated into project plans, thereby establishing credibility not only with the regulatory body but with the affected public as well. Regardless of who identifies the need, it is useful to have a set of criteria to assist in this determination (Box 3.2). When determining need, consideration must also be given to the time and human and financial resources involved, as well as to the values of the affected public (Austin, 2000).

Box 3.2 Determining the Need for EIA Follow-up

A proposed Canadian follow-up framework (Baker and Dobos, 2001) sets out the following considerations for determining need (influenced by Sadler, 1996):

- where there is a regulatory (legal) requirement to do so
- where there is limited experience by the proponent in implementation of the type of project proposed
- for issues of high public concern
- in environmentally sensitive areas
- where there is some reasonable uncertainty in the accuracy of the analysis and predictions
- where the proposed mitigation measures may not fully address the predicted effects (i.e. residual effects will occur)
- where new or unproven technology or techniques are proposed, including mitigation, analytical or modelling techniques
- where significant cumulative effects are predicted to occur
- the sensitivity or scale of the project in relation to the risk associated with failure of proposed mitigation measures
- where adaptive management is being proposed in the EIA as a mitigation approach.

In relation to the pre-decision EIA process (Figure 3.1), the need for follow-up should optimally be determined early in the EIA phase, during the stages where impact predictions are being made and mitigation measures are being proposed. It may be evident from the identification of key issues during Environmental Impact Statement (EIS) preparation that some level of follow-up is required. Consequently, this may be the most effective time to design the follow-up programme (step 2).

Follow-up programme design (step 2)

Once the need for follow-up has been established, the critical design phase of the follow-up programme begins. This step involves the determination of roles and responsibilities, the scope of follow-up issues, and the tools and methodologies to be used in the follow-up programme (Figure 3.1). Careful consideration of these factors is critical for ensuring effectiveness and efficiency of the entire follow-up process. Ideally, if more thought and effort is put into the design phase, then fewer problems should arise in the latter part of the follow-up programme.

Determination of roles and responsibilities

A clear understanding of the roles and responsibilities of all stakeholders is crucial for implementing efficient follow-up programmes; if no one is accountable then the tasks are unlikely to be completed satisfactorily. It can be expected that many participants in the pre-decision EIA process will want to participate in the follow-up programme, some by necessity, others voluntarily. Determination of roles and responsibilities may depend upon the reasons for conducting the follow-up. If the follow-up is a requirement of a project approval, then the regulator will play a significant role in all aspects of the follow-up. The determination of roles and responsibilities is likely to be project specific. There are some good examples of the various roles and responsibilities that stakeholders can play (Morrison-Saunders et al, 2001, 2003), as subsequent chapters demonstrate.

Decision-maker/regulatory authority

Regulators may provide significant input into the design of the follow-up programme, primarily discussing with the proponent the requirements and conditions that must be included, but also assisting in the design of components that will improve the overall performance of the follow-up programme. Appropriate authorities with specialist or expert knowledge may be consulted for their input at the design stage, as well as later at the evaluation stage. Regulators may try to ensure that proponents fulfil their follow-up requirements by including these in authorizations, licences, permits or approval conditions. If follow-up is a legal requirement, then the responsibility to determine the acceptability of the design lies with the regulatory agency. A good example of this is found in Hong Kong, where the follow-up programme (known formally as Environmental Monitoring and Auditing) clearly defines the roles and responsibilities of the proponent, the Environmental Protection Department, and the public (EPD, 2002; Chapter 9). In The Netherlands, the regulator is primarily responsible for conducting follow-up and the proponent is obliged to cooperate (Van Lamoen and Arts, 2002).

Proponent

Proponents, more often than not, are designated the responsibility of designing and implementing the follow-up programme. For example, recent changes in Canadian EIA follow-up practice allow for the regulator 'to require the proponent to plan for a follow-up programme early in the planning stages of a project and to ensure its implementation' (CEAA, 2002). Although the majority of the design and implementation responsibility may rest with the proponent, these steps should not be done in isolation, but in consultation with all stakeholders, including the affected public. Marshall (2001) provides a good description of roles and responsibilities of the proponent in situations where follow-up is not a regulatory requirement, but rather a (voluntary) means of project management that integrates EIA recommendations into project plans. Public participation and consultation are still very important to this approach. Morrison-Saunders et al (2003) suggest that the self-regulatory initiatives of proponents may fill the gap in EIA regulations in some jurisdictions.

Community and affected public

Community participation is a critical element of the EIA process, and therefore should be a key consideration in any follow-up programme. Austin (2000) suggests that EIA follow-up activities that involve local communities are opportunities for recognizing and enhancing local environmental, social and cultural awareness and knowledge, examining project impacts on that knowledge, and then incorporating that knowledge into the decision-making process. She also concluded that a major consequence of community participation in the follow-up activities was enhanced and better-informed communication about projects within communities and regular communication between communities and the regulatory authorities. Chapter 8 describes the potential roles and responsibilities of an appointed independent third-party monitoring agency made up of regulators, the proponent, academics, aboriginal persons and community members along with the successes and shortcomings of such an arrangement. Other examples of the use of community and local knowledge in EIA follow-up can be found in Denis (2002) and Morrison-Saunders et al (2003). Further suggestions for the role of the community in follow-up are provided later.

The stakeholders involved in follow-up may be collectively organized into a formal follow-up committee. If this is the case, then it may be useful to develop some basic guidelines that define the roles of the committee so that people can decide if they want to be, or can be, involved. One of the challenges facing follow-up committees is that often they are formed in response to a particular issue. Over time, as the initial issue is addressed and others arise, the interest level in the committee often declines, and it is difficult to ensure the effectiveness of the committee over long periods of time (Gagnon et al, 2002). It may be useful to note that O'Beirne et al (2000) found that having senior project decision-makers on the coordinating committee made it possible to respond quickly and effectively to environmental management requirements as they arose.

Determination of scope of issues

In some jurisdictions, such as The Netherlands, follow-up has to be conducted for all projects that undergo an EIA process (Chapter 4); however, this is not realistic for most jurisdictions, given the number of projects developed each year and/or the magnitude of the projects that warrant significant efforts with respect to follow-up. As is the case in scoping an EIA, there is a need to focus on the important issues, not necessarily on all the issues. Furthermore, the scope of issues to be followed up should focus on collecting the appropriate information at an appropriate scale and effort. The scope of the follow-up programme may depend on the potential significance of the impacts and the uncertainties about predictions and outcomes (Sadler, 1996). Selection criteria that might be used in the scoping of EIA follow-up are presented in Box 3.3.

Box 3.3 EIA Follow-up Scoping Criteria

The selection criteria used to identify critical issues in EIA follow-up programmes may include focusing on situations where (Baker and Dobos, 2001):

- residual effects may occur
- the effects are considered to be most adverse, including cumulatively
- valued ecosystem components are likely to be affected
- gaps in knowledge exist
- there is a significant level of predictive uncertainty
- there is public sensitivity to an issue.

The level of effort put into the follow-up programme will likely be project-specific and issue-specific and should be customized. There is likely no need to address every issue to the same level of detail. The level of detail should be appropriate to the scale, sensitivity and complexity of the issue, and should be reflected in the choice of methodologies (which is also part of the design stage).

Ideally, the scoping of follow-up issues should be undertaken as an integral part of the pre-decision EIA process, possibly conducted at the same time that mitigation measures are being proposed. As mitigation is proposed for various predicted impacts, it should become apparent (based on the scoping criteria established) whether follow-up is likely to be necessary for each issue identified. The final decision on the scope of follow-up requirements should be made prior to project approval so that such requirements may be incorporated into the terms and conditions of the project approval.

Selection of methodologies and tools

In addition to determining who will be involved, to what degree, and what issues will be addressed, there needs to be thoughtful consideration of the question of how each issue will be addressed. Several approaches and tools can be used to implement an EIA follow-up programme (Box 3.4). This list is

---

Box 3.4 Methodologies and Tools for Follow-up Programmes

A wide range of methodologies and tools may be employed in EIA follow-up at the project level including:

- environmental monitoring (base-line, effects and compliance)
- environmental audits
- site visits or inspections
- proponent's environmental manager and environmental management system
- multi-stakeholder advisory committees (may be an independent third party appointed by the decision-maker or may be community based)
- use of written agreements or contracts between regulators, proponents and other stakeholders
- integration of follow-up terms and conditions into authorizations, licences, permits or approvals
- an adaptive management approach (must be integrated with the proposed mitigation strategy)
- financial assurances, staged approvals or progressive funding arrangements
- regional environmental initiatives
- area-wide monitoring (general state of the environment monitoring schemes)
- analysis of (secondary) monitoring data, documents, calculations, modelling, mapping and expert judgements
- field research, inventories, interviews with people and registrations of activities
- project log books (deviations from regular development/operation)
- complaints register
- camera or monitoring equipment streaming images or data onto a publicly accessible internet site.

EIA follow-up closely parallels activities undertaken during the preparation of EISs for which many text books have been written on methodological aspects.

---

not exhaustive; it is merely intended to provide some ideas for the designers of EIA follow-up programmes. Several of these tools and approaches are described in detail in other chapters and so a description of each will not be provided here.

The selection of methods is dependent on various factors, including the scope and type of project, the nature of the issues to be addressed and the extent to which stakeholders are involved in the follow-up process. Thus, selection must be project specific. Other methodological factors to consider may include likely costs and benefits and the actual feasibility or practicality of carrying out the EIA follow-up.

There is no evidence to suggest that any one of these tools is more effective than the others. However, the selection of tools and methods to be used in implementing the follow-up programme should be considered carefully. For example, experience from South Africa (O'Beirne et al, 2000) demonstrated that the success of implementation of mitigation measures was dependent not just on describing the mitigation measures but on determining the mechanisms that would ensure their implementation.

Follow-up programme documentation

Ideally, the design phase of the follow-up programme should be completed (partially or fully) and documented prior to a consent decision being made so that it can be taken into consideration during this decision-making process. A 'preliminary' follow-up programme could either be incorporated into the EIS itself or be provided as a separate document. Providing this information prior to a consent decision being made would allow it to influence the outcome, resulting in better-informed decisions. Under the framework of Figure 3.1, this follow-up programme would be finalized only after the consent decision has been made. The programme should be amended in light of the consent decision to accommodate any recommendations and conditions attached to the approval, prior to project implementation. The incorporation of commitments made by proponents and recommendations made by other stakeholders into a legally binding decision is a common feature in some jurisdictions, such as Western Australia (Bailey, 1997), Hong Kong (EPD, 2002) and The Netherlands (Chapter 4). The final follow-up programme should be formally documented to help ensure accountability for the programme by all stakeholders involved.

Implementation (step 3)

The implementation step of the framework is simply the beginning of the post-decision stages of EIA in which the follow-up programme, as agreed at the design stage, is put into operation. This is the phase that most practitioners identify as 'follow-up'. For example, this is the step where mitigation measures are put into place and impact monitoring and/or audit programmes begin.

Implementation of the follow-up programme may start along with project construction, or it may not be necessary until operations begin; again, this determination is project specific. Implementation initially consists largely of data and information collection, which should allow for verification of impact predictions and implementation of mitigation measures. Specific requirements of the implementation stage are solely dependent on the nature of the follow-up programmes and are, therefore, project specific.

Evaluation of findings (step 4)

The submission of EIA follow-up reports is often where the follow-up process stops. Unfortunately the evaluation of the outcomes and results from the follow-up is often not conducted, but this analysis should be carried out as it is a critical step in the process. An analysis of the data collected should be conducted to ensure that the information provided is useful for the targeted audience. Data itself is not necessarily useful information; the meaning of the data needs to be extracted.

Overall, the evaluation stage needs to identify the lessons learned from the EIA follow-up programme. This involves not only continuing with the subsequent steps, but, ultimately, addressing the question: did the advice provided protect the environment and/or mitigate the environmental effects?

More specifically, the evaluation of the EIA follow-up results should determine the completeness and adequacy of the information provided. Results and outcomes need to be compared to base-line information collected prior to project implementation, as well as to EIA predictions in order to determine the accuracy of the assessment and the effectiveness of the mitigation measures. Where possible there will need to be a comparison of the monitoring or audit results with any existing guidelines to determine compliance. Any unforeseen effects need to be noted for further assessment, if deemed necessary.

The evaluation of results (including an analysis of the quality of the information provided) could be conducted by any one or several of the follow-up participants, depending upon the programme, the conditions of the follow-up programme and any agreements. Often the appropriate regulatory authorities will be involved to some degree in the evaluation process, but in some unique situations, the evaluation of findings is not in the hands of the proponent or the regulators. For example, results of the follow-up programme in Hong Kong are independently evaluated by a third party (EPD, 2002). In another example, a unique arrangement set up in northern Canada provides for an independent monitoring agency, comprising the government, proponent and aboriginal community members, to be the overall evaluators of the follow-up information (Chapter 8). This arrangement is also unique in that it evaluates the actions of the regulatory agencies as well as those of the proponent.

The steps involved in the evaluation stage are likely to be project specific and dependent upon the methods and tools that were selected to implement the programme. However, there are some generic steps that should occur to ensure that an evaluation is completed (Box 3.5).

Box 3.5 Four Steps in the Evaluation of EIA Follow-up

1   The responsible agency (regulator or proponent) should ensure that all requested information has been submitted by the proponent in a timely manner, according to the agreed schedule.

2   The responsible agency should ensure that all materials submitted are reviewed by the respective experts and committees as set out at the beginning of the follow-up programme.

3   Once the responsible agency has reviewed the material it should determine whether further measures are necessary (through consultation with all stakeholders or follow-up committee members).

4   Outcomes from the evaluation stage should be documented as appropriate. If further mitigation measures are identified as being necessary during the evaluation stage, then this should be discussed with the proponent and interested stakeholders.

Regardless of the design of the programme, findings should be submitted to those appointed responsible for the programme in a formal follow-up report. These reports should be submitted to the regulatory agency responsible for the project and should be distributed by the stakeholder who has agreed to take the lead role in the EIA follow-up programme to all other stakeholders. This will ensure accountability among the participants in the follow-up programme and maintain a transparent and credible process.

Issue management (step 5)

The evaluation stage of the EIA follow-up programme may determine that further steps are needed in order to manage the issues identified. There are numerous reasons and situations that may warrant taking further actions, however; in general these may include situations in which:

* proposed mitigation measures have not been implemented or were not effective
* the EIA follow-up identified unexpected environmental impacts
* the EIS was incorrect in its predictions of the anticipated effects of the project and adverse environmental effects occurred
* proposed methodologies have been implemented and are proving to be ineffective or inappropriate.

Depending upon the findings of the evaluation, further measures may involve adapting the follow-up programme and then re-implementing the revised programme (Figure 3.1). Revisions may be needed for any number of aspects of the design, such as a re-evaluation of mitigation measures, project construction or operations, or the methodologies in the follow-up programme. A useful approach for managing such situations is the implementation of an adaptive management approach at the outset of the EIA. This approach works best when designed during the planning stage of the project and implemented during the start of construction or operational start-up (O'Beirne et al, 2000). However, it may also prove to be useful as a measure to manage follow-up issues that are identified during the evaluation stage of the follow-up programme (Chapter 7).

To remedy problems identified during follow-up, modification of project construction activities, operations or decommissioning activities may be required. Such measures will require flexibility on the part of the proponent with respect to monitoring programmes, other follow-up approaches and tools, as well as to project operations.

Once the appropriate management measures have been agreed, a schedule should be developed to complete implementation of these actions and should be discussed and agreed by those involved. If there are no problems identified in the evaluation stage, then the management step in the follow-up process is not necessary.

To close off the follow-up process, a report or some form of written communication should be presented to the appropriate agencies and stakeholders, identifying specific findings of the follow-up programme, any management measures taken to address outstanding issues, and the conclusions drawn from the entire process.

Stakeholder communication

Communication with stakeholders, whether it be through verbal communication, written reports or both, is a key component of the follow-up programme, for without it there may be no mechanism of:

- knowing whether commitments were honoured
- knowing whether mitigation and management measures were successful
- ensuring accountability and credibility
- passing on the lessons learned to others for future use.

This aspect of the framework acknowledges that the 'stakeholders' comprise all groups potentially involved in an EIA and the follow-up programme. However, in discussing communication, emphasis is given here to the affected public, as the involvement of the other groups in an EIA (and follow-up programme) is often inherent.

It is not the intention here to determine what is required for ensuring complete and comprehensive communication with stakeholders, nor is there any attempt at defining stakeholder consultation or public participation – such information can be found in the professional and scientific literature (e.g. Petts, 1999). It is necessary, however, briefly to discuss where stakeholder communication and consultation (and consequently, reporting) may be potentially advantageous within the follow-up framework. For the purposes of the framework, the various forms of communication, whether they be informal discussions, formal consultation and negotiations or written reports, are generalized as 'stakeholder involvement'. The nature and extent of specific communication and consultation plans will likely be project dependent.

For the most part, stakeholder consultation should be considered for almost all steps of a follow-up programme (Figure 3.1), beginning with deciding upon the need for follow-up and continuing through the management stage. Public concern over any given issue(s) may often be a key determinant for conducting an EIA, therefore it is obvious that this may also be true for follow-up programmes. Accordingly, it is recommended that the affected public be consulted at the beginning of the framework process when determining need. Stakeholder communication is essential during the design stage to ensure all critical issues are addressed. Once the follow-up is designed and finalized following the consent decision, it is recommended that some form of report be produced and provided to stakeholders. Stakeholder involvement may also be necessary during the implementation stage, especially if unexpected impacts are identified. This will allow for the unexpected issues to be disclosed and for discussion of possible solutions (management). Following the evaluation step, communication with all stakeholders should occur, allowing for discussion and input into possible management measures, if deemed necessary. The final result of the follow-up programme, focusing on findings and management measures, should also be documented for stakeholders.

Reporting

To ensure that reporting of results is not neglected, it is recommended that a formal reporting process be developed, and preferably be agreed at the design stage. Specific reporting requirements for projects should be identified by the regulator, proponent and others as necessary. In general, the reporting requirements may be determined by the magnitude of the issues and by the length of the proposed project phases (construction, operation and decommissioning). It is suggested that the regulator request from the proponent a minimum of one report for each of these phases. If the project has a life of several years, it may be constructive to request an annual follow-up report; some environmental agencies such as that in Hong Kong require more frequent reports (EPD, 2002; Hui and Ho, 2002).

Follow-up documents should report on those components of the EIA follow-up to which the stakeholders have agreed, focusing on the degree to which commitments have been met and on the success and failure of implemented mitigation measures. Results should be accessible to the public. This may be limited if there are a small group of stakeholders, or may be as extensive as the Web-based reporting system found in Hong Kong (Chapter 9).

Reporting is not so much a separate 'phase' of the framework, but rather is a flexible and optional component during the whole process. Having said this, it is strongly recommended that it be incorporated, as a minimum, into the implementation and issue management stages. The reporting scheme should be flexible enough so that any unexpected findings can be acted upon quickly, thus allowing for early warning signs of problems to be dealt with sooner rather than later. A formal reporting scheme should ensure accountability by those responsible for follow-up implementation, thereby ensuring that follow-up activities are not neglected. Such reports are usually provided by the proponent to the regulatory agencies and the stakeholders involved (e.g. a follow-up or management committee if one exists). Reporting at the issue management stages holds not only the proponent but also the responsible (regulatory) agencies accountable for taking action on issues that were identified. Simply put, it should ensure that management actions (or lack thereof) be reported to the affected public.

The suggested contents of a follow-up report are presented in Box 3.6. Reporting should comment on what is working, in addition to what is not working, as this may help ensure that those activities that are positive and effective will be replicated in the future. Reporting should not only provide data and results but should endeavour to facilitate building on existing knowledge, thereby improving the quality of future EIAs. For this reason it is important to remember that reporting and communication is a key component of the follow-up programme, for without it there would be no mechanism of passing on the lessons learned to others.

Box 3.6 Follow-up Reports

The follow-up report should include as a minimum (Arts and Nooteboom, 1999; Arts, 1998; Meijer and van Vliet, 2000):

- purposes of the follow-up
- issues identified
- implementation of the follow-up (mechanisms used to operationalize the programme)
- results (data, information)
- data analysis and evaluation
- management steps that have been undertaken
- further management steps proposed to be taken to deal with outstanding issues effectively
- lessons learned through the follow-up process and recommendations for future EIAs and follow-up programmes.

Relationship between the follow-up framework and the generic EIA process

So far, this chapter has described the framework for EIA follow-up and *how* it might work in practice. The relationship of the framework to the other stages of EIA with respect to the timing and *when* the individual tasks might be undertaken is shown in Figure 3.2.

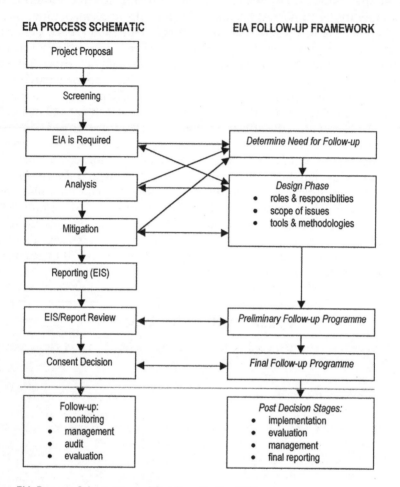

EIA PROCESS SCHEMATIC   EIA FOLLOW-UP FRAMEWORK

Source: EIA Process Schematic modified from Sadler, 1996

Figure 3.2 *Linkage Between a Generic EIA Process and the Follow-up Framework*

There is flexibility in when the various tasks could be undertaken; however, the figure provides some guidance in this matter.

As stated earlier, most EIA practitioners associate follow-up with post-decision actions, aimed largely at monitoring the effects of a project and managing unexpected and unacceptable effects. For the most part, this is an accurate portrayal of follow-up; however, the follow-up framework proposed here recommends that the practitioner plan (design) the follow-up programme prior to any decision being made. Obviously the entire follow-up approach suggested here can occur after the consent decision for a project has been made. Such timing may be necessary in certain circumstances, but given a choice, planning ahead for follow-up prior to a consent decision may yield a more effective and efficient programme.

Overall, the timing of the follow-up activities in relation to the generic EIA process can be summed up as follows:

1   The determination of the need for follow-up and then the design of the follow-up programme should occur during the preparation of the EIS and before the EIS is finalized.
2   It is recommended that some form of follow-up programme be submitted as part of a project application in an EIS. In this manner, a follow-up programme may influence the consent decision, and decision-makers can influence the follow-up work through the terms and conditions of the consent decision.
3   The remaining steps in the follow-up framework will occur after a consent decision has been made.

A few suggestions as to the timing of the pre-decision steps of the framework are indicated in Figure 3.2, but these should not be considered to be rigid. During the initial scoping of the EIA, it may be obvious which issues will require some form of follow-up, thus assisting in determining the need for follow-up. However, the need may not be identified until later in the evaluation stage of the EIA process or until a mitigation measure is proposed; for example, if a proposed mitigation measure has a considerable degree of uncertainty associated with it, then some form of follow-up should be developed to monitor performance.

As for the design of a follow-up programme, the majority of the details will usually be determined during the analysis and mitigation stages of the EIA process. The issues that appear to be problematic will become evident during these steps, and thus, will lead to the development of follow-up measures. Having said this, roles and responsibilities of a follow-up programme may become obvious when determining the need for an EIA; therefore, at least part of the follow-up programme design will begin early in the EIA process. It is important to keep in mind that unexpected effects of a project, identified through follow-up, may later change roles and responsibilities in the follow-up work.

A 'preliminary' follow-up programme should be prepared and provided to reviewers (regulators) and stakeholders at the same time as the EIS. Such timing will allow the follow-up programme to influence the conclusions of the EIS and the consent decision. Similarly, input from the affected public may also influence the final programme, if they have not already had an opportunity to do so.

The remainder of the generic EIA process (Box 1.1) is summarized as 'follow-up'. This component, placed after the consent decision, coincides with the remainder of the 'post-decision' follow-up stages (implementation, evaluation and management). Figure 3.2 also reiterates that some form of final report should be prepared at the conclusion of the follow-up work.

Conclusions

Despite the differences in regulatory approaches to EIA follow-up around the globe, it is possible to identify a generic framework for follow-up that may apply to many EIA systems based on Sadler's (1996) well-established generic EIA schematic. The framework presented here is based upon knowledge and experience of follow-up as found in the scientific and professional literature; it has evolved from previous work conducted for Environment Canada and has been further developed based on other studies, workshops and recommendations from workshop participants at IAIA conferences.

The main issues that need to be addressed are:

- determination of the need
- design of a follow-up programme including the determination of roles and responsibilities
- scope of issues and selection of methodology
- programme implementation
- evaluation of results and findings
- management of issues identified
- reporting/communication.

The framework is a starting point for practitioners to develop their own follow-up programmes suited to project-specific issues and circumstances. It is intended that the framework will be a starting point for further evolution of EIA follow-up practice worldwide.

References

Arts, J (1998) *EIA Follow-up – On the Role of Ex-Post Evaluation in Environmental Impact Assessment*, Groningen, GeoPress

Arts, J, Caldwell, P and Morrison-Saunders, A (2001) 'Environmental impact assessment follow-up: good practice and future directions – findings from a workshop at the IAIA 2000 conference', *Impact Assessment and Project Appraisal*, vol 19, pp175–185

Arts, J and Nooteboom, S (1999) 'Environmental Impact Assessment Monitoring and Auditing', in Petts, J (ed) *Handbook of Environmental Impact Assessment, Volume 1. Environmental Impact Assessment: Process, Methods and Potential*, Oxford, Blackwell Science, pp229–251

Au, E and Sanvicens, G (1996) *EIA Follow up Monitoring and Management. EIA Process Strengthening*, Canberra, Environment Protection Agency

Austin, D (2000) 'Community Participation in EIA Follow-up', presented at *Back to the Future:Where will Impact Assessment be in 10 Years and How Do We Get There? 20th Annual Meeting of the International Association for Impact Assessment*, Hong Kong, 19–23 June 2000, Hull, Quebec, Environment Canada

Bailey, J (1997) 'Environmental impact assessment and management: An underexplored relationship', *Environmental Management*, vol 21, pp317–327

Baker, J and Dobos, R (2001) 'Environmental Assessment Follow-up: A Framework for Environment Canada (draft)', presented at *Impact Assessment in the Urban Context, 21st Annual Meeting of the International Association for Impact Assessment*, Cartagena, Colombia, 26 May–1 June 2001, published on CD ROM: *IA Follow-up Workshop*, Hull, Quebec, Environment Canada

CEAA, Canadian Environmental Assessment Agency (2002) *Follow-up Programmes under the Canadian Environmental Assessment Act*, October 2002, OPS/EPO-6-2002, Gatineau, Quebec, Canadian Environmental Assessment Agency

Denis R (2002) 'The Effectiveness of some Mitigation and Enhancement Measures Carried out along the La Grande Rivière, Downstream and Upstream from the La Grand-I Hydroelectric Generation Station, James Bay, Quebec, Canada', presented at *Assessing the Impact of Impact Assessment: Impact Assessment for Informed Decision Making, 22nd Annual Meeting of the International Association for Impact Assessment*, The Hague, 15–21 June 2002, published on CD ROM: *IA Follow-up Workshop*, Hull, Quebec, Environment Canada

Environment Protection Department (2002) The Operation of the Environmental Impact Assessment Ordinance, Hong Kong, Environmental Protection Department, available at www.epd.gov.hk/eia/operation/index.html

Gagnon, C, LePage, L, Gauthier, M and Cote, G (2002) *Les comités de suivi au Québec: Un nouveau lieu de gestion environnementale?* Chicoutimi, Université du Québec à Chicoutimi

Hui, S and Ho, M (2002) 'EIA Follow-up: Internet-Based Reporting', presented at *Assessing the Impact of Impact Assessment: Impact Assessment for Informed Decision Making, 22nd Annual Meeting of the International Association for Impact Assessment*, The Hague, 15–21 June 2002, published on CD ROM: *IA Follow-up Workshop*, Hull, Quebec, Environment Canada

IAIA, International Association for Impact Assessment and Institute of Environmental Assessment, UK (1999) 'Principles of Environmental Impact Assessment Best Practice', available at www.iaia.org/Non_Menbers/Pubs_Ref_Material/pubs_ref_material_index.htm

Jesus, J (2000) 'Introduction of EIA Follow-up into the New EIA Regulations in Portugal', presented at *Back to the Future: Where will Impact Assessment be in 10 Years and How do we get there? 20th Annual Meeting of the International Association for Impact Assessment*, Hong Kong, 19–23 June 2000, Hull, Quebec, Environment Canada

Marshall, R (2001) 'Application of mitigation and its resolution within Environmental Impact Assessment: An industrial perspective', *Impact Assessment and Project Appraisal*, vol 19, pp195–204

Marshall, R, Smith, N and Wright, R (2001) 'A New Challenge for Industry: Integrating EIA Within Operational EMS', presented at *Impact Assessment in the Urban Context, 21st Annual Meeting of the International Association for Impact Assessment*, Cartagena, Colombia, 26 May–1 June 2001, published on CD ROM: *IA Follow-up Workshop*, Hull, Quebec, Environment Canada

Meijer, J and Van Vliet, J (2000) 'EIA Evaluation: Added-value by Screening and Scoping' presented at *Back to the Future: Where will Impact Assessment be in 10 Years and How do we get there? 20th Annual Meeting of the International Association for Impact Assessment*, Hong Kong, 19–23 June 2000, published on CD ROM: *IA Follow-up Workshop*, Hull, Quebec, Environment Canada

Morrison-Saunders, A, Arts, J, Baker, J and Caldwell, P (2001) 'Roles and stakes in environmental impact assessment follow-up', *Impact Assessment and Project Appraisal*, vol 19, pp289–296

Morrison-Saunders, A, Baker, J and Arts, J (2003) 'Lessons from practice: Towards successful follow-up', *Impact Assessment and Project Appraisal*, vol 21, pp43–56

O'Beirne, S, Clark, M and du Preez, J (2000) 'EIA Follow-up, Perspectives on a Burgeoning Aluminium Industry in Two Developing Countries', presented at *Back to the Future: Where will Impact Assessment be in 10 Years and How do we get there? 20th Annual Meeting of the International Association for Impact Assessment*, Hong Kong, 19–23 June 2000, Hull, Quebec, Environment Canada

Petts, J (1999) 'Public Participation and Environmental Impact Assessment', Petts, J (ed) *Handbook of Environmental Impact Assessment, Volume I. Environmental Impact Assessment: Process, Methods and Potential*, Oxford, Blackwell Science, pp145–177

Sadler, B (ed) (1987a) *Audit and Evaluation in Environmental Assessment and Management, Canadian and International Experience, Volume I. Commissioned Research*, Ottawa, Beauregard Press Ltd

Sadler, B (ed) (1987b) *Audit and Evaluation in Environmental Assessment and Management. Canadian and International Experience Volume II. Supporting Studies*, Ottawa, Beauregard Press Ltd

Sadler, B (1988) 'Evaluation of Assessment: Post-EIS Research and Process Development' in Wathern, P (ed) *Environmental Impact Assessment, Theory and Practice*, London, Unwin Hyman, pp129–142

Sadler, B (1996) *International Study of the Effectiveness of Environmental Assessment, Final Report, Environmental Assessment in a Changing World: Evaluating Practice to Improve Performance*, Canadian Environmental Assessment Agency and the International Association for Impact Assessment, Minister of Supply and Services, Canada

Van Lamoen, F and Arts, J (2002) 'EIA Follow-up for Road Projects: What Do We Want and Need to Know?', presented at *Assessing the Impact of Impact Assessment: Impact Assessment for Informed Decision Making, 22nd Annual Meeting of the International Association for Impact Assessment*, The Hague, 15–21 June 2002, published on CD ROM: *IA Follow-up Workshop*, Hull, Quebec, Environment Canada

4

Designing for EIA Follow-up: Experiences from The Netherlands

Jos Arts and Johan Meijer

Introduction

The saying 'well begun is half done' certainly applies to EIA follow-up. As for EIA generally, careful screening and scoping are crucial steps for getting off to a good start to achieve a well-tailored and practicable EIA follow-up. Screening determines the need and usefulness of EIA follow-up for a specific project while scoping determines the content of the follow-up programme. In addition to these *why?* and *what?* questions posed by screening and scoping respectively, it is important to determine at an early stage *how* the follow-up will be done. Each should be laid down in the EIA follow-up programme.

This chapter focuses on these design steps for EIA follow-up and elaborates on the previous chapter using experiences gained in The Netherlands. The chapter starts with some background information about EIA and follow-up in The Netherlands. Subsequently, it addresses the issues of screening, scoping, organization and timing of EIA follow-up and making follow-up issues operational. This is illustrated with an example of follow-up for a Dutch waste management project.

EIA and follow-up in The Netherlands

Dutch EIA practice

EIA regulations and practice in The Netherlands are generally viewed as relatively advanced in the international literature (Glasson et al, 1994; Sadler, 1996; Wood, 2003). The reasons for this relate to some specific features of the Dutch EIA system, which include (Arts, 1998; Wood, 2003; Box 4.1):

- integration of EIA into the existing decision-making process
- assessment of projects as well as plans
- the advisory role of the independent EIA Commission
- public consultation at an early stage about the scope of the EIS that will be prepared
- the requirement to consider the 'alternative most favourable to the environment'
- the requirement to do EIA follow-up.

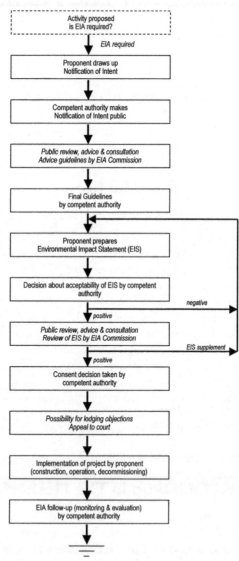

Source: after VROM, 1994b

Figure 4.1 *The EIA Procedure in The Netherlands*

Box 4.1 EIA Regulations in The Netherlands

EIA legislation came into force in 1986 in The Netherlands. Current arrangements are prescribed in the *Environmental Management Act* 1994 (EMA) and the EIA Decree established by the Act (VROM, 1996, 1994a). EIA applies to both public and private activities in The Netherlands. In all cases though, the decisions that require an EIA are government decisions. Mostly the EIA is prepared for an environmental permit and in some cases a land-use plan or route decision. However, these activities may be approved without an EIA procedure if the magnitude of the activity is below the EIA Decree thresholds. The EIA tool links up with the existing decision-making procedures and the Environmental Impact Statement (EIS) can be considered a background document to the consent decision. Extensive spatial planning and environmental regulations already existed before the EIA regulations came into force and continue to apply. The primary aim of the Dutch EIA regulations has been defined by the legislator as: 'to take full account of the environmental interest at stake in the decision-making process on a particular project or plan' (Tweede Kamer, 1981).

The Netherlands EIA procedure is depicted in Figure 4.1. First, the proponent prepares a *Notification of Intent*, which gives a broad outline of the proposed project. The Notification is made public and a first round of consultation, advice and public review starts in order to determine the scope of the EIS. The EIA Commission (a group of independent experts) issues an *Advice with Guidelines* on the basis of which the competent authority prepares the final *Guidelines for the EIS*. The competent authority is usually a municipal or provincial government or a national Ministry (depending on the relevant consent decision).

The proponent prepares the EIS, in which the project proposal and its alternatives are assessed for their impacts, and potential mitigating measures are proposed. An EIS should also include an account of the decision for which it is prepared, other relevant decision-making, methods used, gaps in knowledge and remaining uncertainties (EMA, s7.10). There is no legal requirement for the proponent to devote attention to EIA follow-up in their EIS; however, the guidelines issued by the competent authority usually request this.

The competent authority checks the completed EIS prior to its release for public review along with an application for the consent decision or a draft decision. The EIA Commission evaluates the quality of the EIS and submits a *Review Advice* document to the competent authority.

The competent authority is responsible for the *consent decision* – to grant the environmental permit or to approve the plan. In doing so, it must consider the EIS, the results of the public review and the advice received, and the decision must be made public. Both the proponent and third parties may appeal the decision in court. The competent authority must also *provide a programme for the ex-post evaluation* – i.e. an EIA follow-up programme. This indicates the terms and manner in which the competent authority will perform the evaluation once the project commences.

It has to be borne in mind that EIA in The Netherlands can be considered as simply an 'add-on' to the already extensive environmental regulations and to a very elaborate system for environmental, water management, infrastructure and spatial planning (Arts, 1998). EIA is applied only to activities 'which may have serious, harmful consequences for the environment' (EMA, s7.2(1)) and much attention is devoted to integration with the existing decision-making processes. Screening and scoping of EISs and EIA follow-up programmes are important for this integration process.

EIA follow-up in The Netherlands

Every plan or project for which an EIS has been prepared in The Netherlands must be evaluated during or after implementation as stated in the EMA (s7.39):

> *The competent authority that has taken a decision, in the preparation of which an environmental impact statement was drawn up, shall investigate the effects of the activity concerned on the environment, either during or after its completion.*

The *formal procedure* of this EIA follow-up is quite simple (EMA, s7.37 and s7.39-7.43; Figure 4.2) and much of it is done in parallel with the EIA process itself. When issuing the consent decision, the competent authority provides for an EIA follow-up programme that states in which way (what, when and how) the project will be evaluated. Although implementation of the follow-up programme is the responsibility of the competent authority, the proponent is legally obliged to cooperate. In practice the proponent carries out most of the follow-up work and pays most of the associated costs. This is usually arranged via monitoring and reporting requirements laid down in environmental permits. The competent authority has to prepare a publicly available report on the monitoring and evaluation results. When considered necessary, negative impacts on the environment must be reduced or undone as far as possible (EMA, s7.42(1)). This sequence of investigation, reporting and taking measures is undertaken for as long as is considered necessary in a specific case (Arts, 1998; VROM, 1995).

The EIA follow-up programme compares the effects expected when issuing the *consent decision* with the real effects of the *implemented activity* (EMA, s7.39) to determine whether the real effects lie within the bounds of the decision. Thus, the main subject is the consent decision not the EIS; the latter is merely a source of impact predictions and mitigation proposals. It is only necessary to evaluate the issues relevant to the consent decision. In doing so, sufficient attention needs to be given to intervening developments, particularly because of the dynamic context in which planning is done in the highly urbanized and industrialized setting of The Netherlands.

Despite the clear legal mandate, follow-up has been carried out for only a small proportion of Dutch EIAs. An evaluative study revealed that by 1998

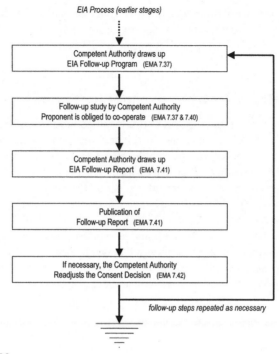

Source: Arts, 1998

Figure 4.2 *Procedure for EIA Follow-up in The Netherlands*

a follow-up study had commenced for only 61 (16 per cent) of the 376 projects that had received a consent decision, and follow-up reports had been published for 22 (6 per cent) projects (Arts, 1998). Half of the follow-up programmes had commenced since 1995, suggesting that the experience with EIA follow-up, though limited, has been increasing in Dutch EIA practice. The main reasons why follow-up practice is limited were identified as (Arts, 1998):

- low policy priority
- lack of external pressure
- lack of surveillance and sanctions
- lack of insight of the benefits of EIA follow-up in relation to the effort needed
- deficiencies in EISs
- inadequate techniques for follow-up
- personnel and time constraints.

Attention has been devoted recently to screening and, especially, to scoping of EIA follow-up in order to address these shortcomings.

The limited extent of formal EIA follow-up practice does not mean that no attention is paid to the follow-up stages in projects in The Netherlands. Outside the EIA framework, many other instruments exist that deal with uncertainties after giving consent to an activity. In short, other control and feedback mechanisms exist that may perform the role of EIA follow-up (Box 4.2).

Box 4.2 Other Avenues for Follow-up

Almost every environmental permit (the most common consent decision to which an EIA is linked) specifies monitoring and reporting requirements for the proponent. Competent authorities frequently audit such requirements. Additional monitoring and reporting often arises from the proponent's environmental management system (EMS; i.e. a form of first party follow-up) or from government area-wide monitoring schemes (e.g. state of the environment reporting), and this is the case whether or not a project has been subject to EIA. This (additional) information can be very useful for situations in which EIA follow-up does occur – bearing in mind that not all monitoring and evaluation activity will be applicable at the individual project level. Linking up with these other evaluative instruments is an important consideration in screening and scoping for EIA follow-up in The Netherlands.

Screening: Determining the need for EIA follow-up

The relevance of the objectives for EIA follow-up

The first task needed in follow-up is *screening* to determine the need for and usefulness of follow-up, in short to ask: *Why* should EIA follow-up be done? EIA follow-up may generally be appropriate if it can achieve one or more of several objectives (Chapter 1):

1 *Controlling* of the project and its environmental impacts (checking), which is perhaps the most important objective and reason to start EIA follow-up (Box 4.3)
2 Maintaining decision-making *flexibility* and enabling adaptive management (adjusting action). Control is only possible if the activity can be adjusted when follow-up outcomes indicate a need. If there is no means to address the follow-up outcomes, most likely there would be no reason to do follow-up.
3 Improving scientific and technical *knowledge* (learning) may provide considerable added value to the EIA follow-up for proponents and government regulators alike, but alone would rarely justify follow-up for an individual project.
4 Improving *public awareness and acceptance* (informing, communication) is important for politically or socially sensitive projects. It may serve as an additional assurance of sound implementation and management, even when scientific or information uncertainties are not significant.

5   *Integration* with other existing information sources (streamlining information). This may not in itself be a reason to initiate EIA follow-up, but added value may be realized if follow-up becomes an 'umbrella' under which various monitoring and evaluative activities are brought together, thereby providing an integrated assessment of otherwise scattered information (Figure 4.6). The extent to which EIA follow-up may help to meet this objective is dependent on the specific legislative and administrative context and has proven to be very relevant to practice in The Netherlands (Arts, 1998; Meijer and Van Vliet, 2000).

The objectives of follow-up will be determined by the parties involved (discussed later) and will also play an important role in scoping.

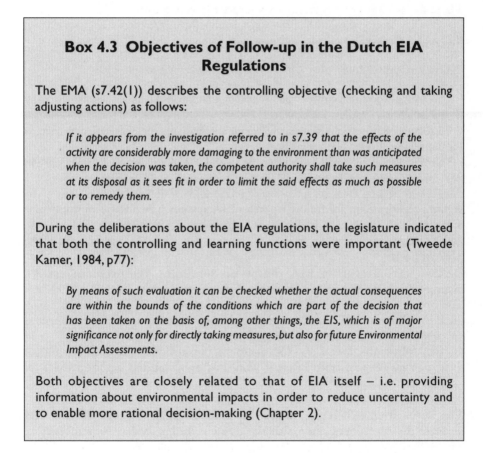

Box 4.3 Objectives of Follow-up in the Dutch EIA Regulations

The EMA (s7.42(1)) describes the controlling objective (checking and taking adjusting actions) as follows:

> If it appears from the investigation referred to in s7.39 that the effects of the activity are considerably more damaging to the environment than was anticipated when the decision was taken, the competent authority shall take such measures at its disposal as it sees fit in order to limit the said effects as much as possible or to remedy them.

During the deliberations about the EIA regulations, the legislature indicated that both the controlling and learning functions were important (Tweede Kamer, 1984, p77):

> By means of such evaluation it can be checked whether the actual consequences are within the bounds of the conditions which are part of the decision that has been taken on the basis of, among other things, the EIS, which is of major significance not only for directly taking measures, but also for future Environmental Impact Assessments.

Both objectives are closely related to that of EIA itself – i.e. providing information about environmental impacts in order to reduce uncertainty and to enable more rational decision-making (Chapter 2).

Screening thresholds

In addition to the five general EIA follow-up objectives, the following factors may be taken as screening thresholds, indicating a need for EIA follow-up in relation to a particular EIA project (Van Eck, 1997; Arts and Nooteboom, 1999; Chapter 3):

- degree of uncertainty in the EIS, including new EIA techniques or models
- degree of uncertainty of the effectiveness of mitigation measures
- complexity and magnitude of a proposed activity, involvement of new or unproven technologies
- sensitivity of the area where the activity is proposed
- degree of risk if the activity is not correctly implemented
- political and/or societal sensitivity
- intervening developments and events.

These are similar criteria as for EIA screening generally.

Forms of screening requirements

Screening requirements for EIA follow-up may take various forms:

- *no* formal requirement for follow-up for EIA projects, as is the case in many jurisdictions (Sadler, 1996; Wood, 2003)
- a formal requirement *always* to *undertake* follow-up for every EIA project, as is the case in The Netherlands
- a formal requirement to *screen* for the need for EIA follow-up, as is the case in Canada (Chapter 3) and which is developing in Dutch practice.

While a requirement for follow-up in an EIA system seems to be an important prerequisite for successful EIA follow-up practice (Morrison-Saunders et al, 2003), the most useful approach is to *screen for follow-up* and to act on the basis of need.

Two variants of an EIA follow-up screening requirement can be distinguished depending on where the onus of proof rests (Van Eck, 1997):

- EIA follow-up, *if...* – follow-up only has to be carried out if it is expected to add value to the specific EIA project
- EIA follow-up, *unless...* – follow-up should always be carried out unless it can be demonstrated that it would offer no added value to the EIA project.

The latter approach is favourable for protecting environmental interests because the proponent and/or the competent authority has to demonstrate why there is no need for EIA follow-up in order to avoid it.

Screening for follow-up not only needs explicit screening criteria but also should be undertaken early (preferably in the EIS stage) and with public disclosure. Openness and accountability are especially important if the proponent and/or the competent authority proposes that there is no need for EIA follow-up.

Screening for EIA follow-up in The Netherlands

Current EIA regulations in The Netherlands do not call for screening of the need for EIA follow-up. Instead it is assumed that if a proposal warrants EIA, then it will be useful to carry out an ex-post evaluation of the actual environmental impacts. However, results of an evaluative study suggest that EIA follow-up will not always be useful (Arts, 1998). In some cases other (legal) instruments already provide for follow-up of actual environmental impacts. Not surprisingly, therefore, in practice for many EIA projects in The Netherlands no EIA follow-up has been initiated, despite the legal requirement to do so. This may be considered a form of implicit screening but whether this is always justified remains unclear. Proposals for introducing a formal screening step and moving to a discretionary requirement for EIA follow-up have been advocated (VROM, 1998, 2003) but not yet implemented.

An example of screening for follow-up: The Province of South Holland approach

Guidelines for how to do EIA follow-up in the Province of South Holland, including a screening step, have been prepared by the provincial authority (PZH, 2001a, b). By allowing for selective EIA follow-up, the Province of South Holland has acted in advance of proposed changes to the Dutch EIA regulations. The Province felt the need to tackle the growing number of completed EIA projects in their jurisdiction which formally required follow-up and the wish to do follow-up carefully, but only for projects where it would provide added value. Without added value there was no (political) support and also the available budgets were limited. The screening approach focuses on control, knowledge and communication aspects of follow-up (Box 4.4). The type of project is also an important consideration (e.g. whether the project is at strategic, locational or operational level) as well as the existence of other evaluative instruments that may achieve follow-up purposes.

As part of its action plan, the Province of South Holland screened all 56 EIA projects to which it had granted consent by the end of 2000 (PZH, 2001b). They found EIA follow-up to be especially useful for operational EIA projects (e.g. industrial projects, waste management projects or infrastructure projects) while evaluation of strategic and locational level EIAs was considered of limited relevance.

For various EIA projects at the operational level, follow-up was no longer relevant as they were never realized, had not yet been implemented, or were already decommissioned. For 15 projects a form of follow-up was considered relevant but could be accomplished via the normal monitoring and surveillance of environmental permits. For the rest of the projects an EIA follow-up will be carried out or a screening decision will be made at a later stage. The Province concluded that EIA follow-up is especially relevant for projects subject to public concern, projects applying complex environmental techniques and projects with an important nature conservation component

---

Box 4.4 Screening for EIA Follow-up in the Province of South Holland

Three purposes of EIA follow-up are applied (Wachelder, 2002; Meijer and Van Vliet, 2000):

- *Control* – the larger the magnitude of environmental impacts, the more relevant it is to evaluate them. If environmental impacts occur in sensitive areas, then extra attention is needed. However, if no remedial measures can be taken, follow-up for controlling is of little use.
- *Knowledge* – if there are important uncertainties and/or gaps in knowledge in the EIS for significant impacts, it is useful to carry out EIA follow-up focusing on these. If it is evident that certain impact predictions could be very useful for similar projects in the future, then follow-up to determine the reliability of the predictions is worthwhile.
- *Communication* – EIA follow-up may contribute to external accountability, internal integration and harmonization as well as gain support for newly proposed projects. If there is public concern about environmental impacts, follow-up may alleviate these concerns and ensure that appropriate mitigation occurs. Where multiple consent decisions and/or competent authorities are involved, EIA follow-up may fulfil an important coordinating and integrating role.

Note: These three purposes correspond to the five EIA follow-up objectives discussed previously where 'control' corresponds to checking (1) and taking adjusting action (2), 'knowledge' corresponds to learning (3) and 'communication' corresponds to informing (4) and streamlining information (5).

(PZH, 2001b). During preparation of the guidelines, the Province carried out pilot follow-ups for two waste projects, one of which is discussed later in this chapter.

For strategic level activities, the Province argued that the cyclic nature of decision-making makes it unsuited for follow-up. Before a new policy plan is prepared, the Province evaluates the previous one. In some cases a new EIA will also have to be prepared for the new policy plan. The Province concluded that EIA follow-up has little added value at the strategic level (PZH, 2001a). In other contexts, however, strategic level follow-up can be useful (Chapter 10).

For locational level projects, the Province assumes that the follow-up is restricted to the location choice that has been the subject of EIA. However, location choice is often irreversible: once a road, housing or industrial estate has been built, this intervention cannot be easily changed. For these locational projects, often another EIA has to be prepared at the operational level.

Consequently, the monitoring and evaluation of the actual environmental impacts at the location can be carried out as part of EIA follow-up at the operational level. It has to be stated, however, that for some locational projects, no EIA eventuates at the operational level – e.g. road construction projects. For such projects, the EIA considers both the locational and operational level and EIA follow-up would be very relevant (Van Lamoen and Arts, 2002).

Scoping: Defining the content of EIA follow-up

The place of scoping

Once it has been decided that follow-up *is* useful for an EIA project, it has to be determined *how* the follow-up will be carried out. As with EIA itself, there is a need to focus on the important issues. Scoping is crucial for carefully determining the objectives, functions and the relevant issues of EIA follow-up. It reveals the benefits or incentives of EIA follow-up and how EIA follow-up can be done in a specific situation (e.g. which methods and techniques are relevant and which problems and obstacles may be encountered along the way). In short, careful scoping is essential to achieve a fruitful and feasible EIA follow-up. Additionally, it provides a mechanism for linking EIS preparation, the project plan and the consent decision with project implementation and management (Figure 4.3).

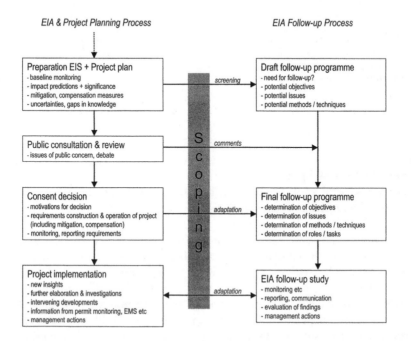

Figure 4.3 *Scoping for EIA Follow-up – The Link with the EIS, the Consent Decision and Project Planning*

How to carry out scoping for EIA follow-up

Objective-led scoping

In order to be useful, the generation and selection of follow-up issues has to be guided by the objectives the follow-up has to meet (i.e. an objective-led scoping approach). Different objectives may be relevant to different parties, and consequently the selected follow-up issues will differ. For example, the performance of new environmental protection techniques may be an important issue for EIA follow-up with the objective of controlling. In the same vein, the condition of specific species may be important when the objective is to enhance knowledge about the relationship between the activity and such species. If the objective of follow-up is legitimization, gaining public support or communication about the project, it may be relevant to include issues under political or public debate (e.g. nuisance). Where a screening stage is utilized, these objectives should already be clear. From this point, scoping involves a mixed process of *generating* a list of potentially important issues for evaluation and then *selecting* the issues which will actually be evaluated (Figure 4.4).

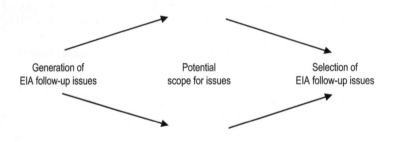

Source: after EIA Commission, 1994

Figure 4.4 *The Diverging and Converging Process of Scoping of EIA Follow-up Issues*

Generating follow-up issues

There are several sources that can be used to generate possible issues for follow-up, including (VROM, 1995):

- *Environmental impacts predicted in the EIS* – Only those impacts that relate to the consent decision are relevant to follow-up (i.e. those associated with the chosen alternative). Other relevant information contained in the EIS includes the original state of the environment (base-line monitoring).
- *Gaps in knowledge described in the EIS* – There may be (too) little known about certain aspects of the activity, its impacts, the likely effectiveness of mitigation measures and the state of the environment. In The Netherlands, a competent authority may issue the consent decision when such knowledge gaps exist provided they are not crucial (i.e. would change the consent

decision). The EIA Commission plays an important role in identifying and appraising knowledge gaps and their review advice often indicates whether these should be monitored and evaluated in the EIA follow-up.

- *Mitigation and compensation measures* – Usually, mitigation and compensation measures are indicated in the EIS as well as in the final consent decision. These are relevant issues, especially if these measures are technically complex, their effectiveness is uncertain or unfamiliar, and/or considerable risks are involved if they do not perform as expected.
- *Issues under discussion when the decision was made* – These can be described in the grounds for the decision, in the preamble to the decision or in explanatory memoranda. Issues for discussion can also arise from input from the public, from the EIA Commission and from others.
- *Further investigations and environmental management plans (EMPs)* – A consent decision may identify specific environmental or project-related aspects that need further investigation and scrutiny by regulators prior to project implementation. This may include preparation of EMPs that further elaborate on mitigation measures.
- *External, intervening events* – External events in the vicinity of a project (e.g. new investigations, projects, plans, policy documents or regulations) may lead to changing insight into environmental and project management, which may affect the ongoing follow-up.
- *Enforcement of environmental permits* – Where the consent decision is an environmental permit, relevant follow-up issues can arise from inspections, surveillance, reporting and other enforcement activities carried out in light of the permit. Additionally, evaluation issues can arise from complaints by people living in the vicinity or by other interest groups (e.g. patterns and trends in complaints).
- *New initiatives developed by the proponent* – Additional issues may become apparent if there is an application for modification or extension of the activity.

The mixture of pre-decision and post-decision sources of issues for follow-up highlights the need for a flexible and adaptive approach to be taken.

It is neither possible nor useful to include all conceivable issues in the EIA follow-up. First, it is inherent to scoping that the issues generated will provide a picture only at a given moment in time. Therefore, it is important to enable new (unexpected) relevant issues in later phases of the project development to be included in the EIA follow-up (e.g. by monitoring issues and complaints brought forward by other parties). Second, the follow-up study has to be selective because of efficiency considerations (e.g. environmental effectiveness and limited budgets and staff resources). EIA follow-up should not become a goal in itself.

Selecting follow-up issues

In selecting issues to incorporate in EIA follow-up, the relevant follow-up objectives are central. In addition, several criteria can be used which are closely related to the thresholds for screening and include:

- *Relevance to decision-making* – Issues important to decision-makers, the public or other stakeholders (e.g. the EIA Commission) may warrant follow-up attention. These can be found in the permit, its provisions, review reactions and complaints or the EIS (likelihood and magnitude of impact, uncertainty of prediction).
- *Relationship of the issue with the environment* – EIA follow-up should concern significant environmental issues and impacts. In the Dutch EIA system, the environment is broadly defined to include (VROM, 1994b): protection of humans, flora and fauna, goods, water, soil and air; the relations between them (ecosystems, climate); protection of historical and cultural values (archaeology, landscape, monuments); and consequences for humans (physical health and psychological health as quality of life). Issues related to economic aspects such as efficiency or legal concerns such as liability do not have to be included in the EIA follow-up (but this might be done voluntarily for specific reasons).
- *Phase of project development* – Many projects proceed in phases, each of which may be associated with specific issues which change over time. Thus, the focus of follow-up may need to change (e.g. construction of protective facilities to mitigate nuisance resulting from operation).
- *Relevance to future uses* – Can the results of the follow-up of this issue be used for future activities, decision-making, or EIAs, and is this considered important (by the competent authority)?

Feasibility of follow-up

While an objective-led approach to EIA follow-up is vital when determining the purposes of EIA follow-up, consideration of feasibility is also essential to the scoping process. There is inevitably some tension between what is desirable and what is possible in practice. The issue of feasibility raises questions such as: How much effort (in terms of time, staff resources or money) is required to monitor and evaluate the issue? Is it reasonable to expect the organization to make such an effort? Do the results of including the issue in the EIA follow-up outweigh the effort required?

Feasibility of follow-up includes methodological, informational, juridical, organizational and financial aspects and raises questions such as (Arts et al, 2001):

- Is it possible to measure and test the issue? This relates to the issue of causality (i.e. being able to attribute clearly an environmental impact to a project) and the availability of information and appropriate methods.
- Is it financially and/or organizationally achievable to monitor and evaluate the issues? EIA follow-up will only be successful if appropriate budgets and staff resources are provided.
- Is it justifiable to evaluate an issue and then take additional measures? This may regard juridical procedures and competencies of the proponent and regulatory bodies.

- What is the potential to react? The capacity for implementing remedial measures, adaptive environmental management, or to learn from experience are important considerations here.

In particular, the *potential to adjust* is an important guiding principle in scoping. In The Netherlands this relates to s7.42 of the EMA, which deals with taking remedial measures to limit environmental impacts. In the scoping process there are interactions between objectives and functions, available methods and techniques, available budget, time, capacity and the expected results and outcomes of EIA follow-up (Figure 4.5).

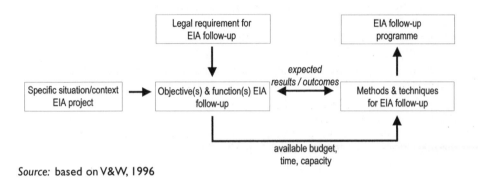

Source: based on V&W, 1996

Figure 4.5 *Determination of the Scope of EIA Follow-up for Road Construction Projects*

Relevance to various parties

The relevance of specific issues may differ among the parties involved in EIA, and this can be illustrated by considering the relationship between follow-up objectives and the various parties. A competent authority may emphasize the controlling objective because of the need for checking compliance with the consent decision. Members of the public may consider the communication objective to be most important in order to be kept informed about the impacts of a particular activity. Integration with other available information (streamlining function) can be relevant to competent authorities and proponents alike. For the competent authority, it may allow an integrated assessment of the environmental performance of an activity; for the proponent, it may be useful in streamlining the monitoring and evaluation requirements that are imposed. The importance attached to the functions and objectives of EIA follow-up may not only differ but the functions and objectives may also be interpreted differently. For example, the controlling objective of EIA follow-up may be relevant to the competent authority in checking compliance with the consent decision, to the proponent in implementing an EMS for the project, and to third parties as they seek to secure their interests. Ultimately, transparency in the scoping stage is vital because the various parties attach more or less importance to the various objectives, functions and issues of EIA follow-up.

The process of scoping for EIA follow-up

It is important to start scoping for follow-up early and to lay down the results in a formal programme (i.e. what is to be investigated, why, when, how and by whom?). In The Netherlands, the EMA (s7.37) requires the competent authority to determine the scope of follow-up at the consent decision stage. However, the process should ideally start earlier than this. Preparation for follow-up should occur during EIS preparation, and the proponent can submit a draft follow-up programme as part of the EIS (Chapter 3). Not only would this ensure that EIA follow-up is transparent, but it would also enable refinement and improvement during the review and decision-making process. In this sense, all parties in the EIA process engage in their own scoping of EIA follow-up programmes at some point. There are clear advantages to the proponent for commencing follow-up design early in the EIA process since they will be responsible for most of the work required. Thus proponents may attune the EIA follow-up to their own monitoring and evaluation activities and EMS.

A potential drawback to early EIA follow-up scoping relates to the frequent criticism of inadequate EISs. The proponent might commit to only a minimal EIA follow-up programme to save on costs or effort. Also, it may not be clear which alternative in the EIS will be chosen and thus which issues are relevant. Although the review and decision-making process should be able to redress this, a bad start may determine the discussions afterwards. Currently the Dutch EMA does not require the proponent to include a proposal for follow-up in the EIS, although in practice most advice guidelines contain some general statements to this effect. Unfortunately, however, the quality of the sections on EIA follow-up in both EISs and consent decisions often proves to be of poor quality (Arts, 1998), indicating that there is considerable room for improvement here.

EIA follow-up has to be done in a *dynamic context*. After the follow-up programme has been prepared, intervening developments may give cause for additional follow-up issues to be included in the programme. Similarly, issues that were relevant at the time of initial scoping may become irrelevant. Although the focus of scoping for follow-up lies in the early stages, this will always be a snapshot in time, and some form of *ongoing scoping* is needed to keep EIA follow-up useful for the specific project and its context (Figure 4.3).

An example: Scoping for EIA follow-up of road projects in The Netherlands

So far this chapter has emphasized screening and scoping for EIA follow-up on an individual project basis. For some categories of EIA projects it may be possible to make some generalizations with respect to relevant follow-up issues. For example, the Dutch Ministry of Transport distinguishes two categories of issues for EIA follow-up scoping of road projects (V&W, 2003; Van Lamoen and Arts, 2002). These categories (Table 4.1) set a standard for

Table 4.1 *Scoping Categories Relevant for EIA Follow-up of Road Projects*

'Yes', unless	'No', unless
Noise	Nature conservation (flora and fauna)
Air pollution	Landscape
External safety	Social impacts (e.g. barrier effects, liveability)
Mitigation measures	Archaeology and cultural heritage
Compensation measures (Traffic)	Soil (including geomorphology and geology)
	Water (including surface and groundwater)

Source: after V&W, 2003

scoping for all road projects of the Ministry, but still leave room for tailoring to specific project needs.

The items in the first category ('yes', unless) have a strong legal basis, either national or European, such as noise and air pollution. Most of them are directly linked to traffic intensities, which itself will be closely linked to the objective of a road project (e.g. improving traffic capacity, decreasing congestion and/or traffic safety). They also act as an indicator for subsequent effects (e.g. noise can be used as an indicator for disturbance of fauna). All of the items in this category should be included in the EIA follow-up programme, unless they are clearly irrelevant to the project and/or the consent decision.

The second category ('no', unless) contains all other environmental issues normally found in EISs for road development projects, such as nature conservation, cultural heritage and soil and water issues. Effects for these aspects are mostly diminished by mitigation or compensation measures and may not always warrant follow-up. In specific cases though, it can be relevant to incorporate them directly into the monitoring and evaluation programme for the EIA follow-up. Sometimes, the initial monitoring and evaluation may be followed by an in-depth study on triggered aspects. Box 4.5 provides an example of scoping for an EIA follow-up programme for a road construction project in The Netherlands in which a staged approach was used.

The result of screening and scoping: A follow-up programme

The results of the steps of screening and scoping should be laid down in the EIA follow-up programme. A practicable programme should also clarify how the follow-up should be done, including the operationalization of the issues and the organization and timing of the follow-up study.

Making the follow-up issues operational

When discussing the *feasibility* of including certain issues in the scope of the EIA follow-up, the way the issues are measured must also be taken into account.

Box 4.5 EIA Follow-up Programme for the A50 Road Construction Project

For the construction of the A50 road between Eindhoven and Oss (RWS North Brabant, 1991, 1995), the primary objective and function of the EIA follow-up was to check whether the actual impacts were within the bounds of the original decision. An important additional objective was learning for future EIA projects. However, testing methods and models for impact predictions were not part of the follow-up study. The evaluation section included in the EIS (RWS North Brabant, 1991) has been the basis for the detailed scoping and elaboration of a follow-up programme that commenced in 1995 (RWS North Brabant, 1995).

The scope of the EIA follow-up programme concerned both the construction and operational phases. The first investigations commenced in 1996, one year before the actual road construction started, and mainly involved an inventory of birds in a nature conservation area and monitoring of hydrological and soil issues. These investigations were conducted to provide base-line data (a reference benchmark for EIA follow-up results) as well as to provide information additional to the EIS for detailed road design and construction purposes.

The scope of the EIA follow-up programme has been discussed during the project's implementation. Details have been (and will be) further elaborated and adjusted during the construction and operational phases (RWS North Brabant, 1998, 2003). For instance, in the operational phases, noise and traffic flows will be monitored. For the selection of follow-up issues, various criteria have been used, such as degree of uncertainty of EIS predictions, possibilities for adjustment (technical, administrative and juridical), magnitude of the impact, the interests involved and the results of external consultation (RWS North Brabant, 1995). Other principles used for making the EIA follow-up operational are to measure as closely as possible to the disturbing source, to select issues that are directly related to the A50 project (because of causality issues), and to keep the effort reasonable in terms of finances and staff resources (TMC, 2004). During the period of follow-up, in all spanning a period of some 12 years between 1996 and 2008, the road developer (Rijkswaterstaat North Brabant, Ministry of Transport) will periodically prepare reports containing the monitoring and evaluation results, at which time it will be determined whether the programme needs adjustment. The scoping approach to the A50 project has been a flexible one, leaving room for adaptation of the follow-up programme. The long period involved made the organization of the follow-up difficult. Because of this, the EIA follow-up for this road development has been conceived as a series of separate 'well-delineated, project-like compact actions' (V&W, 1996).

For example, it must be determined which variables are to be considered, which methods are to be used (Box 3.4), where, when and how often measurements will be carried out, which data are already available, and who will be doing the research. Additionally, the criteria that will be used for evaluating the follow-up results need to be specified.

The *objectives* to be met are also significant with respect to making the issues operational. This relates to such aspects as the level of detail, the timing and the methodological quality (rigour) of the required follow-up results. For example, to gain better insight into dose–effect relationships (with the objective of learning), it is conceivable that more-extensive and precise measurements of a follow-up issue are needed than for an issue that is included in order to communicate about the activity to the public. In the latter case, the quick availability of follow-up results might be more relevant. For the controlling objective, the way that follow-up issues are measured is relevant, particularly if the authority and/or proponent wants to take additional measures and has to deal with juridical requirements.

Various *sources of data* (about, for example, construction and functioning of facilities, emissions, state of the environment) may be relevant for making the follow-up issues operational including:

- measurements, registrations and reporting pursuant to the environmental permit provisions (or other consent decisions)
- descriptions in the EIS (with respect to use of indicators, level of detail, expected impacts)
- monitoring and auditing because of a proponent's EMS or annual environmental report
- general investigations of the state of the environment
- other investigations and reports on relevant issues including complaint data.

These various sources need to be considered when determining data collection needs. It is important to identify what data has already been collected and by whom, how overlap of work can be avoided, and thus what data needs to be generated specifically for the EIA follow-up.

In The Netherlands, much data is often already available and usually few investigations have to be carried out specifically for EIA follow-up. For this reason, EIA follow-up can have an important function in streamlining information flows. It may bring added value by acting as an 'umbrella' under which various monitoring and evaluative activities can be integrated and managed – an integrated assessment of otherwise scattered information (Figure 4.6). This is especially true for more complex projects for which an integrated appraisal of the environmental performance through EIA follow-up may have clear added value above the other monitoring and evaluative activities already in place. However, this factor will usually not be a reason in itself to start EIA follow-up. As EIA follow-up may extend over a long time span, it is important to note carefully the way these incoming flows of measurement and registration data are archived.

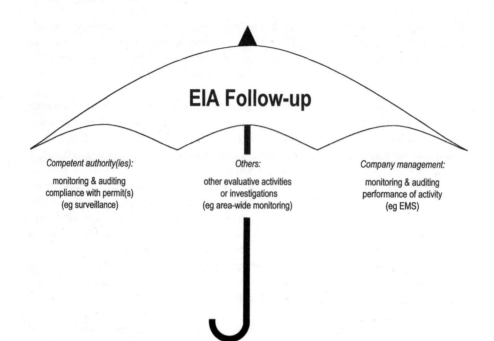

Source: after Arts, 1998

Figure 4.6 *EIA Follow-up as an Umbrella – Integration of the Various Flows of Information*

The design of monitoring programmes is also important for operationalizing EIA follow-up. Here, it is useful to focus EIA follow-up on those issues that are easily measured and can unambiguously be appraised against clear criteria – measuring indicators related to emissions and the performance of protective facilities (laid down in permits or regulations) rather than final impacts on flora, fauna, landscape and humans. In this way, problems related to causality may be prevented, because it can be very difficult to link unambiguously environmental changes to a project (because of complex measuring methods, synergism, accumulation etc.). This may also enable an adequate and timely response to slow processes involving long-term impacts (e.g. groundwater pollution affecting 'downstream' habitats). Project specific impact monitoring in this manner may be combined with area-wide monitoring or registration of complaints in order to keep track of the changes in the environment (scanning the state of the surrounding environment), resulting in a sort of 'two-track approach' to monitoring. If important environmental changes are discovered, this may warrant having an in-depth monitoring and evaluation of the specific issue to assess whether the impacts are caused by the project (re-scoping), corresponding to the 'mixed-scanning approach' to planning of Etzioni (1967; Chapter 2). The technical and methodological aspects of monitoring are well covered elsewhere (Green, 1979; Chapter 5) and are not further discussed here.

Organizational aspects of EIA follow-up

Organizational aspects need to be clearly outlined in the EIA follow-up programme, including:

- the parties involved, including the divisions of an organization and the persons involved
- the division of tasks, roles and responsibilities between proponent, competent authority, the public and others (e.g. contractors, consultants, advisory bodies)
- planning of the activities for the follow-up study
- timely reservation of necessary capacity and budgets to provide for the costs of EIA follow-up (Box 4.6).

Box 4.6 Costs of EIA Follow-up

The costs of EIA follow-up include (VROM, 1995; Arts, 1998):

- *research costs* – determined by the number of investigations needed for the follow-up issues (these may be reduced if existing information can be used)
- *organizational costs* – mainly related to the costs of staff involved
- *procedural costs* – mainly related to the costs of producing follow-up reports, other communication and decision-making
- *costs of implementing remedial measures* – in response to unacceptable impacts.

Usually the latter will be borne by the proponent in accordance with the 'polluter pays' principle, but remedial measures can only be asked from the proponent if they are 'fair and reasonable' and it is clear that the impacts are caused by the project.

Timing aspects in EIA follow-up

Timing is another important scoping-related issue and should be specified in the follow-up programme. Different issues may require different frequencies of monitoring as well as different time periods over which measurement is relevant. Feedback may occur over a large or small number of a project's life cycle phases (Arts and Nooteboom, 1999). Some issues may require continuous monitoring and a direct management response, while for others an evaluation at the end of the project may be all that is needed. In many jurisdictions, follow-up is limited to rapid cycles of compliance monitoring of project implementation and/or EMS (Sadler, 1988).

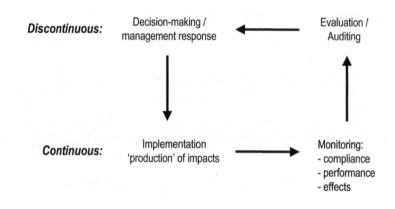

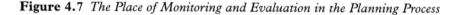

Source: after Arts and Nooteboom, 1999

Figure 4.7 *The Place of Monitoring and Evaluation in the Planning Process*

Figure 4.7 shows that the effects of consent decisions may be monitored by means of a continuous monitoring programme. Implementation, compliance, performance and impact monitoring is usually done on a continuous basis. A follow-up report is prepared at intervals (i.e. discontinuous) to evaluate all the monitoring data of the previous period. This will be the basis for decision-making about remedial action or other management responses. Their implementation may result in changes in impacts of the project on the environment that in turn can be monitored.

In the life cycle of an EIA project, several phases and related *evaluative moments* that are relevant to follow-up can usually be distinguished:

- *Pre-construction phase* – representing the base-line situation before the project has been implemented. Usually the EIS contains a description of this, however, sometimes additional work may be needed following the consent decision but prior to project commencement (e.g. an EMP).
- *Construction phase* – when the project and its facilities are built, particular environmental effects may be experienced (e.g. habitat loss) and the construction of protective facilities can be monitored.
- *Operational phase* – when the project is actually operated and in use. For projects with a long operational phase this may result in a number of evaluative moments (e.g. periodic reporting requirements specified in permits, EMS or other self-regulation cycles, project modification or upgrades etc.).
- *Decommissioning phase* – when a project is dismantled and the site is rehabilitated or redeveloped. Not all projects are decommissioned (e.g. roads and other transport infrastructure), thus sometimes the operational phase is essentially permanent.

The follow-up programme

Combining all of the elements of the previous discussion, the contents of an EIA follow-up programme established by screening and scoping include:

- objectives and functions of follow-up (as well as a description of the EIA project)
- follow-up issues
- manner of investigation (indicators, methods, techniques)
- sources of data
- monitoring design (period, moments, frequency)
- framework for evaluation (criteria, standards, requirements, predictions, expectations etc.)
- moments for evaluation and reporting of follow-up results
- organization of the follow-up including division of roles and tasks (e.g. planning, capacity and finances).

Once the screening and scoping stages have been completed the actual follow-up study can start. Subsequent chapters in this book provide several examples of follow-up implementation from around the world. A practical example of EIA follow-up screening and scoping for a case study from The Netherlands follows.

The Derde Merwedehaven waste disposal facility

Background

The Derde Merwedehaven waste disposal facility is located in a highly in-dustrialized, densely populated urban agglomeration in the province of South Holland that is confronted with serious environmental pollution. The waste facility itself is situated in an industrial harbour complex constructed in the 1960s near the cities of Dordrecht and Sliedrecht (Figure 4.8). The industrial development of this harbour area has been limited, and since 1971, contaminated dredging sludge was dumped in the harbour, which was undertaken without protective measures that could have prevented the spread of pollution (BKH, 1991).

The realization by the end of the 1980s that there would be too little capacity for disposing of waste in the province of South Holland led to the proposal to develop a waste disposal facility at the Derde Merwedehaven site. In this way, the project could also provide for protective structures to prevent further spread of the previously dumped contaminated dredging sludge. In January 1989, the EIA procedure commenced and two years later the EIS and the applications for permits were published. Subsequently, construction of the waste disposal facilities commenced and part of the site has been in operation since June 1993 (PZH, 1994). During the public review and advice round,

Source: BKH, 1991

Figure 4.8 *Location of the Derde Merwedehaven Waste Disposal
Site near Dordrecht*

many comments were submitted which advocated following-up certain EIA
issues.

A major issue that arose during the planning process of the Derde
Merwedehaven development concerns the protective facilities. This issue
was discussed intensively during the EIA procedure. For this project a new
and technically complex solution has been applied for the geohydrological
insulation of the waste facility. The proponent did not use a sealing-off structure
at the bottom of the disposal area as is usually done in The Netherlands, since
the bottom of the existing harbour at the location was already polluted by
previously dumped dredging sludge. It was decided to isolate the entire waste
disposal facility from the surrounding area by building a vertical sealing wall
of sand bentonite (a natural clay material with very low permeability). The
wall extends almost 30m underground until it reaches a natural horizontal
impermeable layer (the 'layer of Kedichem') and is intended to isolate the
waste dump from more deeply situated groundwater layers (Figure 4.9).
The combination of the sealing wall and the layer of Kedichem results in a
sort of tub. The water within this tub is constantly pumped up via drains,

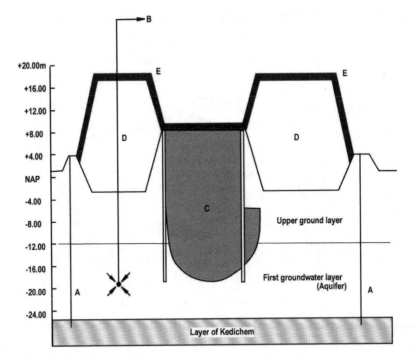

KEY

NAP   Normal Amsterdam Level (ordinance level)

A   vertical sealing wall of sand bentonite

B   groundwater pumped up

C   dump for dredging sludge

D   dump for dry waste

E   cover seal

Source: BKH, 1991

Figure 4.9 *Sketch of Structure of the Derde Merwedehaven Waste Disposal Facility*

creating a zone of 'hydrological under-pressure'. This inwardly directed flow of groundwater should keep contaminated water from spreading out of the disposal facility into the surrounding area.

Other structures built for this project are a treatment installation for the extracted waste water and covering layers to seal off the upper surface after part of the waste dump is filled to capacity. The environmental permit provided for the disposal of wet waste (dredging sludge) into the former harbour and for the disposal of dry waste (industrial, construction and demolition waste) onto the grounds around the harbour (Figure 4.10).

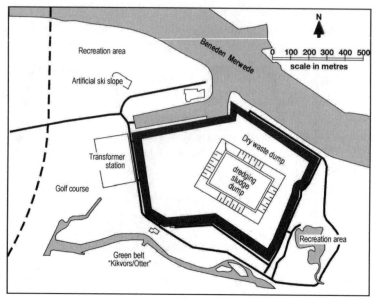

Source: BKH, 1991

Figure 4.10 *Site Layout of the Derde Merwedehaven Waste Disposal Facility*

Screening for EIA follow-up

In accordance with the EMA, a follow-up study was mandatory. With respect to the screening for follow-up, the competent authority (the Province of South Holland) included the Derde Merwedehaven development as a pilot study for gaining experience with selective EIA follow-up (PZH, 2001b). Other reasons not directly related to this project gave impetus to its follow-up. For instance, a personal factor seemed to be important in that some administrators within the provincial government were clearly committed to the concept of EIA follow-up, to the extent that the provincial authority has developed its own 'Guidelines for Selective EIA Follow-up' (PZH, 2001a).

In the environmental permit, explicit attention was given to EIA follow-up, and the relations between the EIS results and the reactions of the EIA Commission and the public were laid out along with the monitoring and registration requirements under the permit provisions. The Province distinguished two follow-up objectives for this project: controlling of the activity's environmental impact and enhancing knowledge (about odour and health impacts as well as carrying out EIA follow-up itself). Later on, the objective of communication was added, which was related to odour and health complaints (PZH, 2001b).

The scope of the EIA follow-up

The Province of South Holland initiated and coordinated the EIA follow-up and cooperated closely with other relevant authorities (such as the water board and municipalities in the region) and the proponent who had most of the information relevant to the follow-up study. Relevant follow-up issues (Table 4.2) were derived from the EIS, the review advice of the EIA Commission, the environmental permit (including its provisions, its explanatory memorandum and the public submissions) and complaints reported by people living in the area (PZH, 1994; CSO, 1994). To check whether enough attention was given to certain topics, the main patterns of people's complaints were examined.

Table 4.2 *EIA Follow-up Issues for the Derde Merwedehaven Project*

Site construction and management aspects	• Construction and performance of the dump heap: distance to bottom of dump and groundwater level ('sagging'), settling of the dump heap • Construction of hydrological control system: hydrological isolation, check by external experts • Performance of hydrological control system: hydrological isolation, extent of water flows, composition of percolate water • Supply and acceptance of waste: development supply, acceptance and control, ratio of different modes of transport in the supply of waste (road/water)
Environmental aspects	• Physical changes: levels of groundwater, settling around the dump • Surface water and bedding of water (in former harbour): emissions and (mitigating) measures • Mitigation of nuisances: noise, air, odour and dust emissions • Spread of litter, nuisance caused by vermin • Serious incidents, accidents

Source: PZH, 1994

The first EIA follow-up study focused on the construction phase and the first year of waste disposal operations (the period until April 1994). As soil and water issues were considered to be particularly important (VROM, 1995), the isolation, containment and control of contamination of groundwater and soil received much attention, as did the construction and performance of related protective facilities such as sealing structures and drains. Specific attention was given to the complex construction of the vertical sealing wall. The facility's geohydrological isolation was investigated by carrying out a sensitivity analysis and a large-scale drain test after the completion of the sealing. Additional investigations were carried out on the most important gaps in knowledge indicated in the EIS (subsoil structure, soil and groundwater quality). Additionally, the study considered the supply and acceptance of waste as well as an analysis of complaints.

Issues such as landfill gas (methane), the structures for completion of the disposal facility, and the way the waste dump fits into the landscape were not part of the first EIA follow-up study. For other issues, such as the quality of air, surface water, or flora and fauna (although the latter received much attention in the EIS), it was not possible to establish unambiguous causal relationships between these issues and the activities at the waste disposal site (PZH, 1994). The EIA follow-up study was designed to focus explicitly on the construction and performance of protective facilities and emissions from the waste facility rather than measurement of impacts in the surrounding environment, in order to prevent causality problems when evaluating the follow-up results.

Making the follow-up issues operational

The environmental permit provisions and the EIS provided useful starting points for making the follow-up issues operational. The permit outlined accepted measurements and calculation methods and provided criteria (standards) for evaluating the follow-up results for most issues. Other regulations such as the Dutch Decree on Dumping also proved to be important. The level of detail of the follow-up study was linked to the level of detail in the EIS and additional investigations. The follow-up study focused on the general outlines of construction and those operational aspects that were relevant from an environmental point of view. Technical details were checked as part of enforcement of the environmental permits. The follow-up research was mainly concerned with how the activity as implemented deviated from what had been stated in the EIS, the additional investigations and the permits (PZH, 1994).

For *evaluation*, follow-up results were compared with the standards laid down in the permit provisions and the regulations as well as with the EIS predictions and descriptions of the base-line situation. Reports prepared after the EIS was finished were also consulted. Some of these had been used to decide whether or not to grant the environmental permits themselves, while others had to be prepared because of permit provisions. They included a risk analysis, a report on the detailed design, a rule book for waste disposal at the site, a checklist for site controls, evaluation reports made by the proponent (part of their EMS) and evaluation reports made by the Enforcement Department of the Province of South Holland (PZH, 1994).

Results of the first EIA follow-up study

When the results of the first EIA follow-up study were compared with the predictions and expectations in the EIS, a number of deviations came to light (PZH, 1994) including:

- Difficulties in constructing the vertical sealing wall made it necessary to adjust the design, though without loss of quality.
- The drainage system was installed at a higher level than planned as the deeper soil proved to be contaminated.

- Drainage water from the bottom of the disposal site was more polluted than was expected in the EIS.
- A higher proportion of organic material was evident in the waste composition, resulting in higher odour and gas emissions.
- A higher proportion of waste was trucked in by road rather than arriving by ship, although absolute traffic movements were lower than expected.

In general, it appeared that the permit provisions were observed, apart from some deviations:

- Some permanent departures from the design plan and the plan for disposing of waste were made because of practical problems (which were approved by the competent authority after the original consent was granted).
- The share of waste trucked in exceeded the limit set.
- The production of landfill gas was greater than the maximum allowed.

The competent authority concluded that the deviations from the EIS and the permit provisions which had been recorded were not of such a nature that they would require reconsideration of the original decision or for the environmental permits to be revoked.

The second follow-up study

A second EIA follow-up study was undertaken for the waste disposal facility in 1998 with a focus on the operational phase from 1994 to 1997. The organization of this follow-up study was comparable to that of the first. Use was made of the extensive performance-monitoring programme operated by the proponent as part of their EMS along with information collected by the competent authority from the surveillance and enforcement activities (PZH, 1998).

In view of the first follow-up report, the *scope of the second EIA follow-up study* was changed. It included (PZH, 1998; PROAV, 1998) intervening developments (policy developments, new activities planned at the site), waste supply (composition and supply of waste), geohydrology (construction and performance of isolation facilities, drainage water), construction and performance of the waste dump (settling and subsidence), soil and groundwater (quality and amount of water flows) and local environmental pollution (noise, odour, landfill gas, dust and accidents).

Among these issues, the focus of the second EIA follow-up was on odour control and geohydrological isolation. One of the key findings of the first EIA follow-up regarding the odour problems was related to the supply of waste being different than expected. On the basis of that outcome, a system for draining landfill gas had been constructed at the waste disposal site. The results of the second EIA follow-up indicated that the system for removing landfill gas seemed to perform as expected, although this issue needs to be monitored in the future.

Since the first EIA follow-up study, the vertical barrier had been finished and subjected to a drainage test and it was concluded that it performed well (PZH, 1999). However, the horizontal underground Kedichem layer that should have isolated the disposal site from more deeply situated groundwater layers proved to be less impermeable than was assumed when designing the facility. Much more deep groundwater has had to be pumped out in order to maintain the 'geohydrological under-pressure'. As this water is not polluted (the water percolating through the waste is drained away directly below the bottom of the waste) it is discharged into the surface water. However, this situation is less desirable because of provincial water policies which seek to limit drainage of fresh groundwater in order to prevent saltwater intrusion.

The second follow-up report concluded that the waste disposal facility complied with the environmental permits apart from some minor deviations (PZH, 1999). However, it indicated that the complaints of people living nearby needed to be addressed. Specifically, prevention of odour problems and a careful system of dealing with complaints was advocated.

The second EIA follow-up report has formed a basis for granting (adjusted) environmental permits. One reason is that the owner of the waste disposal facility wished to increase the total amount of waste dumped at the site (from 10.3 million to 11.3 million cubic metres) and to extend the period of dumping (from 2003 to 2017, as the supply of waste was less than expected in the EIS). The environmental permit was accordingly revised in 2002 on the basis of the follow-up studies carried out. The revised permit included extra monitoring requirements (with respect to odour) and requirements regarding facilities for landfill gas emissions. Furthermore, the proponent had plans to start new activities relating to storage, treatment and separation of waste flows which triggered a new EIA procedure. However, these development proposals were withdrawn and the new EIA procedure was cancelled before the EIS was published.

The Province has planned a third EIA follow-up study and the initial preparations for this have been carried out (PZH, 2001b). The focus will be the performance of the facilities for geohydrological isolation, emission facilities (especially odour) and health issues. The third follow-up study will also have a communication objective in relation to the public complaints because the geohydrological isolation and emissions (odour) have become issues of intense public debate (PZH, 2001b). However, parallel to the EIA follow-up, specific studies have been carried out into these issues (especially into health) and specific monitoring activities have been initiated because of the environmental permit. Because these investigations have provided answers to the major issues of the third EIA follow-up study, commencement of that study has been delayed.

Lessons learned

Various lessons can be learnt with respect to screening and scoping for EIA follow-up from the Derde Merwedehaven project (CSO, 1994; Meijer, 1994, 1995; PZH, 1994, 1999):

- Because of the dynamic context of the project, scoping for follow-up has been an ongoing and iterative process.
- Much information was already available because of permit provisions and the proponent's EMS. There was a greater need to make this information accessible and to interpret it than to collect new data. The EIA follow-up provided a useful integrated analysis of the development.
- Reservation of resources was important. The availability of reserved budgets for the evaluation proved to be a major stimulus to the actual carrying out of the EIA follow-up.
- Over time the relevance of follow-up specifically related to the original EIS and consent decision declined. The original project became part of the regular operations of the company, with other monitoring and evaluative instruments (e.g. EMS) taking over the role of EIA follow-up.

Conclusions

An early start to screening and scoping for follow-up is vital for an EIA follow-up that is effective, efficient and useful. A timely and explicit screening and scoping for EIA follow-up may enhance the openness of the follow-up process to other parties. In this way, checks and balances are built in, thereby preventing the scope from being distorted or overly narrow and taking into account follow-up issues relevant to the different parties.

It is crucial to do a good job of tailoring the scope of EIA follow-up to the EIA project at hand. Follow-up can easily become complex and require much effort as issues may have to be monitored over long time periods. EIA follow-up should not become a goal in itself; instead, an objective-led approach to screening and scoping for follow-up is important. It is useful to focus the EIA follow-up on those issues that are easily measured and can unambiguously be appraised against clear criteria, thus avoiding problems of causality.

In general, the consent decision and the EIS may provide useful information for guiding EIA follow-up. It is important for the follow-up study itself to link up with existing monitoring and evaluation activities such as environmental permit provisions, EMS and area-wide monitoring schemes. EIA follow-up may provide an 'umbrella' under which various information sources can be integrated and coordinated.

EIA follow-up can be seen as a balancing act between what one wants (objectives) and what one can achieve (feasibility) in order to result in practicable and cost-effective follow-up. Important points include: a clear division of roles, tasks and responsibilities irrespective of who has the lead in follow-up; reservation of earmarked budgets, time and capacity; and careful planning of the follow-up study.

EIA follow-up occurs in a dynamic context with different issues being relevant in the planning, construction, operation and decommissioning phases of the project. This warrants a flexible approach utilizing ongoing scoping. Although EIA follow-up is a finite process, it may be continued by blending the EIA project-specific follow-up into ongoing project management and/or by forming the start of a new cycle of planning and decision-making.

References

Arts, J (1998) *EIA Follow-up – On the Role of Ex-post Evaluation in Environmental Impact Assessment*, Groningen, GeoPress

Arts, J and Nooteboom, S (1999) 'Environmental Impact Assessment Monitoring and Auditing', in Petts, J (ed) *Handbook of Environmental Impact Assessment Volume 1. Environmental Impact Assessment: Process, Methods and Potential*, Oxford, Blackwell Science, pp229–251

Arts, J, Caldwell, P and Morrison-Saunders, A (2001) 'EIA follow-up: Good practice and future directions: Findings from a workshop at the IAIA 2000 Conference', *Impact Assessment and Project Appraisal*, vol 19, pp175–185

BKH Adviesbureau (1991) *Milieu-Effectrapport Afvalberging Derde Merwedehaven (EIS for Waste Disposal at the Derde Merwedehaven Site)*, prepared for the Municipality of Dordrecht and PROAV, The Hague

CSO Adviesbureau voor milieuonderzoek (1994) *Notitie over evaluatie m.e.r. Derde Merwedehaven (Memo on EIA Follow-up for the Derde Merwedehaven Project)*, Prepared for the Province of South Holland, Maastricht

EIA Commission (1994) *EIA Methodology in The Netherlands, Views of the Commission for EIA*, Utrecht, EIA Commission

Etzioni, A (1967) 'Mixed Scanning: A "Third" Approach to Decision-making', reprinted in Faludi, A (ed) (1973) *A Reader in Planning Theory*, Oxford, Pergamon Press, pp217–229

Glasson, J, Therivel, R and Chadwick, A (1994*) Introduction to Environmental Impact Assessment*, Natural and Built Environment Series 1, London, UCL Press

Green, R (1979) *Sampling Design and Statistical Methods for Environmental Biologists*, New York, John Wiley

Meijer, J (1994) *Interne notitie over organisatorische aspecten inzake evaluatie m.e.r. Derde Merwedehaven (Internal Memo on Organizational Aspects of the EIA Follow-up of the Derde Merwedehaven Project)*, The Hague, Province of South Holland

Meijer, J (1995) '*Evaluatie bij m.e.r.-projecten: typen, reikwijdte en uitvoeringsaspecten' (EIA Follow-up of EIA Projects: Typology, Scope and Aspects of Implementation)*, presented at a VVM workshop, 28 November 1995, Haarlem, The Hague, Province of South Holland

Meijer, J and Van Vliet, J (2000) 'EIA Evaluation: Added Value by Screening and Scoping', presented at *Back to the Future: Where will Impact Assessment be in 10 Years and How do we get there? 20th Annual Meeting of the International Association for Impact Assessment*, 19–23 June 2000, Hong Kong, published on CD ROM: *IA Follow-up Workshop*, Hull, Quebec, Environment Canada

Morrison-Saunders, A, Baker, J and Arts, J (2003) 'Lessons from practice: Towards successful follow-up', *Impact Assessment and Project Appraisal*, vol 21, pp43–56

PROAV, Provincial Waste Disposal Company, South Holland (1998) *Notitie ten behoeve overleg evaluatie MER afvalberging Derde Merwedehaven, 11 maart 1998 (Memo for EIA Follow-up for the Derde Merwedehaven Project)*, internal memorandum, Dordrecht

PZH, Province of South Holland (1994) *Evaluatie MER Afvalberging Derde Merwedehaven (EIA Follow-up Report for Waste Disposal at the Derde Merwedehaven*

Site), Bureau Coördinatie, Vergunningen en M.e.r., drafted by Kleijn, C E and Groenewoud, H E (CSO Adviesbureau voor Milieuonderzoek), The Hague, Province of South Holland

PZH, Province of South Holland (1998) *Vragenlijst tweede m.e.r. evaluatie Afvalberging Derde Merwedehaven (List of Questions for the Second EIA Follow-up for the Derde Merwedehaven Project)*, Internal Memo, The Hague, Province of South Holland

PZH, Province of South Holland (1999) *Evaluatieverslag milieu-effectrapportage Derde Merwedehaven periode 1 april 1994 t/m 31 december 1997 (EIA Follow-up Report for the Derde Merwedehaven Project for the Period 1 April 1994 – 31 December 1997)*, Drafted by Grip, S and Meijer, J (Directie Water en Milieu), The Hague, Province of South Holland

PZH, Province of South Holland (2001a) *Handreiking Selectieve MER-evaluatie (Guidelines for Selective EIA Follow-up)*, July 2001, The Hague, Province of South Holland

PZH, Province of South Holland (2001b) *Plan van aanpak evaluatie afgeronde m.e.r.-projecten; gebaseerd op Handreiking Selectieve MER-evaluatie (Action Plan for Selective EIA Follow-up)*, July 2001, The Hague, Province of South Holland

RWS North Brabant (Public Works Council, North Brabant) (1991) *Tracénota en Milieu-effectrapport A50 Eindhoven-Oss/Ravenstein (Route Plan and EIS for the A50)*, Hertogenbosch

RWS North Brabant (Public Works Council, North Brabant) (1995) *Evaluatie achteraf (art. 7.39 Wm) voor de A50 Eindhoven-Oss, Concept Projectvoorstel (Project Proposal for EIA Follow-up of the A50 Project)*, Hertogenbosch

RWS North Brabant (Public Works Council, North Brabant) (1998) *M.e.r.-evaluatie A50 Eindhoven-Oss, Projectplan (Project Plan EIA Follow-up for the A50)*, Hertogenbosch

RWS North Brabant (Public Works Council, North Brabant) (2003) *M.e.r.-evaluatieprogramma A50 Eindhoven-Oss, Projectplan (EIA Follow-up Programme for the A50)*, prepared by Van der Vlies, M, Hertogenbosch

Sadler, B (1988) 'Evaluation of Assessment: Post-EIS Research and Process Development' in Wathern, P (ed) *Environmental Impact Assessment, theory and practice*, London, Unwin Hyman, pp129–142

Sadler, B (1996) *International Study of the Effectiveness of Environmental Assessment, Final Report, Environmental Assessment in a Changing World: Evaluating Practice to Improve Performance*, Canadian Environmental Assessment Agency and the International Association for Impact Assessment, Hull, Quebec, Minister of Supply and Services

TMC, Transportation/EIA Centre (2004) *Quick scan evaluatie m.e.r. (Quick Scan EIA Follow-up)*, drafted by Nijsten, R and Arts, J, Delft, Ministry of Transport, Public Works and Water Management

Tweede Kamer der Staten Generaal, Dutch Lower House (1981) *Memorie van Toelichting Uitbreiding van de Wet algemene bepalingen milieuhygiëne (Regelen met betrekking tot milieu-effectrapportage) (Explanatory Memorandum to the EIA Bill)*, Vergaderjaar 1980–1981, 16814 no3, The Hague, Staatsuitgeverij

Van Eck, M (1997) *Discussienotitie over evaluatie achteraf bij milieu-effectrapportage (Discussion Paper on EIA Follow-up)*, Memorandum prepared under the responsibility of the Working Programme EIA, February 1997, Utrecht, EIA Commission

Van Lamoen, F and Arts, J (2002) 'EIA Follow-up for Road Projects: What Do We Want and Need to Know?', presented at *Assessing the Impact of Impact Assessment: Impact Assessment for Informed Decision Making, 22nd Annual Meeting of the International*

Association for Impact Assessment, 15–21 June 2002, The Hague, published on CD ROM: *IA Follow-up Workshop*, Hull, Quebec, Environment Canada

VROM, Ministry of Housing, Physical Planning and Environment (1994a) EIA Decree 1994, *Bulletin of Acts, Orders and Decrees*, 1994/no 540, The Hague

VROM, Ministry of Housing, Physical Planning and Environment (1994b) *Handleiding milieu-effectrapportage (Guidance on EIA)*, drafted by Van Haeren, J J F M and Gravendeel, J W (DHV) and Samkalden, D and Van Tilburg, R (Twijnstra Gudde), Lelystad, Koninklijke Vermande

VROM, Ministry of Housing, Physical Planning and Environment (1995) *Handleiding evaluatie m.e.r. afvalstortplaatsen (Guidance on EIA Follow-up for Waste Disposal Projects)*, EIA series 51, drafted by Arts, J (Rijksuniversiteit Groningen), The Hague

VROM, Ministry of Housing, Physical Planning and Environment (1996) *Environmental Management Act*, English Text of the Environmental Management Act dated 1 August 1996, The Hague

VROM, Ministry of Housing, Physical Planning and Environment (1998) *Effectiever met milieu-effectrapportage, Toekomstvisie, korte termijnmaatregelen en reactie van het kabinet op het tweede ECW-advies op het instrument milieu-effectrapportage (More-Effective EIA: Vision on the Future, Short-term Measures and Reaction of the Cabinet on the Second Advisory Report of the ECW on the EIA Regulations)*, final draft, 11 May 1998, The Hague

VROM, Ministry of Housing, Physical Planning and Environment (2003) *Evaluatie m.e.r. (Evaluation study on EIA)*, drafted by Van Kessel, H, Boer, T, Roelofs, B and Klein Koerkamp, K (Novioconsult), The Hague

V&W, Ministry of Transport, Public Works and Water Management (1996) *Hand-reiking evaluatie m.e.r. weginfrastructuur (Guidance on EIA Follow-up for Road Infrastructure Projects)*, drafted by Klink, Th F and Eijssen, P H M (DHV), Rijkswaterstaat DWW series, Delft

V&W, Ministry of Transport, Public Works and Water Management (2003) *Werkwijzer evaluatie milieueffecten hoofdwegenprojecten, Leidraad voor de evaluatie achteraf bij m.e.r. (Guidelines for EIA Follow-up of Road Projects)*, drafted by Arts, J and Van Lamoen, F (Transportation/EIA Centre), Delft

Wachelder, B (2002) 'Selective Subsequent EIA Follow-up (Evaluation)', presented at *Assessing the Impact of Impact Assessment: Impact Assessment for Informed Decision Making, 22nd Annual Meeting of the International Association for Impact Assessment*, 15–21 June 2002, The Hague, published on CD ROM: *IA Follow-up Workshop*, Hull, Quebec, Environment Canada

Wood, C (2003) *Environmental Impact Assessment – A Comparative Review*, 2nd edition, Harlow, Pearson Education Ltd

5

Appraising Effects of Mitigation Measures: The Grand Coulee Dam's Impacts on Fisheries

Leonard Ortolano and Christine L. May

Introduction

Following the initial establishment of practices and procedures for impact assessment, which characterized much of the early years of EIA during the late 1970s and into the 1980s, attention swung to evaluating the quality of EIAs, and the first follow-up studies appeared (Caldwell et al, 1982; Bisset, 1984; Sadler 1987a, b). In the wider EIA literature at this time, much was written about the scientific integrity of EIA (Caldwell, 1982; Beanlands and Duinker, 1984; Culhane et al, 1987). Debate included the role of science in EIA and how scientific approaches could be utilized to overcome uncertainties concerning predicted environmental effects and to achieve rational outcomes. The use of scientific approaches in EIA is equally relevant to follow-up activities. This chapter focuses on scientific approaches to EIA follow-up monitoring for a major case study project in the US which attempted to determine environmental impacts and the effectiveness of mitigation measures.

This chapter uses the Grand Coulee Dam (GCD) on the Columbia River in the US to address a central issue in EIA follow-up work: determining post-project impacts when the underlying scientific knowledge is incomplete. This chapter uses material from an evaluation of GCD conducted originally by a team of 13 planners and natural and social scientists for the World Commission on Dams (Ortolano and Cushing, 2000). We are pleased to acknowledge the contributions of our colleagues on the study. Our analysis, which concerns impacts on salmon fisheries, also examines how failure to account for cumulative effects of related projects has adversely impacted indigenous peoples and biodiversity. Scientific uncertainty and cumulative effects are closely related in this case because the effects of GCD are difficult to isolate from the effects of more than a dozen other dams built on the Columbia River following construction of GCD. However, the effect of multiple dams is only one of several factors making it difficult to isolate impacts of GCD on fisheries.

The following question is basic for any EIA follow-up study: was the proposed mitigation programme implemented? In the GCD case, the answer is 'yes'.

A second fundamental question is: did the mitigation programme succeed in meeting its goals? This question can be investigated because there is an extensive time series of fisheries run size data. However, causes for temporal shifts in salmon population cannot be identified definitively because many external factors influence the Columbia River ecosystem and the requisite scientific knowledge for distinguishing the effects of different factors is incomplete.

Interestingly, post-project monitoring and mitigation of GCD's effects on fisheries were undertaken during the 1930s, long before the advent of EIA as a formal set of procedures. Anticipated adverse economic impacts on commercial fisheries motivated the post-project follow-up work. Notwithstanding that the initial monitoring and mitigation were undertaken in the absence of formal EIA requirements, those requirements (imposed during the 1970s) eventually influenced project operations. We begin by providing background information on GCD and the role played by US EIA requirements since GCD was constructed.

Introduction to GCD and CBP

The Grand Coulee Dam and the associated Columbia Basin Project (CBP) were originally viewed as one project, but people now refer to them separately. GCD constitutes the dam and power plant; the reservoir, called Lake Roosevelt; and ancillary facilities at the dam. CBP constitutes the system to pump water from Lake Roosevelt to irrigate 416,000 hectares (ha) of land in the semi-arid region in the State of Washington known as the Columbia Plateau. Figure 5.1 shows the location of GCD in relation to other dams on the Columbia River's main stem.

The concept of building a dam on the Columbia River to irrigate the Columbia Plateau had been discussed seriously since the early 1900s. By the early 1930s, the State of Washington, the US Army Corps of Engineers ('the Corps') and the Bureau of Reclamation ('Reclamation') each had plans for a dam near a canyon known as the Grand Coulee. It was only after Franklin Roosevelt was elected president in 1932 that a particular project was selected for construction. The plan supported by Roosevelt was intended to put unemployed people to work building the dam, to provide inexpensive public power and to irrigate part of the Columbia Plateau.

Figure 5.1 *Location of the Grand Coulee Dam*

GCD, which is 1.6km wide and 107m high, has a generating capacity of 6809MW and is the largest producer of electricity in the US. The first stage of GCD's construction, including the dam and two power houses, was started in 1933 and completed in 1951. The second stage, consisting of the third power plant, began in the mid-1960s and was completed in 1975.

World War II caused delays in constructing CBP. Irrigation works were initiated in 1945 and settlement began in 1949. The last addition of lands to CBP occurred in 1985. Box 5.1 contains a timeline of key events concerning EIA and the preparation of Environmental Impact Statements (EISs) related to GCD and CBP.

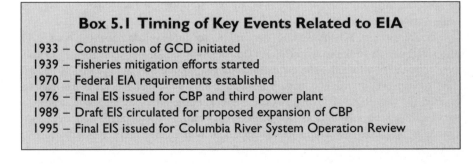

Box 5.1 Timing of Key Events Related to EIA

1933 – Construction of GCD initiated
1939 – Fisheries mitigation efforts started
1970 – Federal EIA requirements established
1976 – Final EIS issued for CBP and third power plant
1989 – Draft EIS circulated for proposed expansion of CBP
1995 – Final EIS issued for Columbia River System Operation Review

Environmental Impact Statements for GCD and CBP

The US *National Environmental Policy Act* of 1969 (NEPA) introduced EIA procedures for federal projects, and all federal actions on GCD and CBP after 1969 were subject to the statute's provisions. NEPA's principal EIA-related requirement concerns an EIS process that is initiated whenever a federal agency makes a decision that can have a significant impact on the quality of the human environment. Although some ex-ante impact assessments were made for GCD and CBP, the original project pre-dates NEPA. Since 1970, however, three EIS's have been prepared in the context of GCD and CBP.

The EIS process to implement NEPA was heavily influenced by court actions during the 1970s. In that decade, critics of federal infrastructure projects frequently sued federal agencies alleging that agencies had not prepared required EIS's or that their EIS's were inadequate. Judicial decisions in these cases influenced the US Council on Environmental Quality (CEQ), the agency created by NEPA to oversee the EIS process. In 1978, CEQ formalized much of its earlier EIS guidance by issuing binding regulations detailing what agencies must do to comply with federal EIS requirements (CEQ, 1986).

CEQ's regulations include general provisions for post-project mitigation and monitoring. They require that a federal agency's 'record of decision' (ROD) for a proposed action shall:

> *State whether all practicable means to avoid or minimize environmental harm from the alternative selected have been adopted, and if not, why they were not. A monitoring and enforcement programme shall be adopted and summarized where applicable for any mitigation (CEQ 1986, s1505.2(c)).*

Box 5.2 displays portions of the CEQ regulations that define mitigation, and it indicates EIA follow-up steps that the 'lead agency' must employ. The mandate in Box 5.2 was confusing to some, and CEQ responded by issuing clarifying guidance that calls on agencies to consider a broad range of mitigation measures (Box 5.3). This guidance does not require that all possible mitigations be implemented. CEQ hoped that by mentioning mitigations that agencies were not legally obliged to implement, others would be encouraged to act. The only mitigations that *must* be carried out are those listed in RODs issued by agencies.

As mentioned, NEPA was not applicable to the original planning for GCD and CBP, which took place in the 1920s and 1930s. The first EIS for GCD was issued in 1975, when the third power plant was being installed (USBR, 1976). The new power plant was nearly complete in 1975, but Reclamation issued an EIS for the original CBP plus the new power plant. The EIS was largely a pro-forma exercise that was not directed at influencing a particular decision. Under conditions prevailing in the 1970s, it was prudent for Reclamation to

Box 5.2 Portions of CEQ Regulations Pertaining to Mitigation

Definition of mitigation

CEQ Regulations define 'mitigations' to include measures for:

- avoiding the impact altogether by not taking a certain action or parts of an action
- minimizing impacts by limiting the degree or magnitude of the action and its implementation
- rectifying the impact by repairing, rehabilitating or restoring the affected environment
- reducing or eliminating the impact over time by preservation and maintenance operations during the life of the action
- compensating for the impact by replacing or providing substitute resources or environments.

Required EIA follow-up procedures

Agencies may provide for monitoring to assure that their decisions are carried out and should do so in important cases. Mitigation and other conditions established in the EIS or during its review and committed as part of the decision shall be implemented by the lead agency or other appropriate consenting agency. The lead agency shall:

- include appropriate conditions in grants, permits or other approvals
- condition funding of actions on mitigation
- upon request, inform cooperating or commenting agencies on progress in carrying out mitigation measures which they have proposed and which were adopted by the agency making the decision
- upon request, make available to the public the results of relevant monitoring.

Source: CEQ, 1986 (s1505.3 and 1508.20)

do this as many federal projects under construction at that time were being challenged successfully in courts if they lacked an EIS.

In 1989, Reclamation produced a draft EIS for a proposal to irrigate additional CBP lands (USBR, 1989). The EIS process catalysed debate. Some people criticized Reclamation's proposal because it had an unfavourable benefit–cost ratio. Others felt the expansion of irrigation would jeopardize efforts to increase in-stream flows to support Columbia River salmon and steelhead (i.e. salmonids). During the late 1930s, steelhead averaged less than 3 per cent of the total number of salmonids passing Bonneville Dam (Fish,

---

Box 5.3 CEQ Follow-up Guidance

What is the scope of mitigation measures that must be discussed?

Mitigation measures discussed in an EIS must cover the range of impacts of the proposal. The measures must include such things as design alternatives that would decrease pollution emissions, construction impacts, aesthetic intrusion, as well as relocation assistance and other possible efforts.

How should an EIS treat the subject of available mitigation measures that are (1) outside the jurisdiction of the lead or cooperating agencies, or (2) unlikely to be adopted or enforced by the responsible agency?

All relevant, reasonable mitigation measures that could improve the project are to be identified, even if they are outside the jurisdiction of the lead agency or the cooperating agencies, and thus would not be committed as part of the RODs of these agencies. This will serve to alert agencies or officials who can implement these extra measures, and will encourage them to do so. In addition, the EIS and ROD should indicate the likelihood that such measures will be adopted or enforced by the responsible agencies.

What is the enforceability of a Record of Decision?

Agencies will be held accountable for preparing RODs that conform to the decisions actually made and for carrying out the actions set forth in the ROD. The terms of a ROD are enforceable by agencies and private parties.

Source: CEQ, 1981 (Questions 19a and b and 34d with minor editing)

1944). As a partial response to critics, Reclamation chose not to finalize its draft EIS. This allowed for the possibility of expanding the irrigated area in the future.

The third GCD-related EIS, issued in 1995, was for a Columbia River System Operation Review (USDOE, USACE, USBR, 1995). This EIS covered operations of GCD in tandem with operations at 13 other federal dams in the US portion of the Columbia River Basin. Issues related to salmon overshadowed the review process as the prospect increased that certain species of salmon would become listed as 'endangered' under the Endangered Species Act (ESA). The EIS process began to be eclipsed by ESA-related issues. Indeed, the Biological Opinion issued in 1995 by the National Marine Fisheries Services heavily influenced the system operations strategy that was eventually adopted (NMFS, 1995). Actions specific to GCD included insuring availability of water to meet summer flow targets at downstream dams.

Notwithstanding the significance of the aforementioned EISs, they are peripheral to the main arguments herein because they were produced decades after the key decisions relating to GCD and CBP had been made, and, except for the system operations review, they had no effect on EIA follow-up activities. Our main concern is the impact of GCD's salmon and steelhead mitigation plans. At the time the plans were created, there were no requirements for EIA and mitigations. Federal officials felt mitigation measures were needed because GCD's impacts would adversely affect commercial fishing for salmonids.

Mitigation of impacts on Columbia River salmonids

Salmon and steelhead are anadromous: they are hatched in freshwater, migrate to sea after several months, live anywhere from one to five years at sea, and then migrate back to the freshwater environment of their birth in order to reproduce and die (the time spent before migrating to the sea, and the time spent in the ocean varies among species of salmonids). As physical barriers, dams typically impede both migrations. Young salmon have trouble getting past dams on their way to the sea, and mortality rates are typically between 2 and 15 per cent per dam (NPPC, undated, p3). Average juvenile mortality rates can be as low as 2 per cent if fish bypass facilities are employed, but the juveniles must be able to locate the bypass systems and avoid getting swept into intakes leading to turbines. An average of 15 per cent of juveniles migrating to sea on the main stem (as opposed to tributaries) of the Columbia River are killed in passage though a dam's turbines. Adults have problems negotiating fish passage facilities on their way back to spawning grounds, with mortality rates of about 5 per cent per dam. For instance, at a fish ladder, a commonly used fish passage facility, adults returning to spawn must locate the ladders and have the physical strength to traverse them.

Because of the height of the dam above the downstream water (107m), GCD did not include fish passage facilities. A formal EIA was not conducted, but predictions were made of how the dam would influence the salmon and steelhead that once spawned upstream of the dam site.

Estimated impacts of GCD

Annual salmonid populations in the Columbia River Basin have fluctuated widely, and estimates vary significantly. Prior to white settlement in the 1800s, the basin supported a population estimated at between 7 and 30 million salmonids, with annual runs to the Upper Columbia (i.e. the portion of the basin above GCD) of between 500,000 and 1.3 million (NRC, 1995). In 1938, *before* GCD blocked migrating salmonids, the basin-wide run of salmonids was 2.2 million and the run to the Upper Columbia River was about 25,000 (Calkins et al, 1939). By that time, over-harvesting and habitat destruction had taken a toll on some species (Chapman et al, 1982; Mullan, 1987).

Because no fish passage facilities had been planned for GCD, returning adults would be unable to reach their native spawning grounds and would therefore fail to reproduce. Without a fisheries mitigation programme, the average annual Upper Columbia migration of 25,000 salmon and steelhead would have been lost. The monetary value of fisheries adversely affected by GCD was estimated to be about US$250,000 to $300,000 in 1937 dollars. This anticipated economic loss was the driving force behind GCD's fisheries mitigation and monitoring programme.

Reclamation recognized the commercial importance of Columbia River fisheries, but the agency was unable to reach agreement with the US Department of Fisheries and the State of Washington on a fisheries mitigation approach. Uncertainties over how the two downstream dams – Bonneville and Rock Island – would affect the run size of salmonids made matters more complex. Some predicted that Bonneville Dam would eliminate 90 per cent of the salmon and that Rock Island Dam would cause additional damage (Pitzer, 1994). This represents an early example of issues that would become increasingly complex as more dams were built in the Columbia River Basin: what are the combined effects of multiple dams on salmonids and is it feasible to isolate the effects of any one dam?

In 1937, the dam's foundation was completed and salmonid runs were blocked, but a plan to mitigate the effects of GCD on fisheries had not yet been devised. While discussions about fisheries mitigation continued, government officials paid little attention to the significance of salmon to indigenous peoples in either the US or Canada.

Following the practices of the period, the US did not have a formal process for involving affected indigenous people in GCD's decision process, and no effort was made to gain their consent for destroying tribal fisheries. Although the federal government had, in the early 1930s, assured affected indigenous people that their rights in lands and fisheries would be considered, there was no follow-up on those assurances (Ortolano and Cushing, 2000, p 3.7–5).

In retrospect, the social and cultural impacts of eliminating salmon above GCD were devastating. By blocking the spawning runs, the project severely disrupted the way of life for indigenous people in the Upper Columbia Basin. Important salmon-based cultural and ritual ceremonies were eliminated, parts of language and crafts associated with fishing disappeared, and tribal members' diets changed significantly. For the Spokane and some of the tribes of the Colville Confederation, salmon probably accounted for about 40–50 per cent of their daily diet before GCD. As a result of moving to foods high in fat, sugar and salt, rates of heart disease, diabetes and other diet-related illnesses have increased significantly on the reservations (see Ortolano and Cushing (2000) for further details).

GCD's fisheries maintenance programme

In January 1939, the Secretary of the Interior appointed a three-person Board of Consultants to create a plan for mitigating GCD's effects on salmonids. The

Board developed the Grand Coulee Fish Maintenance Program (GCFMP), which entailed trapping migrating adult salmonids as they reached the top of fish ladders at Rock Island Dam and transporting them in specially equipped trucks to four tributaries in the Middle Columbia for natural propagation and to four hatcheries located on these tributaries for artificial propagation (Calkins et al, 1939). The four Middle Columbia tributaries are the Wenatchee, Entiat, Methow and Okanogan Rivers (Figure 5.2).

The process of trapping migrating adult salmonids at Rock Island Dam and transplanting them in the Middle Columbia tributaries was to be repeated for several years until salmonids that once spawned above GCD were retrained to spawn in the tributaries. The process only needed to be repeated for several years because that is how long it would take before the last of the adult salmonids born above GCD would have attempted to return to the place of their birth to spawn. Thereafter, the returning salmonids would be those born in the Middle Columbia tributaries, and they would return to those tributaries instinctively to spawn. The concept behind the plan was that the commercial value of the fishery could be maintained by shifting the Upper Columbia runs to a location below GCD. The Board recommended that GCFMP be approached as a *scientific experiment*. A fisheries management programme of this magnitude had not been previously attempted (Netboy, 1980).

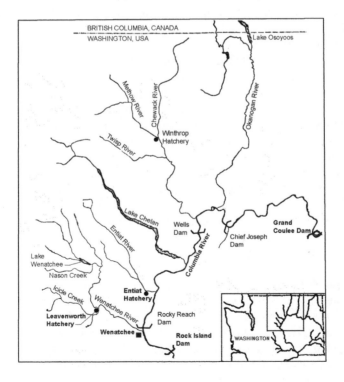

Figure 5.2 *Middle Columbia Tributaries and GCFMP Hatcheries*

Based on an average of the annual runs counted at Rock Island Dam from 1933 to 1938, the Board reckoned that about 25,000 adult salmonids migrated to the Upper Columbia in a typical year. The Board also estimated that less than 2500 fish spawned naturally in Middle Columbia tributaries, a number judged as unimportant compared with the total number of fish involved, i.e. 25,000.

In establishing its goals for GCFMP, the Board recognized that several stringent in-river fish harvesting restrictions were being considered at the time, and that implementation of those regulations could increase the run size beyond 25,000. Nevertheless, the Board had to size GCFMP's facilities without knowing the outcome of deliberations on harvesting regulations. In the end, the Board sized its truck fleet, hatcheries and other facilities to accommodate a target run size of 36,500 migrating adult salmonids.

Implementing GCFMP

The natural propagation element of the Board's plan involved trapping (at Rock Island Dam) salmonids migrating to spawn in the Upper Columbia and then taking the trapped fish by truck to holding areas on the four Middle Columbia tributaries, where they would spawn naturally. This programme began in 1939 and was discontinued in 1944 because the Board assumed that 5 years was sufficient to retrain the salmonids to spawn in the four tributaries indefinitely.

The natural propagation programme faced difficulties, but they were managed using the adaptive management strategy suggested by GCFMP; outcomes of GCFMP were observed and then actions to offset unexpected adverse effects were undertaken. For example, GCFMP staff observed high concentrations of returning adult salmonids in small downstream sections of the natural propagation areas. This clustering problem, which was caused by natural obstacles in the tributaries impeding upstream migration, was solved by modifying stream channel cross sections to eliminate barriers. Despite the problems, natural propagation was considered a success. Based on recorded fish counts at Rock Island Dam from 1938 to 1947, most returns from the relocated runs exceeded expectations (Fish, 1944; Fish and Hanavan, 1948).

Artificial propagation, the second key element in the Board's plan, began in 1940 with the opening of Leavenworth National Fish Hatchery (NFH) on Icicle Creek. One year later, additional hatcheries were completed on the Entiat and Methow rivers. From 1940 to 1944, some fish trapped at Rock Island Dam were transferred to the hatcheries instead of the holding areas in the tributaries. These fish were held in ponds until they spawned or their eggs were collected manually. The fertilized eggs were incubated and the resulting offspring were raised until ready for release. As with wild salmon, only a small percentage of the released hatchery-reared salmonids reached maturity in the ocean and made it back to the hatchery to spawn. Those that returned provided eggs for the next hatchery season.

The Board's view of GCFMP as a scientific experiment proved accurate in the context of artificial propagation. Difficulties were encountered with the original hatchery designs in the early years of operations, but adaptive management strategies were employed to resolve some of them. For example, migrating adult fish could not reach the Entiat and Methow river hatcheries because of inadequate fish passage facilities between the tributaries and the hatcheries. This was solved with the addition of fish ladders. Some problems, however, were intractable: during winter, freezing temperatures and the lack of a sufficient and suitable water supply interfered with the ability to rear fish; during summer, the water supply was too low to support full-capacity operation. All three hatcheries consistently ran at less than 10 per cent of their original design capacities.

Scientific studies were undertaken to improve the success rate of the artificial propagation programme. The primary focus was on reducing adult fish mortality. Some adult fish required two to nine months of residence at the hatchery (depending on the species) before reaching sexual maturity. During this time, fish suffered high rates of fungal illness, and pre-spawning mortality rates often exceeded 50 per cent (Fish, 1944).

The hatcheries also experienced shortfalls in egg supply, and continual egg supplementation from neighbouring river systems and hatcheries was necessary. As a result of this breeding across systems, it became impossible to retrieve the genetic uniqueness of Upper Columbia stocks.

Difficulties in isolating effects of GCD and GCFMP

A basic question in any evaluation of an impact mitigation plan like GCFMP concerns whether the proposed plan was carried out. In this case, with one minor exception, the Board's plan was fully implemented. The exception concerns the Board's proposal for a hatchery for the Okanogan River. The only suitable site was in Canada, and the hatchery was not built because of international complications and the building restrictions in place during World War II.

Another fundamental query concerns whether the mitigation programme met its goal, which in the GCFMP's case was to sustain an annual run of 36,500 migrating adult salmonids. During the late 1990s, the total number of salmonids passing Rock Island Dam (based on the five-year average from 1994–1998 in Figure 5.3) was estimated as 48,700. But can all or part of the 48,700 run size be attributed to GCFMP? This question cannot be answered because the effects of GCFMP cannot be distinguished from the effects of other variables that influence run size: harvesting, other dams and hatcheries, climate and ocean conditions, and habitat. Each of these factors has changed significantly since the 1930s.

Fish harvesting, which is affected by both regulations and technology, has a direct impact on the number of adult salmonids able to migrate past Rock Island Dam. Consider, for example, the increased regulation of in-river

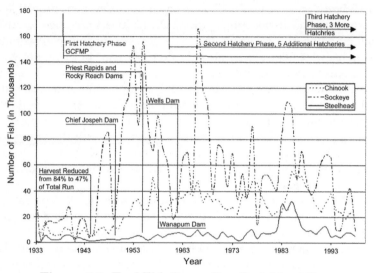

Figure 5.3 *Total Fish Counts Past Rock Island Dam*

commercial fishing. In the 1940s, selective season closures led to increased run sizes during those seasons. By the 1960s, in-river fishing seasons had become shorter, and the total in-river harvest was minimal (Chapman et al, 1982). However, as in-river harvests were scaled back, ocean fishing increased. Improvements in boat and fishing technologies allowed boats to range farther, stay out longer and exploit areas of the ocean that were previously unfished.

Additional *dams and hatcheries* have also affected the size of salmonid runs. Since the late 1930s, many fish mitigation efforts (linked to new dams) have been undertaken in the Middle Columbia, and these activities contribute to difficulties in isolating the effects of GCD and GCFMP. Before construction of GCD, only Bonneville and Rock Island Dams existed on the main stem. Each of these two dams had fish passage facilities, but fish mortality occurred on both upstream and downstream migrations through the dams. Although facility design changes made over the past 60 years have reduced mortality rates during passage of any one dam, there are more dams that salmonids must traverse to reach the four Middle Columbia tributaries. For example, salmonids that spawn in the Wenatchee River must migrate past seven main-stem dams, while those spawning in the Methow and Okanogan must traverse nine.

Construction of many of the new dams was accompanied by development of new hatcheries and corresponding increases in hatchery releases. For example, between 1961 and 1967, four hatcheries and one satellite facility were built in the Middle Columbia Basin to offset losses associated with four new dams. Another phase of mitigation was initiated in 1989 with construction of three hatcheries and seven satellite facilities in the Middle Columbia.

Variations in *ocean and climate conditions* contribute further to the problem of isolating the effects of GCD and GCFMP. The Pacific Ocean undergoes a fluctuation, on a 20–30 year timescale, know as the Pacific Decadal Oscillation (PDO). In the so-called 'positive' phase of the PDO, the eastern wedge of the Pacific (including the portion near Oregon and Washington) warms, and this is accompanied by a decrease in stocks of the US Northwest salmon and an increase in Alaskan salmon stocks (Mantua et al, 1997). During the 'negative' phase, the Pacific's eastern wedge cools, and this provides favourable conditions for US Northwest salmon, and declining conditions for Alaskan salmon.

Over the past century, four major PDO shifts have been observed. The PDO was in a phase providing poor conditions for US Northwest salmon in two periods: 1925–1946, and 1977–1999. In contrast, the PDO was in a phase providing favourable conditions for US Northwest salmon from 1947 to 1976. The PDO recently shifted to a phase favourable to US Northwest salmon, and salmon populations in the Columbia River experienced record returns in 2000 and 2001 (Yuasa, 2001).

Based on correlations between PDO and production patterns of pink, coho and sockeye salmon in the Columbia River, Hare et al (1999) argued that a lack of immediate response to salmon restoration efforts may be misconstrued as failures in salmon mitigation programmes, when, in fact, poor results may be explainable by unfavourable ocean conditions.

Other important variables concern changes in *habitat*. Consider, for example, Chief Joseph Dam, which was constructed downstream of GCD in the 1950s and did not contain fish passage facilities. It eliminated 81km of main stem salmonid spawning habitat. Moreover, salmonid habitat within the four Middle Columbia tributaries – the Wenatchee, Methow, Entiat, and Okanogan – has been degraded continually as a result of forest fires, logging, shoreline development, irrigation withdrawals and shoreline vegetation removal.

As a consequence of the types of changes described above, it is virtually impossible to isolate the influence of GCD and GCFMP on the size of the salmon and steelhead runs above Rock Island Dam. In principle, research could have been implemented to try to isolate the influence of GCD and GCFMP on salmonids (e.g. using research designs distinguishing between impact sites and control sites and employing both pre- and post-project data in the manner advocated by Green, 1979 and Osenberg and Schmitt, 1996). However, such research was not undertaken. Moreover, given the intense pace of development in the Columbia Basin in the decades following GCD's construction, it is not clear that even the most carefully designed post-project biological assessment studies would have been successful in isolating the influence of GCD and GCFMP from the effects of other variables.

Irreversible and irretrievable impacts of GCD on salmon

Notwithstanding the above-noted difficulties in estimating GCD's effects on run size, some effects of GCD on salmonids were unambiguous. In particular,

GCD blocked salmonids from over 1770km of Upper Columbia habitat. This change is virtually irreversible since the possibility that GCD will be dismantled is practically nil: the dam is the centrepiece of the Columbia River hydropower system.

In the Columbia Basin, habitat limits salmonid run size. In the 1930s, extensive habitat areas were available above the GCD site. Much of that habitat had not changed significantly since the late 1800s, and Scholz et al (1985) argued that a cessation in commercial fishing could have restored the Upper Columbia runs to much more abundant numbers. The Board's plan made it infeasible substantially to increase population sizes of Upper Columbia stocks in the Middle Columbia tributaries because GCFMP was developed around a habitat area that cannot support significant population increases. Little prospect exists for increasing the size of salmon runs by restoring habitat in the four Middle Columbia tributaries (Mullan, 1987).

Hatcheries such as those that are part of GCFMP influence wild salmon: interbreeding between wild and hatchery salmon tends to homogenize the population with a consequent loss of particular stocks of wild salmon. More-over, hatchery fish compete with wild salmon for food and habitat.

In the 1930s, the distinction between wild and hatchery fish was not a major concern. The primary goal of GCFMP was to reach a target population size. The origin of the fish was immaterial. Today, biologists attach importance to the differences between hatchery and wild fish, and only wild salmon are of concern under ESA. Currently 60 to 80 per cent of the population (i.e. roughly 48,700) is attributable to hatchery stocks (Busby et al, 1996; Gustafson et al, 1997; Myers et al, 1998).

An irreversible effect of GCFMP is that many original salmon stocks have been lost. This resulted from homogenization of the Upper and Middle Columbia stocks, hatchery egg supplementation, and inter-breeding and competition between wild and hatchery salmon. In comparison to the 1930s, biologists today are concerned about specific stocks and the diversity and genetic information they provide. If the ecological significance of distinct stocks of salmonids had been recognized at the time, this large-scale homogenization would probably not have been performed. As a result of GCD construction, a number of Upper Columbia fish populations or stocks were completely lost (e.g. Arrow, Slocan and Whatshan sockeye). GCFMP adversely affected the Okanogan sockeye population since it called for harvesting Okanogan sockeye for hatchery brood stock and genetic mixing of wild and hatchery stocks.

The Board of Consultants that created GCFMP could not have anticipated the importance currently attached to wild salmon and individual salmon stocks. And it could not have expected that many people today would want to restore salmon runs back to historical abundance. Moreover, the Board could not possibly have predicted that many US Northwest citizens attach value simply to knowing that salmon exist in the Columbia River.

One final point regarding impacts of GCD relates to *cumulative effects* of GCD and other Columbia River dams on salmonids. GCD was built at a time when only two dams existed on the Columbia. However, the Corps had already prepared plans for many other dams (USACE, 1933). Those early plans later served as a blueprint for developing the US portion of the Columbia as an integrated hydroelectric power system.

The Corps' failure to conduct a cumulative effects assessment (CEA) represents a missed opportunity, but one that is understandable. Although the Corps had responsibility for determining the feasibility of a sequence of dams on the main stem of the Columbia, it did not have authority to implement the basin-wide plan that it had delineated, and it did not assume responsibility for examining the effects of the basin-wide plan on salmonids. The Corps left the task of mitigating fisheries impacts to state and federal fisheries agencies, which, for many years, dealt with mitigation issues one dam at a time.

Another factor complicating the assessment of cumulative effects concerns the absence of regional planning institutions to support such an assessment. Dams on the Columbia have been constructed by a myriad of entities, including the Corps, Reclamation, and a host of non-federal organizations, and, for the most part, decisions were made one dam at a time. Neither a basin-wide water resources agency nor a regional planning framework existed to account for cumulative effects. Moreover, during the late 1920s and early 1930s, EIA did not exist as a formal activity, and the concept of cumulative environmental impacts did not enter the vocabulary of planners until the 1970s.

Conclusions and policy implications

We raised two main questions, the first of which concerned whether the mitigation programme had been carried out. Our analysis shows that, with minor exceptions, GCFMP had been implemented as planned.

Our second question was: did GCFMP meet its own annual target of 36,500 adult salmonids migrating above Rock Island Dam? Our assessment shows that with the data available, it is virtually impossible to distinguish the effects of GCD and GCFMP from other variables that influence salmon runs in the Columbia: harvesting practices, other dams and hatcheries, climate and ocean conditions, and habitat. The average run size of 48,700 salmonids exceeds the target, but it is impossible to say what fraction of the 48,700 salmonids can be attributed to GCFMP.

Adaptive management

During the late 1930s, before additional dam and hatchery construction took place, a before-and-after control-impact study might have provided useful information about the influence of GCD and GCFMP on salmonid run size. However, given the changes since the 1930s and the recently identified significance of ocean conditions on salmonids, it is not clear that even a careful research design could have distinguished the effects of GCD and GCFMP from other variables that influence run size. Moreover, the cost and time associated with implementing such a careful research design would have been high.

Given the circumstances, the adaptive management approach taken by the Board and the scientists who implemented GCFMP appears reasonable. The overall approach advocated by the Board – dealing with mitigation as an experiment that may require modification in response to follow-up monitoring – deserves to be emulated, particularly when important resources are at stake.

The EIA literature offers two main reasons for post-project monitoring related to impact prediction: (1) observations of an intervention's effects can improve the ability to make predictions, and (2) observed outcomes can be used to initiate (or modify) mitigation programmes to deal with unanticipated impacts. These reasons are not mutually exclusive. The EIA literature reflects differences of opinion regarding the importance of quantitative predictions. For example, Beanlands and Duinker (1984) argue that EIA practitioners should avoid vague, qualitative predictions of ecological impacts and that they should use unambiguous, testable predictions instead. In contrast, Morrison-Saunders and Bailey (1999) indicate that '[a] high level of scientific rigor in impact prediction may not result in more or improved environmental management' (p293). They argue that even vague, descriptive predictions in EIA can alert managers to important issues requiring their attention, for example, devising environmental management plans. Notwithstanding these differences of opinion regarding the significance of scientifically rigorous predictions, all four authors agree on the importance of follow-up monitoring in EIA. However, in the case of GCD's impacts on salmonids, the emphasis throughout has been on finding practical solutions to fisheries management problems. Scientists associated with GCFMP were not preoccupied with checking the predictions of GCD's impacts because the only predicted impact – that the Upper Columbia salmonid run would be lost unless mitigation measures were undertaken – was clearly valid.

Experience with GCD and GCFMP provides strong support for an adaptive environmental management strategy similar to that advocated by Holling (1978) and his colleagues. However, it also raises fundamental questions about the effectiveness of projects and mitigations that are planned in isolation, outside of a regional development framework.

Cumulative effects assessment

More generally, experience in the Columbia River Basin indicates that assessments of cumulative impacts need to be undertaken to avoid the types of resource management problems that have occurred so often during the past half-century. In recent years, considerable progress has been made in developing practical methodologies for conducting cumulative effects assessment (CEA). An example is the work of CEQ (1997), which augmented its NEPA regulations with special guidance on CEA.

Although methodological challenges persist, one of the main difficulties in conducting CEAs relates to the lack of incentives for regulatory agencies and project proponents to conduct CEAs. Project proponents often fail to embrace CEA because they fear it will increase costs and uncertainties in the project approval process. And government regulators often lack the mandates and resources needed to account for cumulative effects. For example, when the Corps planned a series of dams on the Columbia in the late 1920s and early 1930s, it had no mandate to look at basin-wide fisheries management issues. Indeed, those planning studies ignored completely the salmon fisheries question (USACE, 1933). The Corps assumed that state and federal fisheries agencies would manage salmon problems linked to dam building. Although fisheries agencies eventually implemented fisheries mitigation measures for the sequence of dams on the Columbia, they did so one dam at a time.

The inadequacy of incentives to conduct CEA has not changed substantially as a result of passage of the *National Environmental Policy Act* of 1969. CEQ (1986) regulations implementing NEPA require an assessment of cumulative effects, but the mandate is both general and ambiguous. CEQ does not spell out what must be done, and federal agencies are often able to ignore the CEA requirement without penalty. Under the circumstances, many agencies are reluctant to allocate their scarce resources to conducting CEA. This reluctance is pronounced when agencies responsible for conducting EIAs are also project proponents because CEA may delay their projects.

Another important impediment to conducting CEA is the absence of regional planning and management frameworks. Foreseeable future projects often involve actions by a diverse array of private organizations, as well as state, federal and local agencies. Unless these organizations share information and coordinate their activities, it will be difficult to conduct meaningful CEA. Moreover, actions to mitigate adverse effects may also require coordinated efforts involving numerous public and private organizations. Regional planning institutions are essential for orchestrating the needed inter-organizational coordination. In the US, regional planning institutions with the stature and authority to manage cumulative effects are scarce.

The volume edited by Kennedy (2002) contains examples demonstrating how inter-organizational cooperation can be instrumental in conducting CEA, and it highlights the importance of regional planning and management frameworks in CEA work. Significantly, the volume also points out the potential for using strategic environmental assessments (specifically, regional and sectoral environmental assessments) as a basis for integrating cumulative effects into decision processes.

If a regional environmental assessment had been conducted for dams proposed in the Corps study of 1933, it could have highlighted the Columbia River Basin salmonid problems decades before those problems, which include numerous species threatened with extinction, reached their current state. Moreover, a regional environmental assessment might have clarified how the effects of dams and other basin-wide changes on salmonids would adversely affect indigenous peoples.

Public consultation

The devastating impacts of GCD on indigenous peoples resulted from a failure to engage in meaningful dialogue with affected parties, and the inability of those parties to press for a full study of environmental and social impacts, including GCD's irreversible effect in blocking salmonids from the Upper Columbia. Reclamation's failure to consult meaningfully with affected indigenous people during the planning of GCD has led to great bitterness on the part of many tribal members.

Relationships between indigenous people and federal agencies responsible for managing the Columbia River Basin's resources have been strained ever since GCD was constructed. For example, in 1951 the Colville Confederated Tribes sued the US government alleging that the government had failed to compensate them for fish they would have been able to consume in the absence of GCD. The tribes won this case. In a different 1951 case, one alleging that the US government failed to keep its promises to provide tribes a share of power revenues from GCD, the Colvilles eventually won a lump sum of $53 million (in 1994 dollars) and annual payments of US$15 million. The Confederated Colville tribes, along with the Spokane tribe, have also contested decisions of the National Park Service concerning the management and jurisdiction of lands in the national recreation area centred on Lake Roosevelt, the reservoir created by GCD. Unlike Native Americans, Canada's indigenous people have not had access to the US courts to gain mitigation and compensation for their salmon losses, but they are actively seeking their long-term goal of salmon restoration.

As a result of NEPA, federal agencies in the US are no longer able to act without considering the environmental and social consequences of their decisions. And as long as NEPA remains a statute, future generations will not be placed in the position faced by indigenous peoples affected by GCD – being left out of deliberations on potentially negative actions taken by US federal agencies. The EIS process established under NEPA requires federal agencies to consult with all parties affected by proposed agency actions that may significantly affect the quality of the human environment. This consultation gives affected parties, including those in Canada and Mexico who may be influenced by projects in the US, the opportunity to participate in scoping as well as the public review and comment on a draft EIS (Bass et al, 2001) In addition, parties within the US who believe that a federal agency has failed to implement the EIS process properly can use the courts to press their claims. Citizen participation is widely viewed as a cornerstone of the EIS process.

References

Bass, R, Herson, A and Bogdan, K (2001) *The NEPA Book*, 2nd edition, Point Arena, California, Solano Press

Beanlands, G and Duinker, P (1984) 'An ecological framework for environmental impact assessment', *Journal of Environmental Management*, vol 18, pp267–277

Bisset, R (1984) 'Post-development audits to investigate the accuracy of environmental impact predictions', *Umweltpolitik*, vol 4, pp463–484

Busby, P, Wainwright, T, Bryant, G, Lierheimer, L, Waples, R, Waknitz, F and Lagomarsino, I (1996) *Status Review of West Coast Steelhead from Washington, Oregon, and California*, NOAA Technical Memorandum NMFS-NWFSC-27, Seattle, Washington, US Department of Commerce

Caldwell, L (1982) *Science and the National Environmental Policy Act: Redirecting Policy Through Procedural Reform*, Tuscaloosa, Alabama, University of Alabama Press

Caldwell, L, Bartlett, D, Parker, D and Keys, D (1982) *A Study of Ways to Improve the Scientific Content and Methodology of Environmental Impact Analysis*, Advanced Studies in Science, Technology and Public Affairs, School of Public and Environmental Affairs, Bloomington, Indiana University

Calkins, R, Durand, W and Rich, W (1939) *Report of the Board of Consultants on the Fish Problems of the Upper Columbia River Section*, 7 March 1939, Stanford, California, Stanford University

CEQ, Council of Environmental Quality (1981) *Forty Most Asked Questions Concerning CEQ's NEPA Regulations*, Washington, DC, Council of Environmental Quality

CEQ, Council of Environmental Quality (1986) *Regulations for Implementing the Procedural Provisions of the National Environmental Policy Act, 40 Code of Federal Regulations, Parts 1500–1508* (as of 1 July 1986; initial version issued in 1978), Washington, DC, Council of Environmental Quality

CEQ, Council of Environmental Quality (1997) *Considering Cumulative Effects Under the National Environmental Policy Act*, Washington, DC, Council of Environmental Quality

Chapman, D, Van Hyning, J and McKenzie, D (1982) *Alternative Approaches to Base Run and Compensation Goals for Columbia River Salmon and Steelhead Resources*, prepared for Chelan County PUD, Grand County PUD and Douglas County PUD; Battelle, Pacific Northwest Laboratories, Richland, Washington

Culhane, P, Friesema, H and Beecher, J (1987) *Forecasts and Environmental Decision-Making, The Content and Predictive Accuracy of Environmental Impact Statements*, Boulder, Colorado, Westview Press

Fish, F (1944) *The Retention of Adult Salmon with Particular Reference to the Grand Coulee Fish–Salvage Program*, Special Scientific Report No. 27, Washington, DC, US Fish and Wildlife Service

Fish, F and Hanavan, M (1948) *A Report on the Grand Coulee Fish Maintenance Project, 1939–1947*, Special Scientific Report No. 55, Washington, DC, US Fish and Wildlife Service

Green, R (1979) *Sampling Design and Statistical Methods for Environmental Biologists*, New York, John Wiley

Gustafson, R, Wainwright, T, Winans, G, Waknitz, F, Parker, L and Waples, R (1997) *Status Review of Sockeye Salmon from Washington and Oregon*, NOAA Technical Memorandum NMFS-NWFSC-33, Seattle, Washington, US Department of Commerce

Hare, S, Mantua, N and Francis, R (1999) 'Inverse production regimes: Alaskan and West Coast salmon', *Fisheries*, vol 24, pp6–14

Holling, C (ed) (1978) *Adaptive Environmental Assessment and Management*, Chichester, John Wiley

Kennedy, A (ed) (2002) *Cumulative Environmental Effects Management: Tools and Approaches*, Edmonton, Alberta Society of Professional Biologists

Mantua, N, Hare, S, Zhang, Y, Wallace, J and Francis, R (1997) 'A Pacific interdecadal climate oscillation with impacts on salmon production', *Bulletin of the American Meteorological Society*, vol 78, pp1069–1079

Morrison-Saunders, A and Bailey, J (1999) 'Exploring the EIA/environmental management relationship', *Environmental Management*, vol 24, pp281–295

Mullan, J (1987) *Status and Propagation of Chinook Salmon in the Middle Columbia River through 1985*, Biological Report, Washington, DC, US Fish and Wildlife Service, pp87–111

Myers, J, Kope, R, Bryant, G, Teel, D, Lierheimer, L, Wainwright, T, Grand, W, Waknitz, F, Neely, K, Lindley, S and Waples, R (1998) *Status Review of Chinook Salmon from Washington, Idaho, Oregon, and California*, NOAA Technical Memorandum NMFS-NWFSC-35, Seattle, Washington, US Department of Commerce

Netboy, A (1980) *The Columbia River Salmon and Steelhead Trout*, Seattle, Washington, University of Washington Press

NMFS, National Marine Fisheries Services (1995) *Biological Opinion, Endangered Species Act-Section 7 Consultation. Reinitiation of Consultation on 1994–1998 Operation of the Federal Columbia River Power System and Juvenile Transportation Program in 1995 and Future Years*, Seattle, Washington, National Marine Fisheries Services, Northwest Region

NPPC, Northwest Power Planning Council (undated) *Numerical Estimates of Hydropower-Related Losses, Columbia Basin Fish and Wildlife Program*, Portland, Oregon, Northwest Power Planning Council

NRC, National Resource Council (1995) *Upstream: Salmon and Society in the Pacific Northwest/Committee on Protection and Management of Pacific Northwest Anadromous Salmonids, Board on Environmental Studies and Toxicology, Commission on Life Sciences*, Prepublication Copy, Washington, DC, National Academy Press

Ortolano, L and Cushing, K (2000) *Grand Coulee Dam and Columbia Basin Project, USA*, Prepared for the World Commission on Dams, Cape Town, South Africa

Osenberg, C, and Schmitt, R (1996) 'Detecting Ecological Impacts Caused by Human Activities', in Schmitt, R, and Osenberg, C (eds) *Detecting Ecological Impacts: Concepts and Applications in Coastal Areas*, San Diego, California, Academic Press

Pitzer, P (1994) *Grand Coulee: Harnessing a Dream*, Pullman, Washington, Washington State University Press

Sadler, B (ed) (1987a) *Audit and Evaluation in Environmental Assessment and Management, Canadian and International Experience Volume I. Commissioned Research*, Ottawa, Beauregard Press Ltd

Sadler, B (ed) (1987b) *Audit and Evaluation in Environmental Assessment and Management. Canadian and International Experience Volume II. Supporting Studies*, Ottawa, Beauregard Press Ltd

Scholz, A, O'Laughlin, K, Geist, D, Uehara, J, Field, L, Kleist, T, Zozaya, I, Peone, T and Teetsatuskie, K (1985) *Compilation of Information on Salmon and Steelhead Run Size, Catch and Hydropower Related Losses in the Upper Columbia River Basin, above Grand Coulee Dam*, Upper Columbia United Tribes Fisheries Center, Department of Biology, Cheney, Washington, Eastern Washington University

USACE, US Army Corps of Engineers (1933) 'Columbia River and Minor Tributaries: letter from the Secretary of War Transmitting Pursuant to Section 1 of the River and Harbor Act approved January 21, 1927, a letter from the Chief of Engineers, US Army, Dated March 29, 1932, submitting a report, together with accompanying papers and illustrations, containing a general plan for the improvement of the Columbia River and minor tributaries for the purposes of navigation and efficient development of its water power, the control of floods, and the needs of irrigation', Army Corps of Engineers. 73rd Congress, 1st Session, House Document No. 103, Washington, DC, US Government Printing Office

USBR, US Bureau of Reclamation (1976) *Environmental Impact Statement: Columbia Basin Project*, Boise, Idaho, US Department of the Interior

USBR, US Bureau of Reclamation (1989) *Draft Environmental Impact Statement: Continued Development of the Columbia Basin Project, Washington*, Boise, Idaho, US Department of the Interior

USDOE, USACE and USBR, US Department of Energy, US Army Corps of Engineers and US Bureau of Reclamation (1995) *Columbia River System Operation Review Final Environmental Impact Statement Main Report*, DOE/EIS-0170, Portland, Oregon, US Department of Energy

Yuasa, M (2001) 'Columbia River Salmon Forecast Strong for 2002,' *The Seattle Times*, Fishing, Thursday, 13 December 2001

6

Can Industry Benefit from Participation in EIA Follow-up? The ScottishPower Experience

Ross Marshall

Introduction

Proponent-led initiatives (first-party follow-up) can play an important role in achieving and enhancing follow-up outcomes (Chapter 1). This chapter presents the experiences of a proponent based in the UK using self-regulation instruments to maximize positive environmental outcomes through sound implementation of mitigation measures for both major and minor development projects (not all of which required Environmental Impact Assessment (EIA) or follow-up by regulators). It presents both a theoretical perspective and case study examples of the role of industry self-regulation in EIA follow-up.

Proponent-driven EIA follow-up

EIA follow-up refers to the controlled activities undertaken during and following the construction and implementation phases for new developments. It can encompass a broad spectrum of activities, from regular site inspections and surveillance, through compliance statements, to a very formal, systematic process of monitoring and audits. Applying follow-up within EIA is no longer an option but a sound precaution and proactive measure in today's heavily regulated industrial environment, in which the announcement of new development is often treated with dismay and opposition by local residents. For the astute proponent, all the evidence suggests that EIA follow-up has a valuable role to play in good developmental practice, encouraging the integration of environmental perspectives into developmental programmes, the systematic implementation of mitigation and the triggering of environmental risk responses posed through construction activities.

Proponents engaged in EIA must have a clear idea of the objectives of the exercise and the steps required to achieve the development objectives. In the past, developmental success has been judged on whether planning consent was granted or refused, and it can be argued that this focus on gaining consent has been the primary factor motivating proponents to participate either voluntarily or through statutory controls in EIA follow-up. Under such circumstances a proponent will be agreeable to the imposition of EIA follow-up, if the economic costs of follow-up are not disadvantageous and if such activity results in consent. However, this narrow view limits the use of EIA follow-up to that of an imposed control on development and degrades the contribution that EIA follow-up can make to developmental projects.

Increasingly, successful development is viewed in terms of its final result – operational environmental performance, acceptance by stakeholders, contribution to sustainable development, and the magnitude of environmental impact over all life-cycle phases. EIA has become increasingly expensive and resource hungry, demanding escalating consultancy services, budget and time. There is a need to safeguard the returns (i.e. the probability of consent, environmental benefits and quality of decision-making) against the capital expended. This demands that proponents resist the traditional emphasis on consent acquisition, and direct attention across all phases of development, in particular the construction and implementation phases. To sustain EIA performance, proponents must constantly re-evaluate their approach and attitude to developmental planning.

ScottishPower

A good example of this is ScottishPower, an international energy company employing nearly 14,000 people and serving over five million customers in the US and UK. PowerSystems, one of its subsidiary companies, provides asset management expertise and the day-to-day operation of the company's UK transmission and distribution electricity networks. PowerSystems has always promoted the concept of environmental care in its corporate policy and the strategic consideration of the environment in its operational activities (PowerSystems, 2001a). This has resulted in PowerSystems becoming the first UK electrical utility formally accredited to ISO 14001, and reference to the company's approach to EIA has been made in UK Planning Advisory Notes (Scottish Executive, 1999, 2000).

In 1998, PowerSystems adopted a proactive approach to EIA follow-up based on self-regulation. They recognized that EIA could be utilized as an important pre-construction planning tool for new infrastructure, and that EIA could act as a mechanism for self-regulation, in which design attributes, site and routing strategy, areas of conflict and mitigation strategies could be closely examined prior to finalized design and project costing. EIA follow-up was perceived as a strategic tool that could be adopted in-house to avoid unnecessary stakeholder confrontation. PowerSystem's motivation was driven by an internal environmental ethos, its reputation for delivering on promises and the desire to demonstrate continuous improvement in its ISO

14001-compliant environmental management system (EMS) and corporate governance programmes.

The concept of corporate governance, in particular that of environmental governance, has become an increasingly important factor in the business behaviour of companies listed on national stock markets. In the UK and the US, corporate governance has come to prominence as a result of several high-profile corporate failures. The focus in the UK has been on structure and processes, whereas concern with shareholder rights has characterized the US position. Environmental governance is concerned with ensuring that environmental issues are directed, controlled and managed to enhance shareholder value (ICA, 1999).

EMSs form that part of the overall management system that includes organizational structure, planning activities, responsibilities, practices, procedures, processes and resources for developing, implementing, achieving, reviewing and maintaining environmental policy (BSI, 1996). An EMS is a voluntary tool that a company adopts to improve corporate governance and environmental practice. In contrast, EIA has become a critical statutory component of major planning activities and development. PowerSystems have started to view EIA follow-up as one of the few strategic processes that can provide a practicable link between EIA and the company's operational and environmental management systems. The role of EIA follow-up here is to augment environmental decision-making, construction management, compliance with consent requirements and the implementation of mitigation strategies (Marshall, 2001). Visible and verifiable implementation is the preferred approach to residual impact management, and self-regulated EIA follow-up is the preferred mechanism that will enable this to occur.

Chapter structure and signposts

In the absence of legislative mandates for EIA follow-up in the UK (and in most other national EIA frameworks), the purpose of this chapter is to explore factors that can motivate proponent participation beyond that of public or stakeholder pressure to do so. It also explores how active management of EIA follow-up activities can benefit proponents in commercial and reputation terms.

EIA follow-up is perceived as a strategic link between the pre-decision and post-decision phases of development (Figure 6.1). Building on this critical concept, which underlies this entire chapter, subsequent sections seek to examine how proponents can utilize EIA follow-up to promote developmental practice, to examine the benefits that can be achieved from a proactive approach, and to examine how such programmes can be instigated practicably. After introducing the legislative basis for EIA follow-up and its application under UK land use planning laws, this chapter examines various forms of EIA follow-up from a proponent's perspective using ScottishPower case studies as examples. The final section discusses how Environmental Management Plan (EMP) frameworks can be designed to implement EIA follow-up.

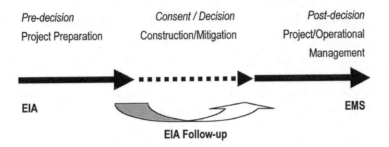

Figure 6.1 *EIA Follow-up as Linkage Between EIA and Operational Management*

UK EIA regulations and follow-up practice

UK development consents are granted through two tiers of government – planning permission subject to local planning authority control and statutory consents granted by central government decision-making bodies (DMB, e.g. Secretaries of State, Scottish Ministers, National Assembly of Wales).

In the UK, EIA regulations constitute a central framework for the environmental screening of major developments prior to the granting of consent, with the various Land Use Planning Acts and regulations providing the legal framework against which the acceptability of development is then assessed. Proponent success will be greatest where development complies with planning policy, or when design factors mitigate stakeholder concerns regarding environment degradation.

Draft proposals for the European Commission's (EC) EIA Directive recognized the beneficial effects of monitoring and the technical shortcomings of an EIA Directive that made no provision for monitoring residual effects. However, the decision was taken that no need existed at that time to adapt the rules to provide for systematic monitoring of the circumstances in which the development consent decision was taken or for monitoring of the proposed corrective measures to avoid, reduce or offset adverse effects on the environment (CEC, 1994). The UK's EIA Regulations, following the EC's model, are therefore silent on the issue of monitoring and contain no specific requirement for EIA follow-up (Box 6.1). This does not preclude the occurrence of monitoring, especially implementation monitoring, as it is customary for DMB to impose planning conditions with developmental consent and to check these to some extent. Although EIA follow-up has no mandatory basis under UK planning law, conditions reside within existing land use planning frameworks that can be utilized to dictate consent conditions, legal agreements to secure works, or the financial contributions necessitated by development proposals.

Box 6.1 The Statutory Basis for EIA Follow-up in the UK

Central or local governmental parties have a duty to consider the environmental implications of an action prior to granting developmental consent. This process limits the formal status of the Environmental Impact Statement (EIS) when compared to other national EIA regulations. Under UK planning law, the process of EIA is the formal means through which the proponent provides a body of required environmental information to the decision-maker; an EIS is just a commonly accepted format in which it is submitted. A DMB is not obliged to pay any attention to the proponent's EIA findings (although it is unlikely to ignore it in practice), as it is legally possible for a DMB to reach an adequate decision point if the environmental data submitted by other agencies or interested parties is deemed adequate to their decision-making purposes.

Pre-consent decision

A pre-consent decision arises if a stakeholder considers that EIA follow-up is likely to be necessary or practicable during initial consultation. It must be made as a specific request to the proponent at the *scoping* stage of the EIA. The proponent has no obligation to transfer such a request into a proposal for inclusion within the EIS, although omission or refusal to do so may be valid material grounds for consent refusal.

Consent decision

A DMB can arrive at three potential decision points when reviewing an application: 'Refuse', 'Accept', and 'Accept subject to conditions'. The third is the most commonly applied decision, and consent is granted subject to a number of planning conditions, i.e. agreed methodologies, working times, access areas, management practices or agreement over final design principles. If EIA follow-up is regarded as necessary and appropriate, then a statutory agency or stakeholder must make specific representation to the DMB requesting its inclusion as a necessary consent condition. If the DMB agrees or wishes to insert EIA follow-up under its own volition, this is accomplished through the insertion of specific permitting conditions in the final consent documentation. Until the final consent conditions are written down as an attachment to the consent and the consent is effectively signed off by the DMB, nothing is agreed under UK planning law.

However, this does not exclude voluntary implementation of EIA follow-up by the proponent or the possibility that legal agreements between the proponent and a third party may require follow-up activities. Section 106 of the *Town and Country Planning Act* 1990 allows the drafting of agreements (known as planning obligations) between the DMB and the proponent. Under these obligations, the proponent and the DMB enter into a legal agreement to undertake follow-up activities necessary to resolve perceived differences or to ensure action. They can be used for a variety of compensatory, mitigation, monitoring or audit purposes.

Post-consent decision

Under UK planning law, non-conformance by a proponent in respect of consent conditions pertaining to EIA follow-up would provide the DMB with a clear legal mandate for declaring the development in breech of its planning condition.

EIA follow-up activities are by no means common in the UK, and are often confined to 'bad neighbour' developments such as landfill sites, power stations or road schemes. In a study of EIA methods and techniques Wessels (2002) could identify no formal linkage between the implementation of EIA follow-up activities such as impact monitoring and the earlier stages of the EIA process. The study did however perceive that voluntary proponent auditing was increasing in importance within the UK.

Under UK planning law, EIA follow-up proposals inserted by a proponent into the EIS are not valid, neither are they regarded as an integral component of the consent or planning permission. Stakeholders can only be reassured that EIA follow-up programmes will be enacted if the DMB expressly incorporates them into the developmental consent, approves plans that clearly incorporate follow-up or mitigation controls, or if the proponent voluntarily exerts sufficient self-regulation to implement such programmes. UK planning law does not prohibit a DMB from setting conditions that refer directly to EIS sections that set out follow-up proposals; however, parties opposed to the development can legally challenge this decision if the EIS proposals are vague in context or procedurally undefined. Post-decision there is no formal right of appeal if implementation monitoring reveals unsatisfactory omissions or impacts, but monitoring results can be used to bring pressure to bear on proponents and/or environmental authorities (Wood, 2003).

Benefits of EIA follow-up for industry: Motivating factors for proponents

The sustained supply of infrastructure for society's needs and requirements are essentially problematical in democracies. This is particularly true where responsibility for the planning and installation of essential infrastructure (e.g. electrical networks, water systems, roads) has been entrusted to privatized entities. Since the advent of privatization in the UK, new infrastructure development is complicated further where DMBs or residents perceive no immediate benefit to themselves through the siting of necessary infrastructure, or where schemes benefit members of society distant from the site of development.

The pressure for EIA follow-up will be greatest where inherent uncertainty in impact assessment requires supplementation, or where stakeholders require a controlling framework for the implementation of mitigation or impact management. The regulator's motivation to impose EIA follow-up will be bound up with the desire to control compliance, to reduce uncertainty, to verify earlier predictions and ultimately to improve the decision management of future EIA processes. The individual or community's desire to initiate follow-up will be based on the desire for the controlled management and/or communication of issues of concern. Under such circumstances a proponent will be agreeable to the imposition of follow-up if the economic cost of follow-up is not disadvantageous and if it results in developmental consent. This simplifies the complex interactions between stakeholders, but highlights an area where the practicalities of the situation will result in proponent acquiescence.

This implies that the proponent's relationship with regulators/stakeholders is typically reactive, with the imposition of consents, monitoring programmes or audits of management controls acting as regulatory *sticks* with which to beat the proponent into environmental compliance. While this may be true, it is worth examining closely what other potential opportunities (*carrots*) follow-up can hold for the astute and proactive proponent. Four key activities can be identified as the primary building blocks for EIA follow-up processes and participation (Arts et al, 2001; Chapter 1): monitoring, evaluation, management and communication. Re-examination of these four activities in an industrial context identifies seven distinct proponent-oriented concepts or functions of EIA follow-up of potential benefit (Table 6.1). These are examined in greater depth alongside specific case studies.

Deriving value from EIA follow-up: ScottishPower's experience and case studies

The following sections outline ScottishPower's experience and application of EIA follow-up, in particular by its PowerSystems division. The case studies (Figure 6.2), representative of issues that commonly face proponents when developing new projects, have been chosen to demonstrate how EIA follow-up can have value beyond that of basic compliance with imposed conditions.

Monitoring for conformance

Monitoring for conformance is one of the commonest forms of EIA follow-up that proponents engage in, either voluntarily or via DMB-applied statutory measures or agreements. The requirement will arise where stakeholder concerns exert pressure on the DMB to ensure that demonstrable control is maintained over a specific area of impact post-decision.

Table 6.1 *EIA Follow-up: Motivating Factors for Proponents*

Key activities in EIA follow-up	Proponent-oriented forms of EIA follow-up	Description
Monitoring	Monitoring for conformance	The collection of data and comparison with standards, predictions or expectations that provide proof of technological, management or operational control against a specific consent requirement or voluntary mitigation measure
	Monitoring for compliance post-decision	Monitoring and audit activities that are developed by the proponent to demonstrate through environmental management frameworks how the collective body of consent conditions or voluntary mitigation measures will be enacted and complied with
Evaluation	Evaluation for future knowledge	The appraisal of the impact or impact mitigation with standards, predictions or expectations in environmental performance for one development that can address areas of impact encountered in future developmental EIA
Management	Management for future consents and licences	Monitoring and evaluation activities during EIA that facilitate operational or environmental permitting in subsequent stages of the development's life cycle
	Management for liability avoidance	Monitoring and evaluation activities arising from EIA that offset future risk of liability or compensation issues
Communication	Communication for consent closure pre-decision	Anticipatory proposals that detail management, monitoring or evaluation proposals submitted pre-decision. Their objective is to foreclose concerns and positively to increase the likelihood of the development being granted statutory consent
	Stakeholder communication	Activities integrated within the EIA process that inform stakeholders or communities and enhance the relationship between the developer and such interested parties to pre-empt concerns or foreclose objections

Note: 'Key activities in EIA follow-up' adapted from Arts et al, 2001

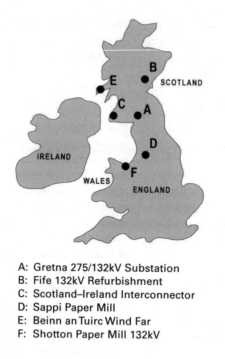

A: Gretna 275/132kV Substation
B: Fife 132kV Refurbishment
C: Scotland–Ireland Interconnector
D: Sappi Paper Mill
E: Beinn an Tuirc Wind Far
F: Shotton Paper Mill 132kV

Figure 6.2 *Map of ScottishPower Case Studies*

EIA is a predictive tool, thus by default conclusions concerning residual impact and the likely effectiveness of mitigation are submitted in advance of their final evaluation. Given that the object of EIA should be to reduce adverse effects to levels where they can no longer be considered significant in terms of environmental adversity, monitoring for conformance seeks to impose control over as yet unquantified impacts. It requires the proponent to collect data or provide proof of technological, management or operational control over a specific environmental aspect of concern.

No internationally accepted methodology exists for conformance monitoring. However, the structured application of monitoring or management systems, applied as EIA follow-up, can improve understanding and acceptance of controversial development. Linked to specific consenting requirements or forming the core objectives of EIA follow-up, these management systems can form a bridgehead between EIA and the construction programme of the final development, ensuring that mitigation is implemented to the satisfaction of concerned stakeholders.

Case study 1: The Scotland–Ireland interconnector

The Scotland–Ireland Interconnector was developed in partnership between ScottishPower and the Northern Ireland Electricity Company. Project need was founded on the existing state of the Irish electrical system, its isolation, higher electricity costs and a lack of diversity in its supply. Principal interconnector elements were a 64km 275kV overhead transmission line, a 26km sub-sea connection and two converter substations. PowerSystems' responsibility was to produce the EIS for the cable and overhead line and to gain planning permission for the Scottish converter station. During the course of the EIA, a large number of mitigation proposals were developed (ScottishPower, 1997).

PowerSystems proposed the concept of a 'Mitigation Handbook' (Box 6.2) to reassure the DMB and other stakeholders about the way individual consent proposals would be implemented. This is a controlling document that would set out and detail how individual applications agreed as EIA follow-up had been completed and agreed with stakeholders before the start of construction. The project was ultimately granted consent in 1998 after review at a Public Inquiry, and construction was completed in 2001. The Mitigation Handbook became the main reference document for use between interested parties, landowners, the contractor and PowerSystems during construction.

Box 6.2 Mitigation Handbook Design and Contents

The Mitigation Handbook sought to create a conformance programme between individual stakeholders and PowerSystems in which design characteristics, operating procedures and defined timescales for specific mitigation aspects were identified along specific sections of the overhead line route or at substations. At these locations actions to exert technical, management or operational control were clearly set out. For example:

Visual and landscape impact – At substations and within treed areas, extensive landscaping proposals were agreed individually with stakeholders. On agreement, landscaping maps and plans were bound into the Handbook and incorporated within construction design programmes.

Access – Constraint maps for operational sites and contractor movements were developed and incorporated into the Handbook and then integrated into the contractual arrangements agreed with the developer. The maps and plans restricted access and allowed for only the minimum removal of landscape features such as trees, hedges and walls.

Remediation activities – Post-construction restoration and remediation activities were agreed with stakeholders. Measures included the restoration of landscape features (hedges and walls).

Archaeological and cultural aspects – Protocols to be implemented pre-construction, during construction or specific to individual features were developed. Where professional archaeological monitoring would oversee the excavation of foundations, briefs were developed and protocols agreed with heritage bodies. At minor sites of archaeological interest where damage was unavoidable, recording of exposed sections were made prior to the resumption of construction.

Proof of the Handbook's value was demonstrated during the outbreak of foot-and-mouth disease (FMD), a virulent animal disease in livestock necessitating extreme statutory restrictions and hygiene precautions, in the UK during 2001. During this period the Handbook was revised to include specialized FMD-operating protocols and landowner entry onto land consent forms. This reflected its acceptance by all concerned parties as a trusted and controllable working mechanism for environmental conformance.

Monitoring for consent compliance post-decision

Planning consent is rarely granted on the grounds that the physical shell of the development or its operation will have minimal impact on surroundings. Land use planning is a more subtle art and perceives that approval is granted on the basis that the development and its subsequent operation will have an impact that can be accommodated within the existing balance of human evolution. In terms of environmental governance and sustainable development, it is thus beholden on both the grantor of consent and on the recipient of that consent to ensure the minimization of residual environmental effect post-development. It is clear that the environmental consent conditions imposed by a DMB are of little value if they are not implemented. Only through a proponent's compliance with imposed or voluntary consent conditions will the planning process have demonstrated its true environmental merit in safeguarding stakeholder concerns.

PowerSystems has realized that the ability to demonstrate control over impact has become an important factor in planning for successful development and one that accords with the fundamentals of EIA follow-up. As an industry engaged in the long-term provision of electricity supplies, it is important to the company's reputation and relationship with stakeholders that mitigation cited in response to envisaged significant adverse effects, or which assisted in gaining consent, are implemented post-decision. However, with this realization arose the need for practical EMS frameworks that can deliver these objectives across the scope of consented conditions or voluntary mitigation measures. Transferring what is envisaged to what will be proven as effective in practice requires active management (including well-timed and practicable management activities). EIA follow-up applied through EMS is the tool that the company has selected to ensure that this will happen.

Case study 2: The Fife 132kV refurbishment and rationalization project

The Fife 132kV refurbishment and rationalization programme has secured electricity supplies for the next 40 years in Central Scotland for 160,000 customers. In developing the programme, PowerSystems was aware that proposals for new overhead transmission lines would attract concerns regarding visual impact, electromagnetic fields and ecological disturbance. The EIA identified a number of significant adverse impacts typically associated with new overhead line construction and the dismantling of old towers and conductors (PowerSystems, 1999). Approval was granted to the project in recognition of its strategic benefit to Central Scotland, and a range of consent conditions were applied to the new overhead transmission line.

The company developed a project-specific EMP to implement the consent conditions and EIA-mitigation strategies (outlined later on). The objective for the EMP was to ensure that all consent requirements and mitigation proposals were complied with and could be verified through one operational procedure post-construction.

Evaluation for future knowledge

Although EIA follow-up is a tool that commonly revolves around the monitoring and control of site-specific environmental impacts, in specific cases, lessons learnt through follow-up may be transferred and used to quantify environmental risk in future development scenarios. This application to facilitate future risk management will be dependent on the occurrence of comparable risks. These arise where new forms of development demand knowledge of environmental aspects that are new to proponents, DMBs or stakeholders. The promotion of renewable energy since the 1990s, in particular the utilization of wind power, has given rise to considerable debate regarding specific environmental impacts on nature conservation, landscape and noise not previously encountered in conventional energy development siting programmes.

For the proponent, follow-up programmes may assist the transfer of best practice, essential research impact data or valuable lessons learnt from mistakes to future projects. Although a proponent's motivation to conduct such studies may be inhibited by the perceived expense of the initial follow-up programme, in the long-term it may be cost-effective in terms of applied risk management. Follow-up may facilitate the monitoring of impact management, allow controls to be tracked and evaluated across the form of development, or be used to verify the scale of residual impact.

Case study 3: Beinn an Tuirc wind farm

The Beinn an Tuirc wind farm, situated on Scotland's Mull of Kintyre, is one of the UK's most productive wind farms. However, initial scoping rapidly established that the site formed part of a golden eagle's territory, a species listed on Schedule 1 of the *Wildlife and Countryside Act* 1981 and Annex 1 of the EU Directive on the Conservation of Wild Birds. The ecological impact assessment identified that the eagles were occupying a marginal territory where food resources were scarce. The birds had only bred successfully twice in the previous 15 years. This low success rate was attributed to a decline in prey availability linked to a twelvefold increase in commercial forest area over the previous 12 years.

ScottishPower conducted a two-year detailed monitoring programme into all aspects of the eagle's ranging behaviour (CRE Energy, 1998). Although the EIA identified that the birds were actively hunting within the site at certain periods of the year, it was concluded that the proposed wind farm site did not provide an important hunting area for the golden eagles. To mitigate the risk of an eagle collision, but more importantly, to improve the overall situation for the golden eagles, ScottishPower developed an innovative habitat management plan to increase prey availability within the eagles' territory. Large scale removal of immature plantation, forestry and heather management, and the creation of prey 'hotspots' were designed not only to shift eagle activity away from the wind farm but also to make the eagle territory sustainable in the longer term.

ScottishPower's analysis of the ecological data recognized the singular value of such an approach and its future application at other upland wind farm sites. On this basis, the decision was made to extend the EIA's ecological and eagle monitoring programmes through follow-up for an additional 5-year period. This time frame included the construction and initial operational years of the wind farm. The ecological data obtained as part of the EIA process, supplemented by post-decision monitoring on-site into habitat management schemes, have started to form a valuable database that can be used in the siting and development of future wind farms. The Beinn an Tuirc wind farm has effectively become an extensive *open-air laboratory* for the company.

Access to this extensive monitoring data bestows on the company a competitive advantage unavailable to its competitors. The wealth of follow-up data being obtained from the 30MW Beinn an Tuirc wind farm has allowed ScottishPower to proceed in its stated objectives of developing a renewable generation portfolio equivalent to 10 per cent of its total output (equivalent to 4500MW installed renewable energy plant) by 2010 and to become one of the UK's leading suppliers of green energy (ScottishPower, 2001). The follow-up data for the Beinn an Tuirc wind farm is now directing future EIA assessments for wind farm projects totalling over 600MW. It has allowed the company to argue strongly on the basis of proven scientific fact regarding the true scale or magnitude of the ecological effects of wind farms.

Management for future consents and licences

In the UK, the environmental and operational activities of industry are seldom regulated through one integrated consent; instead a number of distinct licences and consents must be obtained from statutory bodies or governmental departments. For a thermal power station, consent for development will be followed by the necessity of gaining an integrated pollution permit prior to operation (which monitors discharges to air, water and land), a licence to burn specific fuels (such as natural gas) and licences to manage waste arising or to store fuel oil on-site. At the end of its operational life, the power station will require additional licences to cease operations or to surrender its existing operational licences (e.g. waste management licences, permits for on-site fuel tanks).

Prior to starting EIA a proponent should consider whether the environmental assessment of a specific parameter or effects might also be required under other regulations. Where more than one regime applies, proponents can save unnecessary time, money and effort if they identify and coordinate the different assessments required. For ScottishPower, relevant regulations include the Habitats Directive (92/43/EEC), Wild Birds Directive (79/409/EEC), Integrated Pollution Prevention and Control Directive (96/61/EC) and Control of Major Accident Hazards Directive (96/82/EC). Although the statutory requirements for these and for the EIA Directive are independent of each other, there are clearly links between them in respect of their requirement for impact assessment (ODPM, 2001). The considered management of follow-up within EIA can provide structured links that meet the data demands of developmental EIA as well as subsequent statutory data requirements.

Case study 4: The Sappi Paper Mill CHP plant

The Sappi Paper Mill Combined Heat and Power (CHP) plant is a 60MW gas-powered venture in Blackburn, England. A voluntary EIS was prepared to accompany application for consent to build and operate a thermal power plant under the *Electricity Act* 1989 (UK). ScottishPower was also aware that prior to commercial operation, the plant would have to obtain an integrated pollution permit as it would be a prescribed process under the *Environmental Protection (Prescribed Processes and Substances) Regulations* 1991 (now the *Pollution Prevention (England and Wales) Regulations* 2000, which implement Directive 96/61/EC).

During the EIA scoping and consultation phases, local residents expressed concerns about the impact on local air quality, particularly in the vicinity of a local primary school. Recognizing that a lack of data regarding local ambient air quality existed, and that the potential for localized air pollution would be an important factor in the determination of the consent, a proposal was put to residents. ScottishPower proposed that a combined weather/nitrous oxide monitoring station would be installed on the roof of the primary school. Data connections would ensure that local air quality could be monitored on-line continuously and these data would be freely available to the school (for local residents), the DMB's environmental health department and ScottishPower. Subsequently, these 'in-situ' data were combined with data obtained through prescriptive atmospheric dispersion modelling to evaluate the proposed plant's impact on local air quality.

Building on the base-line data gathered for the purposes of EIA, the programme was subsequently extended post-decision through construction and commissioning trials. This follow-up data have allowed the company to build up a picture of ambient air quality for the area, to verify the predictions of the EIA, and to negotiate final permit and licensing conditions with the UK's Environment Agency under the Pollution Prevention (England and Wales) Regulations 2000.

The monitoring station remains in place and the 'win–win' advantages to stakeholders through this follow-up programme remain important to ScottishPower. Local residents retain access to the data and are reassured regarding the plant's environmental impact. The school has gained an additional teaching aid through the weather station, and the DMB has acquired a continuous monitoring station that contributes directly to its Local Air Quality Plan. Importantly, the company's operational data needs have been met and the programme has established ScottishPower as a 'good neighbour' in the area.

Management for liability avoidance

Although the majority of proponent-oriented forms of EIA follow-up are demonstrated through case studies specific to ScottishPower's experience, in the case of liability avoidance, the work of Ross et al (2001) is best cited.

Case study 5: The Gulf of Guayaquil gas field development

In this offshore natural gas well development in the Gulf of Guayaquil (Ecuador), EIA follow-up was utilized as a defensive strategy to protect the proponent in the event that others polluted important shrimp fisheries, a high-profile economic resource close to the gas field. Utilizing EIA follow-up, the proponent started to gather information about other industrial activities, their ability to manage impact (if at all) and what steps the proponent would have to undertake to offset non-attributable liability. Ultimately a monitoring system and EMS was developed and integrated with operations, a monitoring programme that would protect the company from liability in the event of adverse impact to the shrimp fisheries (Ross et al, 2001). The Gulf of Guayaquil case is of note in that it is a rare published example of a proponent using EIA follow-up to foresee events and to determine a strategic pathway during future operational phases.

Communication for consent closure pre-decision

For projects with high community visibility and significant environmental impact it is important to maintain community acceptance and understanding. It is common for proponents to find that their development plans are dominated by a small number of factors whose importance is regarded as significantly greater than other attributes. This aspect of development, termed 'issue attention' by Downs (1972), is a recognized factor of EIA.

With issue attention, stakeholder attention concentrates on a small number of perceived adverse effects that begin to dominate the review and decision-making process, raising their profile rapidly once the scheme becomes public knowledge. It is the perceived significance of such issues that results in initial opposition by stakeholders to a development proposal. Regardless of their true environmental effect, these issues may polarize parties over the perceived environmental consequences. An essential factor in the final analysis of a development will thus be the degree to which the consent conditions and mitigation settle such issues.

Issues of impact uncertainty in pre-decision EIA may start to make the concept of the proposed development unacceptable to stakeholders, where:

- true effect data is unobtainable
- final design or construction criteria cannot yet be determined
- mitigation strategies require further development
- statements regarding future mitigation effectiveness cannot be substantiated.

Ultimately it is not the predictive effects of development but the residual effect of development, if it proceeds (with or without mitigation), that will be relevant. The pre-decision development of EIA follow-up programmes by the proponent can provide a controlling vehicle for progress to be made in resolving such issues, while safeguarding aspects of environmental concerns of relevance to stakeholders. In such circumstances, it is in the proponent's interest to work with stakeholders towards a solution that can reassure interested parties that residual effect will be no greater than predicted or that proposed mitigation will be sufficiently durable.

Communication for consent closure involves the proponent adopting a proactive stance and seeking to anticipate the issues that are likely to dominate the decision-making process and through which means a positive outcome to the issue can be proposed. Often this will involve submitting detailed proposals for EIA follow-up management, monitoring or evaluation. The proponent's objective will usually be to foreclose concerns that present a risk to the granting of developmental consent. The challenge is then to anticipate the nature of the concerns and to proactively submit solutions that will be accepted as valid, effective and practicable by the stakeholders, and ultimately by the DMB.

Case study 6: the Gretna Green 275/132kV substation

The Gretna 275/132kV substation project on the Scotland–England border was necessitated by the threatened closure of a strategically important regional nuclear power station. The time allocated to obtain planning permission and the substation's construction was critical, for without reinforcement of the network, the nuclear plant's closure would threaten the security of electricity supplies in South Scotland. PowerSystems sought to fast-track the planning process by pre-empting likely concerns that could delay the planning application or delay the setting of consent conditions.

The company prepared a detailed in-house EIS and undertook scoping and consultation exercises with local stakeholders. This non-statutory EIS evaluated the existing environmental base-line and sought to identify all environmental aspects that would be of material significance to the planning application. In anticipation of stakeholder concerns, and in a variation from existing practice, the company decided to produce a 'control of environmental effects' (CEE) document (PowerSystems, 2001b). The document sets out proposed consent conditions, frameworks for their management, and protocols to guide mitigation implementation during construction. The document was also designed to act as a public statement on how PowerSystems intended to:

- control environmental effects arising if the scheme was granted planning consent
- meet its environmental commitments and duties
- follow good construction practice
- follow up any proposed consenting conditions.

The CEE document was submitted as part of the planning consent, and the DMB (Dumfries and Galloway Council) were invited to set and reference the document as part of the planning consent, which they duly did. Ultimately, the CEE document was submitted to contractors in 2001 as a component of the project requirements.

Stakeholder communication

Debate or controversy will surround any area of perceived environmental conflict linked to development, and an EIS will be scrutinized by a variety of interested parties. Controversy polarizes opinions and can jeopardize the likelihood that objective communication between stakeholders will then take place. In the UK, proponents should never forget that the concept of environmental harm is a valid material consideration in planning terms when deciding whether to grant consent, and legitimate grounds for refusal (Ball and Bell, 1995). Consequently, the mitigation of anticipated adverse effects becomes an important area for resolution post-decision. EIS mitigation statements will be evaluated in respect of their 'usefulness', which should be equated with their relevance for the respective reader or their information requirements. It is thus in the proponent's interest to ensure that mitigation strategies are communicated clearly and concisely to stakeholders.

If the EIS contains unresolved areas of technical design, omissions or undefined mitigation strategies, then responsibility for these exclusions lies with the applicant. Regardless of other social, economic or land use considerations, unless the environmental effects of development are deemed to lie within discerned boundaries of environmental and political acceptability, developmental consent is unlikely to be granted.

Case study 7: Shotton Paper Mill 132kV transmission line

The EIA involved a new overhead line extension into an existing industrial area in Northeast Wales to support the local system. The engineering principles of the new line were relatively straightforward and the DMB supported the strategic economic advantage to the region of the line. However, the transmission line's route was complicated by the presence of winter wading birds and common terns (*Sterna hirundo*) breeding and colonizing existing cooling water lagoons on the site of a steel rolling mill close to the terminal substation.

During scoping, local conservationists expressed concern about disturbance and displacement impacts on the terns, in particular the colony's future breeding success if the line was implemented. In consultation with this group and the statutory nature conservation body (Countryside Council for Wales), PowerSystems proposed that as part of the EIA and for follow-up purposes an independent consultancy (the British Trust for Ornithology) be commissioned to study the issue. This was acceptable to the conservationists and a programme of bird monitoring was subsequently developed. PowerSystems felt that such an open approach would improve communication with the conservationists, who valued their independence and who were nervous about compromizing their initial stance of opposition, to resolve the issue.

Pre-decision, one of the study's initial conclusions was that limitations in the number of existing breeding sites in the lagoons were curtailing future tern population expansion (Balmer et al, 2002). In response PowerSystems proposed, as compensation and as part of the mitigation programme, to construct a new breeding site. The site selected would also alter the terns' existing flight-line into the lagoons taking them further away from the proposed overhead line. The subsequent two-year follow-up monitoring programme has indicated no significant impact on bird displacement or disturbance. No avian collisions with the new line have been recorded and local bird populations have adapted to its presence. One of the most pleasant surprises is that the terns have colonized the new breeding site at a faster rate than the conservationists anticipated.

The previously discussed CEE document (Gretna substation case study) required stakeholder communication to ensure the fast-tracking of the consent application, and was thus designed to pre-empt regulator and statutory consultation concerns across the scope of the project and to demonstrate how stakeholder interests would be protected. In the Shotton Paper Mill case, economic necessity enhanced the political presumption that the DMB would grant developmental consent. However, the proponent recognized that there were reputation and community relations advantages in pre-empting specific stakeholder concerns, and through follow-up to engage with interested parties to foreclose areas of objection prior to submission of the consent application.

The lessons learnt from the case studies of proponent-oriented forms of EIA follow-up are presented in Box 6.3. The remainder of the chapter focuses on management aspects of proponent-led follow-up.

The management of EIA follow-up: Improving practice

Since the 1970s, when it was first introduced into the UK, practitioners have observed EIA to develop into the pre-eminent regulatory requirement for major development. It serves to provide information to DMB, other regulators and stakeholders. EIA also enables proponents to set their own environmental standards and to ameliorate adverse environmental impacts. EIA follow-up can play an important role in this process and remove the consideration of these aspects by a DMB as material grounds for consent refusal. Through monitoring, audit or evaluation of management control, EIA follow-up

---

Box 6.3 Lessons Learnt from Proponent-oriented Forms of EIA Follow-up

- Individually, or collectively, the design commitments that mitigate environmental effects or that assisted in the gaining of consent must be carried out. Follow-up enables this to occur (*monitoring for conformance, monitoring for compliance post-decision*).
- Proponents can utilize the data from follow-up programmes to enhance their scientific knowledge of processes and activities, notably those environmental aspects that have a bearing on future development activities. Follow-up can allow impacts to be verified and the benefits of mitigation to be identified and quantified in hard risk capital terms (*evaluation for future knowledge*).
- EIA follow-up can make commercial sense where future development or operational consents are necessary. Components of EIA may also assist additional statutory obligations, and follow-up can facilitate this future data requirement (*management for future consents and licences*).
- EIA follow-up can be used to foresee risk and liability and manage follow-up activities to determine a strategic pathway during future operational phases (*management for liability avoidance*).
- One of the simplest and most transparent drivers for the inclusion of follow-up will be the open desire to agree terms that grant consent while offsetting aspects of uncertainty identified pre-decision. This process can be enhanced through the application of EIA follow-up linked to environmental management systems (*communication for consent closure pre-decision*).
- A proponent should recognize what is significant to the stakeholders and how follow-up can resolve such issues. Through this means, EIA follow-up can improve community communication, reduce confrontation and benefit all stakeholders. The use of an independent body to develop and monitor follow-up can improve relationships between the proponent and stakeholders (*stakeholder communication*).

---

can ensure that the expected post-decision benefits of the EIA process are achieved. Chapter 2 discussed the *implementation gap* that exists between project plans and their implementation. Best practice in EIA follow-up will require proponents to close this gap through the imposition of management controls to safeguard follow-up programmes, and the establishment of practical linkages between the *envisaged* and what is to be *implemented* (Figure 6.1). Follow-up programmes therefore demand procedures that move mitigation or developmental consents into operational management systems during construction or operation post-decision.

Formal EMSs form that part of a company's corporate governance or management systems that control and implement structures, activities, procedures and tasks for promoting environmental responsibility. The risk-anticipatory processes of EIA may be viewed as an important component of a company's EMS framework, and yet, despite three decades of EIA experience it is clear that a linkage gap often separates internal EIA and EMS processes within many companies. Although many EIA-proponent companies have subsequently adopted formal EMSs (e.g. the ISO 14000 series), it is suspected that only a few of these companies will have considered incorporating the EIA process within the EMS's scope of control. This linkage gap exists because most EMSs are oriented towards the day-to-day activities of companies, and fail to consider the environmental implications of new developmental activity. In addition, companies involved in EIA often perceive EIA to be above and beyond the normal scope of operational activities, as it is rare for companies to possess staff familiar with both EIA and EMS.

This last point may best be demonstrated by the example of a UK pharmaceutical plant and the experience of its bemused environmental manager who related this cautionary tale to the author after appreciating this fundamental weakness in his existing EMS. The case involved the company's proposals for a significant extension to the site's capability and manufacturing capacity. Environmental consultants working directly for the company's engineering department had prepared the EIS and the consent application for the proposed plant extension. The local planning authority granted the consent and the plant was constructed. However, a subsequent ISO 14001 compliance audit could identify no direct contact between the pharmaceutical plant's internal environmental group and the new facility's development team during the design and construction phases of the project. It became apparent during the compliance audit that the internal environmental group's responsibility for the new facilities and its EMS compliance would only start once the site had been formally commissioned and handed over by the contractors. The dictates of the company's EMS thus had had very little impact on the considered design of the plant. The auditor considered this a major non-conformance within the existing EMS.

In-house systems may seek to promote best practice systems individually within EMS and on occasion EIA, but direct transition and linkage between them may not exist at a sophisticated or practicable operational level. PowerSystems' ISO 14001-certificated EMS compels the company to adopt a consistent and methodical approach to known environmental risks. The EMS thus forms a base-line for generic environmental requirements during operation, maintenance and construction projects. However, specific major infrastructure developments will have clearly defined environmental effects or implications above and beyond the scope of the generic EMS. Design and construction decisions are made in direct response to circumstances that are site-specific and often transitory during a particular phase of activity. Therefore development projects must also remain *dynamic* in the manner in which they react to such issues, circumstances or events. In contrast, the operational EMS mechanisms in-situ within established activities such as maintenance or operational production are much less dynamic, the introduction of new operational patterns of work slowly becoming more *static* as activity settles down into organized patterns of staff behaviour. To contain all such decisions or risk protocols in the corporate EMS would be time consuming and bureaucratic.

There is therefore a need for forms of EMS that are simpler and less bureaucratic than formal systems such as ISO 14001, and that focus solely on significant environmental aspects arising directly from EIA-related development. Such 'EMS-*lite*' forms of environmental management need to provide uncomplicated controlling mechanisms that directly implement project/site-specific environmental controls. Environmental Management Plans (EMP) provide one example of a modified EMS-framework and a practical means of providing this simple bridging mechanism. They can address what is environmentally significant, allowing project managers the flexibility to impose mitigation or controls that are risk and site specific, and that are flexible in their application. Where the need for EIA follow-up exists, EMPs provide a mechanism to incorporate, implement and discharge this requirement.

The preceding sections have outlined a number of EMS/EMP approaches that have been developed and evaluated by PowerSystems (e.g. CEE documents, the Mitigation Handbook and the project-specific EMP). On the basis of their practical structure, effective management control, and integration within the company's EMS, PowerSystem's concentration is now directed towards project-specific EMPs as the preferred mechanism to implement post-decision EIA follow-up.

EMPs are an effective means of implementing EIA follow-up. As management tools they have the flexibility to suit individual project circumstances and to adapt with experience. Their simplicity allows proponents to incorporate new frameworks for monitoring, auditing or evaluating the effectiveness of EIA follow-up programmes. Flexibility was a factor recognized by Wlodarczyk (2000) when he proposed that EIA follow-up improvements need to be made in an incremental but continuous fashion. Critically, EMPs can control aspects of EIA follow-up while forming a direct management link between the development and the EIA processes (Figure 6.3).

The remainder of this chapter examines how the EMP is designed and put into practice to implement EIA follow-up.

A practical framework for environmental management plans

The time span and timing of EIA follow-up activities

Any EMP directed towards the controlled implementation of EIA follow-up must take note of, and encompass, the time frame within which the development will operate. Effects anticipated in an EIA may be long term or short lived, transitory or permanent, and specific to particular aspects of development. In response, the timing of EIA follow-up activities may be

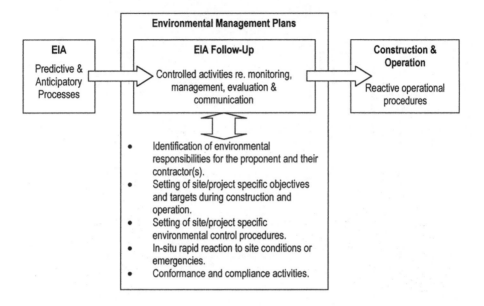

Figure 6.3 *The Perceived Role, Interaction and Objective of Environmental Management Plans*

spread across the time frame of the development's life, from its 'cradle' to its 'grave'. It is not uncommon for the consenting requirements of certain forms of developments, such as wind farms and open-cast mineral extraction sites, to address proposals regarding the final decommissioning of the site. Consent conditions may seek the planned restoration or rehabilitation of the site on its closure, and details on how these will be monitored. The time frames for EIA follow-up are thus not limited solely to the construction phase, but can encompass all post-decision phases through to eventual decommissioning (Table 6.2).

Table 6.2, which is based on data obtained from a study of mitigation proposals contained in 100 Scottish EISs between 1980 and 1999 (Marshall, 2000), outlines the potential range of follow-up activities that can be utilized across the specific life stages of a development or forms of mitigation activity. It is against this time frame and range of activities that management structures must be implemented to control and direct individual activities.

Interlinking EMS and EIA processes

A feature of EMS design, when considering the use of EMPs, is how best to integrate both into existing engineering or project management systems. Can the EMP integrate seamlessly with existing procedures or do new procedures have to be developed? This has important implications when a proponent is seeking to close the implementation gap for EIA follow-up and is trying

Table 6.2 *The Scope for Mitigation Post-decision and its Interaction with EIA Follow-up Activities*

	Potential design and management forms for mitigation and impact control				
	Pre-determination of impact	Project alternatives	Physical design and abatement measures	Operational management	Stakeholder communication pathways
Authorization (consenting conditions, planning agreements)		C	†C	†~AC	†~AC
Pre-construction (detailed design)	†	†	†C		
Construction (site preparation, material stockpiling, construction, completion activities)			†~AC	†~AC	†~AC
Site transference (commissioning and testing)	~		~A		~C
Operational activity (site management, environmental management systems, contingency and emergency planning)	†~AC		†~AC	†~AC	†~AC
Decommissioning	~AC	~A	~AC	†~AC	~AC
Restoration/rehabilitation	†~AC	~AC	~AC	†~AC	~AC
Alternative projects/future consents			†	†A	†C

Note: shading denotes scope for follow-up post-decision. EIA follow-up activities denoted by: † = Monitoring; A = Audit/Evaluation; ~ = Management; and C = Communication

Source: after Marshall, 2000

to assess how readily staff or contractors involved in the management of EIA follow-up will adapt to, accept and implement new EMS and EMP procedures.

Although an EIA can identify the need for environmental control, it is not often practical or necessary to greatly amend the day-to-day operational focus of a company's core EMS to provide the necessary site-specific controls that are demanded. EMS frameworks are intended to provide organizations with the elements of an effective EMS, which can be integrated with other management requirements, to assist the organization achieve its environmental and economic goals. Redirecting such systems to provide temporary or transitory site-specific management can be labour intensive and disruptive to the overall function of the organization's EMS.

The concept of EMP was promoted initially for significant works undertaken on behalf of bodies such as the World Bank (1991), and in the UK the concept has been adapted for use by the UK's Environment Agency for flood defence construction (Environment Agency, 1999). PowerSystems' EMP framework, adapted from the Environment Agency's model, has been developed to form a practical link between the wider management structures of the company's ISO 14001-compliant EMS and the anticipated environmental controls motivated by consented conditions, EIA follow-up programmes and stakeholder requests for electricity transmission and distribution projects. PowerSystems' EMP protocol is focused towards aspects of project management involving environmental criteria, and the monitoring and auditing of consented/mitigation commitments post-decision (ScottishPower, 1999; Marshall, 2002).

EMPs – as EMS-*lite* systems, focusing only upon what is significant to that project – can act as a simple linking interface between the formal certified EMS and the EIA/project development. However, this places a clear duty on the proponent to develop procedural systems in their EMS to encompass EIA/EMP activities, and for the EMP to set out clear documented links on how EIA-specific actions are to be enacted. Successfully thought through, project-specific EMPs possess a number of benefits for proponents; however, the key to their success remains dependent on:

- developing strong documented linkage with EIA/consent requirements
- how they address practical issues of communication and human interactions
- the working interface between the EMS and the project-specific EMP.

EIA follow-up schemes and their methodology are unlikely to follow any set pattern if no national or state-specified scheme exists. In the absence of statutory requirements, their development will be motivated by a proponent's individualistic desire to satisfy specific project requirements or for them to fit within existing management frameworks. Companies like ScottishPower do not expect or particularly require formalized protocols to be developed for their benefit. As the previous case studies demonstrate, individual projects will throw up specific issues, only a few of which may have applications in other arenas. However, where a generic environmental or industry sector problem is perceived and acts as a barrier to development, then proponents will welcome governmental or academic support for innovative or issue-specific EIA follow-up methodologies.

Modern construction practice and PowerSystems' approach to EMPs for EIA follow-up

In the initial phase of all PowerSystems' major developments requiring EIA, the need for the proposed transmission or distribution system will have been established by internal studies conducted by system design engineers. Strategic planning (which may involve Strategic Environmental Assessment) will then identify the preferred alternative technical solution. Once this has been determined, an internal project team (involving system design engineers, construction engineers and environmental planners) sets in motion the process of outlining the project's design, conducting the EIA and gaining consent. On the granting of consent, a development project team of construction engineers, aided by the environmental planners, prepare the tender documentation and set out the requirements for follow-up. A project engineer is then allocated to oversee and monitor the progress of construction.

Construction practices and contractor management

In tandem with most UK utilities, PowerSystems is becoming increasingly dependent on contractors to design and construct new infrastructure projects. This increases demands on in-house project management staff to ensure that EIA follow-up programmes addressing mitigation commitments or consented conditions are instigated. Although some proponents continue to design and project manage construction phases in-house, 'design and build' (DB) and 'turnkey' contracts have become commonplace as companies increasingly seek to streamline construction practices and procedures.

In a DB project, one contractor will serve as both the design professional and the constructor. By overlapping design and construction activities, traditionally performed sequentially, the project duration can be shortened. The single contractor takes responsibility for the entire project overcoming all challenges that the client may face from the onset of the project, thereby reducing the client's management and administration burden. Turnkey projects follow similar principles; however, the distinction is that the contractor, rather than the client, has sole responsibility for all decisions regarding the final design. Rather than resolving issues as they arise, the client's role is effectively limited to the issue of a 'fit-for-purpose' design tender of what is required and the inheritance of the completed project (i.e. when they 'turn the key' to enter). Using the turnkey approach reduces the number of potential contractor claims (legal actions), as the contractor has overall responsibility for the final design and therefore cannot claim for a changed condition, enforced delay or design error due to design incompleteness.

The turnkey and DB approaches, as well as projects that are designed and managed by internal staff, are used by PowerSystems across the range of its major infrastructure programmes. The decision to adopt a particular approach is determined by the current internal workload, project complexity, scale and in-house experience. When seeking to interlink EIA follow-up within these schemes, the challenge for PowerSystems is to implement management controls that align EIA follow-up programmes closely and in tandem with the development phases. This demands practical management frameworks that are simple, clear and effective (Figure 6.4).

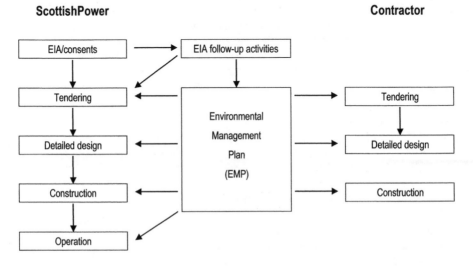

Figure 6.4 *Contractor–client Interactions and the Linkage Role of EMP*

Closing the implementation gap: PowerSystems EMP structure and content

As the connecting framework, the EMP is intended to be the interface through which all significant environmental aspects and obligations are enacted. Post-decision, the objectives and content of the EMP are prepared. Table 6.3 outlines the generic components of an EMP and its structures. Consent conditions, EIA follow-up obligations and actions to safeguard stakeholder concerns are collected and compiled into the '*Table of Site-specific Environmental Actions*' (Table 6.4).

The '*Table of Site-specific Environmental Actions*' forms the core of the EMP. Dependent on the scale of the development, the table of actions is often subdivided into three distinct post-decision phases for larger schemes (before, during and after construction), which equate to construction stages used by PowerSystems engineers. Within each phase, further subdivision by relevant environmental impacts or aspects (e.g. water quality, ecology) is possible (Table 6.4).

Table 6.3 *PowerSystems' EMP Structure and Content*

Parameter	Information
Introduction	Project description, commitment to mitigation implementation and consent fulfilment during construction phase.
Generic environmental actions	Reference to the standard documents contained within PowerSystems' ISO 14001 EMS relating to construction activities, waste management and control of contractors.
Environmentally significant changes	The procedure, protocol and consultation process to be followed where environmentally significant changes to the project design are encountered and where potential amendments to the EMP are required. Identification of responsibility for overseeing the changes to the EMP and ensuring that these changes do not conflict with any consenting or planning conditions.
Project team roles and responsibilities	The role of the individual project team members is defined. Information should include their name, title, affiliation (i.e. staff, contractor or environmental consultant), specific on-site responsibilities, environmental and auditing duties. The project manager is ultimately responsible for ensuring that the EMP is adequately translated into contract documents and adhered to during all phases of the project.
Liaison and consultation requirements	Details and contact addresses for required liaison between the project team and the relevant external consultees and authorities to ensure that environmental issues are fully closed out.
Consents and permissions	A record of all required environmental licences and permissions prior to the start of construction.
Table of site-specific environmental actions	A table of site-specific environmental actions of significance to the project, i.e. mitigation commitments and consenting conditions. Each condition is uniquely identified and grouped chronologically or according to its specific environmental receptor (e.g. nature conservation, noise) and the action required. Columns are included to allow for a cross-reference of EMP actions with consent conditions or proposed mitigation actions, and contract document clauses. A column is included for the individual actions to be 'signed off' upon successful completion.
Changes during construction	A register of variations record details of changes and environmental implications and is linked to a variation document appended to the EMP as a controlled document.
Monitoring programme	Details and schedules of monitoring, including equipment calibration responsibilities.
Appendices	Variation documents, key contacts, audit schedules and findings, waste management 'duty of care' register.

Source: Marshall, 2002

Table 6.4 *PowerSystems' Template for the 'Table of Site-specific Environmental Actions' with Hypothetical Entries*

No	Objective	Action	Responsible person	Achievement criteria	Contract reference	Consent/ mitigation reference	Completed (initial and date)	Notes/ further action
				Actions during construction				
Nature conservation								
12	To avoid disturbance to moorland	Vehicle movement should be restricted to track or coarse grassland below the moorland	Contractor	No significant long-term damage to moorland	Doc 13F/2.3	ES Ref. 3 (sect 6.9)		
13	To avoid disturbance to moorland	Materials and traffic to be kept off Field A where green orchid resides	Contractor	No evidence of transport or material movement	Doc 13F/2.4	Section 37 Ref. No 3		
Landscape								
14	To reduce visual effect at No 27 the Larches	Planting of screening belt along Wood Lane during construction	Contractor	Material evidence of complete planting scheme		ES Ref. 6 (sect 11.7)		
Water quality								
15	To reduce risk to Mid Burn	Installation of oil protection floating boom	Site engineer	Photograph of boom in position		S37.13		Verify presence of oil spillage kit

Table 6.4 (continued)

No	Objective	Action	Responsible person	Achievement criteria	Contract reference	Consent/ mitigation reference	Completed (initial and date)	Notes further action
	Recreation and amenity							
	Actions following construction (including monitoring)							
34	To maintain the privacy of local residents	Restricted working hours during weekend	Project manager	No valid out-of-hours complaint		ES Ref. 7 (sect 10.3)		
35	To reduce visual effect at Crudville playing fields	Lopping and replanting of trees at Crudville Spinney	Contractor	Material evidence of completed works	Doc 13F/6.1	ES Ref. 6 (sect 11.8)		

The mock template examples presented in Table 6.4 are taken from PowerSystems internal guidance document for setting up an EMP (ScottishPower, 1999). They are generic in character and are included solely to allow the reader to understand how the table is used. The key issue for PowerSystems' staff is that in response to significant aspects, the controlling objectives, methodologies and approaches to be enacted in follow-up are entered into the table and are recorded. Contractors and consultants engaged within the follow-up programme are assigned roles and deliverables in the table, and their individual approach and methodologies are made transparent.

The value of EMPs

One of the fascinating aspects of EIA is its flexibility; few other methodologies can be adapted so readily to wide ranging forms of development or perceptions of environmental effect. No company can allow or afford its EMS to stifle such initiative and ingenuity, but equally it is to a company's advantage to demonstrate through documented controls the decision-making processes and actions that have been initiated, mitigated and controlled. Seeking to enhance the practical aspects of EMS to control the quality of EIA and EIA follow-up provides yet another means by which motivated proponents can lead from the front. Management frameworks for EIA follow-up can only be truly successful when they are absorbed into the risk control and management strategies of a company. When integrated into EMS structures, the findings and conclusions of the EIA can be successfully implemented (Box 6.4).

The key to successful EMP is to adopt a system that is not prescriptive and that allows individual project managers to retain the initiative. The perceived benefits in applying EMP frameworks to EIA follow-up are that it:

- concentrates resources on what is significant in terms of regulatory requirements, environmental care and stakeholder concern
- encourages systematic and explicit approaches to the controlled amelioration of adverse environmental effects
- identifies management and contractual responsibilities
- integrates planning consent conditions and mitigation measures into construction programmes
- is an auditable programme that addresses aspects of environmental and consent condition compliance
- provides a means of engaging stakeholders in constructive project dialogue.

Discussion and conclusions

EIA follow-up will be required where ecosystems are sensitive or lack resilience to change, and where population pressures are greatest – particularly where both exist in a precarious balance. Thus it may not be too much of a surprise

---

Box 6.4 Lessons Learnt: Management of Proponent-based EIA Follow-up

- Mitigation proposals are of no environmental value if they remain only as a series of proposals in an EIS; only through their delivery via EMPs and EMS will the EIA have demonstrated its value to all stakeholders.
- The post-decision management of EIA follow-up programmes requires the instigation of site-specific management controls, the implementation of defined actions and the assignment of responsibilities.
- EMP, operating flexibly within EMS frameworks, can provide comprehensive frameworks to successfully implement EIA follow-up programmes and close the *implementation gap* between project plans and their implementation.

---

that pressure on proponents has been most intensive in densely populated countries such as Hong Kong and The Netherlands, or where ecosystems lack environmental resilience (Au, 2001; Arts et al, 2001; Baker and Dobos, 2001).

In such conditions, stakeholders opposing new development often regard the proponent as a Machiavellian figure. Plans are treated with suspicion and an air of mistrust permeates interactions between the parties. In such circumstances the proponent may thus be wise to remember Machiavelli's famous advice to his prince that: 'In the actions of all men, where there is no impartial arbiter, one must first consider the final result' (Machiavelli, 1532). This phrase, often presented in shorthand as 'the end justifies the means', is as relevant today as when it was written. As outlined in the introductory section, questions regarding 'the final result' are now an essential component of development, and by association of EIA follow-up. In seeking to promote change through action and development, the proponent as the instigator of that change is best advised to consider the ultimate environmental consequences of their actions. The process of follow-up has direct applicability in this process.

Although questions of residual impact are of moral interest to the proponent, it is apparent that for many EIA proponents it is the gaining of developmental consent that acts as the over-riding driver. For EIA follow-up practice and application to become integral facets of EIA practice for proponents, recognizable gains above and beyond that of simple conformance or compliance with imposed follow-up programmes must be discerned. The desire to agree to conditions that deliver future consents and licences will always remain the prime motivation for proponent participation, but EIA follow-up is more than just a mutually convenient way of agreeing developmental terms. For proponents who are concerned about their environmental performance or reputation, it can form a strategic link between EIA and formal environmental management practices. Once embraced, EIA follow-up starts to define the very approach adopted for EIA, stakeholder communication, impact mitigation and the EIS format. To be truly motivated, industrial EIA practitioners must perceive that follow-up can be a positive factor in development and one that can result in improved risk management, reputation and in specific circumstances economic benefit.

The UK's land use planning laws and regulations pertaining to EIA contain no specific requirement for EIA follow-up. Thus, motivated proponents are forced to develop their own approach. ScottishPower has recognized that a proactive approach to EIA follow-up can enhance developmental success and 'keep an eye' on the final outcome. This results in success not only in material terms regarding timescale, delivery and the efficient use of resources, but also in terms of subjective values such as trust, reputation and stakeholder recognition. The final result is thus reflected not only through individual project success but through its contribution to the sustained economic growth of the company in the long-term (Figure 6.5).

ScottishPower accepts that the strict self-regulation of behaviour is the price it must pay as an electrical utility to achieve long-term transmission

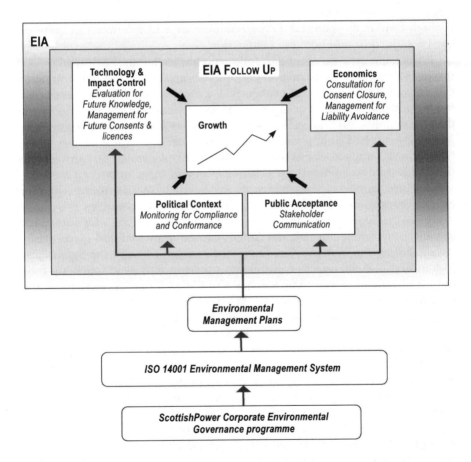

Figure 6.5 *Key Drivers in PowerSystem's Participation in EIA Follow-up*

network solutions that ensure secure and reliable supplies of electricity to customers. The company is aware that its ability to deliver such programmes will be closely associated with stakeholder impact and how stakeholders perceive the company's attitude to environmental care. Follow-up frameworks sensibly applied through self-regulated mechanisms can significantly improve stakeholder acceptance of proposed developments and have reduced direct opposition to projects. Box 6.5 presents some motivations for proponents to engage voluntarily in EIA follow-up.

The recognition of EIA follow-up has strengthened the need for in-house management frameworks, such as PowerSystems' corporate EMS and its approach to EMP. The case studies, notably those for the Scottish–Irish Interconnector and the Fife reinforcements, outline practical pathways for the controlled implementation of EIA follow-up post-decision either singularly or across the broad sweep of mitigation/consent activities. EIA-anticipated effects may be transitory or consequence specific in developmental pathways. EMPs are one practical way that the company has found to control and direct environmental management after completion of the EIS. Implemented through EMP in an open and transparent manner, EIA follow-up programmes can be audited or monitored to completion.

Embracing the concept of EIA follow-up has encouraged ScottishPower to improve control over construction programmes and to integrate environmental care into its decision-making processes in a manner that is cost-effective and holds out strategic gains. For example the lessons learnt in specific EIA follow-up programmes, such as at Beinn an Tuirc wind farm and the Sappi Paper Mill, have resulted in approaches that can be used in future developmental programmes. Impact assessment data on the displacement and disturbance of wind farm developments on golden eagles and other important moorland species have important consequences for ScottishPower's future renewable energy programmes. The data arising from the follow-up studies at Beinn an Tuirc have assisted the company in setting out an approach for future EIA in which environmental risk assessment can be improved and given greater weight during the EIA process. Experience gained through the Sappi Paper Mill project and the direct involvement of the community in follow-up monitoring of local air quality impacts has also added a new approach to public consultation and direct participation in major developments. Both case studies have had positive advantages that have led to the gaining of developmental consent, but equally important, these case studies and the others referenced have resulted in direct improvements to corporate and project environmental management systems. As a result, the company has benefited from improved interaction with stakeholders, an expansion in the knowledge bases required for future development and licences, and positive adjustments in staff and contractor attitudes to the controlled management of environmental impact.

In conclusion, it is clear that a proactive approach to follow-up, practised through self-regulated EMS frameworks can enhance the power of EIA and contribute directly to a proponent's developmental success and corporate reputation.

Box 6.5 Motivating Proponents

A proponent's self-motivation to participate in EIA follow-up can be rewarded in a variety of ways.

Consent closure can be achieved through the agreement of terms, using EIA follow-up activities such as monitoring and audit, that grant consent (or that are inserted as a condition of consent being granted) to offsetting aspects of impact concern or uncertainty. Using EIA follow-up, a proponent's visible **conformance** with individual consents, mitigation strategies or obligations can improve stakeholder acceptance of controversial development. Similarly a proponent's overall **compliance** with the total suite of developmental obligations can demonstrate environmental responsibility and willingness to offset the adverse aspects of development. In the absence of statutory or consent requirements to undertake follow-up, there is a reputation advantage to the proponent in undertaking self-regulated follow-up, such as monitoring and audit that provide proof of technological, management or operational control. A proponent's reputation for proactive conformance and compliance can overcome areas of impact uncertainty and prevent barriers to the granting of consent.

Future knowledge of areas of impact uncertainty inherent in development and that can enhance future development project appraisal can be gained through EIA follow-up activities. This knowledge can be used to enhance the proponent's scientific knowledge of processes and activities, notably those environmental aspects that have a bearing on future development activities. Adverse impacts can be verified and the benefits of mitigation quantified in hard risk capital terms.

Future consents and licences can be assisted through monitoring and evaluation activities during the EIA that facilitate statutory applications at future operational stages resulting in a financial saving or streamlining of data requirements.

Liability avoidance is provided through the use of follow-up monitoring and evaluation activities arising from EIA that are used to offset future risk of liability or compensation issues.

Stakeholder communication activities integrated within the EIA process can inform stakeholders or communities, enhancing the relationship between the developer and such interested parties to pre-empt concerns or foreclose objections. Follow-up programmes can recognize what is significant to stakeholders and demonstrate how safeguards can resolve such issues. The use of independent bodies to develop and monitor follow-up can significantly improve relationships further.

In promoting EIA follow-up, the application of structured EMS frameworks within EIA follow-up to control impact or ensure mitigation implementation can provide comprehensive frameworks to successfully implement EIA follow-up programmes and close the implementation gap that can exist between project plans and their implementation.

References

Arts, J, Caldwell, P and Morrison-Saunders, A (2001) 'EIA follow-up: Good practice and future directions: Findings from a workshop at the IAIA 2000 Conference', *Impact Assessment and Project Appraisal*, vol 19, pp175–185

Au, E (2001) 'Latest Developments of EIA Follow-up in Hong Kong', presented at *Impact Assessment in the Urban Context, 21st Annual Meeting of the International Association for Impact Assessment*, 26 May–1 June 2001, Cartagena, Colombia, published on CD ROM: *IA Follow-up Workshop*, Hull, Quebec, Environment Canada

Baker, J and Dobos, R (2001) 'Environmental Assessment Follow-up: A Framework for Environment Canada (Draft)', presented at *Impact Assessment in the Urban Context, 21st Annual Meeting of the International Association for Impact Assessment*, 26 May–1 June 2001, Cartagena, Colombia, published on CD ROM: *IA Follow-up Workshop*, Hull, Quebec, Environment Canada

Ball, S and Bell, S (1995) *Environmental Law* 3rd edition, London, Blackstone Press

Balmer, D, Holloway, S, Burton, N and Clark, N (2002). *A Study of the Risk of Collision with Powerlines by Common Terns and Water Birds at Shotton Steel Works, North Wales*, British Trust for Ornithology Research Report No.280, Thetford, British Trust for Ornithology

BSI, British Standards Institution (1996) *Implementation of ISO 14001:1996 – Environmental Management Systems – Specification for Use*, London, British Standards Institution

CEC, Commission of the European Communities (1994) *Proposal for a Council Directive Amending Directive 85/337/EEC on the Assessment of the Effect of Certain Public and Private Projects on the Environment*, COM(93) 575 final, Brussels

CRE Energy (1998), *Beinn an Tuirc Windfarm: Environmental Statement*, Glasgow, CRE Energy

Downs, A (1972) 'Up and down with ecology: the "issue attention cycle"', *The Public Interest*, vol 28, pp38-50

Environment Agency (1999) *Environmental Action Plans – Good Practice Guidelines*, Environment Agency, Anglia Region

ICA, Institute of Chartered Accountants in England and Wales (1999) *Internal Control: Guidance for Directors on the Combined Code*, London, ICA

Machiavelli, N (1532) *The Prince*, Translation: Bondenella, P and Musa, M (ed and trans) (1979) *Il Principe*, Oxford, Oxford University Press

Marshall, R (2000) *The Concept and Role of Mitigation in EIA, With Particular Reference to Scottish Legislation and Practice*, PhD thesis, Glasgow, University of Strathclyde

Marshall, R (2001) 'Application of mitigation and its resolution within environmental impact assessment: an industrial perspective', *Impact Assessment and Project Appraisal*, vol 19, pp195–204

Marshall, R (2002) 'Professional practice on developing environmental management systems to deliver mitigation and protect the EIA process during follow-up', *Impact Assessment and Project Appraisal*, vol 20, pp286–292

ODPM, Office of the Deputy Prime Minister (2001) *Environmental Impact Assessment – A Guide to Procedures*, 7 February 2001, HMSO

PowerSystems (1999) *Fife 132 kV Refurbishment and Rationalisation Program, Environmental Impact Statement*, Glasgow, ScottishPower

PowerSystems (2001a) *Environmental Policy*, Env-01-001, Issue No.4, Glasgow, ScottishPower

PowerSystems (2001b) *'The Gretna Substation - Control of Environmental Effects During the Construction Phase'*, submitted as an accompanying document to the statutory planning application for the *'132kV Gretna Substation'* to Dumfries and Galloway Council, 20 April 2001, Glasgow, ScottishPower

Ross, W, Green, J and Croal, P (2001) 'Follow-up Studies in Cumulative Effects: Management Implications in Developing Nations', presented at *Impact Assessment in the Urban Context, 21st Annual Meeting of the International Association for Impact Assessment*, 26 May–1 June 2001, Cartagena, Colombia, published on CD ROM: *IA Follow-up Workshop*, Hull, Quebec, Environment Canada

Scottish Executive (1999) *Planning Advice Note 58 – Environmental Impact Assessment*, Edinburgh, Scottish Executive

Scottish Executive (2000) *Planning Advice Note 45 – Renewable Energy Technologies*, Edinburgh, Scottish Executive

ScottishPower (1997) *Scotland–Ireland Interconnector – Environmental Statement*, Glasgow, ScottishPower

ScottishPower (1999) *Construction Projects: Environmental Guidance and Construction of an Environmental Management Plan*, Glasgow, ScottishPower

ScottishPower (2001) *ScottishPower Environmental Report 2000/01*, Glasgow, ScottishPower

Wessels, J (2002) *EIA Methods and Techniques*, Masters Programme in Environmental Analysis and Management, School for Environmental Science and Development, Potchefstroom University for CHE. Potchefstroom

Wlodarczyk, T (2000) 'Improving Monitoring and Follow-up in Canadian Environmental Assessments', presented at *Back to the Future: Where Will Impact Assessment be in 10 Years and How Do We Get There? 20th Annual Meeting of the International Association for Impact Assessment*, 19–23 June 2000, Hong Kong Convention and Exhibition Centre, Hong Kong

World Bank (1991) *Annex C - Operational Directive 4.01 - Environmental Assessment*, Washington, DC, World Bank

Wood, C (2003) *Environmental Impact Assessment – A comparative review*, 2nd edition, Harlow, Pearson Education

7

EIA Follow-up and Adaptive Management

Angus Morrison-Saunders, Bryan Jenkins and John Bailey

Introduction

The previous chapter highlighted the importance of mitigation in Environmental Impact Assessment (EIA) follow-up and the role of the proponent in a largely self-regulation context. This chapter also focuses on the role of proponents in environmental management with a particular emphasis on adaptive environmental management. It provides a theoretical and practical perspective on the importance of EIA as an environmental management tool based on review of the follow-up literature and a case study from Western Australia. In terms of the contextual framework in which EIA follow-up occurs, it showcases a regulatory setting which promotes proponent responsibility for follow-up during both the pre- and post-decision stages of EIA. It also advocates a focus on environmental outcomes rather than on the extent of mitigation implementation, compliance with consent decision conditions or scientific analysis of EIA techniques.

The concept of adaptive environmental management was advanced by Holling (1978) as an alternative to EIA for renewable resource management problems. It emphasizes the importance of environmental management and the cyclical role of impact monitoring with appropriate modification of management programmes in response. The need for adaptive environmental management in EIA is a result of the uncertainty associated with changing states of the environment and the imprecision of impact prediction. Holling (1978, p133) noted that impact prediction processes will never be perfect and that no amount of observation prior to a project will reveal what impacts the project will eventually have. He therefore advocated that EIA activities should be an ongoing investigation into impacts (not a one-time prediction exercise) accompanied by appropriate ongoing environmental management responses.

In this chapter, use of the term adaptive management is somewhat broader than that of Holling. As defined in Chapter 2, it simply refers to changing project and environmental management activities in response to either actual impacts that have occurred or to avoid potential impacts. Adaptive management may also come about due to technological advances or new initiatives in best practice EIA.

The chapter discusses the importance of environmental management in EIA and the relationship between environmental management and follow-up activities, using case study examples from Western Australia. Means for promoting an adaptive management approach in EIA and follow-up are then explored. Future directions for adaptive EIA follow-up are discussed, including how it can incorporate the precautionary principle through contingency planning, illustrated using a case study on harbour development. This is a proactive approach to follow-up and project management. The chapter ends with some lessons learnt on the process of adaptive management during EIA follow-up in Western Australia.

The importance of environmental management

Despite the early recognition of the importance of environmental management in EIA by Holling and others, many of the early follow-up studies focused on the technical and regulatory aspects of EIA. The main emphasis was on auditing EIA predictions and compliance with EIA approval conditions including proposed mitigation measures. As can be seen in Chapters 8 and 9, which focus on practice in Canada and Hong Kong, these continue to feature in EIA follow-up regulations. Impact prediction audits determine the accuracy and outcomes of predictions made in Environmental Impact Statements (EIS) once a proposal is actually implemented. Early prediction accuracy audits were carried out by Bisset (1984) and the extensive study of Culhane et al (1987). Prediction accuracy audits require an analysis of impact monitoring results against the original prediction statements. Compliance audits address the regulatory aspects of EIA by determining the extent to which approval conditions (e.g. for impact mitigation) have been implemented by proponents once projects are operational. Like prediction audits, they require examination of impact monitoring results as well as operational checks on implemented works and activities.

While prediction and compliance audits may provide useful learning from experience about technical and practical aspects of EIA, they generally fall short of determining environmental management outcomes (Box 7.1). As Bailey and Hobbs (1990) asked: 'What point is there in correctly predicting 99 per cent of impacts if none of them gets managed properly?' This point was taken up by Carbon (1995) who stated that:

'Those who are concerned with the accuracy of environmental predictions should focus instead on the effectiveness of management processes to protect the environment. The important question to ask afterwards is "was the environment protected?"

It is more useful for environmental protection purposes to have an EIA follow-up process that focuses on environmental management outcomes and that promotes an adaptive approach to project and impact management as envisaged by Holling (1978). The results of follow-up studies focusing on environmental management outcomes in Western Australia are discussed in the following section.

Box 7.1 Limitations of Prediction and Compliance Audits in Relation to Environmental Performance

Prediction audits

Prediction audits compare predicted impacts with actual consequences in order to compare the accuracy and utility of different prediction methods (Bailey and Hobbs, 1990). Since EIA decision-making is largely based upon the likely or foreseeable consequences of a particular proposal, impact predictions are seen to lie at the heart of successful EIA. It is therefore desirable that a high level of prediction accuracy is attained in practice. In most studies, prediction accuracy is expressed as a percentage and results to date have been variable, but generally not impressive. For example in descending order of recorded prediction accuracy, the following results have been reported:

- Luecht et al (1989) – 80 per cent
- Wood et al (2000) – 79 per cent 'accurate' or 'nearly accurate' (of 56 per cent overall auditable)
- Bailey et al (1992) – 78 per cent (of 53 per cent overall that were auditable)
- Bernard et al (1993) – 70–75 per cent of water quality, morphology and hydrology impacts within a subset of aquatic resource predictions
- Bisset (1984) – 47 per cent (of 12 per cent overall that were auditable)
- Buckley (1991) – 44 per cent (±5 per cent) for the quantified, critical and testable predictions
- Henderson (1987) – 44 per cent of predictions recorded as being correct with an additional 10 per cent partially correct or uncertain
- Culhane et al (1987) – 30 per cent were found to be 'fairly accurate'.

The problem with recording predictive accuracy is that it does not provide any real information on environmental performance or outcomes. This is illustrated in the following chart.

Type of predictive statement		Prediction outcome		Environmental outcome
No impact predicted	→	Accurate	→	No impact
Impact expected	→	Inaccurate	→	No impact
No impact predicted	→	Inaccurate	→	Impact occurs
Impact expected	→	Accurate	→	Impact occurs

For predictive statements where no impact is expected to occur which prove to be accurate, a high percentage of predictive accuracy refers to no change in the environment from the proposed action. Clearly from an environmental performance point of view, this is a desirable outcome. However for predictive statements where an impact was expected to occur, but they are found to be inaccurate, there is also no change in the environment. Here, a high proportion of *inaccurate* predictions is an indicator of positive environmental performance.

Compliance audits

A similar problem occurs with compliance audits. Here the number of approval conditions complied with is also often expressed as a percentage. It is assumed that implementing proposed mitigation measures as planned actually protects the environment, but this may not be the case. For example, checking compliance with a pollution emission standard focuses attention on the waste emission itself rather than the receiving environment. Through cumulative or synergistic effects, it is possible that the receiving environment is adversely impacted, but this may not be examined during a compliance audit.

An additional problem with both prediction and compliance audits where results are expressed as percentages is that it assumes that all predictions or mitigation measures have equal weighting. Even if 99 per cent of impacts are identified correctly and mitigation measures are put in place for them as intended during the pre-decision stages of EIA, an unacceptable adverse negative impact may be associated with the remaining 1 per cent. Hence, from an environmental management point of view, it would be inappropriate to conclude that a high level of predictive accuracy or compliance equated with environmental protection.

EIA follow-up and environmental management in Western Australia

Background

Salient elements of the present EIA system in Western Australia, including follow-up requirements, are summarized in Box 7.2 and Figure 7.1. There has been a strong tradition of emphasis on environmental management aspects of EIA in Western Australia. The concept of ongoing environmental management was incorporated into the Western Australian EIA procedures in 1980 through the use of an EIS document specifically known as an Environmental Review and Management Programme (ERMP). It was intended that an ERMP would place considerable emphasis on the identification of ongoing environmental management and monitoring activities to be undertaken during project implementation, in addition to the prediction of potential environmental impacts (DCE, 1980). The preparation of an EIS by a proponent is not intended to represent a 'snapshot' approach to EIA, a criticism frequently levelled at EIA of projects elsewhere. In current Western Australian practice, the Environmental Protection Authority (EPA) identify 'relevant environmental factors' for proposed actions and establish management objectives for these during the screening and scoping stages of EIA.

The EPA is a statutory body, comprising of five members, which is independent from government. It is responsible for overseeing the EIA process in Western Australia. It plays a key role in determining whether or not to assess development proposals (i.e. screening) and in determining the level of assessment that will apply for proposals that are subject to EIA (details on the various assessment options can be found in Government Gazette, 2002; for simplicity, the generic term EIS is used here). The EPA also assess projects and provide advice to government on whether or not proposals should be granted approval and what conditions should apply to proposals that are implemented.

In Western Australia, proponents are charged with the responsibility for environmental management of their proposals and with demonstrating in their EIS documents that the environmental factors can be satisfactorily managed to meet the EPA's management objectives. Following public review, the subsequent EPA assessment and advice to the Minister for the Environment and Heritage focuses on the ability to manage the proposal so as to meet the EPA objectives for each relevant environmental factor (Morrison-Saunders and Bailey, 2000a). Proponent commitments in the EIS and EPA recommendations for management become legally binding conditions of approval served on proponents by the Minister.

During the post-decision stages of the process, compliance auditing focuses on the extent to which there has been compliance with the Ministerial conditions. Proponents are typically required to submit regular compliance reports to the EPA and are expected to adapt their management programmes as required to satisfy the Ministerial conditions.

A mechanism is provided for in the legislation to review and amend approval conditions and the subsequent process involves evaluation by the EPA and public reporting of their advice to the Minister. Conditions may be altered to extend time limits (e.g. if a proponent has not initiated implementation of their proposal within 5 years of receiving Ministerial approval, the approval is rescinded), to enable project changes (e.g. extend mining lease areas, increase production volumes, alter processing techniques etc.) and/or to adapt management practices. In the five year period from 1996 to 2000, the process for changing approval conditions was called upon on 22 occasions (based on an appraisal of EPA report and recommendation documents published in this period). Of these, 13 involved explicit changes to environmental management practices, mainly in connection with project changes. Additionally, for several of the other projects, all of which involved extensions to time limits, additional environmental management requirements were imposed to reflect 'current environmental standards and practice'. The ability to modify approval conditions in Western Australia is clearly also an important mechanism for providing for adaptive environmental management.

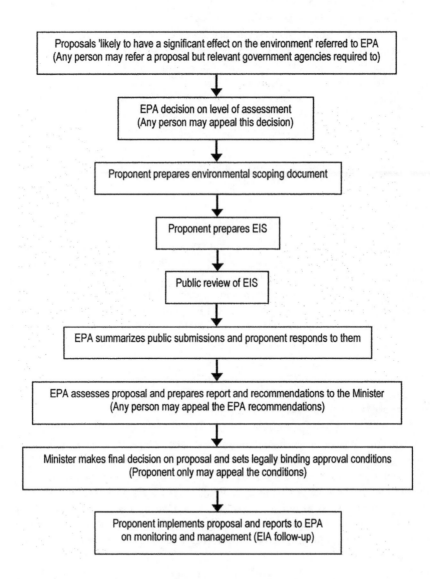

Figure 7.1 *EIA Process in Western Australia*

Box 7.2 EIA and Follow-up Requirements in Western Australia

Objectives of EIA in Western Australia

The EPA has five objectives for EIA in Western Australia (Government Gazette, 2002). Several of these are relevant to follow-up and adaptive management:

- ensure that proponents take primary responsibility for protection of the environment influenced by their proposals
- ensure best practicable measures are taken to minimize adverse impacts on the environment, and that proposals meet relevant environmental objectives and standards to protect the environment and implement the principles of sustainability
- encourage proponents to implement continuous improvement in environmental performance and the application of best practice environmental management in implementing their proposals.

The other two objectives concern public participation in EIA and the provision of advice to Government for decision-making purposes.

Follow-up requirements

As part of the EIS preparation, proponents are required to 'include an audit table with environmental management commitments that will form part of the conditions of approval and will become legally binding and be audited if the proposal is implemented' (Government Gazette, 2002, s6.3.6).
Following public review of the EIS and EPA assessment of a proposal, under the terms of the *Environmental Protection Act* 1986 (s44), the EPA is required to prepare a report to the Minister for the Environment and Heritage on:

- the environmental factors relevant to that proposal
- the conditions and procedures, if any, to which any implementation of that proposal should be subject.

The Act establishes that subsequent approval conditions served by the Minister are legally binding on proponents (s45) and that it is an offence for proponents not to comply with them (s47). The Act provides for the Chief Executive Officer of the Department of Environmental Protection (DEP) or a relevant decision-making authority to monitor 'the implementation of any proposal insofar as that implementation is subject to any [approval] conditions or procedures'. Audit procedures are outlined in a (non-legal) advisory document prepared by the DEP (1997).

Adaptive management and follow-up

Adaptive management is not specifically prescribed in the legally binding procedures for EIA in Western Australia. Rather it evolves during project implementation because of the way in which approval conditions are based around environmental objectives established for relevant environmental factors by the EPA. Compliance audit requirements are legally provided for and are tied to the approval conditions which emphasize environmental performance objectives rather than prescribed actions to be undertaken by proponents or standards to be met. Thus the problems identified with compliance audits in Box 7.1 are largely avoided.

In Western Australia, approval conditions themselves are not necessarily fixed. First, a five-year time limit is placed on project approvals as one of the Ministerial conditions of approval. If a project is not implemented within that period, then the approval lapses. Second, provision exists in the Act (s46) to change environmental conditions and allow time extensions to project approvals to be considered. Sometimes such changes are adaptive management (i.e. new or improved project management strategies).

EIA follow-up studies in Western Australia

Several follow-up studies based on case studies from Western Australia have explored the relationship between follow-up and adaptive environmental management and are summarized here.

When discussing their proposed framework for conducting EIA audits, Bailey and Hobbs (1990) suggested that it is more important to understand whether the EIA procedural framework results in good management, rather than focusing on the scientific evaluation of impact predictions alone. In their subsequent environmental audit of artificial waterway projects in Western Australia, Bailey et al (1992) recorded both predictive success and the management response to the impacts that were observed in practice. They found that predictive accuracy had no bearing on environmental management activities. Management responses were just as likely to be implemented for impacts that were inaccurately predicted or were not predicted at all in EIA documents, as for those that were accurately forecast during the pre-decision stages of the process. They concluded that impact identification and the implementation of associated environmental conditions was of greater significance than formal impact prediction processes.

In subsequent work, Bailey (1997) examined the theory and practice of EIA with respect to project-based environmental management in an approach that was in keeping with Culhane's (1993) management-by-objectives model of EIA. Bailey (1997) did not engage in a formal EIA follow-up study; rather he provided anecdotal examples from his own experience as a member of the EPA over a nine-year period in which some 500 individual impact assessments were undertaken. He gave examples of approaches to EIA that encourage or facilitate ongoing environmental management such as:

- The encouragement of proponent commitments for environmental management (Box 7.2).
- The specific incorporation of environmental management considerations in the EIA process (e.g. the use of an ERMP as the form of EIS document required for major development proposals).
- The establishment of environmental objectives by the EPA that proponents are legally required to comply with, but for which the means of compliance are not specified. This enables flexibility in project implementation and management. It encourages proponents to continue to plan and design their project over time.
- The requirement for proponents to prepare detailed Environmental Management Programmes (EMPs) following the approval decision, but prior to project implementation, for major or complex proposals. Brew and Lee (1996) suggest that an EMP describe the management systems and the monitoring and auditing arrangements required to ensure both the proper implementation of agreed mitigation measures and the verification of predicted environmental impacts. Leaving the final details of environmental management to be resolved after the approval decision has been granted encourages a flexible approach by both proponents and regulatory authorities.

The work of Bailey (1997) led to a detailed follow-up study in Western Australia to determine the relationship between EIA and environmental management activities (Morrison-Saunders and Bailey 1999). The purpose was to determine where environmental management responses originate during EIA. To explore this further the EIA process was divided into three stages based around the principal approval decision (Figure 7.2). The *pre-decision*

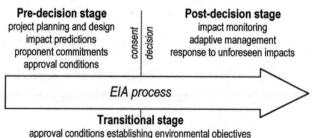

Pre-decision stage
project planning and design
impact predictions
proponent commitments
approval conditions

consent decision

Post-decision stage
impact monitoring
adaptive management
response to unforeseen impacts

EIA process

Transitional stage
approval conditions establishing environmental objectives
environmental management programmes (EMPs)

Source: Morrison-Saunders, 1997

Figure 7.2 *A Management Model of EIA*

stage occurs up to and including the approval decision itself. It includes initial project planning, base-line studies, preparation of EIS documents and their assessment by the public and competent authorities. The *post-decision* stage refers to activities that take place after the approval decision such as project implementation including mitigation and management actions and impact monitoring and reporting. The third EIA stage is a *transitional* one that overlaps both the pre- and post-decision stages of the process. Establishment of environmental objectives by the EPA to be resolved by the proponent during project implementation and the requirement for an EMP to be prepared following the approval decision but prior to project implementation are examples of transitional stage activities. In analysing these three stages of EIA, the emphasis of the investigation was on management actions and environmental outcomes (Box 7.3).

Findings from an environmental management follow-up study

Six projects that had undergone EIA in Western Australia and had been in operation for at least five years were examined using the methodology outlined in Box 7.3. The projects comprised a wastewater outfall into the ocean, two water supply dams, a mineral sands processing plant, a sodium cyanide manufacturing plant and an offshore oil and gas extraction project with processing facilities located on a nearby island. The following results were previously reported in Morrison-Saunders and Bailey (1999); full case study details are in Morrison-Saunders (1997).

Impact predictions and environmental management

Not all predicted impacts had a proposed management action associated with them. However predictions addressing issues considered to be important by the EPA (e.g. they were specifically identified in scoping guidelines for the EIS or influenced project decision-making) were more likely to have a corresponding management action than the others. Hence it appears that the EIA process was successful at focusing attention and effort onto important issues.

All six projects provided examples in which the implementation of planned environmental management actions successfully avoided the occurrence of predicted impacts. These ranged from 6 to 22 per cent of predicted impacts for each project. They mainly concerned management of project construction activities and project design elements.

Construction activity examples included:

- watering construction sites to avoid dust generation
- tunnelling beneath busy roads for pipeline installation to avoid traffic disruption
- sourcing construction materials for dam infrastructure from future reservoir inundation areas to avoid unnecessary habitat destruction

Box 7.3 Methodology for EIA Follow-up with Environmental Management Emphasis

This methodology for EIA follow-up is based upon four aspects of EIA (Morrison-Saunders and Bailey, 1999): impact predictions, actual impacts recorded during project implementation, impact monitoring programmes and environmental management activities. For each project under investigation, the following steps were taken:

1 The identification of potential impacts in pre-decision EIA documents (scoping guidelines, the proponents' EIS and the EPA's assessment report). These impact predictions provide the basis for environmental management and monitoring activities as well as providing guidance for identification of the actual impacts that occurred in practice.
2 The identification of management actions proposed in pre-decision and transitional EIA documents (e.g. EMPs) to avoid or minimize the occurrence of predicted impacts.
3 Evaluation of impact monitoring programme results (i.e. post-decision reports) to identify documented environmental impacts that had occurred as well any new environmental management actions taken in response to these. New or evolving management actions in response to observed impacts is evidence that adaptive environmental management is occurring.
4 Interviews with project managers and regulatory authorities to identify monitoring and management activities and project impacts not documented in post-decision reports.
5 Site visits to inspect first-hand some of the key impact sites and environmental management initiatives.

By comparing predicted impacts (1) with actual impacts (3) in light of proposed management actions (2), it is possible to determine which potential impacts were avoided or minimized through successful mitigation measures. This is one measure of effective pre-decision EIA. Steps (3)–(5) serve to identify the actual impacts that occurred and to record the environmental management response to them. The intention is also to evaluate the extent to which the environment has been protected and managed. Site visits and direct contact with project managers and regulators are important to obtain first-hand insight as well as to learn about the many small or minor issues and incidents that may not be included in post-decision reports but which nevertheless provide useful information on the effectiveness of EIA measures and procedures.

Project design aspects that avoided impacts included:

- rerouting recreational trails around a construction site so tourists were not affected
- route selection (of roads and pipelines) to avoid private property and sites of cultural heritage and remnant vegetation
- releasing water from a dam to maintain water quality in downstream pools and another reservoir
- landscaping to avoid noise and visual impacts from industrial operations
- installation and operation of pollution control equipment to avoid air quality impacts and leak detection and recovery systems for effluent dams.

In terms of impact predictions made in pre-decision EIA documents, the number of predicted impacts that did occur in practice ranged from 33 to 53 per cent for the six projects. Most of these were inevitable outcomes of project construction and implementation (e.g. clearing of habitat, emission of pollutants and employment of personnel).

There were numerous examples of accurate predictions of no impact for each of the case studies (14–25 per cent of predicted impacts). Examples of predictions that expected an impact to occur but proved to be inaccurate were only evident for two of the projects (4 and 11 per cent respectively). There was only one case study for which it was possible to verify all the impact predictions. For the remaining five case studies, 4–24 per cent of the predicted impacts could not be verified due to the absence of impact monitoring programmes or other lack of information about project outcomes. In almost all circumstances, these concerned ecological issues (e.g. predicted impacts on fish and wildlife). These would require relatively sophisticated and expensive scientific monitoring programmes to determine whether impacts had occurred compared to changes to the physical environment (e.g. evident from simple observation) or impacts on people (e.g. evident from complaints received).

In terms of the actual impacts that occurred in practice, there was no case study in which all of the impacts were accurately predicted. The range of accurately predicted impacts was 40–80 per cent, with the proportion of inaccurately predicted impacts ranging from 20 to 50 per cent. There was only one case study for which some inaccurately predicted impacts turned out to be *better* than predicted in the pre-decision EIA documents. In all other cases, the resulting outcomes were *worse* than predicted. Three reasons why actual impacts differed from the original impact predictions were recorded in approximately equal measure:

- inadequacies in predictive methods and techniques
- changes to project design or operation
- inadequacies in project and impact management.

As with other prediction audits discussed previously, the accuracy of impact predictions was not as high as EIA practitioners would wish. The uncertainty evident in pre-decision impact prediction highlights the importance of more general issue identification and the value of putting appropriate mitigation measures in place.

Impact mitigation and environmental management performance

The vast majority of environmental management actions recorded for the six projects were originally identified during the pre-decision stages of the EIA process (87–100 per cent). The remainder evolved during the post-decision stage either in response to unexpected impacts or because the management actions that had been implemented were not adequate to protect the environment (i.e. evidence of an adaptive approach).

Effective environmental performance relies on mitigation measures being implemented (and implemented well). Most of the pre-decision management proposals were subsequently implemented in practice (83–97 per cent). For two of the projects, all proposed management actions that could have been implemented were implemented in practice. In four of the projects, some proposed management actions were not implemented (3–6 per cent) as had been promised in pre-decision documentation. In some cases site conditions did not permit implementation of mitigation measures (e.g. it was not possible to source all required construction materials for dam construction from the reservoir inundation zone and a fish trap could not be installed at one dam site due to the naturally rocky terrain). In other cases, alternative management measures to the original proposal were implemented instead (e.g. switching water supplies to a groundwater scheme rather than using multilevel off-takes to minimize turbidity in the water supply following flood inflows into the reservoir and installing manual shut-down stations rather than an automatic system connected to emission testers for the sodium cyanide manufacturing plant). There were several situations however, where proposed management actions should have been implemented; for example:

- a commitment to ensure that normal emissions of nitrogen oxides at one of the industrial plants would be within particular recommended guidelines had not been complied with, although the proponent was planning to install further pollution control equipment that would address this issue at the time of audit
- a commitment to limit the height of certain buildings to minimize visual impact was not complied with (although no complaints had been received on this issue)
- change in plans for the burial of solid waste to an on-site instead of an off-site location
- breach of a commitment to avoid discharge of liquid waste to the environment, when an overfull evaporation dam was pumped out.

Additionally a number of proposed management actions were not applicable at the time of the follow-up study (0–5 per cent) as the requisite conditions had not occurred. Some of these related to project decommissioning and rehabilitation actions. Others concerned contingency plans for predicted events that had not eventuated (e.g. there was no need for animal control measures at one of the dams as no problems with dingo or kangaroo numbers had been encountered, and no oil spills had occurred at the offshore oil and gas facility so various oil spill contingency plans had not been put into action). One recommended mitigation action proposed by the EPA concerning safeguards for the ammonia supply pipeline to the sodium cyanide plant had been successfully appealed against by the proponent, so the original management proposal was no longer applicable.

For two of the projects, it was not possible to determine whether particular management actions had been implemented in practice due to lack of information (2 and 6 per cent respectively). Overall though, the high implementation rate of management actions indicates that the six projects proceeded largely as proposed during the pre-decision stage of EIA.

An interesting finding was that proposed management actions tied to legally binding approval conditions were not any more likely to be implemented in practice than those with voluntary or recommendation-only status. This result is contrary to the work of others (e.g. Gibson, 1993; Ortolano and Shepherd, 1995; Sadler, 1996) who suggest that an important determinant of the effectiveness of EIA is having legally binding approval conditions. It is also contrary to the work of Bailey et al (1992) who previously found that compliance with legally binding approval conditions was statistically higher than the others. Morrison-Saunders and Bailey (1999) suggested that the clear expectation that proponents should account for the environmental performance of their projects may be sufficient to ensure that proposed management activities are implemented in practice. In contrast Hui (2000) reported on the increasing need for regulatory controls on project management for projects in Hong Kong. It seems that the cultural context in which EIA takes place may also have an important bearing on environmental protection and management outcomes (Morrison-Saunders et al, 2003). Additionally, industry-led management initiatives such as environmental management systems and commitment to self-regulation may play an important role here (Chapter 6).

For two of the projects examined by Morrison-Saunders and Bailey (1999), all the observed impacts had previously been identified in impact predictions (although they were not all accurately predicted). The number of unexpected impacts recorded for the other two projects ranged from 5 to 10 per cent. The possibility exists that other environmental impacts may have occurred in practice for any of the six projects but which have not been recorded due to deficiencies in monitoring programmes (e.g. some potential impacts identified in predictions were not able to be verified).

Many of the observed impacts did not require a subsequent environmental management response (25–90 per cent). These impacts comprised the beneficial outcomes of projects for which no management was necessary as well as the inevitable or otherwise unavoidable adverse impacts of project implementation accepted by decision-makers (e.g. habitat loss arising from project construction and operation). Only three impacts from the six projects were not responded to by project managers where a response could reasonably have been implemented. This result, combined with the limitations of some monitoring programmes (i.e. the unverifiable impact predictions) and the small number of proposed environmental management actions not implemented in practice represent the overall deficiency in the ongoing environmental management of the six projects.

A management response was implemented for the remaining impacts that occurred in practice (10–62 per cent). Many of these were inaccurately predicted or were unexpected (approximately 25 per cent overall). The fact that they were responded to by managers suggests that the EIA process is effective from an environmental protection perspective. Morrison-Saunders and Bailey (1999) suggested that simple impact or issue identification and the establishment of environmental management programmes during the pre-decision stages of EIA may be all that is necessary for ultimate environmental protection purposes. However, it must be realized that for environmental issues and processes that are not well understood it may be necessary to engage in detailed scientific investigation and rigorous impact prediction to tackle these successfully.

Monitoring programmes were found to be deficient for the six projects in that it was not possible to verify some impact predictions. However, a strong relationship between monitoring and management activity was evident. This provides the opportunity for adaptive environmental management to eventuate. It is possible for appropriate environmental management to be undertaken even in the face of uncertainties in monitoring findings. Such an approach is one way in which operational EIA can be made consistent with the expectations of the precautionary principle.

With respect to the three stages of EIA (Figure 7.2), Morrison-Saunders and Bailey (1999) found that the majority of environmental management activities originated during the pre-decision stage of EIA (71–91 per cent). However the transitional stage activities (6–21 per cent), which mostly related to management objectives set by the EPA for proponents to meet or the requirement to prepare an EMP and the new environmental management actions that originated during the post-decision stage (0–13 per cent), also played an important role for the six projects. Morrison-Saunders and Bailey (2000b) provided some examples of successful environmental management originating from each of the three stages of the EIA process, demonstrating that all three stages are important. In particular, it is the transitional and post-decision stages which give rise to adaptive environmental management.

Having discussed the results of EIA follow-up aimed at understanding environmental management performance and understood which stages of EIA contributed to adaptive environmental management, it is interesting to reflect on the factors that encourage or enable adaptive management to occur.

Factors promoting adaptive environmental management in EIA

A number of approaches to EIA and subsequent follow-up may promote adaptive environmental management in practice (Box 7.4).

Holling (1978) and Beanlands and Duinker (1983) advocate treating impact predictions as scientific hypotheses rather than absolute statements, thereby inviting a flexible open-minded follow-up approach to verify them. In this way, a proposal is framed as an ongoing experiment. From a rational-scientific perspective, this notion is very appealing, but it risks placing too much emphasis on the impact prediction process, which prediction audits have repeatedly found to be unreliable.

Instead, follow-up studies in Western Australia have suggested that impact identification may be all that is required to ensure that appropriate environmental management is put in place. The emphasis here is on management of potential impacts rather than engaging rigorous impact prediction techniques. Making it clear that responsibility for project and impact management remains with the proponent, but in a non-prescriptive fashion, is an important part of this approach. The recent practice in use in Western Australia is for the EPA to identify relevant environmental factors and establish objectives for these, but

Box 7.4 Ways to Promote Adaptive Environmental Management

Approaches to EIA and follow-up that encourage an adaptive environmental management approach include:

- focus on impact management activities
- proponents clearly responsible for environmental management
- establish management objectives for important environmental issues during the scoping stage of EIA
- permit the preparation of EMPs after a proposal is approved but prior to commencement in which details of environmental management strategies are provided
- require proponents to report on their progress in meeting environmental objectives
- encourage proponents to adopt EMS
- involve the public, especially local communities, in follow-up programmes
- link environmental monitoring programmes to mitigation and environmental management activities
- have legally enforceable follow-up requirements, but which permit a flexible rather than prescriptive approach.

to leave the details up to the proponent to resolve (Morrison-Saunders and Bailey, 2000a). The role of the EPA and its supporting department responsible for administering EIA is to make judgements of the acceptability of environmental management proposals and outcomes for projects. The EPA has striven to avoid a fixed prescriptive approach to environmental management; licence conditions for pollution emissions relating to established standards are an exception to this.

To encourage the meeting of environmental objectives in a flexible way, the EPA encourages use of EMPs. A major advantage of EMPs from a proponent perspective is that approval can be granted in the absence of detailed design specifications on the basis that these will be resolved in a subsequent EMP that is approved by the EPA prior to proposal implementation. This means that proponents can secure funding for their proposals (an easier task with an EPA approval granted) and invest the time and money required for detailed project design specifications, knowing that the project will now proceed. Environmental considerations can be built into the design specifications for all aspects of project construction and operation. Given that there is normally a time lag between project approval and subsequent implementation, having the in-between step of an EMP provides the proponent with more time to fine tune mitigation and monitoring elements than if this process ended when the EIS was finalized.

Another mechanism that can promote adaptive management by proponents, and which may work in tandem with an EMP approach (Chapter 6), is industry self-regulation instruments such as environmental management systems (EMS). A goal of environmental agencies such as the EPA in Western Australia is to ensure that proponents not only take responsibility for project and environmental management but also seek to achieve continual ongoing improvements in environmental management; a goal that lies at the heart of EMS certification. Continual improvement requires ongoing follow-up investigations and an adaptive environmental management approach. With an EMS approach, proponents are self-directed to achieve this.

Adaptive environmental management may also be promoted through public pressure and involvement in EIA. In further analysis of the case studies reported previously, Morrison-Saunders (1998) found that public influences made an important contribution to the identification and implementation of environmental management activities during EIA for the six projects. For example, a public submission on an EIS led to an approval condition which required the proponent to conduct ongoing monitoring and reporting on the effectiveness of the management measures taken for a particular impact. This resulted in adaptive management when the initial mitigation attempts were found to be unsuccessful. Public pressure during the post-decision stages of the EIA process was also found to influence environmental management practices. This included both explicit opposition to unacceptable odour emissions for one project and the implicit public pressure through the fear of negative publicity for another project. In each case the proponent adapted their original management programmes to accommodate the needs or desires of the community. Overall public involvement was an important mechanism for ensuring that the environment was protected and managed as intended by the EIA process for each of the six projects (Morrison-Saunders, 1998).

Having opportunities for public involvement in EIA and transparency in decision-making and project outcomes is important for adaptive environmental management. Public participation is also important in EIA follow-up programmes for the same reasons (Chapters 8 and 9).

Future directions for EIA follow-up and adaptive environmental management

This chapter has shown how follow-up for environmental management performance can be undertaken in practice and how environmental management objectives are factored into EIA decision-making in Western Australia. Extrapolating from these two approaches, it is possible to conceive an EIA process that promotes adaptive management based upon meeting environmental management objectives in which follow-up emphasizes environmental management outcomes. The central column of Figure 7.3

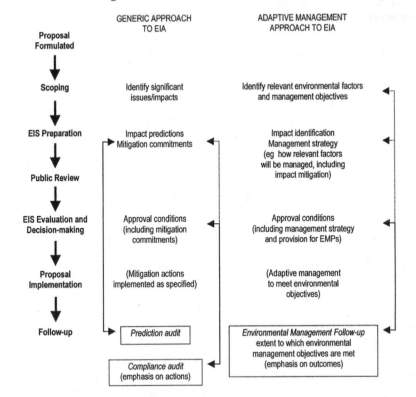

Figure 7.3 *Comparison of Conventional and Adaptive Management Approaches to EIA and Follow-up*

depicts a generic EIA process in which prediction and compliance audits are carried out. The right column shows how a slight change to the emphasis of the process can result in adaptive environmental management and follow-up of environmental outcomes.

Adaptive management and the precautionary principle

The environment is clearly complex and dynamic. Base-line studies and predictive models are usually incapable of accounting for this. Consequently the practical goal of EIA is to understand enough about the environment and the likely consequences of a proposed action in order to make an informed decision about it. However, some level of uncertainty is inevitable with respect to proposal implementation and subsequent environmental outcomes (Chapter 2). Utilizing an adaptive environmental management approach to EIA and subsequent follow-up activities provides a means of proceeding with proposed actions in the face of uncertainties.

Uncertainty in EIA may give rise to application of the precautionary principle. For decision-making purposes the precautionary principle suggests that when there is uncertainty in available information concerning possible adverse environmental effects, then the decision should come down in favour of the environment. This may mean a proposal should not be permitted to proceed. However, the precautionary principle also has relevance for environmental management strategies. Jenkins (1993) notes that where there is uncertainty of outcome, an appropriate environmental management strategy is to devise a contingency plan to accommodate it (this approach is also applied in other jurisdictions such as Hong Kong, where such a contingency plan is known as an 'event action plan'; Chapter 9). If the contingency plan is capable of accommodating the 'worst case scenario', then it will be acceptable to proceed with the proposal. However, the intention is that implementation of the contingency plan or other corrective action is taken depending upon the results of monitoring. Hence provision for adaptive management during follow-up is consistent with taking a precautionary approach. An example of a case study in which contingency plans were put in place to address uncertainties and then subsequently enacted follows.

Harbour development in Cockburn Sound, Western Australia

Formal assessment was required of the proposal to extend the breakwater in Northern Harbour within Cockburn Sound, in the southern metropolitan region of capital city Perth, Western Australia (Halpern Glick Maunsell, 1996). The breakwater extension was to protect shipbuilding facilities from west-northwest ocean swells.

The key environmental factor in the EPA's evaluation of the proposal was water quality in the harbour (EPA, 1996). Cockburn Sound has a history of algal blooms due to increased nitrogen loads from effluent discharges and groundwater inflows containing elevated nitrogen levels.

In the area of Northern Harbour, groundwater seepage into Cockburn Sound contains nutrients injected from a starch manufacturer and the biosolids storage facility of a sewage treatment plant. Construction and operation of these two plants pre-dated EIA requirements in Western Australia. The emergency overflow outfall for the sewage treatment plant also discharged into Northern Harbour. The construction of the breakwater would have the effect of increased residence time for the nutrients entering the harbour from groundwater.

The effects of increased residence times and groundwater inflows were assessed using a well-mixed, annual-average, first-order total nitrogen model. Under 'worst case' conditions it was estimated that the breakwater would increase the residence time from 2.4 to 5 days and increase the nitrogen elevation above background from 70µg/litre to 140µg/litre (Halpern Glick Maunsell, 1996). The proponent did not consider that these increases would result in unacceptable water quality in the harbour. The proponent also proposed monitoring of water quality as part of its environmental management plan. The EPA considered that there was uncertainty in relation to water quality and sought commitment by the proponent for a contingency plan to be prepared and implemented if the water quality in the harbour became unacceptable (EPA, 1996).

Further industrial infrastructure and harbour development was proposed in Jervoise Bay to create another harbour to the south of Northern Harbour. This proposal, termed 'Southern Harbour', was also subject to formal EIA (Halpern Glick Maunsell, 1997).

Soon after the release of the EIS for the Southern Harbour, there was a significant algal bloom within the Northern Harbour with breakwater extension. Three cycles of algal species occurred with counts over 5×10^6 cells/litre from 6 January to 10 February 1998. Nitrogen levels in the harbour were measured at 370µg/litre above background (Halpern Glick Maunsell, 1998).

This event triggered the contingency plan requirement as a condition of the Northern Harbour approval and led to a significantly revised breakwater layout for Southern Harbour to facilitate water circulation (Figure 7.4). It also led to the development of a groundwater recovery system to meet the contingency plan requirement as well as the EPA water quality objective for Southern Harbour to maintain or improve the quality of marine water (EPA, 1998).

The modified breakwater layout for Southern Harbour changed the flushing time from 9.5 days under the original proposal to just 2 days. This was still higher than the existing pre-harbour flushing time of 0.4 days and meant that the groundwater recovery system had to cover both harbours to meet the EPA water quality objectives.

The groundwater recovery scheme involves 4 recovery bores, 27 coastal monitoring bores for saltwater intrusion and nutrients, and 8 inland monitoring bores for nitrogen sources and drawdown near market garden supply bores. There is also monitoring in Northern Harbour for nitrogen and chlorophyll *a* concentrations.

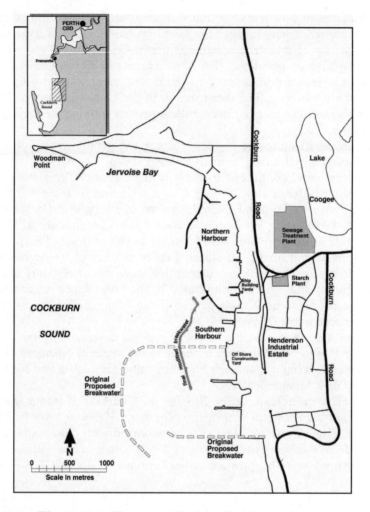

Figure 7.4 *Changes to Harbour Breakwater Layout*

After two years of operation, 90 tonnes of nitrogen have been recovered with the recovery bores intercepting 40–50 per cent of the load to the harbours. Nitrogen levels in the harbours have decreased by around 25 per cent (Parsons Brickerhoff, 2003).

This example demonstrates the value of having a contingency plan requirement when impact predictions turn out to be inaccurate. This precautionary approach during EIA and subsequent follow-up activities promoted adaptive environmental management. The contingency plan was linked to a clear environmental objective and made legally binding in the approval conditions. The revision to the breakwater layout is also a reflection of adaptive management in response to EIA follow-up monitoring. The introduction of the groundwater recovery system was another element of contingency planning and adaptive management for this project. It plays an important role in reducing the nitrogen load in Northern Harbour with consequent reductions in nitrogen in the marine water quality.

Conclusion

There are a number of lessons learnt from EIA follow-up experience in Western Australia. This chapter has highlighted the benefits of tailoring EIA follow-up activities to environmental management objectives so as to promote flexible and adaptive management outcomes. This has significant advantages in terms of achieving sound environmental performance compared to follow-up directed at prediction accuracy or compliance determination alone. Clearly there is an important role for EIA regulators to play here with respect to the style and content of EIA approval conditions. However, this chapter has also highlighted the important role that proponent self-regulation and external public pressure can play in achieving adaptive environmental management.

Taking an adaptive approach to EIA and follow-up works hand in hand with application of the precautionary principle. Projecting a 'worst case' scenario during the impact prediction stage of EIA enables contingency plans to be incorporated into project approval conditions. These plans are only implemented by proponents if and when EIA follow-up monitoring identifies a need for further environmental management measures to be put in place. For circumstances in which the 'worst case scenario' never eventuates, there are clear cost advantages to the proponent. Equally, however, appropriate environmental safeguards have been provided for in the event that problems arise. And ultimately, the purpose of EIA and EIA follow-up is to ensure that the environment is adequately protected.

References

Arts, J, Caldwell, P and Morrison-Saunders, A (2001) 'EIA follow-up: Good practice and future directions: Findings from a workshop at the IAIA 2000 Conference', *Impact Assessment and Project Appraisal*, vol 19, pp175–185

Bailey, J (1997) 'Environmental Impact Assessment and management: An under-explored relationship', *Environmental Management*, vol 21, pp317–327

Bailey, J and Hobbs, V (1990) 'A proposed framework and database for EIA auditing', *Journal of Environmental Management*, vol 31, pp163–172

Bailey, J, Hobbs, V and Saunders, A (1992) 'Environmental auditing: Artificial waterway developments in Western Australia', *Journal of Environmental Management*, vol 34, pp1–13

Beanlands, G and Duinker, P (1983) *An Ecological Framework for Environmental Impact Assessment in Canada*, Institute for Resource and Environmental Studies, Dalhousie University, Quebec, Canada, Published in cooperation with Federal Environmental Assessment Review Office

Bernard, D, Hunsaker Jr, D and Marmorek, D (1993) 'Tools for Improving Predictive Capabilities of Environmental Impact Assessments: Structured Hypotheses, Audits and Monitoring', in Hildebrand, S and Cannon, J (eds) *Environmental Analysis: The NEPA Experience*, Boca Raton, Florida, Lewis Publishers, pp547–564

Bisset, R (1984) 'Post-development audits to investigate the accuracy of environmental impact predictions', *Umweltpolitik*, vol 4, pp463–484

Brew, D and Lee, N (1996) 'Monitoring, environmental management plans and post-project analysis', *EIA Newsletter*, vol 12, pp10–11

Buckley, R (1991) 'Auditing the precision and accuracy of environmental impact predictions in Australia', *Environmental Monitoring and Assessment*, vol 18, pp1–23

Carbon, B (1995) 'EIA – an overview', *Australian Journal of Environmental Management*, vol 2, pp62–64

Culhane, P (1993) 'Post-EIS environmental auditing: A first step to making Rational Environment Assessment a reality', *The Environmental Professional*, vol 15, 66–75

Culhane, P, Friesema, H and Beecher, J (1987) *Forecasts and Environmental Decision-Making, The Content and Predictive Accuracy of Environmental Impact Statements*, Boulder, Colorado, Westview Press

DCE, Department of Conservation and Environment (1980) *Procedures for Environmental Assessment of Proposals in Western Australia*, Bulletin 38, Perth, Western Australia, Department of Conservation and Environment

DEP, Department of Environmental Protection (1997) *Auditing Environmental Conditions: Guidelines for Proponents*, Perth, Western Australia, Department of Environmental Protection, available at www.epa.wa.gov.au/docs/1040_EIA_ ADENCON97.pdf

EPA, Environmental Protection Authority (1996) *Breakwater Extension, Northern Harbour Precinct, Jervoise Bay – Report and Recommendations of the Environmental Protection Authority*, Bulletin 836, Perth, Western Australia, Environmental Protection Authority

EPA, Environmental Protection Authority (1998) *Industrial Infrastructure and Harbour Development, Jervoise Bay – Report and Recommendations of the Environmental Protection Authority*, Bulletin 908, Perth, Western Australia, Environmental Protection Authority

Gibson, R (1993) 'Environmental assessment design: Lessons from the Canadian experience', *The Environmental Professional*, vol 15, pp12–24

Government Gazette (2002) *Environmental Impact Assessment (Part IV Division 1) Administrative Procedures 2002*, Government Gazette, Western Australia, No. 26, 8 February 2002, pp561–580, available at www.epa.wa.gov.au/docs/1139_EIA_ Admin.pdf

Halpern Glick Maunsell (1996) *Breakwater Extension: Northern Harbour, Jervoise Bay – Consultative Environmental Review*, Perth, Western Australia, Prepared for the Department of Commerce and Trade

Halpern Glick Maunsell (1997) *Industrial Infrastructure and Harbour Development Jervoise Bay – Public Environmental Review*, Perth, Western Australia, Prepared for the Department of Commerce and Trade in association with LandCorp and Main Roads WA

Halpern Glick Maunsell (1998) *Investigation of Water Quality in the Jervoise Bay Northern Harbour: December 1997 – March 1998*, Perth, Western Australia, Report E4443A(2) to Department of Commerce and Trade

Henderson, L (1987) 'Difficulties in impact prediction auditing', *EIA Worldletter* vol May/June, pp9–12

Holling, C (ed) (1978) *Adaptive Environmental Assessment and Management*, Chichester, UK, John Wiley

Hui, S (2000) 'Environmental Monitoring and Audit: Past, Present, Future', presented at *Back to the Future: Where will Impact Assessment be in 10 Years and How Do We Get There? 20th Annual Meeting of the International Association for Impact Assessment*, 19–23 June, Hong Kong

Jenkins B, (1993) 'Viewpoints on the Precautionary Principle: The Precautionary Principle as an Information and Environmental Management Strategy', in Institute of Environmental Studies, *The Precautionary Principle: A New Approach to Environmental Management Conference Papers*, Conference 20–21 September 1993, University of New South Wales, Sydney, Institute of Environmental Studies

Luecht, D, Adams-Walden, L, Bair, R and Siebert, D (1989) 'Statistical evaluation of predicted and actual impacts of construction grants projects in three river basins of United States Region 5', *The Environmental Professional*, vol 7, pp160–170

Morrison-Saunders, A (1997) *The Influence of EIA on Environmental Management in Western Australia*, PhD thesis, Murdoch University, Western Australia

Morrison-Saunders, A (1998) 'The Effect of Public Pressure During Environmental Impact Assessment on Environmental Management Outcomes', presented at *Sustainability and the Role of Impact Assessment in the Global Economy*, 18th Annual Meeting of the International Association for Impact Assessment, 19–24 April 1998, Christchurch, New Zealand

Morrison-Saunders, A and Bailey, J (1999) 'Exploring the EIA/environmental management relationship', *Environmental Management*, vol 24, pp281–295

Morrison-Saunders, A and Bailey, J (2000a) 'Transparency in EIA decision-making: Recent developments in Western Australia', *Impact Assessment and Project Appraisal*, vol 18, pp260–270

Morrison-Saunders, A and Bailey, J (2000b) 'Exploring the EIA/Environmental Management Relationship: Follow-up for Performance Evaluation', presented at *Back to the Future: Where will Impact Assessment be in 10 Years and How Do We Get There? 20th Annual Meeting of the International Association for Impact Assessment*, 19–23 June 2000, Hong Kong, Hull, Quebec, Environment Canada

Morrison-Saunders, A, Baker, J and Arts, J (2003) 'Lessons from practice: Towards successful follow-up', *Impact Assessment and Project Appraisal*, vol 21, pp43–56

Ortolano, L and Shepherd, A (1995) 'Environmental impact assessment: Challenges and opportunities', *Impact Assessment*, vol 13, pp 3–30

Parsons Brickerhoff (2003) *Jervoise Bay Recovery Bores, Monitoring Review No. 6, August to November 2002*, Perth, Western Australia, Report to Department of Industry and Technology

Sadler, B (1996) *International Study of the Effectiveness of Environmental Assessment, Final Report, Environmental Assessment in a Changing World: Evaluating Practice to Improve Performance*, Canadian Environmental Assessment Agency and the International Association for Impact Assessment, Minister of Supply and Services, Canada

Wood, C, Dipper, B and Jones, C (2000) 'Auditing the assessment of the environmental impacts of planning projects', *Journal of Environmental Planning and Management*, vol 43, pp 23–47

8

The Independent Environmental Watchdog: A Canadian Experiment in EIA Follow-up

William A. Ross

Introduction

There is a real danger in Environmental Impact Assessment (EIA) that involvement of the public is one of informing rather than truly engaging in public participation. This can continue into the follow-up stages. As noted in Chapter 3, the minimum position should be one of reporting and informing stakeholders of EIA follow-up outcomes. This minimum position is not sufficient. There is a well-established social impact assessment literature, including best practice principles (Vanclay, 2003), which advocate a fully participative involvement of the public in all aspects of EIA planning, investigation, decision-making and follow-up.

This chapter presents a case study of a major mining project in Canada in which the public played an intrinsic and central role in the EIA follow-up programme. It highlights the strengths and weaknesses of the programme in which EIA follow-up was carried out by a body independent of both the proponent and government, thereby allowing the performance of both parties to be evaluated and for these stakeholder groups to be held accountable for their actions. This is an example of third party EIA follow-up (Chapter 1).

The Ekati Diamond Mine is Canada's first diamond mine. It went through a high level of environmental assessment and one of the conditions of approval recommended was the creation of an independent watchdog. The Environmental Agreement for the mine, signed by the proponent BHP Billiton Diamonds Inc. (BHPB), the Canadian federal Government and the Government of the Northwest Territories (GNWT), required the creation of the *Independent Environmental Monitoring Agency* (henceforth the Agency) to oversee both the project and the project's government regulators. This approach to follow-up is an innovative Canadian experiment in monitoring and management for a major northern project. The Agency reports to the public and, especially, to the four aboriginal communities most directly affected by the mine. Other interesting approaches to follow-up for the mine have also been used. One reported on here is involvement by the affected communities.

This chapter reports on the follow-up programme for the mine and the involvement of the affected communities in monitoring and specifically on the mandate and operation of the Agency, created in 1997. It briefly describes the mine, the EIA process used to review the mine, the follow-up requirements required as a result of the review, the environmental concerns associated with the mine and, especially, the Agency. Some emphasis is placed on how the follow-up programmes have been able to manage the environmental impacts, including the involvement of the affected communities in monitoring and management for the mine. It also describes the successes and failures of that Agency as judged by the author, a member of the Agency since its inception. The overall effectiveness of the follow-up for the mine is also evaluated.

Ekati Mine

The Ekati Mine produces gem quality diamonds and is located in Canada's North, on the barren lands near Lac de Gras about 300km northeast of Yellowknife, Northwest Territories and close to Nunavut Territory (Figure 8.1). Construction of the mine commenced in 1996 and production started in October 1998.

The mine involves extraction of kimberlite, the ore containing the diamonds, from 'pipes', usually found under lakes. The kimberlite is processed on site and the diamonds are sent through Yellowknife to market. In order to get at the kimberlite ore, which is done primarily by surface mining techniques, the lakes must be drained, or 'dewatered'. Explosives are used to blast the surrounding rock, which is sent to waste rock piles, while the kimberlite is sent to the processing plant. Capacity of the processing plant is now 9000 tonnes per day, which will be increased to 18,000 tonnes per day in a few years. The processed kimberlite is sent to a large tailings pond where it is allowed to settle onto the bottom and to become encased in permafrost (permanently frozen ground). It is possible that the tailings will be revegetated with local plant species (less expensive and environmentally preferred if this option proves feasible), although the currently approved abandonment and reclamation plan calls for covering the tailings with rock.

There is an on-site work camp, which accommodates approximately 650 persons. Thus, there are impacts of the mining, of the processing and of the largest 'hotel' in the Northwest Territories. Planes fly to and from the site from Yellowknife every day (weather permitting) and there is road access during the winter (over the ice on the 'winter road') for a few months each year.

Figure 8.1 *Location of the Ekati Diamond Mine*

EIA process for the Ekati Mine

The Ekati Diamond Mine was subject to a full panel review (the highest level of assessment under the Canadian environmental impact assessment process; Box 8.1) carried out from 1994 to 1996. The Environmental Assessment panel held scoping meetings in early 1995 in eight NWT communities and received over 50 written submissions and heard from approximately 125 presenters at that stage of the process. It then issued the final guidelines for the Environmental Impact Statement (EIS).

Box 8.1 EIA Classes in Canada

There are three EIA classes used in Canada:

- screening – assessed relatively quickly (~6000 annually)
- comprehensive study – projects that have potential for greater environmental impacts (~20 annually)
- review panel – more major project impacts; review by an independent panel (a few annually).

Source: Canadian Environmental Assessment Act

When the EIS had been accepted, the panel held 18 days of project review public hearings in nine different communities in early 1996. The panel received over 75 written submissions and heard approximately 260 presentations.

Approval also required hearings in Yellowknife before the Northwest Territories Water Board. The panel made recommendations to the Government of Canada and the Water Board determined conditions of the water licence issued to BHPB. The Environmental Assessment panel (MacLachlan et al, 1996, p 1) concluded that:

> The environmental effects of the Project are largely predictable and mitigable. Effects not predicted can be detected by monitoring and can be addressed by the Proponent's proposed environmental management plans and adaptive management strategy.

At the end of the process, the project was approved subject to a number of conditions (MacLachlan et al, 1996).

The main people affected by the project were determined to be aboriginal groups from the surrounding regions: the Kitikmeot Inuit Association (based in Kugluktuk on the Arctic Ocean); the Dogrib Treaty 11 Council (based around Behchoko, also known as Rae-Edzo, north of Yellowknife); Akaitcho Treaty 8 (based in Lutsel k'e to the east of Yellowknife and in Yellowknife itself); and the North Slave Metis Alliance (based in Yellowknife). These aboriginal groups traditionally used the area where the mine is now located. They are also based in the communities closest to the mine. In the Northwest Territories, and especially in neighbouring Nunavut (which includes Kugluktuk), aboriginal people are a large proportion of the population (in Nunavut, a majority). These groups have special status in the environmental management of the mine.

BHPB's main means of managing environmental impacts was 'adaptive environmental management' (MacLachlan et al, 1996), in effect, to monitor results, evaluate them and manage any unacceptable results to make them acceptable. This approach made it all the more important to have an effective monitoring and management programme in place for the mine.

Follow-up requirements for the Ekati Mine

Because there are relatively few panel reviews and because these reviews are primarily for projects likely to have major environmental impacts, there is no 'standard' requirement for follow-up for such projects. Specialized attention is given to them by the environmental assessment panel and subsequently by the regulators, and normally there is a substantial follow-up requirement imposed as a condition of approval. Details of the follow-up programme will follow from the environmental review. More information on follow-up studies under the Canadian Environmental Assessment Act is available from CEAA (2002).

There are several authorizations for the Ekati Mine. The important ones for the purpose of follow-up requirements are the class A water licence (for Panda, Koala, Koala North, Misery and Fox pipes), the authorization for works or undertakings affecting fish habitat, the class A water licence for the Sable Pidgeon and Beartooth pipes, and the Sable and Pidgeon land use permits. All these documents are available from the Agency (IEMA, 2002d). Most importantly for the purposes of this chapter, the approval was subject to the conditions of an Environmental Agreement signed by the proponent, the Government of the Northwest Territories and the Government of Canada (IEMA, 2002e).

Other monitoring and management requirements were attached to the approval as well. The approval by the Northwest Territories Water Board (since replaced by the Mackenzie Valley Land and Water Board) required water quality monitoring. The approval under the Fisheries Act (dewatering of the lakes) required fish studies. Approval by the Ministry of Renewable Resources of the Northwest Territories required wildlife monitoring, although this requirement and the monitoring of aquatic effects is handled mainly through the Environmental Agreement. BHPB also must provide and constantly update its operating environmental management plan (consisting of air quality management plans; materials management plans, including a contingency plan for on-site and winter road spills; wildlife management plans, including caribou management, grizzly bear management and the effects of esker disturbance on wildlife; traffic management plans; aquatic life management plans; waste management plan; quarry management plans; and environmental monitoring programmes). BHPB also has bilateral (socio-economic) impact benefit agreements with each of the four aboriginal groups. These are based on the principle that the project causes impacts on the communities and so the company also provides some compensating benefits as developed in consultation with the individual communities. The environmental assessment panel recommended 'that all parties set the timely negotiation, conclusion and implementation of Impact and Benefits Agreements as a priority' (MacLachlan et al, 1996, p 3). The content of the impact benefit agreements is confidential and the agreements are outside the mandate of the Agency and of the Environmental Agreement. These monitoring requirements, except for those imposed through the Environmental Agreement, are fairly conventional;

they are of the type that would normally be imposed on any large development project in Canada.

The proponent has made the following observation about its monitoring programmes (BHPB, 2002a, p 87):

> *The main objective of the Aquatic Effects Monitoring Program (AEMP) is to identify any effects that the EKATI™ Mine is having on the surrounding aquatic environment. Results are incorporated into BHP's overall Environmental Management Plan such that actions can be taken to minimize any effects from mine operations.*

This link between the monitoring programme and environmental management at the mine is consistent with the adaptive environmental management approach taken by BHPB (Box 8.2).

BHPB recently received approval for an expansion of the project. It obtained authority to mine three other pipes not previously approved. The proposal went before the Mackenzie Valley Land and Water Board, which held hearings at which it sought input regarding conditions of approval, such as monitoring programme details. The Agency participated actively in this review.

Box 8.2 Follow-up Requirements for the Ekati Mine

Source: BHPB, 2001

Wildlife effects monitoring

- distribution, behaviour and activity patterns of wildlife are observed
- study area of 1600km²
- caribou, wolves, grizzly bears, wolverines, upland birds, loons, raptors, and wildlife habitat
- continually refined by annual workshops to improve the programme.

Aquatic effects monitoring

1. 'Surveillance Network Programme':
   - required by water licence
   - ~20 active stations
   - compliance monitoring – to ensure compliance with regulations
   - monitored parameters vary – usually include pH, total suspended solids, metals scan
   - water licence regulations cover ammonia, aluminium, arsenic, copper, nickel, total suspended solids, pH, BOD5, and oil and grease
   - frequency varies from weekly (during open water) to ~160 samples annually.
2. Aquatic Effects Monitoring Programme:
   - required by both water licence and Environmental Agreement

- meteorology, hydrology, lake water quality, stream water quality, physical limnology, phytoplankton, zooplankton, lake benthos and stream benthos
- continually refined by annual workshops to improve programme
- before-after-control-impact (BACI) statistical design – analysis of variance:
  i   before and after project (compare base-line and after project start)
  ii   control is a monitoring site far from the mine so no effect is expected
  iii impact is a site that could be affected by the mine.
3 Special Effects Monitoring Programmes:
  - Panda Diversion Channel:
    i   required by Fisheries authorization (channel was constructed to provide fish habitat)
    ii   evaluate predictions made concerning the effectiveness of the channel
    iii fish studies (mainly Arctic grayling)
    iv   fish habitat studies.
  - Kodiak Lake:
    i   identify nutrient-related effects on the aquatic environment of Kodiak Lake
    ii   assess the recovery of the lake from the input of nutrients
    iii water quality, phytoplankton and zooplankton biomass, and dissolved oxygen.
4 Fish Out Studies:
  - required by Fisheries authorization
  - catch all fish when draining lakes
  - confirm predictions of fish impacts.
5 Meteorology:
  - automated weather stations (two)
  - since 1993 (base-line plus post project)
  - average annual temperature −7.3 to −8.5°C
  - evaporation pan to measure evapotranspiration
  - snow surveys
  - wind surveys being done to explore use of wind power.
6 Hydrology:
  - Four stream hydrology stations plus two control stations (continuously operated).

Air quality monitoring

- mass balance emission calculations (NO_x, SO_2, greenhouse gases)
- total suspended particulate sampling:
  i   two high volume air samplers
  ii   operate continuously for 24 hours every six days
  iii 23 measurements at each station May to September.

Management of environmental impacts

The range of environmental issues associated with the mine include wildlife impacts, aquatic effects, impacts associated with mine waste and cumulative effects (IEMA 2001, 2002a). MacLachlan et al (1996) observed 'potential effects on wildlife, in particular caribou, and water were the most important environmental issues in this review'.

The wildlife impacts are dominantly concerns for impacts on caribou, as the Bathurst caribou herd is the largest herd in Canada (population about 300,000) and thousands to tens of thousands of caribou migrate through the mine lease area twice annually. The main concern is that the mine will disrupt caribou during their migrations. Caribou are of great importance for aboriginal people. Bears, wolves, wolverines, birds, loons and raptors are also species of concern for which monitoring and management is carried out.

Aquatic effects (Dillon, 2000; Rescan, 2000a, b) are created when lakes are drained or bypass channels are created. Monitoring requirements have been created by various legal instruments including the water licence, the Environmental Agreement and the Fisheries authorization (IEMA, 2002b). Both the dewatering of lakes and the creation of new channels must be carried out in such a way as to create 'no net loss of fisheries habitat', in accordance with the requirements of the Canadian Fisheries Act. There have been special studies carried out in association with deposition of nutrients into Kodiak Lake, the lake adjacent to the dormitory and processing plant and to determine the effectiveness of the Panda diversion channel for fish habitat (Rescan, 2000a). The addition of nutrients from treated sewage, from dewatering the adjacent Panda Lake and from silt loading from the Panda diversion channel, resulted in a change in the trophic status of Kodiak Lake from unproductive to moderately productive. Associated changes in dissolved oxygen under winter ice created potential problems for fish. Indeed, the fisheries expert in the Agency was looking at the measured results for dissolved oxygen under ice in Kodiak Lake and noticed that they were dropping quite rapidly. He pointed this out to BHPB. Adaptive environmental management was applied and changes were made to protect the fish. This was one of the early examples of a possible problem being avoided by careful monitoring (collection of dissolved oxygen data), evaluation programmes (assessment of what it means – dropping values) and management programmes (sewage diversion from Kodiak Lake to the tailings pond, aeration of Kodiak Lake).

One of the crucial lessons to be learned from this impact is the importance of monitoring an early warning indicator (dissolved oxygen in the water column, rather than finding dead fish in the lake). Another lesson found for this impact is the importance of watching not just the level of a monitored parameter, but also its trend (the oxygen levels were still satisfactory when observed, but the rapid decline indicated that anoxic water would soon be dominant and fish deaths would result in the absence of corrective action).

Impacts associated with the mine waste include the runoff from the waste rock pile. The rock could be acid generating (acid mine drainage), in which case acidic runoff may need active management. This possibility is being investigated; some monitoring results suggest that this was a real danger (a few seeps from the rock pile have low pH and high sulphate levels). This was a concern for a year or two, but no longer seems to be serious. Indeed, the Agency (IEMA, 2002a) concluded that 'BHPB's technical consultant has developed a robust approach to identifying and analysing the [acid drainage] problems that have arisen'. Again, water quality monitoring of 'seeps' from the Panda waste rock pile provided the indication of a possible problem. This led to a revised (much more intensive) monitoring programme to understand better what was happening and what should be done about it. These more detailed studies combined with three workshops involving stakeholders led to improved understanding of waste rock chemistry and better options for managing different types of waste rock. This understanding is proving useful for waste rock piles associated with other pits where rock geochemistry is different. Examples of management actions include the choice of where to place different rock types on the rock pile and monitoring to ensure rapid permafrost penetration into the rock piles so that any water entering the rock pile will freeze permanently.

There are still minor concerns about the possible toxicity of the kimberlite tailings on fish. Preliminary studies suggest this may not be a problem, but studies continue. One of the interesting options to limiting the size of the tailings pond is to use the kimberlite tailings to fill in the mined-out pits. This will only be possible if the tailings are not toxic to aquatic life. Currently, studies are being conducted comparing the growth of benthic invertebrates on a substrate of kimberlite tailings with the growth on a natural lake bottom. If the growth on a kimberlite substrate is successful, the option of putting it into the pits before reclaiming the lakes will look more promising.

Cumulative impacts, the impacts of the Ekati Mine in combination with the impacts of other human activities in the region, are another concern. While the region is certainly undeveloped compared to most industrial areas, the aboriginal people have a strong desire to protect the environment and wish it to remain as a high-quality refuge from industrial pollution. There are several other activities that could contribute to cumulative impacts on wildlife or aquatic effects. These include exploration for diamonds (carried out by BHPB as well as by several other companies), the development of the recently approved Diavik Mine approximately 30km to the southeast of the Ekati Mine, other diamond mines currently being planned, expansion of the Ekati Mine by the addition of three new kimberlite pipes (recently applied for), the winter road used to transport equipment to several mines in the area, and the possible construction of an all-weather road to service more mining development.

Indeed, the only 'significant adverse effect' noted by the Agency was a cumulative effect, the effect of the Ekati Mine, the Diavik Mine and a camp operated for the winter road on the local wolverine population (IEMA, 2001). In 2001, BHPB noted that: 'since January 1998, there have been 16 wolverines relocated or destroyed in association with mining activities in the Lac de

Gras area' (BHPB, 2002b). The Agency noted that 'the repeated relocation or destruction of wolverines in the Lac de Gras area, relative to poor waste management practices by a number of operators in 1998–2001, indeed represents a significant adverse cumulative effect on the local population of wolverines'. The Agency also observed that 'improved waste management practices by BHPB in 2002 have decreased its contribution to the cumulative effect on wolverines' (IEMA, 2002c).

It should be noted that the wolverine is also the symbol of the Agency (Figure 8.2). A wolverine is a predator that becomes very aggressive when challenged. It has sharp teeth. The Agency Chair, Red Pederson, has indicated that the best thing to do with sharp teeth is to smile with them, thus showing others how sharp they are, while remaining friendly.

Figure 8.2 *Wolverine Symbol of the Independent Environmental Monitoring Agency*

Effectiveness of environmental management at the Ekati Mine

In its annual report of 2000, the Agency made the following observation about the effectiveness of BHPB's environmental management (IEMA, 2000):

> *[BHPB's] environmental management and compliance has, to date, been good and improving. [BHPB], the regulatory authorities, the Aboriginal organizations and the Agency contribute to the ongoing improvement of the environmental management at [Ekati]. The company has made efforts to comply with the terms of its authorizations, as is evident from the available inspection reports. Overall [BHPB] has responded well to facing the challenges of being the first operating diamond mine in the North.*

It is my view that the intervening years have not changed this evaluation. The significant adverse effect on wolverines has occurred, but, as noted above,

BHPB has responded well to that problem. Other than the wolverine impact, there have been no identified significant adverse impacts to date. There will likely be other impacts discovered in the future, but the company is making efforts to avoid them, as are others.

Independent Environmental Monitoring Agency

The Environmental Agreement, among other things, established the Agency as a watchdog for environmental management for the Ekati Mine. The Agency is to watch over both the mine operator, BHPB, and the regulators, the various agencies of the Government of Canada and the Government of the Northwest Territories. It is this role as watchdog that makes the Agency unique. There have been many advisory bodies, but the Agency has the mandated responsibility to recommend action by BHPB and by the regulators to improve environmental management at the mine. These recommendations must be responded to publicly.

The Environmental Agreement also obliges BHPB to report annually on environmental programmes and every three years to prepare an environmental impact report. The annual report must 'include the results of BHPB's ongoing compliance with this Agreement and applicable legislation, instruments and agreements for the preceding Reporting Year and providing the Minister, the GNWT, the Agency and the Aboriginal Peoples with all supporting information and data from the environmental monitoring'. The three-year environmental impact report must present the longer term effects of the project, the results of environmental monitoring programmes and the actual performance of the project in comparison to the results predicted in the EIS and to evaluate how BHPB's adaptive environmental management has performed. In its environmental management of the mine, BHPB is also required to give full consideration to the traditional knowledge of aboriginal people; a responsibility the Agency is required to 'review, report, or make recommendations on'. More information on community involvement aspects appears in the following section.

The full text of the Environmental Agreement is available on the Agency web site: www.monitoringagency.net (IEMA, 2002d). There are seven members to whom the Agency is responsible: BHPB; the Government of Canada; the Government of the Northwest Territories; and the four aboriginal groups in the region – the Kitikmeot Inuit Association, the Dogrib Treaty 11 Council, Akaitcho Treaty 8, and the North Slave Metis Alliance. These seven members comprise the Society. There are seven Agency Board members appointed by these seven members. Three are jointly appointed by BHPB and the two governments, while the aboriginal groups each appoint one member. While Agency Board members may be so appointed, we are not representatives of those who appoint us. We all have the same mandate, the mandate spelled out in the Environmental Agreement. The background of the Agency Board members is briefly outlined in Box 8.3.

Box 8.3 Composition of the Independent Environmental Monitoring Agency

The Agency Board members and the member(s) who appointed them are:

- a retired senior politician from the Government of the Northwest Territories (Kitikmeot Inuit Association)
- a retired fisheries consultant with extensive Northern experience (BHPB and Governments)
- a university professor specializing in wildlife biology (BHPB and Governments)
- an environmental consultant with impact assessment experience, mostly working for aboriginal consultants (Dogrib Treaty 11 Council)
- a university professor specializing in environmental impact assessment (BHPB and Governments)
- the vice president of the North Slave Metis Alliance, who is also the chair of a similar Agency recently put in place for the Diavik Mine (North Slave Metis Alliance)
- a consultant with extensive Canadian Arctic experience (Akaitcho Treaty 8).

The Board is an active one in that a good deal of the work of the Agency is carried out by Board members, although we are ably assisted by two members of staff (a manager and an environmental analyst) who run the office in Yellowknife and carry out much of our analysis and day-to-day work. The Agency operates with an annual budget of approximately CAN$500,000 provided by BHPB, in accordance with the Environmental Agreement. The tasks of the Agency, as specified in the Environmental Agreement are outlined in Box 8.4.

Box 8.4 Tasks of the Independent Environmental Monitoring Agency

The tasks of the Agency include:

1. reviewing and commenting on monitoring and management plans and the results of these activities
2. monitoring and encouraging the integration of traditional knowledge of the nearby aboriginal peoples into the mine's environmental plans
3. participating in regulatory processes directly related to environmental matters involving the Ekati Mine, its impacts and its cumulative effects
4. bringing concerns of the aboriginal peoples and the general public to the Ekati Diamond Mine operators and to government
5. keeping the aboriginal peoples and the public informed about Agency activities and findings
6. writing an annual report with recommendations that require the response of BHP and governments.

In order to carry out these tasks, the Agency engages in the activities outlined in Box 8.5. It is worth explaining some of these further. Two tasks to which Board members dedicate the bulk of their time are reviewing documents (BHPB annual reports, applications for mine expansions, annual monitoring reports, regulatory reports and the like) and reviewing and commenting on regulatory approvals. The latter is illustrated by the application for a new licence to mine three new kimberlite pipes which were not included in the original approval and went through a separate two-year approval process. An EIS was prepared for the Mackenzie Valley Environmental Impact Review Board, which held hearings and made recommendations. The Agency reviewed the EIS, offered advice to the Review Board and participated in the hearings. While this was a much more modest EIA review process than was used for the original mine application, it was still very demanding of Agency, regulator and industry time. The final approvals were carried out by the Mackenzie Valley Land and Water Board, which again solicited input from the Agency and held a short hearing in which we participated fully.

Box 8.5 Activities of the Independent Environmental Monitoring Agency

In order to meet its mandate, the Agency:

- monitors and reviews environmental management plans and reports by BHBP and government agencies
- analyses issues to promote the identification, evaluation and management of environmental impacts
- reviews the activities of regulatory agencies and their interactions with BHBP
- monitors the progress of traditional knowledge studies funded by BHP and conducted by aboriginal organizations
- facilitates interaction between BHP and aboriginal organizations to integrate traditional knowledge into BHP's management plan
- participates in technical workshops involving environmental management at the Ekati Mine
- meets and corresponds regularly with BHBP and regulators about environmental issues at Ekati
- reviews and comments on regulatory approvals sought by BHBP that relate to environmental matters
- reports to aboriginal organizations and the public at large
- maintains a publicly accessible library of all materials regarding environmental management of the Ekati Mine
- publishes newsletters, a web site, a brochure and annual reports
- holds an annual general meeting for members of the Agency.

Community involvement in follow-up studies

It was noted previously that BHPB had a formal requirement under the Environmental Agreement to include consideration of traditional knowledge in its mine environmental management. It has done so in a variety of ways.

BHPB strives to incorporate traditional knowledge into its environmental programmes. In an effort to do so, representatives from the communities have visited the mine site to see first-hand the success of our mitigation measures. During their visit we encourage them to share with us their understanding of the land and its wildlife. Elders from various communities are flown up to site, housed in staff accommodations, and accompany environmental staff during their monitoring duties. In 2001, for example, visitors from Kugluktuk, Lutsel k'e, North Slave Metis Alliance, Treaty 11, and the Yellowknives Dene came to site to observe the caribou migration, provide input on environmental management programmes and to become familiar with the site (BHPB, 2002b, p17).

One of the wildlife monitoring requirements agreed to is to do snow track surveys (a common means of counting animals in the winter) of wolverine regularly. The question of who is best qualified to do such surveys was asked and the answer was clear. Allen Niptanatiak of Kugluktuk, several hundred kilometres north of the mine, is known as the best wolverine trapper in the area. He was hired by BHPB to do the surveys, thus obtaining the best qualified person for this monitoring responsibility, obtaining direct input from an aboriginal person based on traditional knowledge and hiring someone from one of the directly affected communities; truly a win–win choice. In commuting from his home to the mine site, Mr Niptanatiak often travels by snowmobile over the barren lands with neither a global positioning device nor maps to guide him. Since this happens in the winter (one can only do snow track surveys when there is snow on the ground), the temperature is distinctly inhospitable (often dropping below −30°C at night). The results of his surveys are provided to the environmental consultants for incorporation into BHPB's wildlife effects monitoring programme report.

One of the most successful means of obtaining traditional knowledge from affected aboriginal groups has been bringing elders to the mine site and seeking their advice on matters of environmental concern. Because the caribou are the ecosystem component most valued by northern aboriginal people, much of their input relates to caribou. For example, BHPB is now investigating means of revegetating its tailings pond. According to BHPB (2001, p112):

> The Dogrib have indicated that they would like [BHPB] to discourage caribou from using the revegetated cells and based on their report appear to have some ideas about plants that the caribou do not like to eat. This would appear to be an excellent opportunity for collaboration.

Aboriginal elders have also made other caribou observations when they have visited the mine site. They have expressed concerns about airborne dust (from roads, blasting and the tailings pond) covering vegetation used for food by caribou. As a result of this input, members of the Agency and government regulators have also raised the same question at workshops to improve the monitoring programmes. Such studies of vegetation are now being undertaken by BHPB.

Elders who visit the site during caribou migration have also been taken along haul roads leading to kimberlite pipes being mined at some distance from the main camp. Here the concern is how much the haul road influences caribou migration and hence, the design of future haul roads can be adjusted depending on what is found. The elders, with their trained eyes, are far better able to detect different behaviour by caribou than are road design engineers. While there, elders are able to see many different aspects of caribou ecology. In the summer of 2001, wolves were watched herding caribou into 'boulder fields' (land covered with large boulders where the caribou could not run as fast and where they would be easier prey for the wolves). One caribou had apparently broken its leg and was being ignored by the wolves temporarily. An elder reported the lame caribou as being 'in nature's freezer', as it would remain there, unable to escape, until the wolves wanted it (A. Armstrong, 2001, Environmental Specialist, BHPB Diamonds, Ekati Mine, personal communication).

In addition, Gerry Atatahak, on behalf of the Kugluktuk Agoniatit Association and the Kitikmeot Inuit Association, has carried out much of the work on a BHPB-funded traditional knowledge study that has resulted in a traditional knowledge based GIS system designed for use in preliminary land-use screening (BHPB, 2001). BHPB also is obliged to visit the communities to explain what it is doing and what it has found in its annual report. In this way, it provides feedback on environmental performance.

Evaluation of the Agency

In preparing this chapter, I carried out my own personal evaluation of the successes and failures of the Agency. This evaluation has been shaped in part by an independent evaluation. The Agency contracted with an independent consulting firm, the Macleod Institute, to interview Society members, regulators and other stakeholders, and to conduct an evaluation of the Agency's performance to date. The Macleod Institute (2000) identified the Agency's strengths and weaknesses and made recommendations for improvement. What follows is my assessment combined with their evaluation.

Agency strengths

The strengths of the Agency have been:

1   Improvements to monitoring programmes. The monitoring programmes originally proposed by BHPB were, in the Agency's view, very poor. We

worked immediately with BHPB and its consultants to improve them modestly and encouraged better consultation to make future monitoring programmes better yet. Following the implementation of these annual workshops (see next point), we believe the monitoring programmes are now very good.

2   Annual workshops to improve the monitoring programmes conducted by BHPB involving all stakeholders (BHPB and its consultants, the Agency, government regulators, aboriginal people, interested environmental groups and other industry representatives).

3   Aboriginal liaison to promote traditional knowledge work. We have worked actively with the four aboriginal members and with BHPB to further the development and use of traditional knowledge. With the cooperation and encouragement of all of our members, we facilitated a workshop involving all four aboriginal groups and BHPB.

4   Identification and management of impacts. Agency Board members have identified potential problems and immediately urged BHPB to adjust its management in response to the observed results. We have also made suggestions to BHPB and to government agencies concerning good environmental management practices.

5   Reporting to aboriginal members. We have held meetings in aboriginal communities and have frequently met with these aboriginal groups at our regular board meetings.

6   'The Agency's technical (scientific) contributions are well accepted. A number of Society members expressed a real feeling of comfort that the Agency is ensuring that BHPB's licence conditions are being met' (Macleod Institute, 2000).

7   'Establishing facilities such as a public access library, frequent newsletters and a website' (Macleod Institute, 2000).

Agency weaknesses

The weaknesses of the Agency have been:

1   Inadequate reporting to aboriginal members. In spite of our efforts, we have not generally succeeded in this challenging task. (Note that I believe this is both a strength and a weakness of the Agency's performance).

2   Poor working relationships with BHPB and government agencies. In performing our watchdog role, I believe we have unduly sacrificed the ability to work more closely with BHPB and the government agencies. At the time of this writing, I believe these problems have been significantly reduced. In the beginning, these were more serious.

3   Internal difficulties in reaching decisions we agree on.

One suggestion that the Agency has been seen as being effective by the aboriginal people is illustrated in Box 8.6, which contains a quote from Joe Rabesca, the Grand Chief of the Dogrib (the Dogrib are composed of several distinct communities; the grand chief is an elected chief who represents all the communities). The statement was made at the 1999 annual general meeting of the Society responsible for the Independent Environmental Monitoring Agency.

Box 8.6 Aboriginal Perspective on Follow-up at the Ekati Mine

Joe Rabesca (Grand Chief Dogrib Treaty 11)

This is the kind of work that should have been done a really long time ago. The area between Rae Edzo and Great Bear Lake is my part of the country and mines have historically been bad for us; a complete lack of effort to clean them up. I can see the importance of the work being done and feel BHP working through the Agency is what we all need. There is a lot of uncertainty and that's why we have to work together. If people like the ones in this room can demonstrate that the land will be fine, then we will listen. Diavik did not do this. We must hit these things before the problems happen, but there's no sense talking about it after the fact. Hit it early and plan ahead. We have to keep this land clean. We have one kind of water up there: pure and clean. We want to keep it this way. This is our homeland and I'm not going to move away. I grew up with fish and wildlife and I'm going to keep them around. My kids will have them too. I appreciate what you guys (Directors of the Agency) have done over the past few years and I wanted to give you a pat on the back to say good work and I want you to keep it up. We need to work on these uncertainties. The Dogrib are not against development. A mine gives our people jobs. This mine needs to be a safe and sound place to work. It needs to be a mine that is not polluting the land and water. If we all work together, we can do a lot.

Source: IEMA, 2002f

Another indicator of success is based on recent discussions involving both Agency board members and staff and government regulators. There is increasingly better regulation of the mine based on inputs from the Agency. Conditions of approval recommended by the Agency are being seriously examined and adopted. Recommendations to government regulators in our annual report are agreed with and actions taken. And, there is a general view that an independent watchdog looking over a regulator's shoulder leads to better performance by the regulator.

Similarly, the working relationship with BHPB has improved and the suggestions for improvements in monitoring programmes are being increasingly accepted by both BHPB and the regulators. This acceptance has been coupled with greater tolerance by the Agency and by regulators that expensive monitoring programmes that seem to be providing little information can be either eliminated or, more commonly, cut back.

Perhaps the best indicator of acceptance of the idea of an independent watchdog has been its replication (with some adjustments) for the second diamond mine in Canada, just 30km from the Ekati Mine, (Diavik Diamond Mines, undated). The Diavik Mine also has a similar monitoring agency, the Environmental Management Advisory Board based on an environmental agreement (Environmental Management Advisory Board, undated).

Moreover, the acceptance of using an environmental agreement and a monitoring agency has been so widely accepted in the North that other major projects are likely to use the same tools. Two complications, however, are serious impediments to using such an approach. The first is the need to deal with the cumulative effects (noted previously) of all projects combined. This is complicated if the monitoring agency deals with projects individually, as does (largely) the Agency. The second complication is the duplication of work that would be performed by several different agencies for several different projects.

As a result of the success of agencies and the need for more of them, there has been a recent movement to create a regional monitoring agency to oversee many (preferably all) projects in a region. The current suggestions are to build the regional monitoring agency based on the greater success of the Diavik monitoring agency in working closely with the communities and the greater success of the Independent Environmental Monitoring Agency in its scientific and technical achievements. It is clear that any success the Agency has had has been based on years of developing trust in the community.

References

BHP Billiton (2001) *2000 Environmental Agreement and Water Licence Annual Report*, Yellowknife, Canada, BHP Billiton

BHP Billiton (2002a) *2001 Environmental Agreement and Water Licence Annual Report*, Yellowknife, Canada, BHP Billiton

BHP Billiton (2002b) *EKATI^{TM} Diamond Mine 2001 Wildlife Effects Monitoring Program*, Yellowknife, Canada, Prepared by Golder Associates for BHP Billiton

CEAA, Canadian Environmental Assessment Agency (2002) *Operational Policy Statement: Follow-up Programs under the Canadian Environmental Assessment Act*, available at www.ceaa-acee.gc.ca/0011/0002/followup_e.htm

Dillon Consulting (2000) *Panda Diversion Channel Monitoring Program*, Yellowknife, Canada, Prepared for BHP Diamonds by Dillon Consulting

Environmental Monitoring Advisory Board (undated) *Environmental Monitoring Advisory Board Working With the People, for the Environment*, available at www. emab.ca

IEMA, Independent Environmental Monitoring Agency (2000) *Annual Report 1999–2000*, Yellowknife, Northwest Territories, Canada, IEMA

IEMA, Independent Environmental Monitoring Agency (2001) *Annual Report 2000–2001*, Yellowknife, Northwest Territories, Canada, IEMA

IEMA, Independent Environmental Monitoring Agency (2002a) *Annual Report 2001–2002*, Yellowknife, Northwest Territories, Canada, IEMA

IEMA, Independent Environmental Monitoring Agency (2002b) *Independent Environmental Monitoring Agency: A Public Watchdog for Environmental Management of the Ekati Diamond Mine™*, available at www.monitoringagency.net/

IEMA, Independent Environmental Monitoring Agency (2002c) *Agency's Response to BHPB's Comments Regarding Agency's 2000–2001 Annual Report*, Letter to BHPB by the Independent Environmental Monitoring Agency, Yellowknife, Northwest Territories, Canada, IEMA

IEMA, Independent Environmental Monitoring Agency (2002d) *Independent Environmental Monitoring Agency: Key Documents*, available at www.monitoringagency. net/website/Key%20Documents/New%20Key%20documents%20index.htm

IEMA, Independent Environmental Monitoring Agency (2002e) *Independent Environmental Monitoring Agency: Environmental Agreement*, available at www. monitoringagency.net/website/key%20documents/Environmental%20Agreement/ New_Environmental%20Agreement_menu.htm

IEMA, Independent Environmental Monitoring Agency (2002f) *Agency Annual General Meeting Minutes, 1999*, available at www.monitoringagency.net/website/ agency%20publications/minutes/Annual%20General%20Meeting%20Link.htm

MacLachlan, L, Kenny-Gilday, C, Kupsch, W and Sloan, J (1996) *NWT Diamonds Project: Report of the Environmental Assessment Panel*, Hull, Canada, Minister of Supply and Services, Canada

Macleod Institute (2000) *Independent Environmental Monitoring Agency Evaluation Report*, Calgary, Macleod Institute,

Rescan (2000a) *2000 Kodiak Lake Sewage Effects Study Technical Report*, Yellowknife, Canada, Prepared for BHP Diamonds by Rescan Environmental Services

Rescan (2000b) *2000 Aquatic Effects Monitoring Program (AEMP) Technical Report*, Yellowknife, Canada, Prepared for BHP Diamonds by Rescan Environmental Services

Vanclay, F (2003) 'International principles for social impact assessment', *Impact Assessment and Project Appraisal*, vol 21, pp5–12

9

Learning by Doing: EIA Follow-Up in Hong Kong

Elvis Au and Simon Hui

Introduction

The Environmental Impact Assessment (EIA) system in Hong Kong is characterized by clear requirements for follow-up operating in a strong legislative framework based on a relatively prescriptive system of checks and balances. It has evolved considerably with several major amendments to procedures, particularly concerning follow-up, having been implemented. In addition to having a rigorously enforced EIA follow-up mechanism overseen by the regulator, recent changes to procedures have enhanced communication of follow-up in an innovative but effective approach via electronic media.

This chapter presents the evolution of the EIA follow-up system in Hong Kong both in terms of the regulations and practice; a product of 'learning by doing'. Practical experiences with the process and content of EIA follow-up have alternated with formalization of those experiences into procedures and regulations.

There are three core elements to the chapter which are addressed in turn:

1 regulatory procedures for EIA in Hong Kong that have been introduced on the basis of experiences from practice
2 process innovations which aim to enhance the involvement of stakeholders in EIA follow-up
3 content innovations with respect to the tools and approaches utilized.

A case study example is provided to illustrate some of these innovations. Recent moves towards follow-up for strategic environmental assessments (SEA) are described. The chapter ends with some key lessons learnt from the Hong Kong experience.

Overview of EIA procedures in Hong Kong

The EIA system in Hong Kong started with an administrative EIA process implemented for major development projects in 1986, and has been mandated through the EIA Ordinance 1998 (Government of Hong Kong, 1997). The development of the EIA system has been described previously by Au and Baldwin (1994), Au (1998, 2000) and Wood and Coppell (1999). A recent account of the system can be found in *The Operation of Environmental Impact Assessment Ordinance* (EPD, 2002). Key aspects of the process are summarized in Box 9.1. Figure 9.1 presents a flowchart of the process and Figure 9.2 provides further detail on the current provisions for public participation in the process (more on this issue will be found later in the chapter).

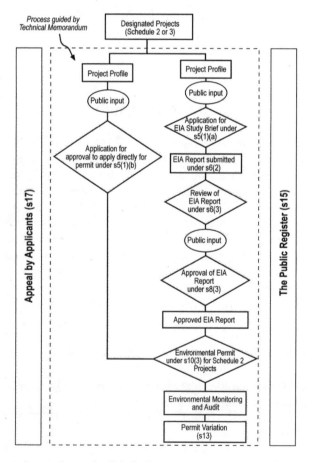

Note: section numbers refer to the EIA Ordinance

Source: EPD, 2002

Figure 9.1 *The Statutory EIA Process in Hong Kong*

Box 9.1 Outline of the Hong Kong EIA Process

Decision-making authority and other stakeholders

It is the responsibility of the proponent (who may be a government department, a private sector developer or a public corporation) to comply with the statutory EIA process and obtain an environmental permit before designated projects listed in Schedule 2 of the EIA Ordinance can proceed. The Ordinance provides for the public and the Advisory Council on the Environment (ACE) the opportunity to be involved at two stages in the EIA process: to comment on a project profile that is prepared by the proponent for the Director of Environmental Protection to issue an EIA study brief, and to comment on the EIA report prepared by the project proponent. The Director of Environmental Protection has the power to:

- issue an EIA Study Brief for projects requiring EIA
- approve or reject a proponent's EIA report
- issue an Environmental Permit which specifies requirements for environmental mitigation and environmental monitoring and audit. Failure to comply with the permit conditions may result in a maximum fine of up to HK$5 million and a maximum of two years' imprisonment for the offender.

The ACE is the Government's principal advisory body on environmental matters. It consists of about 20 members including representatives from industry, government, green groups and academics. The ACE and the public are consulted in relation to Project Profiles and EIA Reports. The Director considers their comments in any subsequent decisions in relation to an application.

Designated projects

Designated projects (i.e. those controlled under the Ordinance) are identified in two schedules. Schedule 2 includes roads and railways, port and marine facilities, waterways and drainage works and other major infrastructure, residential and industrial developments. Such projects must follow the EIA process and also obtain environmental permits before work may begin. Schedule 3 includes mainly engineering feasibility studies of large-scale developments that must also follow the statutory EIA process. Such projects require approval of their EIA reports, but are not required to obtain environmental permits.

Main steps in the process (Figure 9.1)

- Proponents of designated projects prepare a Project Profile which is subject to review by the public and ACE.
- The EPD prepares an EIA Study Brief.
- The proponent prepares an EIA Report, including among other things an Environmental Monitoring and Audit (EM&A) programme.

- The EPD reviews the EIA Report to decide whether it complies with the EIA Study Brief and the Technical Memorandum on the EIA Process. The Technical Memorandum serves as the guide for the Director of the EPD to decide on matters under the Ordinance. It details the procedures to be followed for each step in the EIA process, including the content of each document to be prepared and the guidelines for their review plus the principles, procedures, guidelines, requirements and criteria for the assessment of various environmental factors (e.g. air, noise and water pollution; waste management; ecological impact; fisheries impact; visual and landscape impact and impact on sites of cultural heritage).
- The EIA Report is subject to review by the public and ACE.
- The EPD determines whether the EIA Report should be approved and any conditions which should apply. The proponent can appeal against EPD's decisions to an independent Appeal Board chaired by a person qualified as a District Judge.
- For Schedule 2 projects, the proponent or their contractor applies for an Environmental Permit.
- The Environmental Permit is issued by the EPD. It normally includes a requirement on the submission and implementation of an EM&A Manual outlining the follow-up measures that the Permit Holder is required to implement. It may also include a requirement for the Permit Holder to establish a Project Website for communication of follow-up studies.
- The Permit Holder (i.e. the proponent or the contractor) establishes an Environmental Team (ET) and an Independent Environmental Checker (IEC) for the project.
- During project implementation, the Environmental Team is responsible for ensuring that the Permit Holder complies with follow-up requirements and the IEC is responsible for verifying this. Follow-up results are posted on the Project Website, which is linked to the EIA Ordinance website hosted by EPD (further details on the follow-up system appear later).

Source: EPD, 2002

Need for follow-up

An increased recognition of the need to track EIA study recommendations during project implementation in Hong Kong started in late 1980s. The system of follow-up was initiated as a direct result of the actual application of the EIA process to major development projects such as the US$20,000 million Airport Core Programme projects from 1990 to 1998, which involved ten major individual projects including (Figure 9.3):

- reclaiming a 1248ha airport island
- reclaiming 334ha of land in West Kowloon to support various infrastructure items

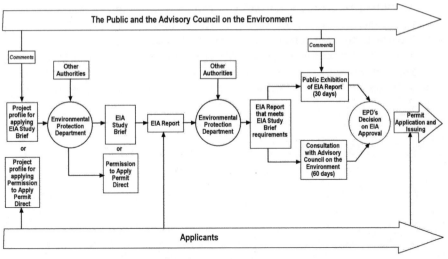

Source: EPD, 2002

Figure 9.2 *Public Participation under the EIA Ordinance*

- a 34km railway from the city to the airport
- a 2160m suspension bridge crossing to Lantau Island carrying both road and rail infrastructure
- a 502m viaduct crossing
- a 820m double-deck concrete–steel composite cable-stayed bridge.

With a tight programme, and because of the sheer scale of the projects involved, the works imposed considerable pressure on the environment. In view of the potentially serious environmental consequences an EM&A system

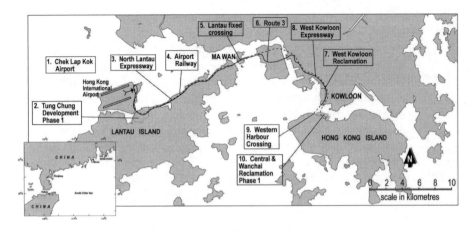

Figure 9.3 *Airport Core Programme Activities*

was developed to ensure environmental objectives would be achieved. The system focused on the early warning of potential problems and a series of action plans to prevent serious problems from happening.

The development of EIA follow-up in Hong Kong is summarized in Box 9.2 (full details appear in Au and Sanvicens, 1995; Au, 1998; Hui, 2000, 2001). It has been characterized as 'learning by doing' and 'trial and error'

Box 9.2 Key Milestones in the History of EIA Follow-up in Hong Kong

1986 The first directive on the environmental review of government projects was issued to apply the EIA process to government projects.

1990 A major environmental monitoring and audit programme was initiated for the Airport Core Programme projects to follow-up three strategic-type environmental assessments and 20 project EIAs.

1992 A government EIA directive was issued with explicit provisions for environmental monitoring and audit requirements for all major public projects and a government circular on the public access to government EIA reports and another government EIA directive on the public access to government EIA reports.

1993 Quarterly summary reports of environmental monitoring and audit results for Airport Core Programme projects were produced and released to the public.

1994 An area-based, proactive follow-up mechanism, titled the Environmental Project Office, was implemented to deal with cumulative environmental impacts from multiple contracts.

1995 Hong Kong EPD completed a review of international practices on EIA follow-up.

1995 The first electronic EIA report on a CD-ROM was produced for a major project and a pilot electronic environmental and monitoring system was tested for some projects.

1998 The Hong Kong EIA Ordinance, its Technical Memorandum on EIA Process and a dedicated website for the Ordinance came into operation, with statutory provisions for environmental permits and EIA follow-up programmes, and with transparent public access to EIA follow-up and management information.

2001 A statutory requirement was introduced for submission and dissemination of electronic environmental monitoring and audit results on the project website.

2002 A statutory requirement was introduced for applying Web cameras for real-time visual monitoring of implementation of some major projects.

Source: various annual reports published by EPD and EIA documents available on the EIA Ordinance website (see EPD, undated(a))

approaches and by pragmatic approaches to practical problems arising from actual implementation of major projects after EIAs were completed. It has been very much driven by the need to avoid and minimize actual environmental problems to the maximum extent possible, by the public aspirations for more effective follow-up mechanisms to protect the community's well being, and by the drive towards greater transparency and accountability.

Initial EIA follow-up phase (1990–1998)

Early experiences with EIA follow-up in Hong Kong are described in Nash (1993), Nash and Deacon (1993), Au and Baldwin (1994) and Sanvicens and Baldwin (1996). In 1992, the EM&A requirements were incorporated into a Government EIA Directive (Planning, Environment and Lands Branch, 1992) and were extended to all major developments in both the public and private sector in Hong Kong. This initial phase was characterized by the adoption of 'learning by doing and trial and error' approaches. There were approximately 100 EM&A programmes for different types of projects in Hong Kong from 1990 to 1998. Many different approaches or practices were tried out during this period: the main ones are discussed later.

There were several reasons why EIA follow-up was initiated in the early 1990s in Hong Kong. Before this, relatively little attention was paid to the actual effects arising from project construction and operation. There was a need to assure and inform the public about what was happening in major projects after the EIA reports were approved and what actions would be taken to follow through the various promises and undertakings made during the EIA study stage. It was recognized that the effectiveness of the Hong Kong EIA system would depend on its ability to provide timely, reliable information for environmentally sound decision-making as well as for protecting the environment. Feedback from the actual implementation of projects after EIAs were completed was considered crucial in checking and enhancing the reliability of information in EIA for decision-making for other similar projects (Au and Baldwin, 1994).

The overall framework of EIA follow-up monitoring and management in Hong Kong currently in use was developed during this initial phase (Au and Sanvicens, 1995; Sanvicens and Au, 1995). The primary purpose of the system was to use various instruments and means to track the implementation of mitigation measures recommended in EIA reports, to follow through the detailed design process, to monitor the actual impacts arising from the implementation of the project, and to provide feedback for improving the EIA process and project planning and development. Follow-up monitoring and management plays an important role in the whole EIA process and project cycle.

In the early applications, the EM&A requirements were identified and defined during the EIA study on an ad-hoc basis. Some projects only had their environmental monitoring and audit requirements introduced into the project just prior to commencement, resulting in some resistance to implementation from both project proponents and contractors. As more experience was gained and the benefits of doing EM&A became obvious, there was an increasing acceptance by all those involved (Au and Sanvicens, 1995).

In the EIAs conducted in the mid-1990s where follow-up was required, a detailed EM&A programme was provided in a separate chapter in the EIA report to facilitate early consensus building by all relevant parties on what needed to be done (Au and Sanvicens, 1995). Through the consolidation of actual experiences, a generic EM&A manual was developed and published (EPD, 1996) to guide the project proponent, the contractors and the professionals involved in preparing and implementing the EM&A programmes. Since mid-1996, a stand-alone EM&A manual has been required for each project in the overall EIA submission package to EPD. As the system was further developed and advanced, quality assurance and impartiality became a prime concern and the IEC system was introduced. This was intended to improve the EM&A programmes for large scale and sensitive projects such as the Route 3 Country Park Section Road Project that linked the North West New Territories with the urban areas (Figure 9.3). Where a number of construction sites were in close proximity and being simultaneously developed in some of the Airport Core Programme projects, an Environmental Project Office (ENPO) was adopted in order to cater for cumulative impacts arising from all the projects (EPD, 1996, 2000).

Also, during this period, EPD staff had been able to learn from and interact with EIA follow-up experts around the world. As part of the contributions to the International Study on the Effectiveness of Environmental Assessment, initiated jointly by the Canadian Environmental Assessment Agency and the International Association for Impact Assessment, the EPD conducted a review of the international practices of EIA follow-up and management (Au and Sanvicens, 1995; Sadler, 1996, pp129 and 135).

Formalization of follow-up through the EIA Ordinance of 1998

In response to the strong public demand for a thorough and effective follow-up system, the *EIA Ordinance* 1998 was enacted. It basically formalized the previous administrative system through various provisions as well as a Technical Memorandum setting out the detailed principles, procedures, guidelines and requirements for various applications, submissions and EIA reports. All statutory EIA reports, all statutory applications and all decisions made by the Director of Environmental Protection under the EIA Ordinance are kept in the Public Register established by the Ordinance. An electronic Public Register (i.e. Internet based) has also been in operation since 1998.

The EIA Ordinance provides the legal framework for assessing the impact on the environment of 'designated projects' (listed in Schedule 2). All construction and operation (or decommissioning, as the case may be) of designated projects requires an environmental permit from the EPD, and proponents must comply with any conditions specified in the permit. Any person who contravenes these requirements commits an offence and is liable to stiff penalties (maximum penalty on first conviction on indictment is a fine of HK$2 million and 6 months' imprisonment; EPD, 2002).

The two main functions of the permit are to ensure that the project will be implemented as assumed in the EIA report and to ensure that the major recommendations in the EIA report will be fully implemented. These two functions are vitally important because when the EIA system fails, it usually happens in the follow-up part. The two most common scenarios are that the project was not implemented according to the assumptions in the EIA report and that promises made in the EIA report were neglected or simply ignored. The legal requirements make these actions (or inactions) an offence in order to ensure that the environmental requirements are met.

Any follow-up requirements are identified in the course of the EIA study in the form of an EM&A programme. Generally speaking, monitoring is normally recommended under the following circumstances:

- where the level of impact identified is very close to a legal standard or criterion
- where the project is located in a sensitive area
- where there is a high degree of uncertainty associated with the assessment methodology used.

Where the need for a follow-up programme is identified, a draft EM&A Manual outlining the proposed programme is provided by the proponent in the EIA report. Such requirements, if approved, will be specified as conditions in the relevant permit. Schedule 4 of the Ordinance addresses matters that may be specified in the environmental permit, and some relevant to EIA follow-up are shown in Box 9.3.

In most cases the carrying out of comprehensive EM&A programmes is only related to those designated projects requiring the conduct of an EIA. Where such need is identified, the proponent will normally prepare a draft EM&A Manual in their EIA report. This should sketch out the objective of the programme; identify what parameters should be monitored, including the monitoring frequencies and locations; and prepare the reporting arrangements and an event action plan. Upon approval of the EIA report, suitable conditions will be specified in the subsequent Environmental Permit requiring the submission of the finalized EM&A Manual and the full implementation of the programme stated in the Manual.

In most permits under the EIA Ordinance that require EM&A programmes, the permit holders are required to engage an Environmental Team (ET) and an Independent Environmental Checker (IEC). Box 9.4 gives an example how this requirement is phrased in practice in a permit condition. Both the ET Leader and the IEC must be environmental professionals having at least seven years of relevant experience. Recently a condition has been introduced that will effectively allow the EPD to demand replacement of the IEC if their performance is found to be less than acceptable.

Box 9.3 Key Provisions under Schedule 4 of the EIA Ordinance for EIA Follow-up

10 Programmes or exercises for monitoring the environmental impact of a designated project or the effectiveness of measures to mitigate its environmental impact, whether such impact may occur within or outside its physical boundary or site, and the review and audit of data and information derived from such programmes or exercises, including specification of:

(a) the parameters or impact to be monitored

(b) the frequency of monitoring, or the procedures, practices, methods or equipment to be used for monitoring, including the maintenance and calibration of such equipment and quality assurance and laboratory accreditation procedures

(c) the standards or criteria to be used for evaluating and auditing monitoring data

(d) plans and procedures for action in response to the results of such monitoring programmes or exercises, including action to intensify or increase monitoring, inspect or investigate revealed or indicated problems, or take remedial measures to address such problems

(e) the nature, format or frequency of the reporting of the results and findings of monitoring or action plans and procedures...

15 The release to the public of reports on monitoring or auditing work or other reports or information in relation to the assessment or carrying out of a designated project.

16 The requirements for carrying out of environmental monitoring by accredited laboratories, or environmental audit by qualified personnel.

17 The requirements of the implementation and completion of mitigation measures to be checked and certified by qualified personnel, and for the submission of certified reports on the status of the implementation of mitigation measures.

Source: Government of Hong Kong, 1997

The Environmental Permit specifies that the IEC must be independent of the ET and the contractor undertaking the project. In a typical project organization, the project proponent will arrange for the contractor to establish the ET while the IEC will be part of their own team of staff or consultants. Experience has shown that this additional feature of the IEC provides a useful checking layer that has helped to prevent any violation of the Ordinance without stretching even thinner the EPD's resource-intensive inspection programme. The IEC also helps to screen submissions under the permit conditions and advises the project proponent on legal and technical environmental requirements concerning design changes during the course of project implementation.

Box 9.4 A Typical Environmental Permit Condition for the Setting Up of an ET and an IEC under the EIA Ordinance

An Environmental Team (ET) shall be established by the Permit Holder no later than one month before the commencement of construction of the Project. The ET shall be headed by an ET Leader. The ET Leader shall be a person who has at least 7 years' experience in EM&A or environmental management. The ET team and the ET Leader shall be responsible for the duties defined in the EM&A Manual submitted and approved under Condition 2.3 of this Permit. The ET Leader shall be responsible for the implementation of the EM&A programme in accordance with the EM&A requirements as contained in the EM&A Manual.

...The ET shall not be in any way an associated body of the IEC for the Project.

An Independent Environmental Checker (IEC) shall be employed by the Permit Holder no later than one month before the commencement of construction of the Project. The IEC shall be a person who has at least 7 years' experience in EM&A or environmental management. The IEC shall be responsible for duties defined in the EM&A Manual submitted and approved under Condition 2.3 of this Permit, and shall audit the overall EM&A programme described in the EIA Report, including the implementation of all environmental mitigation measures, submissions required in the EM&A Manual, and any other submissions required under this Permit. In addition, the IEC shall be responsible for verifying the environmental acceptability of permanent and temporary works, relevant design plans and submissions under this Permit. ...The IEC shall not be in any way an associated body of the Contractor or the Environmental Team for the Project.

Source: various environmental permits available on the EIA Ordinance website (see EPD, undated(a))

While clear regulations are an important prerequisite to establish good EIA follow-up practice (Chapter 1), the process of EIA follow-up and the specific content of follow-up activities and products also need to be given due attention. The next two sections focus on innovations in EIA follow-up processes and their contents that have been put into practice in Hong Kong.

The innovations discussed are based on experience with the actual implementation of more than 100 environmental monitoring and audit programmes for major projects in Hong Kong from 1992 to 2002. A key lesson learned was that the essential steps in post-decision monitoring and management could be a combination of the following elements, depending on the type and scale of the projects and the extent of public or scientific controversies involved:

- inspect and check the implementation of the terms and conditions of project approval
- review or re-assess the environmental implications of any design changes

- monitor the actual effects of the project activities on the environment and the community
- monitor the timing, sequence, location and extent of the actual project activities to anticipate the likely environmental effects
- verify the compliance with regulatory requirements and applicable standards or criteria
- formulate and implement action plans to avoid, reduce or rectify any adverse impacts
- verify the accuracy of the EIA predictions and the effectiveness of the mitigation measures
- provide feedback to project management control to adjust the programming, design or location of the activities or the method of carrying them out
- provide feedback to the EIA process to improve impact prediction and mitigation practices.

Process innovations in EIA follow-up

Various process-based innovations in EIA follow-up (i.e. approaches, tools and techniques) have been developed in Hong Kong. Some of the most important which are addressed here concern:

- management structures for EIA follow-up
- Internet or Web-based EIA follow-up
- the concept of continuous public involvement.

Management structures for EIA follow-up

A schematic of the overall components of the EIA follow-up system in Hong Kong in shown in Figure 9.4. This includes strategic environmental assessment elements and the concept of continuous public involvement, both of which are discussed further later in the chapter. With respect to the implementation of follow-up, different types of management structures have been adopted for different kinds of projects in Hong Kong (EPD, 1998a; Hui, 2000, 2001); there is no single formula in use and a variety of structures have been utilized since the early 1990s (Box 9.5). In consort with the EPD, proponents put forward the types of management structures that can best suit their circumstances and the types of environmental problems in question. The preferred structure is reflected in the EIA report or the EM&A Manual.

Web-based EIA follow-up

Another process innovation in Hong Kong makes use of the Internet to facilitate follow-up. Soon after the implementation of the first EM&A programme it was realized that conventional paper-based reporting is unlikely to be useful as it will take too long for the information to reach all the relevant

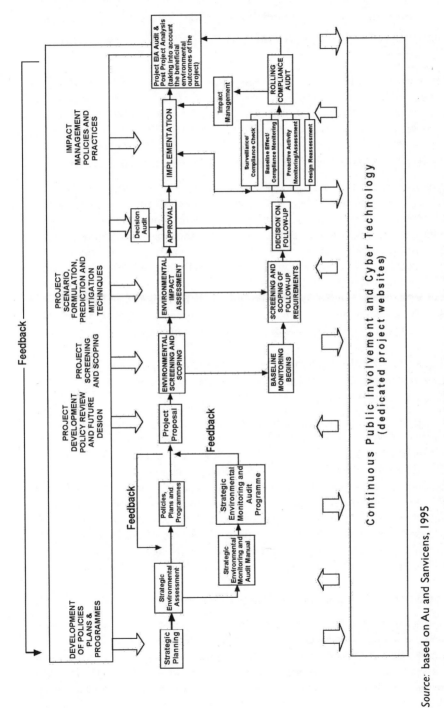

Source: based on Au and Sanvicens, 1995

Figure 9.4 *Schematic Model of the Hong Kong Follow-up System*

Box 9.5 Different Management Structures Used for EIA Follow-up

Type (1) – Project proponent to employ an Environmental Team

Small projects with minimal environmental impacts and public concern are suited to this system. The Environmental Team can be directly recruited into the proponent's resident site staff and, if resources of the proponent permit, an external consultancy can be employed to vindicate the work.

Type (2) – Contractor to employ an Environmental Team

This is one of the earlier management structures used in Hong Kong and has largely been replaced by Type 3. It is simple and straightforward with respect to contractual arrangements with the Contractor undertaking the work on behalf of the proponent by directly employing their own Environmental Team. There is frequently a lack of independence and impartiality compared to other management structures since the Environmental Team is under the direct control of the contractor. The quality of the mitigation measures cannot be ensured and there is a potential for the filtering of data submitted to the reviewing Authority. Additionally, the supply of monitoring equipment is frequently late, thus compromising the quality of the base-line monitoring data.

Type (3) – Project proponent to employ an Independent Environment Checker and contractor to employ an Environmental Team

This is the optimum system for medium to large projects, especially those that are potentially sensitive. The Independent Environment Checker is responsible for auditing the Environmental Team's, work and is professionally independent. The Independent Environment Checker role can be implemented early in the design stage to vet the design submissions and design changes to ensure that EIA recommendations are properly implemented. Moreover, the Independent Environment Checker can manage the handling of public complaints and enquiries. Proponents of projects undergoing EIA studies under the EIA Ordinance are now adopting this type of management structure, and it is anticipated that this system will become the dominant type in the future.

Type (4) – Environmental Project Office

An Environmental Project Office (ENPO) is best suited where multiple developments are occurring and cumulative impacts are of major concern. It is established when there are many different projects or contracts all happening in the same area (e.g. Penny's Bay development area where a future international theme park (HK Disneyland) will be located, and different projects such as the theme park, road links, railway and other essential infrastructure are being built at the same time). The ENPO is set up by the Civil Engineering Department, which oversees the entire development in the area. The ENPO acts as the Independent Environment Checker for individual projects, reporting directly to the proponent of each, and is thus able to deal with cumulative impacts through each proponent. Its success depends on good cooperation and management between all parties concerned.

Box 9.6 A Typical Environmental Permit Condition Requiring the Submission of Electronic Environmental Monitoring and Audit Reports

To facilitate public inspection of the Base-line Monitoring Report and monthly EM&A Reports via the EIA Ordinance Internet Website and at the EIA Ordinance Register Office, electronic copies of these Reports shall be prepared in Hyper Text Markup Language (HTML) (version 4.0 or later) and in Portable Document Format (PDF version 4.0 or later), unless otherwise agreed by the Director and shall be submitted at the same time as the hard copies as described in Conditions 5.2 and 5.3 of this Permit. For the HTML version, a content page capable of providing hyperlink to each section and sub-section of the EM&A Reports shall be included in the beginning of the document. Hyperlinks to all figures, drawings and tables in the EM&A Reports shall be provided in the main text from where the respective references are made. All graphics in the report shall be in interlaced GIF format unless otherwise agreed by the Director. The content of the electronic copies of these Reports shall be the same as the hard copies.

Source: the EIA Ordinance website (EPD, undated(a))

parties, and by the time they receive the information it could be too late for them to do anything about it. Another problem with paper-based systems is a lack of transparency in that it is very difficult for the public to gain access to hard copy EM&A documents.

To address these problems a Web-based system was developed, and since the year 2000, all permits that contain EM&A requirements have also specified the requirement to submit EM&A data in electronic form and to set up a dedicated project EM&A website. Box 9.6 demonstrates how the concept of Web-based follow-up has been transformed into a legal instrument in practice. The website is intended to contain all project information: the full EIA report, the entire Environmental Permit and its conditions, EM&A data, as well as any records of exceedances and subsequent follow-up actions. This technology allows multimedia presentation of EM&A data as well as providing a direct email system for members of the public to communicate with the project engineer.

Box 9.7 A Typical Permit Condition Requiring Project Websites to be Set Up with On-line Environmental Monitoring and Audit Results for Public Access

To ensure a high degree of transparency regarding the monitoring data and results in view of the public concern about the Project, all environmental monitoring and audit data and results, the approved EM&A Manual and all submissions and all performance test data and results required by this Permit shall be made available by the Permit Holder to the public through a dedicated website to be set up by the Permit Holder, in the shortest possible time and in no event later than two weeks after such information is available.

Source: the EIA Ordinance website (EPD, undated(a))

The effectiveness of using Web-based communication in EIA follow-up in Hong Kong in terms of increasing public engagement with the process was reported in Au (2001) and Morrison-Saunders et al (2001). During the period April 1998 to February 2001, some 2200 people physically visited the EIA Ordinance Register Office (the traditional way to view documents or contact officials). In the same period, some 75,000 visits to the Ordinance website were recorded. It is clear that easy access to electronic communication in highly developed places such as Hong Kong has greater potential for public participation in EIA activities, including follow-up, than relying on traditional paper-based approaches.

With the experience gained in implementing the Hong Kong EIA and follow-up system and the ever-growing public demand for more transparency, it is now possible to develop a completely transparent system taking full advantage of Web-based technology (Box 9.7). Starting from 2002, permits for some major sensitive projects have contained a requirement for installation of Web cameras through which the public can see real-time images of what is happening on development sites. This system not only improves accuracy, efficiency and timely feedback to address emerging problems, it also ensures that project engineers are fully alert to the environmental conditions. Public support is maintained through enhancing the public's participation and labour-intensive enforcement programmes are minimized, particularly from the point of view of the EIA regulator.

In addition to providing monitoring data on websites available to the public, it is also possible to install Web cameras and other instruments that stream data onto the Web in real time. Web cameras can even be mounted such that the public can rotate them and zoom in on a particular location they wish to view. In some recent projects assessed in Hong Kong, requirements for Web cameras providing live visual images have been stipulated in the Environmental Permit. To enhance access to information by the public and overall cost-effectiveness, the EPD has developed template websites and other software applications which can be easily customized to individual project needs for general use.

Continuous public involvement

Following on from the opportunities for Web-based EIA follow-up providing data on projects in real time, the EPD is now promoting the Continuous Public Involvement concept for all stages of the EIA process. Rather than consulting the public at the end of the study stage (e.g. as in Figure 9.2), a project proponent can consult throughout the project's life – that is not only in the study stages but also during construction and operation (Figure 9.4). This process will be the ultimate scenario for all public consultation in Hong Kong and will ensure public acceptance and that EIAs are carried out with the best available information.

Previously, public participation involved identifying key interest groups and knowledge bases, with liaison occurring through regular meetings. With the recent advances in computer technology, public consultation and interaction can be more effective and efficient compared with running meetings. The proponent can set up a dedicated project website right from the EIA conception stage through which the entire public can know how information is gathered, which different alternatives are considered and selected and which models are selected for predicting certain impacts. Most of all, members of the public can come in at any point in time to contribute their knowledge and views, ensuring an acceptable product at the end of the process. Special automatic features can be built into the website so that interested individuals can tailor their own requirements such as automatic alerts of new information, customized format of information and direct email linkages to the proponent or other interested groups.

The same website can become the platform for subsequent EIA follow-up communication as discussed previously. By allowing ongoing interaction between the project and the public, it is intended that continuous public involvement occur throughout the EIA process from the early stages through to follow-up.

Content innovations in EIA follow-up

The processes for EIA follow-up will influence the content of resulting programmes to a large extent. This section focuses on tools and techniques that have been adopted in Hong Kong to enhance the quality of EIA follow-up. These revolve primarily around screening and scoping, event action plans and environmental management plans.

Screening and scoping of EIA follow-up requirements

The screening and scoping of the follow-up monitoring and management requirements is undertaken as an integral part of the EIA process in Hong

Kong (EPD, 1996, 1998b). A decision on the follow-up requirements is normally made at the EIA report approval stage. In Hong Kong, screening and scoping of follow-up requirements is not the same as the scoping of issues for impact assessment, though the two are inter-related. The focus of the follow-up process is on those issues of important concern or on valued resources identified during the pre-decision EIA. Criteria for determining follow-up need in Hong Kong are similar to those discussed in Chapters 3 and 4.

Two-tiered event action plans

A two-tiered criteria system of environmental quality performance limits is adopted in effects monitoring and impact management (Box 9.8), with an event action plan set out in the EM&A manual. The first stage is an action

---

Box 9.8 Environmental Quality Performance Limits

Environmental quality performance limits are normally in the form of a set of Action/Limit levels, which are defined as:

Action levels

The levels beyond which there is an indication of a deteriorating ambient environmental quality for a specific parameter (e.g. dissolved oxygen in marine water). Appropriate remedial actions may be necessary to prevent the environmental quality from going beyond the limit levels, which would result in an unacceptable environmental impact.

Limit levels

The levels stipulated in relevant pollution control ordinances, or the Hong Kong Planning Standards and Guidelines or other appropriate criteria established by EPD for a particular project, beyond which the works should not proceed without appropriate remedial action, including a critical review of plant and work methods.

The EM&A system compares impact monitoring during construction of the project with base-line or control station monitoring. The data are audited against trend indicators comprising action levels and limit levels. Once the monitoring results go beyond these limits, an event action plan is initiated where necessary actions will be taken appropriate to the level exceeded. The permit conditions require relevant parties including the proponent, contractor, ET Leader and IEC to initiate actions when the levels are exceeded. Failure to take appropriate actions may lead to enforcement steps being taken by the EPD (as provided for in the EIA Ordinance).

Source: EPD, 1996, 1998a

level trigger (e.g. an emission standard), where action is to be taken before the upper limit is reached. This upper limit is the second stage, the limit level, which should not be exceeded. If the monitoring results demonstrate that the limit level has been exceeded, a predetermined event action plan is initiated to avoid or rectify the problems.

Environmental management plans

The experiences of Hong Kong suggest that the success of the follow-up process depends on whether the assumptions, criteria and mitigation measures developed in the pre-decision stages of EIA are properly translated into enforceable conditions and construction and operational manuals, and on whether monitoring and audit protocols are formulated and written down in a manual or an environmental management plan before the works commence. This is especially important when those involved in the actual project implementation have no involvement in the pre-decision EIA because of the transfer of responsibilities or change of personnel. Environmental monitoring and audit manuals (Box 9.9) or environmental management plans have generated enormous benefits to those involved in the project implementation and greatly enhanced the effectiveness of the monitoring and audit programmes. The benefits include:

- allowing engineers and project managers to focus on significant issues
- developing well planned event action plans to deal with unexpected problems
- delineating clear lines of responsibility.

Case study: Penny's Bay redevelopment

This case study illustrates how the regulations for EIA follow-up combined with some of the process and content innovations discussed previously for a suite of development projects based on the decommissioning of a shipyard and the construction of the Hong Kong Disneyland Theme Park at Penny's Bay in North Lantau (Figure 9.5).

In 1998, the Government of the Hong Kong Special Administrative Region (Government) commissioned a Northshore Lantau Development Feasibility Study covering the area of Northeast Lantau Island including Penny's Bay to formulate preferred development schemes for the study area. In March 1999, after considering the initial findings of the feasibility study, the Government decided that the study area be developed for tourism/recreation development with a world-class theme park in Penny's Bay. An area-based EIA study for the whole Northshore Lantau Development region was subsequently undertaken.

To address public concerns with the proposed theme park, an order was issued under the EIA Ordinance in July 1999 to add to the Schedule 2 list of

Box 9.9 Environmental Monitoring and Audit Manual

1   The EM&A Manual shall contain all the arrangements for implementation of the environmental monitoring and audit aspects and requirements of the Project. Project-specific objectives for environmental management and improvement shall be outlined in an environmental programme, which details the staff responsibilities and the means by which objectives will be achieved.

2   An Environmental Policy Statement issued by the Project's executive management shall be included in a Project's EM&A Manual.

3   There shall be sufficient resources (e.g. staff, equipment, instrumentation and environmental protection/mitigation measures) specified in the Manual, and made available by the Project Proponent for the timely and effective implementation of all the project EM&A requirements.

4   The EM&A Manual shall take full account of the recommendations and requirements laid down in the EIA Report. The proponent shall ensure that the recommended mitigation measures for the potential environmental impacts of the project are accurately translated into effective, quantitative, traceable, measurable and enforceable environmental protection specifications within the project brief and designs.

5   The EM&A Manual shall include a checklist of environmental protection, pollution prevention and control, and mitigation measures in the form of an Implementation Schedule highlighting:
    • why, where, or under what circumstances the recommended impact mitigation action shall be implemented
    • when and for how long the recommended action shall take place
    • who will be the responsible party for the recommended action
    • the details of how the recommended action shall be carried out.

6   The EM&A Manual shall specify the requirements for the submission of environmental monitoring and audit data, including monitoring and audit records, event action plans implemented and follow-up actions, listings of all relevant environmental protection and pollution control legislation and the required licences/permits, communication with regulators vis-à-vis offences under relevant environmental ordinances, waste disposal documentation, incident reports and investigations, public complaints and their resolution, work programmes and methods including any variations to EIA predictions, and provisions for the review of monitoring and audit criteria.

7   The EM&A Manual shall include written mitigation procedures for any major project activities (including construction, design, operation, maintenance, and decommissioning phases) that have potential for environmental impact.

8   The EM&A Manual shall specify the duty list of the Environmental Team and the Independent Checker (Environment).

9   The EM&A Manual shall outline the complaint procedures, clearly stating the complaint receiving set up, case investigation, implementation of corrective measures, communication with the complainant/public, and the requirements of the complaint log/record.

10 The EM&A Manual shall specify the requirements for documentation; both internally, for a concise record of traceable implementation status of committed items, and externally, for the frequency and timing of EM&A report submissions.

Source: EPD, 1996, 1998b

designated projects of the ordinance (i.e. requiring an environmental permit for its construction and operation) any 'theme park or amusement park with a site area of more than 20ha in size'. A stand-alone EIA for the theme park at Penny's Bay and its essential associated infrastructures (e.g. roads and railway) was then conducted in parallel with the Northshore Lantau Development EIA. The two EIA reports were submitted together, and after the statutory public consultation process, were both approved in April 2000.

As multiple construction works under different contracts would be carried out in the Northshore Lantau area at the same time during the construction of the theme park and its associated infrastructure, the Northshore Lantau Development and theme park EIAs recommended that an independent ENPO be established to oversee the cumulative environmental impacts. Under this

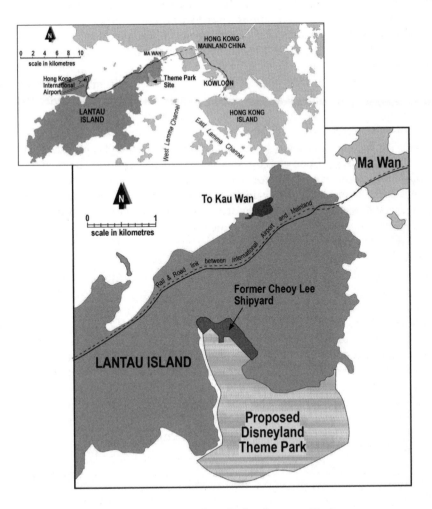

Figure 9.5 *Penny's Bay Redevelopment Projects*

arrangement, the ET, IEC and the project engineers of individual contracts under different proponents would carry out and supervise the EM&A programme of their projects under their environmental permits. The EM&A teams will provide their project information, monitoring and audit results to the ENPO which will also undertake its regular independent inspection and measurements if necessary. In the event of exceedances of environmental quality performance limits or environmental complaints (including those due to cumulative effects), the ENPO will conduct independent investigations, identify the causes and make recommendations to resolve the issues and control environmental impacts.

A third EIA in the Northshore Lantau development area subsequently emerged. The former Cheoy Lee Shipyard was located on the north and eastern shores of Penny's Bay, Lantau Island, with a site area of about 19 hectares of land within the study area of the two EIAs. Although outside the boundary of the theme park, the shipyard was required to be decommissioned to make room for construction of infrastructure for the park (roads, rail and drainage works). A separate EIA study for decommissioning of the shipyard was completed in December 2001. It identified a total of about $87,000m^3$ of contaminated soil that needed to be cleaned up, of which $30,000m^3$ was contaminated with dioxins and the rest by metals, total petroleum hydrocarbons and semi-volatile organic compounds. The EIA study evaluated various treatment options and techniques. It was recommended that soil contaminated only with metals be treated by cement solidification; soil contaminated with petroleum hydrocarbons or semi-volatile organic compounds be treated using a biopiling method; and soil contaminated with dioxins and metals be treated by thermal desorption followed by cement solidification. Dioxin residues generated from the thermal desorption process would be collected and incinerated at a chemical waste treatment centre in Tsing Yi, Hong Kong.

Figure 9.6 shows the management structure of the comprehensive EM&A programme set up for the decommissioning of the shipyard under the environmental permit conditions to ensure environmental compliance of the project. The ET Leader works for a consultancy employed by the contractor to implement the actual monitoring works and site inspections required by the permit and to prepare submissions under the permit. The IEC is a qualified person commissioned by the project proponent to check and audit the works of the ET and submissions by the contractor and to follow up any necessary remediation work. The Project Engineer is responsible for the project design and supervising the contractor's works including EM&A works and any necessary response actions. The ENPO provides the link to other projects in the Penny's Bay area, where the project is located, and a mechanism to deal with cumulative impacts arising from the concurrent activities.

To enhance transparency, the environmental permit for the shipyard project required the setting up of a project website which contains all relevant project information including the EIA report, EM&A Manual, Method Statement, as well as all submissions under the permit. A special Web camera system was also required providing real time continuous visual monitoring accessible by

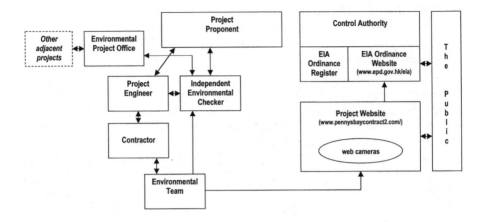

Figure 9.6 *Example of a Comprehensive EM&A Programme in Hong Kong: Penny's Bay Redevelopment Project*

anyone, any time and anywhere (available at www.pennysbaycontract2.com/). Linkage to this and other project websites is also possible via the website of the EIA Ordinance (EPD, undated(a)), which is the electronic equivalent of the EIA Ordinance Register Office set up under the Ordinance. All EIA decisions can be found in the Register and the website, as well as full copies of the EIA reports, the Ordinance and the Technical Memorandum issued under the Ordinance, Guidance Notes, Reference Documents and other useful information.

Follow-up to Strategic Environmental Assessment

Discussion of follow-up monitoring and management in Hong Kong has so far focused only on the project-related EIA. With the emphasis being given to advance and apply the EIA process to policies, plans and programmes, there is a need to develop a commensurate follow-up monitoring and management process to deal with decisions and issues arising from such EIA process applications.

The advent of Strategic Environmental Assessment (SEA) to deal with cumulative impacts and sustainability questions that transcend individual projects demands the development of new types of strategic follow-up. This will involve new management processes and approaches, and new tools and techniques (Chapter 10). Unlike project EIA follow-up, this type of process:

* deals with the aggregate effects of policy or strategy decisions, rather than individual effects of projects
* focuses on tracking the implementation of decisions and the changing circumstances that may result in a policy or strategy review

- deals with the effects on the ecosystem as a whole: i.e. monitors the effects on, or changes to, the environmental carrying capacities, monitors the depletion or protection of the natural capital stock, and monitors and manages cumulative effects.

A possible framework for integrating SEA follow-up into practice in Hong Kong is included in Figure 9.4. Since 1996, there have been several major SEA studies completed in Hong Kong, including SEA for Territorial Development Strategy Review (EPD, undated(b)), Comprehensive Transport Study (Transport Department, 1999) and Railway Development Strategy (Highways Department, 2000). A major feature of the study findings is the inclusion of a strategic environmental monitoring and audit framework to track through major policy, legislative and technical proposals and their assumptions.

For the Transport Study, there is now in place an annual audit of the findings and outcomes of the SEA, including review of major assumptions, checking progress of various initiatives, monitoring key trends and selective reassessment of certain issues and parameters. The audit was conducted by the Transport Department, with management inputs and guidance from the EPD. The results were reviewed by the EPD in conjunction with other departments, and presented to the ACE. It is intended that the results of the review and audit will be fed back to future strategy planning and project formulation. Two key features of this strategic follow-up are as follows (Transport Bureau, 1999):

- The objective of the strategic follow-up programme is to identify any modifications and any studies needed during its implementation and to feed back the results into the future decision-making process. The main aim is to avoid environmental degradation by adopting the precautionary principle for implementation of the recommended transport strategy.
- Up-to-date information on a number of relevant parameters such as vehicle fleet size by vehicle class; vehicle-kilometres travelled; and the related traffic emissions, ambient air quality and noise levels at receivers could act as indicators to highlight the changing environmental conditions arising from the proposed strategy and to chart them against existing and updated forecast conditions. The population, GDP growth, private and goods vehicle fleets and cross-boundary traffic are also fundamental strategic parameters that have been monitored.

Conclusions and lessons learned

The Hong Kong experience shows that clear formal regulations combined with carefully considered process and content details have produced an effective and innovative follow-up system. Key learning points that may be relevant to other jurisdictions can be briefly summarized as follows:

- It is essential to make the EIA follow-up requirements an integral part of the project decision-making.
- There is a need to set realistic goals on what EIA follow-up can achieve. Follow-up monitoring and management cannot turn an environmentally unacceptable project into an acceptable one. But it can certainly help to minimize the actual environmental effects. As a minimum, it should make the impacts no worse than predicted in the EIAs. It should also aim at minimizing the actual adverse impacts, avoiding any further adverse environmental effects, maximizing the environmental benefits of development proposals, and learning from past mistakes to prevent similar problems from occurring in other projects.
- Regular reporting by the proponents on their performance is essential and should be done in a transparent manner.
- It is beneficial to have early discussion and consensus among various stakeholders on the key issues for follow-up, the key environmental attributes to protect, the environmental monitoring and audit protocols, the event action plans and the communication channels.
- A proactive approach to monitor key activities that may result in environmental impacts and to manage impacts and actions is key to success.
- It is crucial to provide proper training for those who have to carry out follow-up monitoring and management, letting them understand the basis of the EIA recommendations and the action plans required.
- Independent surveillance and vetting of monitoring results help to instil confidence and facilitate informed discussion among stakeholders.
- The EIA system and the community can benefit from enhancing transparency, accountability and public engagement through public disclosure of environmental monitoring and audit results and the proactive use of Web technology to widely disseminate EIA and follow-up information and to engage the public in monitoring a project's environmental performance.
- Application of follow-up to the strategic level decisions is necessary to deal with cumulative impacts and sustainability issues above the level of individual projects.

As follow-up practice is relatively new in Hong Kong and is still evolving, there are not too many projects that have fully gone through the entire cycle of planning, design, construction and operation under the EIA Ordinance. The EM&A process focuses mainly on compliance issues and transparency. EIA follow-up activities that need to be further strengthened in Hong Kong are those related to evaluation of the success of various measures and EM&A programmes for both the construction and operational phases, and to the accuracy of predictions after the projects are completed.

Overall, EIA follow-up monitoring and management is regarded as an indispensable part of the EIA system in Hong Kong to ensure that the EIA process actually works to protect the environment and achieve intended outcomes. Practical experience has proved the value of follow-up monitoring and management. Many different techniques and approaches have been adopted in Hong Kong when dealing with the actual environmental outcomes and the emerging environmental issues associated with major developments. The Hong Kong experience is one that can be regarded as learning by doing. EIA follow-up monitoring and management in Hong Kong has become a useful tool for decision-makers and for the public. The recent use of Web-based technologies has improved the efficiency, transparency and effectiveness of the EIA follow-up system in Hong Kong, as well as engaging stakeholders on an almost real-time basis. The goal is to engage the public, the project proponent and the environmental authority in an interactive, innovative manner to ensure the project's environmental performance, to instil public confidence in the system and to create seamless, efficient feedback to project planning and implementation. The recent promotion of a continuous public involvement approach is another important development in this direction.

References

Au, E (1998) 'Status and progress of environmental assessment in Hong Kong: Facing the challenges in the 21st century', *Impact Assessment and Project Appraisal*, vol 16, pp162–166

Au, E (2000) 'Environmental Planning and Impact Assessment of Major Development Projects in Hong Kong' in Wong, W and Edwin, C (eds) *Building Hong Kong – Environmental Considerations*, Hong Kong, Hong Kong University Press

Au, E (2001) 'Latest Developments of EIA Follow-up in Hong Kong', presented at *EIA Follow-up: Outcomes and Improvements Workshop, 21st Annual Meeting of the International Association for Impact Assessment*, 26 May–1 June 2001, Cartagena, Colombia, published on CD ROM: *IA Follow-up Workshop*, Hull, Quebec, Environment Canada

Au, E and Baldwin, P (1994) 'Application of the EIA Process in Hong Kong – Toward a More Effective and Formal System', presented to the *14th Annual Meeting, International Association for Impact Assessment*, 14–18 June 1994, Quebec

Au, E and Sanvicens, G (1995) 'EIA Follow-up Monitoring and Management', in Environment Protection Agency (ed) *International Study of the Effectiveness of Environmental Assessment: Report of the EIA Process Strengthening Workshop*, Canberra, 4–7 April 1995, Environment Protection Agency, available at www.deh.gov.au/assessments/eianet/eastudy/aprilworkshop/paper5.html

EPD, Environmental Protection Department (1992) *Application of the Environmental Impact Assessment Process to Major Private Sector Development Projects*, Advice Note 2/92, Hong Kong, Government Printer

EPD, Environmental Protection Department (1996) *Generic Environmental Management and Audit Manual*, Hong Kong, Environmental Protection Department

EPD, Environmental Protection Department (1998a) *Guidelines for Development Projects in Hong Kong – Environmental Monitoring and Audit*, Hong Kong, Environmental Protection Department

EPD, Environmental Protection Department (1998b) *A Guide to the Environmental Impact Assessment Ordinance*, Hong Kong, Environmental Protection Department

EPD, Environmental Protection Department (2000) *A Collection of Environmental Assessment Experiences in Airport Core Projects*, Hong Kong, Environmental Protection Department

EPD, Environmental Protection Department (2002) *The Operation of Environmental Impact Assessment Ordinance*, Hong Kong, Environmental Protection Department, available at www.epd.gov.hk/eia/operation/index.html

EPD, Environmental Protection Department (undated(a)) *Environmental Impact Assessment Ordinance*, Hong Kong, Environmental Protection Department, available at www.epd.gov.hk/eia/

EPD, Environmental Protection Department (undated(b)) *Territorial Development Strategy Review: Strategic Environmental Assessment of the Medium-Term Options – July 1996*, Hong Kong, Environmental Protection Department, available at www.epd.gov.hk/epd/english/environmentinhk/eia_planning/sea/territorial_dept_02.html

Government of Hong Kong (1997) *Environmental Impact Assessment Ordinance, Cap. 499, no. 9 of 1997*, Hong Kong, Government Printer

Highways Department (2000) *The Second Railway Development Study, Final SEA Report, May 2000*, Railway Development Office, Highways Department, Hong Kong

Hui, S (2000) 'Environmental Monitoring and Audit: Past, Present, Future', presented at *IAIA'00 Back to the Future, 20th Annual Meeting of the International Association for Impact Assessment, 'EIA follow-up Stream'*, 19–23 June 2000, Hong Kong

Hui, S (2001) 'EIA Follow-up: The Hong Kong Approach', presented at the *Canada–Hong Kong EIA Workshop*, 23–25 October 2001, Vancouver, Canada

Morrison-Saunders, A, Arts, J, Baker, J and Caldwell, P (2001) 'Roles and stakes in environmental impact assessment follow-up', *Impact Assessment and Project Appraisal*, vol 19, pp289–296

Nash, J (1993) 'Environmental monitoring and audit of a major construction project in Hong Kong: The West Kowloon Reclamation', *Asian Journal of Environmental Management*, vol 1, pp 23–38

Nash, J and Deacon, R (1993) 'Proactive Environmental Monitoring Audit and Remediation of Major Construction Projects in Hong Kong', presented at *Environmex Asia/Watermex Asia International Conference*, October 1993, Singapore

Planning, Environment and Lands Branch (1992) *Environmental Impact Assessment of Major Development Projects*, Technical Circular 2/92, Hong Kong, Planning, Environment and Lands Branch

Sadler, B (1996) *International Study of the Effectiveness of Environmental Assessment: Final Report, Environmental Assessment in a Changing World: Evaluating Practice to Improve Performance*, Canadian Environmental Assessment Agency and the International Association for Impact Assessment, Hull, Quebec, Minister of Supply and Services, Canada

Sanvicens, G and Au, E (1995) 'Environmental Monitoring and Audit of Airport Core Programme Projects in Hong Kong', Technical Report (EPD/TR 1/95), Hong Kong, Environmental Protection Department

Sanvicens, G and Baldwin, P (1996) 'Environmental monitoring and audit in Hong Kong', *Journal of Environmental Planning and Management*, vol 39, pp429–440

Transport Bureau (1999) *Strategic Environmental Assessment Report for Third Comprehensive Transport Study*, Report (CTS-3), Hong Kong, Transport Bureau

Transport Department (1999) *Third Comprehensive Transport Study – Strategic Environmental Assessment Technical Report*, Hong Kong, Transport Department

Wood, C and Coppell, L (1999) 'An evaluation of the Hong Kong environmental impact assessment system', *Impact Assessment and Project Appraisal*, vol 17, pp21–31

10

Follow-up in Current SEA Understanding

Maria Rosário Partidário and Thomas B. Fischer

Introduction

Follow-up in Strategic Environmental Assessment (SEA) is a new area of increasing interest, largely yet to be formalized. This chapter breaks new ground and many of the issues raised will need further exploration in the years to come. While follow-up is part of good SEA practice, until now there has been little attention given to this subject. Nevertheless, there have been some attempts to experiment with follow-up programmes in informal SEA practice, particularly with respect to monitoring activities, and illustration of such attempts can help to improve current understanding.

This chapter explores the potential scope and limits of SEA follow-up. It starts by analysing current understanding of SEA, focusing in particular on the differences between SEA and Environmental Impact Assessment (EIA), to enable a better focus on the nature of follow-up in SEA. It then identifies the rationale and goals of follow-up in SEA and subsequently identifies possible types of SEA follow-up. An exploration of the meaning of follow-up for different tiers in strategic decision-making is presented. Existing national and European requirements for SEA follow-up are briefly reviewed along with case study examples for a number of policy, plan and programme applications. Both empirical and theoretical elaboration feed into the preliminary methodological guidance to SEA practitioners presented prior to some conclusions on SEA follow-up.

Current understanding of SEA

Debate continues on what SEA actually involves. Several interpretations have been reported, reviewed and discussed in the literature over the past decade

(Lee and Walsh, 1992; Therivel et al, 1992; Sadler and Verheem, 1996; Therivel and Partidário, 1996; Partidário and Clark, 2000; Fischer, 2002a). Likewise, SEA is shaping differently in countries and regions that have formally adopted SEA administrative procedures, such as the USA, Canada, New Zealand, the European Union and its various member states.

Since the early days of SEA, a key question has been: how different is SEA from project-based EIA? With SEA knowledge and experience accumulating, the differences are becoming clearer. SEA is increasingly accepted to be a proactive and objectives-led decision-making support instrument focused on strategic actions (in policy-, plan- and programme-making) and leading to the identification of strategic impacts. Its purpose is to identify, explore, compare and manage the strategic alternative options that enable the achievement of key sustainability objectives, ensuring environmentally sound and sustainable decisions.

Despite this generally acknowledged notion, SEA takes different forms depending on the level of decision-making to which it applies. Three main types of SEA may call for distinct methodological requirements:

- policy SEA – which applies to highest-level proposals
- spatial planning SEA – which applies to proposals with a spatial focus
- sector plan and programme SEA – which applies to proposals for specific sectors.

A growing number of countries exhibit different approaches to SEA and offer case-examples of a diverse nature (Sadler and Verheem, 1996; Therivel and Partidário, 1996; Mens en Ruimte, 1996; Partidário and Clark, 2000; Sheate et al, 2001; Fischer, 2002a). In Europe, since 1996, the discussion around the EU Directive on the environmental assessment of certain plans and programmes has triggered a wave of SEA case studies and research. This has highlighted the differences between approaches to SEA across nations and, most importantly, the relationship between SEA and the decision-making system in place for policy, planning, programme and project EIA (ERM, 1999; EC, 2001a).

It is increasingly recognized that the success of SEA depends on its close articulation with the level and process of decision-making to which it applies and, inherently, with its respective consequences. As a proactive instrument, SEA aims at influencing the policy-making, plan-making and programme-making processes, aiming to improve the consideration of environmental and sustainability issues and concerns in these processes. But like project EIA, SEA also requires that the actual consequences of decisions are checked against the perceived effects, and that impacts are minimized; a function inherently associated with follow-up programmes.

A key difference, however, is that project-based follow-up is based on empirical evidence, particularly the environmental response to project operation. In contrast, for SEA, impacts can not only range from quite vague to very concrete, but can be expected at different relevant tiers of decision-making. Strategic impacts can influence future policies, plans, programmes and also projects (Table 10.1). Follow-up in SEA can only happen if a systematic approach is in place (enabling adequate identification and management of multidirection and multisectoral strategic impacts) which is adjusted to the level of decision where impacts are expected.

Mitigation and compensation measures in SEA must also be strategic in nature, consistent with the level of assessment and the nature of the expected impacts. Its success is therefore not solely dependent on its application as a systematic evaluation process in a pre-decision phase, but also on external circumstances and on action in a post-decision phase.

As Lee and Wood (1978) noted in relation to the scope of EIA, its application can take place at several administrative levels (i.e. national, regional, municipal and local/site-specific levels) and also at several decision levels (policies, plans, programmes and projects). They further suggested that environmental assessment was to be applied in a structured decision-making hierarchy, whenever it is in place, characterized by tiering sequences. These consisted of:

- tiering *at the same* administrative level – across policy-plan-programme-project sequences at national, or at regional, or at municipal, or at local levels
- tiering *between* different administrative levels – a policy at the national level may influence a policy at the local level, or a policy at the regional level may determine the need for a programme at the national level; but also a plan at the regional level may determine the need for a policy at the national level and/or a project at the local level.

This illustrates the complex reality of SEA. It may be applied to just one or two or to all three levels of decision-making above project preparation (policy, plan, programme), and each level is likely to be accompanied by distinct methodological SEA approaches (Fischer and Seaton, 2002). While SEA should always address the strategic component in any policy, plan or programme, the fact is that policies, plans and programmes are different in themselves and will also differ according to the administrative level at which they take place (Partidário, 2000). This means that follow-up approaches will also vary, depending on whether they are linked to either a policy, a plan or a programme and at which administrative level it will take place.

A generic definition of what constitutes a policy, a plan or a programme can help to better understand the universe of actions around which SEA is expected to operate. According to UNEP (2002):

- policy – is a guiding intent, with defined goals, objectives and priorities, and an actual or proposed direction
- plan – is a strategy or a design to carry out a general or particular course of action, incorporating policy ends, options and ways and means to implement them
- programme – is a schedule of proposed commitments, activities or instruments to be implemented within or by a particular sector or area of policy.

Table 10.1 *Main Differences between SEA and EIA*

Aspect	SEA	EIA
Decision-making level	Policy-making, plan-making, programme-making	Plan, programme, project
Nature of Action	Strategic, visionary, conceptual	Immediate, operational
Outcomes	General and often broad brush	Detailed
Relation to decision	Facilitator, mediator	Evaluator, technical/scientific approach
Alternatives	Area-wide, political, regulative, technological, fiscal, economic or social or physical strategies	Specific locations, design, construction, operation
Scale of impacts	Macroscopic, cumulative	Microscopic, localized
Scope of impacts	Sustainability issues, economic and social issues may be more tangible than physical or ecological issues	Physical or ecological issues mainly; to a lesser extent also social and economic
Time scale	Medium to long term	Short to medium term
Key data sources	State of environment reports, sustainable development strategies, Local Agenda 21, statistical data, other policies, plans and programmes	Field work, sample analysis, statistical data
Data	Descriptive, often not clearly quantifiable	Mainly quantifiable
Rigour of analysis	Less rigour, more uncertainty	More rigour, less uncertainty
Assessment benchmarks	Sustainability benchmarks (criteria and objectives)	Legal restrictions and best practice
Public perception	Vague, distant	More reactive (NIMBY)
Post-evaluation	Other strategic actions or project planning	Objective evidence, construction and operation

Source: adapted from Partidário, 2001

These three levels of decision-making can take place at different administrative levels, as initially argued by Lee and Wood (1978). While the form of SEA should be flexibly applied in an appropriate manner to the underlying policy, plan and programme, it should at the same time aim at influencing decision-making in order to improve the consideration of environmental and sustainability issues and concerns at the various administrative levels.

Figure 10.1 illustrates the notion of an impact assessment continuum process, through tiering approaches, across the various levels of decision-making, from policies to projects. In this process, the type of impact assessment instrument varies according to each level, strongly related to the levels of uncertainty and the range of multiple and diverse issues that need to be considered at each different level of decision-making (Partidário, 2000). This emphasizes the need for great adaptability of SEA, particularly considering the range of potential alternatives and the range of site-specific issues involved that determine quite different information needs, as shown in Figure 10.2 (Fischer, 2002b).

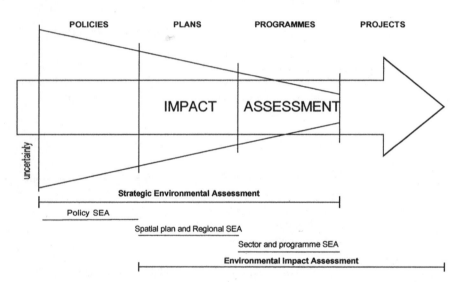

Source: adapted from Partidário, 2000

Figure 10.1 *Impact Assessment across Decision-making Tiers – From SEA to Project EIA*

Key differences between SEA and project EIA can be explained through a number of other aspects, as presented in Table 10.1 (Partidário, 2001). For example, while the nature of actions in SEA situations is strategic and conceptual, in project EIA it is rather immediate and operational, which justifies why SEA yields general outcomes and EIA detailed outcomes. Similarly policies, plans and programmes tend to work on long- to medium-term time scales, leading to longer impact time scales, whereas projects operate

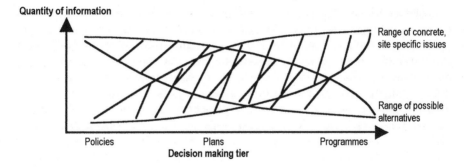

Source: Fischer, 2002b

Figure 10.2 *Quantity of Information Provided by the Three SEA Types*

on medium- to short-term impact time scales. This enables the positioning of SEA differently in relation to the decision-making process. Where SEA should act as a facilitator or a mediator enabling clarification in complex decision-making, in EIA what is relevant is the technical or scientific support to evaluation of proposed actions. With respect to the role of the practitioner, in strategic situations they will usually act as a mediator for negotiations and in project situations act as a technician advocating stakeholder values, particularly in order to avoid NIMBY (not in my back yard) deadlocks (Fischer, 2003).

The range of alternatives to be considered at strategic levels will often relate to spatial alternatives – particularly in plan-level SEA (plan-SEA) – but with a much less site-specific nature than in project EIA. Additionally, strategic decision-making is likely to generate policy-based alternatives relating to social and economic options which may not arise for project EIA. The scale of impacts in SEA will consequently be much less detailed and more likely to relate to issues which are broader in scope than those at the project level. Finally, while EIA focuses much on physical and ecological factors, in SEA economic and social issues may be more tangible than physical or ecological issues, and there is therefore much greater capacity to address cumulative processes and sustainability issues.

The differences between SEA and EIA can also be quite evident with respect to data and information issues, as already highlighted by Figure 10.2. Sources of data in SEA will tend to be more dependent on easily accessible sources such as those provided in annual environmental and sustainability reports. In contrast, for project EIA there is an expectation to have information generated by fieldwork and sample analysis that enables a better quantification of direct and indirect impacts. The rigour of analysis will consequently be less in SEA than in EIA, but also because of the higher levels of uncertainty inherently associated with SEA. This also explains the often less active involvement of the public in SEA processes, where issues being dealt with are more vague because they are long term and not so site-specific.

Finally a key difference between SEA and EIA is related to follow-up processes. The main arguments that justify the difference have already been exposed earlier in this section, relating to the multiple administrative and decision-making levels in which SEA operates, as opposed to project EIA's 'end of pipe' nature. This means that it is much more obvious for projects (even though it may not be immediate) to decide on the evidence that needs to be checked as a consequence of a project, to enable follow-up tracking, than is the case for strategic proposals. For example, a policy can have consequences over a plan, a programme or even a project at national (and even supra-national), regional, municipal or local levels, and in multisectoral contexts. To be feasible, boundaries of accepted evidence need to be established; however, such a decision is difficult to make.

There is one additional point that it is worth exploring in relation to understanding SEA. This concerns whether all three tiers of decision-making above the project level should be considered strategic and therefore bound to be subjected to SEA. This is still a matter of debate and very much dependent on the decision-making context and the practice with planning and project EIA. Practice has shown that project EIA methodologies can be used in the assessment of plans and programmes, with acceptable degrees of success when applied within well developed and systematic systems (Figure 10.1). What results is that the impact assessment tool to be used at any level of decision-making should be the one that makes sense and provides the necessary answers within a particular context. If this is accepted, then it should be stressed that SEA tools should go beyond what project EIA is already doing.

Rationale and goals of follow-up in SEA

Ever since SEA made its first appearances in the early 1990s, most authors have acknowledged the need for follow-up (e.g. Sadler and Verheem, 1996; Therivel and Partidário, 1996; ERM, 1999; Partidário and Clark, 2000; EC, 2001a; Sheate et al, 2001; Fischer, 2002a, b), but usually without clearly stating how this should be done. Arts (1998) made an attempt to explore this issue a little further, comparing follow-up at the operational, spatial and strategic levels. He suggested that SEA follow-up can not only be difficult to carry out but 'the very relevance of doing so can be questioned', (p331) and identified various factors that seriously hamper post-evaluation at strategic levels, including:

- the comprehensiveness and the very high level of abstraction at strategic levels
- the importance of after-linked decision-making and parties other than the leading authority
- the problem of uncertainty
- the difficulty in establishing causal relationships between the content of a strategic plan and the environmental impacts that occur
- the limited value of conformance as an evaluation criterion
- the dynamic, political–administrative context of strategic planning.

Despite these difficulties, follow-up will have an important role to play if SEA is to achieve its acknowledged potential benefits. Without some form of systematic follow-up to decision-making, SEA risks becoming no more than a pro-forma exercise designed to secure a formalized process implementation rather than enhancing its intended benefits and contributing to overall sustainability. SEA benefits include (Wood and Djeddour, 1992; Sadler and Verheem, 1996; Partidário, 1996, 1999; Arts, 1998; and Fischer, 1999):

- the contribution of SEA towards the achievement of integrated and more sustainable and environmentally sound policy, plan and programme decision-making
- the strengthening of project EIAs by better dealing with cumulative and induced impacts.

As indicated previously, an effective SEA follow-up programme is potentially more complex than project EIA follow-up. This is a particularly important point as policies, plans and programmes may often be changed and/or replaced by new ones, and this creates a dynamic cyclical process that calls for new evaluations systematically. Hence the follow-up of an existing policy, plan or programme becomes crucial to the preparation of a new one at the same administrative and decision-making level. At the same time it is also crucial to the development of other stages of decision-making levels, often also at different administrative levels. This is a continuing complex process, where the ex-post evaluation of an existing strategic action links up to the ex-ante evaluation of a new strategic action.

As impacts from projects are substantially different from impacts at strategic levels, the way to measure and describe them will vary. It is important to define exactly what SEA follow-up needs to include. In this context, it is necessary to explore and establish (Mens en Ruimte, 1996):

- What exactly is meant by follow-up in a particular situation, and the expected outcomes?
- When and where should follow-up be applied?
- What are the most appropriate SEA tools for achieving the intended outcome?

Following Tomlinson and Atkinson (1987), Au and Sanvicens (1995) and Ridgway et al (1996), SEA follow-up can broadly be distinguished in terms of goals ensuring conformance with what is set out in the policy, plan or programme and goals dealing with the actual environmental performance, i.e. how actual harm can be minimized and benefits be achieved (Faludi, 1989). However, as argued by Arts (1998), the respective causal links may be difficult to establish, particularly:

- with respect to ensuring *conformance* with what is set out in policies, plans or programmes. It may happen that by the time follow-up is carried out,

the purpose and aims of existing policies, plans or programmes have changed
- with respect to environmental *performance*. The observation of actual environmental harm and benefits may be difficult to obtain, particularly in policy contexts; some indicators may enable some follow-up tracking (e.g. generation of new policies regarding energy conservation) – however, these may be better placed in the context of sustainability indicators and approaches.

A key point in SEA follow-up may be the evaluation of strategic decision-making performance, using criteria that relate to expected conformance, but adapted to the relevance of strategic decisions at the time of the evaluation. Contextual circumstances (e.g. other new policies and orientations) might have changed the reality in which the policy, plan or programme had been established in the first place, and this changing context needs to be incorporated in the evaluation criteria in assessing both conformance and performance of strategic actions.

Additionally, follow-up in SEA can only make sense if specific attention is given to unexpected, unpredicted and uncertainty aspects. This should be one specific goal and benefit of follow-up in SEA, given the volatile, abstract and uncertain context in which SEA operates. Box 10.1 summarizes the four main goals of SEA follow-up.

To support effective decision-making, it is important to identify the mechanisms and instruments that are most suitable to assist SEA follow-up. As will be explained later in further detail, in programme-level SEA (programme-SEA), for example, it is probably easier to define the boundaries of possible effects, as these happen within more contained systems. Therefore, a specific tailor-made mechanism can be established. In policy-level SEA (policy-SEA), however, it is probably not possible to perceive the full extent of potential implications, as it happens within more complex systems. Thus, state of the environment reporting and Agenda 21 related systems can play crucial roles in making SEA follow-up more effective.

Despite the differences between SEA and EIA, there are currently no indications that SEA follow-up should include fundamentally different elements from EIA follow-up (i.e. monitoring, evaluation, management and communication, as defined in Chapter 1).

Types of SEA follow-up

Current difficulties in applying SEA follow-up particularly include contextual uncertainties and unclear relationships with upstream and downstream decision-making tiers (Figure 10.3). A policy will not only have effects downstream to subsequent decision-making tiers, sectors and levels of administration, but may also affect other 'parallel' policies. Likewise, effects of sectoral plans may be seen in the programme implementation of these plans, but it may also be seen in other intra- and inter-sectoral plans and possibly even at policies upstream.

Box 10.1 Goals and Benefits of SEA Follow-up

1 Check on *conformance of terms and conditions* of policy, plan or programme approval. Ensure that conditions of approval are followed in the most cost-effective way, for example, through regular check-ups in a systematic monitoring programme, but also ensure that changing contextual circumstances are considered in the evaluation to be sure of the relevance of the checked conformance, particularly to assess to which point the policy, plan or programme was able to be adapted to the new reality.

2 Check the *satisfactory environmental and sustainability performance* at subsequent stages of decision-making. Assess current expected strategic deliveries, and evaluate through adequate indicators and action plans what may have been possible adverse happenings or trends caused by policies, plans or programmes. Sustainability and environmental benchmarks can act as references for good performance.

3 *Manage actual (as opposed to predicted) impacts*, to deal with uncertainties, unfamiliarities and changes. Apply a systematic and flexible approach to react steadily to critical indicators and enable the possibility for activities to be modified if there are unexpected harmful effects or evidence for trends different from what was planned. Verify the accuracy of past predictions and identify new or revised trends. Review impact management plans or activities regularly and change if necessary.

4 *Disseminate experience for improving the practice of SEA* and decision-making. Carry out general reviews; for example, evaluate prediction techniques in terms of their reliability and review policy, plan and programme conformance and performance according to expected deliveries in accordance with sustainability and environmental benchmarks and management practices.

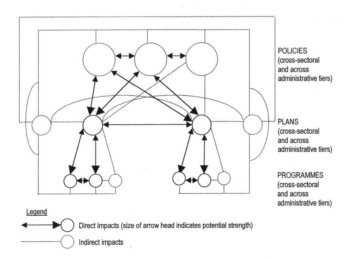

Figure 10.3 *Multi-tier Causal Relationships in SEA Follow-up*

SEA follow-up will need to consider the aggregate, cumulative or synergistic effects of different strategic decisions, and there are particular challenges in tracking the implementation of policy, plan or programme decisions. Changing political circumstances may, for example, result in policy reviews that might in turn have an effect on plan and programme formulation and implementation. Follow-up of a strategic decision needs to look downstream and upstream in the decision-making process, and also to consider an inter-sectoral dimension. Follow-up should not only consider the actual strategic effects but also the inherent impact management responsibilities, including the whole range of institutional, legal, socio-economic, political and biophysical effects. However, the timing, sequence, location and extent of the activities can, and should, be monitored as much as the range of potential effects. Four types of SEA follow-up can be distinguished that are directly related to follow-up goals of conformance, performance, uncertainty and dissemination (Box 10.2).

Tiers in strategic decision-making and consequences for follow-up

Follow-up approaches will vary, depending on whether they take place at a policy, plan or programme decision level. The more pragmatic and concrete the operating level is, the easier it will be to evaluate predictions and pathways of causality. Follow-up is usually more easily achieved if the inherent decision-making level is a programme and the direction of strategic impacts is found to affect the project level directly, or to affect other programme levels (namely in other related sectors, different from the one being assessed). This may also be the case at the plan level, depending on the more deterministic or incremental nature of the plan. Policy follow-up is much more difficult to demonstrate due to larger time lags between policy formulation and actual implementation, and because of the possible multiple outcomes of policy implementation and the changing contextual circumstances (e.g. political changes). Table 10.2 summarizes the different roles of the four types of follow-up in policy, plan and programme situations. These are closely related to the SEA type-specific tasks described by Fischer and Seaton (2002).

Follow-up for policy-SEA

Policy-SEA follow-up needs to consider possible effects at parallel and subsequent tiers. Connecting actual effects with what is laid out in a policy will most likely be a difficult task and outcomes are typically going to be highly complex. Therefore, systematic reporting, focusing on headline-sensitive indicators and covering issues of strategic importance will be needed. State of the environment reporting, sensitivity analysis or similar activities will be of useful assistance. Indicators for policy-SEA follow-up are likely to be of a more general character. Frequency of reporting and public scrutiny may

Box 10.2 Tasks Associated with the Four Types of SEA Follow-up

1   *Conformance follow-up* – Observations of policy, plan or programme developments to demonstrate verification of compliance with objectives, regulatory requirements and applicable standards or criteria. Conformance monitoring can potentially take place within monitoring programmes. It may be difficult in policy situations with large time gaps between policy-making and implementation, as political changes may have led to new policy objectives, unrelated to original objectives.

2   *Performance follow-up* – Measurement of environmental and sustainability parameters and indicators to establish causal relationships with those activities laid out in the policy, plan or programme. Although comparatively straightforward in most situations, in policy situations it may prove to be difficult due to technical and institutional problems, particularly where there are large time gaps between policy-making and implementation.

3   *Uncertainty follow-up* – Reporting on inspections and checks of the policy, plan and programme implementation in subsequent tiers of decision-making, particularly with respect to the environmental and sustainability implications. It requires an impact management programme to be in place to ensure a broad-range observation capable of detecting uncertain, unpredicted and unexpected effects. Detected changes can be reviewed or reassessed in a comprehensive and cumulative manner. Uncertainty follow-up may prove particularly fruitful in policy situations, in which changing political or institutional circumstances may require flexible reactive mechanisms to be in place. In formalized, systematic and pre-determined plan and programme situations, on the other hand, adaptive management might not be feasible.

4   *Dissemination follow-up* – Provide feedback for the design of new policies, plans and programmes, or the methods and approaches of carrying them out, and to improve impact prediction and mitigation practices at all tiers of impact assessment and decision-making. Experience with previous policy, plan or programme SEA needs to be widely disseminated in order to improve future practice.

help to minimize associated uncertainties. Time (short–long term) and scale (local–global) dimensions need to be acknowledged. Good common sense and logic interpretation, rules of thumb and informal evidence may characterize the vaguer nature of policy-level follow-up, yet potentially showing levels of efficiency if adequately conducted.

Follow-up for plan-SEA

Plan-SEA follow-up is likely to deal with concrete spatial environment and socio-economic issues of regions and other territorial boundaries related to

Table 10.2 *Types of Follow-up and their Roles at Different Tiers of Decision-making*

Types of follow-up	Policy	Plan	Programme
Conformance	Check achievement of objectives, particularly legally established targets, recommendations for procedures in follow-up tiers; also check with other sustainability and environmental strategies	Spatial and socio-economic scope – compare planned with real action; Check legally established targets, and recommended procedures in follow-up tiers; check with local agenda 21 initiatives	Check legally established targets, make sure actions are in line with those established in plans and policies, and other strategic terms of reference
Performance	Benchmarking – sustainability and environmental indicators and quality targets (e.g. state of the environment); establish relationships to policy measures	Use benchmarking – sustainability and environmental indicators and quality targets to measure the actual effects of spatial and socio-economic development	Examine prediction accuracy and adopt methodologies accordingly (e.g. multicriteria analysis and cost–benefit analysis)
Uncertainty	Action plans that need to anticipate long-term institutional and political changes and uncertain and unexpected effects	Management plans focusing on uncertain situations and unpredicted effects	Impact and implementation management plans
Dissemination	Regular reporting	Regular reporting	Regular reporting

the plan being assessed. While comparing potential alternative development options, it may refer to economic and social scenarios or to a spatial context, that is, the suitability for different land uses. Ideally, scenarios and spatial alternatives will be a consequence of previously stated policies. As the focus is more concrete, being contained within established boundaries and/or being site specific, causal relationships may be easier to establish than with policy-SEA, and performance, uncertainty and dissemination follow-up may eventually be easier to achieve. Plan-SEA may be dealing with variable alternative scales.

Follow-up for programme-SEA

Programme-SEA identifies development priorities according to a certain development agenda. Follow-up monitoring is likely to focus on ensuring that the chosen options are in line with those identified in the assessment to achieve the highest benefits. Furthermore, policy-SEA and plan-SEA follow-up results should be taken into account if available. Much less uncertainty is expected to occur in comparison with policy-SEAs and plan-SEAs.

Information sources for follow-up

Availability of information is a key issue in SEA follow-up. Direct measurement, whether quantitative or qualitative, may only occur if suitable sources are available. Continuous or ongoing monitoring systems should be in place, irrespective of the policy, plan or programme being assessed. At plan and programme levels, these might be relatively independent, as the focus is more concrete. At policy levels, several policies might be interlinked; thus a more integrated approach is warranted.

Follow-up systems may subsequently be modified or updated, or parallel systems be established in order to enable the monitoring of particular indicators. Current examples of key continuous monitoring systems that can feed into follow-up programmes are state of the environment reports, statistical sectoral monitoring data, spatial monitoring, institutional annual reports, activity plans and other SEAs and EIAs. Other information sources, particularly at the plan and programme levels, might be follow-up programmes of major projects in which integrated water, air, ecology and socio-economic monitoring is undertaken for a major geographical area over a reasonably long period of time. Stakeholders, and particularly responsible authorities, may prove to be significant sources of information. Interviews and workshop brainstorming sessions with stakeholders may provide essential information, particularly in situations where data is not readily available.

Existing requirements for follow-up

Existing requirements for follow-up differ according to the SEA system in place. To appreciate the different perceptions and requirements currently in place, this section briefly reviews the legal or administrative requirements in a few selected regional and national contexts that represent outstanding SEA systems worldwide.

European Union

The European Directive 2002/42/CE adopted in June 2001 required formal impact assessment requirements for plans and programmes to be formulated by all EU member states by 2004, but includes only limited follow-up requirements. Article 10 indicates rather vague monitoring requirements (EC, 2001b):

1   Member States shall monitor the significant environmental effects of the implementation of plans and programmes in order, inter alia, to identify at an early stage unforeseen adverse effects, and to be able to undertake appropriate remedial action.

2   In order to comply with paragraph 1, existing monitoring arrangements may be used if appropriate, with a view to avoiding duplication of monitoring.

The Netherlands

Currently, for most countries in the European Union, there are no formalized SEA systems in place. An exception is The Netherlands, where monitoring is required by the national EIA regulations under section 7.39 of the *Environmental Management Act* 1994 where it states:

> *The competent authority that has taken a decision, in the preparation of which an environmental impact statement was drawn up, shall investigate the effects of the activity concerned on the environment, either during or after its completion'(VROM, 1996; Chapter 4).*

This covers plan and programme environmental assessment as well as project EIA.

Finland

In Finland, the guidelines for SEA indicate that (Ministry of the Environment, 1999):

> *Monitoring should focus on those factors that yield the best indication of the implementation of the chosen alternative and its environmental impacts. Monitoring should be designed in order to address the environmental impact on the target groups and to coordinate the monitoring of environmental and other effects... (e.g... the volume of emissions or the use of natural resources or the state of the environment)... [while] indirect effects can be monitored by examining the trends in production, consumption or decision-making... Annual reports compiled by the authorities should list the targets that have been attained or remain unattained...*

United Kingdom

In the UK, the *Good Practice Guide on Sustainability Appraisal of Regional Planning Guidance* (RPG) mentions the need to monitor the performance and effectiveness of planning outputs and outcomes.

> *The monitoring process will flag up areas where the RPG is not performing to expectations and will raise issues which will need to be addressed in a subsequent evaluation. The results of the evaluation will be fed into subsequent rounds of RPG making, and so on (DETR, 1999).*

The monitoring process will focus on actual strategy performances against the broadly established sustainability and other planning objectives, based on indicators and entering the planning process in a series of 'snapshots'. It is fundamental that the indicators link to the intended purpose of the initially established strategic and sustainability objectives, preferably one indicator per objective. Evaluation is considered to be complex and costly and therefore might need to be infrequent and related to the stages in the planning process.

Canada

No requirements for SEA follow-up are considered in the Canadian Directive for SEA of Policies, Plans and Programmes (CEAA, 1999). However, specific SEA requirements within governmental departments and agencies, such as within the Department of Foreign Affairs and International trade, require that 'an analysis be undertaken which covers... monitoring to control or monitor potential negative environmental effects' (Shuttleworth and Howell, 2000).

South Africa

Guidance for SEA in South Africa identifies monitoring and auditing as one of the key elements of the SEA process, stating that 'resources should be monitored and audited to identify proactively any threat of non-sustainable use and allow for measures to restore sustainability' (CSIR, 2000). This emphasizes the importance of indicators to monitor the achievement of sustainability criteria, the need to have a monitoring and auditing programme in place and the need for feedback in order for SEA to promote continual improvement. Another objective in South Africa is to allow for adjustments of the sustainability framework and the nature of the plan and programme, relating it to the plan and programme development context. This means that other forms of follow-up can be required and should be considered apart from that currently conducted, which include performance and conformance follow-up. Sustainability frameworks may be used as an input to a monitoring and auditing process and should be adjusted as a result.

Follow-up case examples in existing policy-, plan- and programme-making

Five examples for current formal and informal follow-up practice of policy, plan and programme environmental assessment from Hong Kong, The Netherlands (two examples), UK and Germany are outlined here in terms of their purpose, process and monitoring approach. The European examples are drawn from the work of Fischer (2002a, 2004). While all of these examples include some prediction and conformance aspects, none of them explicitly deals with uncertainty management.

Hong Kong Third Comprehensive Transport Study – SEA Technical Report (Transport Department, 1999)

Purpose

- evaluate the effects of policies
- identify further studies and modifications needed during implementation, and feedback into future decision-making

- monitor the assumptions and forecasts used in the SEA against the actual traffic growth and related environmental impacts arising from the transport strategy.

Process

- check environmental changes as well as the implementation of proposed mitigation measures, and recommend new ones if required
- regularly review or update indicators, or keep track of real growth, and compare to projected numbers, triggering a systematic review.

Facilitating agents were identified to oversee the implementation of mitigation measures, namely by initiating feasibility studies showing resource implications and the practicality of proposed mitigation measures in Hong Kong. Facilitating agents should develop an implementation schedule and report on the progress regularly. Indicators were identified to highlight changing environmental conditions. These include vehicle numbers and classes, vehicle-kilometres travelled and related traffic emissions, and ambient air quality and noise levels at sensitive receivers. Other strategic parameters that are used to assess the need to revise the strategy include population, GDP growth, private and goods vehicle fleets and cross-boundary traffic.

Lessons

Given the rather defined and site-specific selected indicators for monitoring, it may be necessary to have a considerable period of continuous monitoring to establish the causal relationship with the socio-economic indicators and enable the evaluation of proposed policies.

The Dutch Policy Plan on Drinking Water Supply – BDIV (Ministerie van Volkshuisvesting, Ruimtelijke Ordening en Milieubeheer, 1993)

Purpose

Follow-up ('ex post evaluation') of the actual impact of the BDIV is formally required by the EIA regulations under the *Environmental Management Act* 1994.

Process

A 'definition study' for the follow-up exercise was conducted for controlling the execution of the BDIV. The starting point was that lower tiers will have to establish their own follow-up systems and report to the Ministry of Environment, which will aggregate the information. This will generate the main instrument for timely and efficient future policy adjustments. Lower tiers submitting monitoring data include the Water Supply Companies. The environmental inspection board and research institutes manage follow-up systems for environmental quality. Indicators to highlight changing environmental conditions include protection of the quality of water resources, quality assurance and reliability, minimization of environmental impact, water saving, choice of resource types and production facilities.

Lessons
It is likely that the information obtained will enable the identification of unexpected or unpredicted situations that may require immediate action, which is a positive outcome. In the longer term, evaluation of the effectiveness of the BDIV itself may also become possible.

The Dutch Second Transport Structure Plan – SVVII (Ministerie van Verkeer en Waterstaat, 1989)

Purpose
Monitor whether certain objectives and targets are achieved. In this context, annual reporting on the change of a selected number of indicators is formally required.

Process
A comprehensive 'to measure is to know' programme (*'meten = weten'*) is in place. This outlines the development of a number of environmental and socio-economic indicators at the national level. An attempt is made to connect the observed patterns with the policy measures proposed in the Second Transport Structure Plan. Among others, these include:

- environmental aspects (NO_x, CO_2, C_xH_y, noise, habitat fragmentation)
- safety issues (mortalities, injuries)
- accessibility (delayed trains, travel time ratios for private and public transport, traffic jams)
- general transport and traffic issues (parking management, bicycle use, public transport and private transport kilometres, public transport subsidies)
- goods transport (road, rail and water traffic, inter-modality)
- economic objectives (competitiveness of national and international infrastructure).

Additionally, a comprehensive national state of the environment report is prepared by the National Institute for Public Health and the Environment (RIVM). This identifies changes in pollution levels, the health of the biophysical environment and the use of resources and is the basis for the national environmental policy plan.

Lessons
The follow-up programme is ongoing. While an attempt is made to connect indicators with the measures proposed in the SVVII (establishing cause–effect relationships), the impact on further action and decisions remains unclear.

Due to the political changes in The Netherlands in 2001 and 2002, there was a significant shift towards different policy objectives than those formulated in the transport plan. These particularly include abandoning the idea of managing demand towards meeting a perceived demand.

Local Transport Plan, Lancashire, UK (Lancashire County Council, 1996)

Purpose
While there are no formal requirements to monitor effects connected with the local transport plan, the underlying strategy identifies the need to follow-up actual developments. This is also a requirement formulated in the Lancashire Local Agenda 21.

Process
An annual, mostly qualitative evaluation exercise is carried out based on the following indicators:

* public transport use, modal shift, pedestrian and bicycle volumes
* traffic speeds, journey times
* pollution, noise, vibration
* accidents
* public opinion.

Lessons
While there is continuous monitoring of certain data sets, in many cases it is unclear how data relate to the proposed action, in other words, cause–effect relationships remain unclear.

Land-use Plan, Ketzin, Germany (Amt Ketzin, 1996)

Purpose
There are formal requirements to monitor the changing spatial development according to the German Federal Construction Law Book. Furthermore, in the *Land* Brandenburg, land-use plans need to identify areas for future compensation in case of any adverse development impacts according to the Federal Intervention Rule. Landscape plans accompany land-use plans and identify environmental and landscape objectives and land suitability.

Process
Future developments have to be in line with land suitability as identified in the land-use plan and landscape plan. The Land Environment Protection Agency (*Landesumweltamt, LUA*) regularly prepares in-depth and qualitative state of the environment reports for the whole area of the *Land* Brandenburg. However, in this context, no direct cause–effect relationships are established.

Lessons

While the kind of spatial monitoring used is effective in terms of sticking to what was originally designed, it does not help to clarify what measures are best suited to meet certain objectives, in other words, no cause–effect relationships are identified.

Types of follow-up used in the case studies

Table 10.3 summarizes the different types of follow-up found in the five case studies. While conformance, performance and dissemination (mainly comprising publicly available reports) follow-up are widely used, there is currently no uncertainty follow-up. A possible explanation is that adaptive management might be at odds with the current planning culture. However, there is a need for further research on this point to establish causes for the lack of uncertainty follow-up.

Table 10.3 *Type of Follow-up in Five Case Studies*

Type of follow-up	Hong Kong	Dutch Water	Dutch Transport	Lancashire Transport	Land-use plan Ketzin
Conformance	+	+	+		+
Performance	+	+	+	+	
Uncertainty					
Dissemination (reporting only)	+	+	+	+	+

Methodological guidance for follow-up

Based on the previous discussion, this section provides preliminary methodological guidance for SEA follow-up for policies, plans and programmes based on three key tasks: definition of purpose, establishment of approaches and reporting on outcomes. Box 10.3 presents those aspects that should be included in a SEA follow-up programme.

Define the purpose

- Check the effects of the implementation of a policy, plan or programme.
- Establish whether objectives were met and what side effects are evident.
- Check whether unexpected events occurred.
- Identify the target audience.
- Identify the mechanisms for dissemination of results.

Establish the approach

- Identify the direction of strategic impacts, and the instruments (other policies, plans, programmes, projects; Figure 10.3).

- Check whether a policy, plan or programme was acknowledged and clearly considered in subsequent tiers (including projects).
- Identify the extent to which objectives are achieved – in this context, use proposed measures and targets, if available.
- If not implemented, or only partially implemented, find out what the underlying reasons are (e.g. using consistency analysis).
- Identify the indicators for monitoring and follow-up.
- Collect the information required by the identified indicators.

Report on the outcomes

- Identify the evidence obtained, namely through the use of indicators.
- Identify the sources of information (e.g. documents, interviews), the timing involved and the techniques used.

Box 10.3 Guidance for SEA Follow-up Programme-specific Activities

- Determine the 'direction' of the impacts within a tiered system; are they between or across policies, plans, programmes and projects.
- Identify the nature, the form and the characteristics of the strategic impacts, and the tiering level at which it is expected to become evident.
- Select appropriate qualitative or quantitative indicators that represent strategic impacts.
- Establish the follow-up programme in terms of the frequency of checking and observing the strategic impacts and the necessary associated methods and techniques.
- Establish the nature and availability of reporting on strategic impacts.
- Define the monitoring process through which the monitoring reporting is to be implemented.
- Ensure that the necessary measures to support positive impacts are in place, and are communicated to the responsible authorities and agents at the appropriate level of decision-making.
- Ensure that action is undertaken to correct the situation, to reverse trends reflected in negative impacts, and increment the positive results.

Conclusions

Practical application of SEA follow-up exists, but so far only to a small extent. However, current practice can be indicative of the potential future shape of SEA follow-up. Based on current evidence and theoretical considerations, preliminary guidance has been formulated on how to conduct follow-up. In this context, the purpose of follow-up needs to be clear, a suitable approach needs to be established and outcomes need to be reported.

The four main types are: conformance, performance, uncertainty and dissemination follow-up. Conformance follow-up focuses on whether developments take place as required, complying with other overall objectives, standards and regulatory requirements. Performance follow-up focuses on the actual effects of strategic actions carried out and compares those with predictions, benchmarks and expected deliveries. Uncertainty follow-up manages unexpected and unpredicted effects, and also addresses situations of uncertainty; subsequently action plans and adaptive management are needed. Dissemination follow-up aims at improving practice by achieving a better understanding of cause–effect relationships. Feedback is of great importance in order to change current shortcomings.

A review of five case studies from Asia and Europe shows that there is currently no uncertainty follow-up evident in practice. This may be due to a difficulty in implementing adaptive management in the current planning culture. It may also relate to the relatively recent application of follow-up in EIA practices. Even though defined in the early days of EIA, follow-up did not receive the same degree of attention to its implementation.

Defining responsibilities for SEA follow-up is not straightforward, but an obvious way to proceed is to align this with those that have the responsibility for carrying out a policy, a plan or a programme. The problem is that SEA is usually a multistakeholder process, especially in policy- and plan-making, involving many people in many different contexts. Consequently, relating the responsibilities of causal effects to the authority responsible for drawing up the policy or plan seems unfair. With programmes there are more direct links and the levels of responsibility are probably easier to identify. It is therefore an issue that requires further elaboration.

Future directions for SEA follow-up may need to be related to the current experience with policy, plan and programme evaluation practices. This is often informal and infrequent. Follow-up may provide opportunities to link SEA with the planning cycle, and show some benefits in terms of methodological approaches, but also in terms of positive synergies of carrying out similar processes simultaneously.

References

Amt Ketzin (1996) *Landschaftsplan Gemeinden Ketzin/Etzin/Falkenrehde/Tremmen/ Zachow (Land-use plan)*, Brandenburg, Ketzin

Arts, J (1998) *EIA Follow-up – On the Role of Ex Post Evaluation in Environmental Impact Assessment*, Groningen, Geo Press

Au, E and Sanvicens, G (1995) 'EIA Follow-up Monitoring and Management', in Environment Protection Agency (ed) *International Study of the Effectiveness of Environmental Assessment: Report of the EIA Process Strengthening Workshop*, Canberra, 4–7 April 1995, Environment Protection Agency, available at www.deh. gov.au/assessments/eianet/eastudy/aprilworkshop/paper5.html

CEAA, Canadian Environmental Assessment Agency (1999) *The Cabinet Directive on the Environmental Assessment of Policy, Plan and Program Proposals*, Hull, CEAA, available at www.ceaa.gc.ca/0011/0002/dir_e.htm#Guidelines

CSIR, Council for Scientific and Industrial Research (2000) *Strategic Environmental Assessment in South Africa – Guideline Document*, Pretoria, Department of Environmental Affairs and Tourism

EC, European Commission (2001a) *SEA and Integration of Environment into Decision-Making*, Final Report, Contract No. B4-3040/99/136634/MAR/B4, Brussels, EC

EC, European Commission (2001b) 'Council Directive on the assessment of the effects of certain plans and programs on the environment (2001/42/EC)', *Official Journal of the European Union*, L197, 21 July 2001

ERM, Environmental Resources Management (1999) *Case-studies on Regional and Sectoral EA: An Analysis of Lessons Learned*, Final Report: Reference 5246, Washington, DC, The World Bank

Faludi, A (1989) 'Conformance vs. performance: Implication for evaluation', *Impact Assessment Bulletin*, vol 7, pp135–151

Fischer, T (1999) 'Benefits from SEA application – a comparative review of Northwest England, Noord-Holland and Brandenburg-Berlin', *Environmental Impact Assessment Review*, vol 19, pp143–173

Fischer, T (2002a) *Strategic Environmental Assessment in Transport and Land Use Planning*, London, Earthscan

Fischer, T (2002b) 'Towards a More Systematic Approach to Policy, Plan and Programme Environmental Assessment – Some Evidence from Europe', in Marsden, S and Dovers, S (eds) *SEA in Australasia*, Sydney, Federation Press

Fischer, T (2003) 'Strategic environmental assessment in post-modern times', *Environmental Impact Assessment Review*, vol 23, pp155–170

Fischer, T (2004) 'Transport policy making and SEA in Liverpool, Amsterdam and Berlin – 1997 and 2002', *Environmental Impact Assessment Review*, vol 24, pp319–336

Fischer, T and Seaton, K (2002) 'Strategic environmental assessment – planning instrument or 'lost' concept?', *Planning Practice and Research*, vol 17, pp31–44

Lancashire County Council (1996) *Transport Policies and Program 1997/98*, Preston, Lancashire County Council

Lee, N and Walsh, F (1992) 'Strategic environmental assessment: an overview', *Project Appraisal*, vol 7, pp126–136

Lee, N and Wood, C (1978) 'EIA – a European perspective', *Built Environment*, vol 4, pp101–110

Mens en Ruimte (1996) *Case Studies on Strategic Environmental Assessment*, Final Report, Vol 1, Brussels, Mens en Ruimte

Ministerie van Verkeer en Waterstaat (1989) *Second Transport Structure Plan (SVVII)*, Part D: Government decision, The Hague, Ministerie van Verkeer en Waterstaat

Ministerie van Volkshuisvesting, Ruimtelijke Ordening en Milieubeheer (1993) *SEA National Plan on Drinking and Industrial Water*, The Hague, Ministerie van Volkshuisvesting, Ruimtelijke Ordening en Milieubeheer

Ministry of the Environment (1999) *Guidelines for the environmental assessment of plans, programs and policies in Finland*, Helsinki, Ministry of the Environment

Partidário, M R (1996) 'Strategic Environmental Assessment: Key issues emerging from recent practice', *EIA Review*, vol 16, pp31–55

Partidário, M R (1999) 'Strategic Environmental Assessment – Principles and Potential' in Petts, J (ed) *Handbook of Environmental Impact Assessment, Volume 1. Environmental Impact Assessment: Process, Methods and Potential*, Oxford, Blackwell Science, pp60–73

Partidário, M R (2000) 'Elements of an SEA framework – improving the added-value of SEA', *Environmental Impact Assessment Review*, vol 20, pp647–663

Partidário, M R (2001). 'Dalla Via a la Vas' (From EIA to SEA), *Archivio di Studio Urbani e Regionali*, FrancoAngeli, anno XXXII – n. vol 71–72, pp187–204

Partidário, M R and Clark, E (eds) (2000) *Perspectives on Strategic Environmental Assessment*, Boca Raton, Florida, Lewis

Ridgway, B, McCabe, M, Bailey, J, Saunders, R and Sadler, B (1996) *Environmental Impact Assessment Training Resource Manual*, prepared for the United Nations Environment Program, Canberra, Environment Protection Agency

Sadler, B and Verheem, R (1996) *Strategic Environmental Assessment – Status, Challenges and Future Directions*, The Hague, Ministry of Housing, Spatial Planning and Environment

Sheate, W, Dagg, S, Richardson, J, Aschemann, R, Palerm, J and Steen, U (2001) *SEA and Integration of the Environment in Strategic Decision-Making*, Final Report to the European Commission, Contract No. B4-3040/99/136634/MAR/B4

Shuttleworth, J and Howell, J (2000) 'Strategic Environmental Assessment within the Government of Canada and Specifically within the Department of Foreign Affairs and International Trade', in Partidário, M R and Clark, E (eds) *Perspectives on Strategic Environmental Assessment*, Boca Raton, Florida, Lewis, pp69–79

Therivel, R and Partidário, M R (eds) (1996) *The Practice of Strategic Environmental Assessment*, London, Earthscan

Therivel, R, Wilson, E, Thompson, S, Heaney, D and Pritchard, D (1992) *Strategic Environmental Assessment*, London, Earthscan

Tomlinson, P and Atkinson, S (1987) 'Environmental audits: Proposed terminology', *Environmental Monitoring and Assessment*, vol 8, pp187–198

Transport Department (1999) *Third Comprehensive Transport Study – Strategic Environmental Assessment Technical Report*, Hong Kong, Transport Department, Government of the Hong Kong Special Administrative Region

VROM, Ministry of Housing, Physical Planning and Environment (1996) *Environmental Management Act*, English Text of the Environmental Management Act, The Hague

Wood, C and Djeddour, M (1992) 'Strategic Environmental Assessment: EA of policies, plans and programs', *Impact Assessment Bulletin*, vol 10, pp3–21

11

On Evaluating the Success of EIA and SEA

Barry Sadler

Introduction

Environmental Impact Assessment (EIA) follow-up encompasses a family of components and tools, as defined in relation to individual proposals. However, follow-up is part of a larger, generic field of ex-post evaluation, which refers here to the analysis of all aspects of EIA and Strategic Environmental Assessment (SEA) effectiveness and performance. Broadly defined, this field is concerned with how well these processes work, what benefits they deliver for decision-making and the environment and which factors contribute to their success or shortfall. A large body of work addresses these themes in one way or another, yielding insights and perspectives that extend and frame the conduct of follow-up studies.

Despite recent improvements, follow-up is poorly developed in many EIA/SEA systems and some activities are carried out superficially or not at all (especially with regard to effectiveness and performance review). As a subset of EIA/SEA follow-up, such reviews provide a policy-oriented interpretation of the lessons of operational experience. So far, only a relatively small number of countries have undertaken this type of review for either individual or system-wide application of the EIA or SEA process, and then typically on an ad hoc basis. Without systematic feedback, EIA/SEA practitioners lack the means to learn by doing and to facilitate adaptation and innovation.

This chapter takes stock of recent progress and experience with different types of EIA/SEA effectiveness and performance review. It looks at selected features, tools and case examples of approaches on three levels of meta-, macro- and micro-evaluation (Chapter 1). The purpose is to unpack key ingredients and proxies of successful EIA and SEA at each level and indicate how findings of meta- and macro-evaluation can reinforce follow-up (and vice versa). A specific aim is to identify organizing concepts, principles, criteria and methods for carrying out effectiveness and performance reviews, recognizing that such issues are difficult to address objectively (Sadler, 1988; Devuyst, 1994; Arts, 1998).

Each level of evaluation and effectiveness review is discussed in turn in the main body of the chapter. Most attention is given to meta- and macro-evaluation since micro-evaluation corresponds to proposal-specific follow-up and is amply covered in the previous chapters. The chapter begins with a brief delineation of key terms, concepts and elements of approach to EIA/SEA effectiveness and performance. It ends with conclusions and recommendations for improving the practice of EIA follow-up, specifically by reference to and use of measures and findings from other levels and types of evaluation. A proposed framework and package for a comprehensive evaluation of the success of EIA implementation and the arrangements under which it takes place is included as Appendix 1.

Organizing concepts and delineation of approach

Effectiveness and performance are interlocking concepts of success in EIA/SEA implementation. Both are broad, aggregate yardsticks or indicators of the extent to which this process achieves its stated aims or meets internationally accepted principles. When referring to EIA/SEA performance, the emphasis usually is on end states and outcomes of process implementation (e.g. what is achieved in terms of realizing environmental objectives and benefits?). The notion of effectiveness refers to the manner of performance, whether and how the EIA/SEA process – either as a whole or in the application of key stages and components – has measured up to its procedural requirements and substantive purpose (which are differently specified in national laws and policies).

The success of EIA/SEA implementation is relative, dependent on the criteria or standards that are set for effectiveness and performance review. A 'litmus test' for determining overall success is the impact of the EIA/SEA process on decision-making at all stages, from the start to final authorization and implementation of environmental terms and conditions. Specifically, does the EIA/SEA process lead to changes to project (plan or policy) design and support informed approval and condition setting, giving effect to appropriate mitigation measures? This is not easily answered, considering that evidence of success is partial, circumstantial, open to argument or may not become apparent for some time, if at all.

A reference guide to evaluating EIA effectiveness and performance is outlined in Box 11.1. When using this guide, reference should be made to the schema of the field of EIA ex-post evaluation outlined in Table 11.1. In this framework, categories of activity are subdivided in accordance with their primary purpose and main elements of approach. Their relationship to EIA follow-up of projects or plans is also shown. At this level, a distinction is made between:

Table 11.1 *A Schema of the Field of Ex-post Evaluation and its Relationship to EIA/SEA Follow-up*

Category	Primary function	Elements of approach
Impact monitoring and management	Proposal-specific EIA/SEA implementation and quality control	Operational or micro level: • surveillance and supervision • effects and mitigation monitoring • compliance and impact auditing • application of EIA follow-up to operational EMS
Effectiveness and performance review	Learning and process development	Operational or micro level: • decision and institutional analysis • quality assurance of methods and procedures • post-project (or plan) analysis System or macro level: • periodic review of the implementation of EIA system • operational and compliance audit of EIA system • comparative analysis of EIA systems
'State of the art' analysis	Better understanding and 'field development'	Generic or meta level: • quality of EIA/SEA reports and studies • practitioner surveys of trends and issues • principles and guidance on EIA/SEA good practice • efficacy of the concepts of EIA and SEA • theory of EIA evaluation and follow-up

Note: The 'operational or micro level' activities correspond to the project level EIA follow-up activities defined in Chapter 1.

• *use of impact monitoring and management for development control,* focusing on corrective actions to address unanticipated or larger than predicted impacts
• *conduct of effectiveness and performance review to learn from doing,* applying the results to future actions.

For EIA projects, this includes integrating impact monitoring and management with Environmental Management Systems (EMS) of the operating facility, which is a key to give effect to an adaptive approach. Similar considerations apply to SEA, although typically policy, plans and programmes require more flexible tracking systems.

Box 11.1 A Reference Guide to Ex-post Evaluation of EIA and SEA

Terms and definitions: Ex-post evaluation here refers to a generic process of review, analysis and interpretation of all aspects of EIA and SEA effectiveness and performance, encompassing the process as a whole and its components, methods, procedures, activities, products, results and their policy and institutional implications. The term *effectiveness*, simply stated, means whether the process or its elements work satisfactorily to meet their intended purpose and *performance* connotes the successful accomplishment or achievement of the task or activity. As such, effectiveness is a broad, aggregate yardstick of the manner of performance.

It encompasses related, subsidiary concepts such as:

- *efficiency* of operations
- *fairness* of procedure and administration
- *cost-effectiveness* or achieving the intended outcome at the least cost
- *efficacy* or relative potential to deliver a particular result, i.e. does EIA/SEA deliver on its potential or could other instruments do the job better?

Concepts and dimensions: A comprehensive approach to ex-post evaluation is built on a 'triangulation test', which relates *policy, practice and performance* (the three Ps). Policy specifies what is required, practice is what actually happens, and performance is concerned with the results and the manner of achievement, relating what happened and what was required. The focus of effectiveness and performance review is on learning from experience and feedback to improve EIA and SEA process and practice in the future.

Such an ex-post evaluation can be undertaken along one or all of three main dimensions:

- *procedural* – Does the EIA or SEA process comply with established provisions and principles?
- *substantive* – Does the EIA or SEA meet its purposes(s) and objectives; e.g. support informed decision-making (immediate aim) and achieve environmental protection (ultimate aim)?
- *transactive* – Does the EIA or SEA process deliver these outcomes efficiently (at least cost and with minimum delay) and equitably (without bias or prejudice to the participants)?

Evaluation principles: The following set of principles provides a framework for a systematic, empirically-based approach to ex-post evaluation:

- place EIA or SEA in the overall context of the decision-making process and the forces and factors bearing on practice and performance
- specify performance criteria, measures and indicators for evaluating the overall effectiveness of EIA or SEA and its operational characteristics
- adopt a multiple-perspective approach, canvassing views of participants to gain a full appreciation of process effectiveness
- recognize that participants' views of success are relative and vary with role, affiliation, values and past experience
- corroborate these views with data and factual information (e.g. from project files, inspection reports, effects monitoring and environmental audits)
- qualify the issues and challenges in comparison to accepted standards of good practice (e.g. complex problem relatively poorly/well handled in the circumstances)
- focus on the 'art of the possible' when drawing conclusions, contrasting what was accomplished with what realistically could be achieved
- identify cost-effective improvements that can be implemented immediately, as well as longer term, structural changes that appear necessary (e.g. to law, procedure and methods).

Source: Sadler, 1998.

In practice, the control and learning functions are not clearly separable in EIA follow-up, and the emphasis changes from one to the other as the follow-up process unfolds. Early activities will centre on supervision and monitoring to check compliance with environmental regulations and terms, when informal evaluation will be part of taking any corrective actions that are necessary. Later, policy-related evaluation of EIA implementation may be carried out as a formal procedure to document effectiveness and performance, focusing on the overall contribution to decision-making or particular strengths and weaknesses. When the focus is on a specific type of development, such as a road or dam, ex-post evaluation corresponds to post-project analysis of experience gained from design to construction (Sadler, 1987; UNECE, 1990).

Only ex-post evaluation of EIA/SEA effectiveness and performance in relation to specific projects and plans meets the strict definition of follow-up (as shown by the demarcation of the micro and macro levels in Table 11.1). However, studies of all levels and categories of ex-post evaluation are needed to draw broader lessons from EIA/SEA follow-up studies. For example, macro-studies of the performance of EIA/SEA systems offer a frame of reference against which to interpret the policy implications of follow-up, which in turn adds to the larger stock of information. Similarly, generic 'state of the art' analyses and particularly work to 'benchmark' EIA principles and standards of good practice are useful for substantiating the wider importance of operational results from follow-up. In turn, these linkages facilitate better understanding and further development of the field, including 'theory building' and methodology of ex-post evaluation and follow-up. Work on this

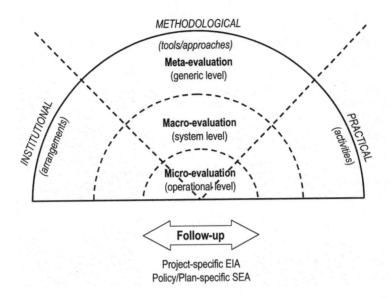

Figure 11.1 *The Anatomy of Success – Scales and Dimensions of Ex-post Evaluation*

subject appears to be limited and largely derived from the planning literature (Sadler, 1990, 1998; Arts, 1998; Emmelin, 1998).

For rounded coverage, the anatomy of success of EIA and SEA needs to be dissected on all three levels of ex-post evaluation and with regard to the institutional, methodological and practical dimensions illustrated in Figure 11.1. The jigsaw puzzle of EIA effectiveness and performance is complex and cannot be reduced to putting together a few pieces, which anyway are subject to different perspectives on what is important. However, certain aspects of meta-, macro- and micro-evaluation can bring particular focus to the wider significance and success of the EIA/SEA process. As such they provide a frame of reference for relating follow-up activities to issues of effectiveness and performance and may be thought of as EIA/SEA follow-up 'writ large'. The elements of success identified in Box 11.2 are particularly important and are discussed in further detail in the remainder of this chapter, beginning with meta level evaluation of the concepts of EIA and SEA.

Meta-evaluation of the success of EIA and SEA as policy concepts and tools

Meta-evaluation specifically addresses 'big picture' issues of whether EIA and SEA successfully measure up to their full potential as policy concepts and instruments for informed decision-making and lead to better project

> ## Box 11.2 Dimensions of Success of EIA and SEA Considered
>
> **Meta-evaluation of the success of EIA and SEA as a policy idea and instrument** – focusing on the efficacy of EIA/SEA as a generic approach to anticipate and manage environmental effects, comparing its potential as a policy instrument with the process as institutionalized worldwide.
>
> **Macro-evaluation of the success of EIA and SEA systems at the jurisdictional (e.g. national) level** – focusing on overall effectiveness and performance of EIA/SEA systems established by particular countries or international agencies, such as the World Bank, which apply to a large number of borrowing countries.
>
> **Micro-evaluation of the success of EIA and SEA application to specific proposals** – focusing on aspects of effectiveness and performance of project-based EIA or SEA of a specific policy, plan or programme proposal.

and policy design, improved environmental protection or more sustainable use of natural resources. It also probes the fundamental approach to impact assessment, including its theoretical underpinnings, rationale, scope and institutionalization (what are the guiding premises, why is this process important, how should it be applied, where and in what form has it been adopted?). Such broad scale questions and issues can be reviewed from a number of standpoints, some normative and some empirical. For present purposes, the focus is on what EIA has achieved and what realistically could have been achieved, looking back over 30 years of practical experience. A sub-text is whether and how other policy tools, applied together with EIA and SEA, may better realize the potential of this process, particularly to address the impacts that matter.

Much of the literature bears on the above theme in some way (e.g. Petts, 1999). Typically, for example, 'state of the art' reviews draw on the 'conventional wisdom' of accumulated experience to document strengths and weaknesses of the field. A survey of the broad contours of field development is undertaken here, focusing on the evolution of EIA and SEA in relation to new demands and policy imperatives, particularly those expressed in international law and agreements. Five 'tests' (Box 11.3) are used to gain a systematic perspective on the success of EIA and SEA as policy concepts or tools and a perspective on future directions and requirements for process strengthening (Table 11.2). When combined, the five tests comprise a set of progressively higher clearance bars for judging relative progress using the indicators also provided in Table 11.2.

Box 11.3   Convergence Tests and Indicators of Success of EIA and SEA as Policy Instruments

The status of EIA/SEA as policy instruments can be evaluated by reference to five tests:

Test 1: Wide adoption and use in different parts of the world?
Test 2: Record of process innovation or improvement?
Test 3: Inclusion of new areas and aspects for consideration?
Test 4: Added value to decision-making and condition-setting?
Test 5: Effective means of environmental protection?

For each test, the degree of relative success or convergence can be evaluated against the following scale:

A   The feature is represented fully and completely.
B   The feature is represented well but there are minor qualifications.
C   The feature is represented but there are a number of reservations.
D   The feature is not represented well.
E   The feature is represented only minimally or incipiently.

Wide adoption and use of EIA and SEA (Test 1)

EIA has been widely adopted and used in different parts of the world, and it substantially meets the first test of success as a policy instrument. Major phases in the evolution of EIA are summarized in Box 11.4. First introduced in 1970 in one country (the US), there were successive waves of take up of EIA leading to its near universal acceptance as an instrument of national decision-making, as specified in Principle 17 of the *Rio Declaration on Environment and Development* (1992). Now in place in more than 100 countries, EIA also is used extensively by the World Bank and other international lending and development agencies. A particularly notable feature of the past decade has been the domestic introduction of EIA by many developing and transition countries. However, EIA take up by lower-income countries remains incomplete.

In contrast to EIA, SEA is still at a relatively early stage of adoption and does not *yet* meet the test of widespread use in different parts of the world. Currently, only a small number of countries, mainly in Europe and North America, have made formal provision for SEA. However, wider adoption and use of SEA is underway; 15 member states of the European Union and 10 accession countries are in the process of transposing the SEA Directive (2001/42/EC) into national legislation (Box 11.4). Once these statutes come into force (July 2004), there will be a doubling of the number of countries with SEA systems, and further expansion is expected to occur as countries ratify the SEA Protocol to the UNECE Convention on EIA in a Transboundary

Box 11.4 Major Trends in EIA and SEA

The *evolution of EIA* can be divided into three overlapping phases:

1 **Introduction and development** (1970–1980) – mandate and foundations laid down by the *US National Environmental Policy Act 1969* (NEPA); basic framework, procedure and methodology still apply; limited adoption by other countries.
2 **Development and diversification** (1980–1992) – scope of EIA extended; procedural and methodological innovation; social, health and other types of impacts given more systematic consideration; supra-national and international EIA frameworks introduced.
3 **'Mainstreaming' and 'up-streaming'** (1992–2002) – take up of EIA by a large number of developing and transitional countries; development of formal SEA systems; inter-sector approach, including new aspects of EIA practice; emphasis now turning towards integrated assessment and sustainability assurance (a new, fourth phase?).

The *evolution of SEA* also can be divided into three overlapping phases:

1 **Formative stage** (1970–1989) – certain legal and policy precedents established in EIA (and related fields); SEA formally applied at the plan and programme level only in US (federal and California EIA systems); some elements of SEA practice in place elsewhere.
2 **Formalization stage** (1990–2000) – SEA provision made by a number of countries and by the World Bank; relatively diversified arrangements and procedure compared to EIA; differentiated forms of SEA practice (as applied to policy or legislation compared to plans and programmes).
3 **Extension and consolidation stage** (2001 onward) – SEA take up and practice in certain countries will be influenced by supra-national and international instruments; EC Directive (2001/41/EC) comes into force in 2004 in member and accession states; an SEA protocol to the Espoo Convention is being negotiated by UNECE countries.

Source: adapted from Sadler 1996, 2001a

Context. So far, the use of SEA in the developing world is largely tied to the requirements of the World Bank or other international development agencies. However, elements of SEA may be in place in some developing countries and there is considerable demand for SEA capacity development, which augers well for future take up.

Record of process innovation or improvement (Test 2)

The development of EIA has been characterized by continued innovation and improvement in law, procedure and methodology and largely meets the second test of success as a policy instrument. However, note that the EIA process was substantially laid down by NEPA implementation and has followed a standard pattern ever since, although over time various minor improvements and adjustments have been made in response to long-standing problem areas. Of particular note are institutional arrangements for EIA quality control and assurance, including strengthened requirements, methods and procedures for follow-up. During the past decade, EIA legislation has been introduced in many developing and transitional countries, and comprehensive reforms have been made in countries that adopted EIA early[1].

SEA process development in the past decade has been impressive and it also largely meets the second test of success as a policy instrument. The arrangements and procedures for SEA are relatively diverse; formal provision is made under EIA or other legislation, administrative order or policy guidelines. Some SEA processes are based on and follow EIA procedure, whereas others apply a modified or minimum procedure. This more flexible approach is adapted particularly to the fluid, iterative process of policy-making. At the level of plans and programmes, EIA-based arrangements are common and further standardization took place when the European Directive on SEA came into force in 2004. The provisions of the Directive have heavily influenced the SEA Protocol of the UNECE[2], which is about much more than transboundary effects and stands as an international procedural benchmark, even though more narrowly cast than some would prefer (Sadler, 2001b).

Inclusion of new areas and aspects (Test 3)

The scope of the EIA process has become progressively broader through the inclusion of new areas and aspects and it largely meets the third test of success as a policy instrument. New demands on EIA have been made as a result of developments in national and international law and policy, as exemplified by the UN Convention on Biological Diversity and the WSSD *Plan of Implementation*. Over the 30-year history of EIA, several trends stand out:

- consideration of other types of impacts and risks (e.g. social, health, visual, gender) which comprise new domains of impact assessment (Porter and Fittipaldi, 1998)
- extension in the scales of assessment to take on more complex, interdependent issues (e.g. cumulative effects, ecological risk, climate change)
- initiation of more interactive forms of public involvement (e.g. mediation, stakeholder dialogue, traditional ecological knowledge)
- application of EIA to new levels and dimensions of decision-making (e.g. strategic, trans-boundary and international lending, assistance).

The scope of SEA has followed a similar evolution to that of EIA and also meets the third test of success as a policy instrument. For present purposes, the inclusion of new areas and aspects of SEA can be grouped into three main phases:

- increase in the type of sectors and spatial plans subject to SEA (as exemplified by the list in the European SEA Directive)
- coverage of other cross-sector or government-wide initiatives, although so far on a relatively limited scale (e.g. trade, investment, macro-economic structural adjustments, national development plans)
- application of SEA across larger spatial scales (e.g. to implement country adaptations to global change or to support international river basin management).

Added value to decision-making and condition setting (Test 4)

EIA and SEA processes are acknowledged as adding value to decision-making in international law and policy; for example, in Principle 17 of the *Rio Declaration on Environment and Development* (which applies only to EIA) and in the preamble to the UNECE Protocol for SEA. Specifically, EIA and SEA provide information on the environmental consequences of proposed actions, thereby leading to more informed choice and, ultimately, to an improved level of environmental protection (Test 5). Generally, these benefits can be traced in most systems, if only on a minimal level, and their distribution is highly variable within and among countries. Of course, such evaluations are based on circumstantial evidence, and are open to different interpretations.

Relatively few surveys of impact assessment professionals have been undertaken to corroborate such findings. One example indicated that EIA was rated as generally successful in ensuring that environmental considerations are taken into account to inform decision-making (Sadler, 1996). However, EIA was considered to be somewhat less influential in establishing terms and conditions of development approval. A more recent survey of International Association for Impact Assessment (IAIA) members indicated that two-thirds considered there had been no improvement in this latter aspect. Less than one-quarter rated current performance in setting terms and conditions of approval as good or better, a slightly larger proportion considered it to be poor or worse, and approximately one-half judged it to be satisfactory (IAIA, 2002).

Similar trends appear to characterize the role of SEA in decision-making, although further qualifications apply. First, SEA is a more diverse, less standardized process than EIA, with variations in influence on decision-making apparent amongst the different types of approach, notably between policy appraisal and the application of EIA-derived procedure to plans and programmes. Second, the relationship of SEA to policy-making and planning typically is less linear and more multidimensional than for EIA, which typically leads to final approval of a specific physical development. Third, because policies, plans and programmes typically encompass a number of components, the role of SEA in relation to setting terms and conditions can be difficult to track and evaluate. Little has been reported on this aspect of SEA practice in the literature on the field.

Effective means of achieving environmental protection (Test 5)

Arguably, EIA and SEA fall well short of being effective means of achieving environmental protection, although this is a complex relationship and needs to be unpacked on a number of levels. First, mitigation is widely considered to be reasonably successful in identifying appropriate measures to avoid, minimize or offset adverse impacts (as indicated by both the surveys mentioned previously). Second, there are reservations, however, about the implementation and enforcement of mitigation measures and their cost-effectiveness[3]. Third, the relationship of EIA (or SEA) implementation to environmental protection 'on the ground' is elusive since it is mediated by many intervening factors, beginning with decision-making and condition setting[4]. Fourth, in part, this reflects on certain deficiencies of EIA follow-up, including the failure to consider the wider implications for effectiveness and performance (using the information from meta-, macro- and other micro-evaluations).

Without such information, a crude proxy of the overall success of EIA and SEA as means to achieve environmental protection can be gained by reference to global or national state of the environment reports. In the third *Global Environmental Outlook*, for example, key trends are described for the 30 year period that EIA has been established. They are also projected forward to 2032 when it is estimated that 70 per cent of the Earth's land surface could be adversely affected by human activity unless urgent action is taken (UNEP, 2002). This sense of impacts becoming more complex and harder to assess was held by 95 per cent and 75 per cent, respectively, of respondents to the IAIA survey (IAIA, 2002). An earlier survey found that EIA is considered to result in environmental benefits but to stop short of providing real safeguards for avoiding irreversible loss or change (Sadler, 1996).

From this perspective, the application of EIA and SEA helps to protect the environment but does not approximate to the lowest common denominator of environmental sustainability (Sadler, 1996, 1999). If so, it heavily qualifies earlier tests of the success of EIA and SEA as policy instruments. Of course, it can be argued that without EIA and SEA, trends in resource depletion and ecological deterioration would be worse. In the end, the issue is not so much the deficiencies of EIA or SEA as means of environmental protection as the limitations of the larger policy and institutional framework that is applied. Only a small proportion of new proposals is subject to EIA or SEA and, more tellingly, most adverse impacts occur as a result of ongoing rather than proposed activities. In this context, EIA follow-up can forge useful linkages between project implementation and environmental management of operating facilities (Sadler and Baxter, 1998).

Retrospect and prospect – towards paradigmatic change

Based on the above evaluation, EIA and SEA are given passing grades in four of the five tests of their success as policy instruments (Table 11.2). Looked at in the round, the progress of the field of EIA from its beginning in one country to its adoption worldwide has been impressive, especially given the relatively short time period over which the instrument has evolved. In the past decade, the development of SEA has been the most striking feature and the field now stands on the threshold of potentially far reaching change. Yet so far, EIA and SEA have failed to measure up along with other tools as effective means for environmental protection, especially against sustainability bottom lines.

This collective indictment has important implications for the future direction of EIA and SEA and the larger field of environmental management. It points towards the need first to further strengthen the integrity of the EIA and SEA process by addressing weaknesses such as follow-up in order to provide better feedback on the outcomes of specific proposals. Second, it indicates the potential value of linking EIA and SEA as part of more integrated frameworks and tools for sustainability appraisal of development proposals and actions. Such approaches are still wanting according to many reports, including *Global Environmental Outlook 3* and the WSSD *Plan of Implementation,* and a number of institutional and methodological constraints remain to be ironed out (UNEP, 2001).

Table 11.2 *Report Card on the Success of EIA and SEA as Policy Instruments*

Aspect evaluated	Score/Rating	
	EIA	**SEA**
Test 1 Wide adoption and use	B+	C
Test 2 Record of process innovation or improvement	B	B
Test 3 Inclusion of new areas and aspects	A–	B–
Test 4 Added value to decision-making and condition setting	C+	C–
Test 5 Effective means of achieving environmental protection	C–	C–?

Note: See Box 11.3 for basis of Score/Rating system

In that context, the evolution of EIA, initially from a 'first' to a 'second' generation SEA process, is indicative of how far this field has come and still has to go. By some accounts, EIA and SEA now are moving towards a 'third' or 'next generation' process of integrated impact assessment or sustainability appraisal (Table 11.3). The terms and scope of this evolving approach vary; it is also called sustainability impact assessment (European Commission), strategic impact analysis (OECD/DAC working group) and integrated assessment and planning for sustainable development (UNEP). It is evident that the three paradigms are at very different stages in their evolution and take up. EIA at the project level is now well established with internationally accepted norms, SEA is at an earlier phase of process evolution and application, and integrated approaches are still at the prototype stage (i.e. not yet institutionalized).

This emerging paradigm appears to be developing along two main avenues, which eventually could converge. First, integrated assessment or sustainability

Table 11.3 *Paradigm Shifts – From EIA to SEA and towards Sustainability Appraisal*

Stage of approach	Focus of approach
First generation – project level EIA	Environmental and related impacts of major development actions
Second generation – SEA	Environmental effects of policy, plans, programmes and legislation
Third or next generation – integrated impact assessment or sustainability appraisal	Economic, environmental and social impacts of project and strategic level proposals or sustainability appraisal if tested against 'triple bottom line' (economic, environmental and social) thresholds or criteria

Source: Sadler, 1996, 1999

appraisal (the former is a basis for the latter but not necessarily the same thing, as Table 11.3 indicates) addresses the full costs and consequences of a proposed action at all levels of decision-making. As such, they bring together economic, environmental and social appraisal, although not necessarily in the form of methodological reconciliation. Second, integrated environmental management addresses the impacts of all actions from both proposed and continuing actions (Table 11.4). An interim or integrative route, termed *environmental sustainability assurance* (ESA) aims to maintain the 'source and sink' functions of natural systems, rather than just minimizing and mitigating impacts (Sadler, 1996, 1999). It links EIA and SEA upstream with environmental accounting and downstream with environmental auditing (Goodland and Sadler, 1996).

These trends have a range of implications for EIA/SEA theory and practice, calling into question basic assumptions and elements of the generic approach (e.g. the scientific rationality and reductionism underpinning the 'before and after' predictive model). In moving in that direction, EIA and SEA are simply going 'back to the future'; back to the concepts outlined in NEPA, which requires federal agencies to 'utilize a systematic, interdisciplinary approach'. Yet such an approach remains demanding, 'never more needed... yet never further away' (O'Riordan, 1998). One way forward is to maintain the integrity and strengthen the EIA/SEA process as one of the analytical streams that are needed to address the full costs and consequences of a proposal and clarify the trade-offs at stake. For example, the report of the World Commission on Dams (2000) has proposed an approach based on identification of rights and interests of those affected, assessment of risks and impacts, ensuring that participation in the decision-making process is commensurate with involuntarily loss and risk bearing, and reconciling competing entitlements by negotiation.

Table 11.4 *Tool Kit for Integrated Environmental Management*

Purpose	Examples of available tools
Integrating the environment into macro-economic and sector policy making and planning	*Macro or trend analysis of environmental impacts* – environmental accounting, ecological footprint analysis, state of the environment reporting *Micro analysis of environmental impacts of proposals* – SEA, technology assessment, comparative risk assessment
Planning and designing environmentally sound projects	EIA, SIA, risk assessment, environmental benefit cost assessment
Environmental management of operations and activities	IPPC (1996 EU-Directive on Integrated Pollution Prevention and Control), EMS (environmental management systems, e.g. ISO 14000 series)
Eco-efficiency of industrial processes and products	Environmental design, life cycle assessment, cleaner production

Source: Sadler, 2002

Within this framework, the emphasis in integration is towards a convergence of elements of approach so that EIA/SEA encompasses (Sadler, 2002):

- *impact science*, taking an adaptive approach to cope with scientific uncertainty
- *civic science*, engaging the people affected by proposals in impact identification and issue resolution
- *'trans-science'*, relating and, where possible, synthesizing facts and values
- *policy science*, informing decision-making and clarifying trade-offs
- *sustainability science*, applying the precautionary principle and the polluter pays principle to ensure that valued resources and ecosystem services are protected, impacts are kept within acceptable levels and losses are made good.

Macro-evaluation of the success of EIA and SEA systems and components

'Macro level' evaluation, focusing on EIA and SEA systems, provides a frame of reference against which EIA follow-up and specific effectiveness and performance reviews can be carried out. At this level, the interpretation of effectiveness and performance is undertaken against the particular legal and institutional regime under which the EIA or SEA process operates.

For example, in the US, NEPA and its implementing Regulations provide 'benchmarks' for making judgements about how well that process works and what it has achieved. EIA arrangements and experience of multilateral lending institutions, member states of the European Union and countries of other regions also have been compared in terms of their common elements and activities (Petts, 1999). Similar comparisons of SEA systems have been made (Sadler and Verheem, 1996) and attention is now turning to SEA capacity and experience of developing and transitional countries (Dalal-Clayton and Sadler, 1998, 2003; Lee and George, 2001).

A number of approaches and instruments can be used for macro-evaluation of the success of EIA and SEA. Of particular interest here are effectiveness or performance-related reviews that incorporate one or more of the following (Sadler, 1998):

- use of evaluative criteria or formal methodologies
- based on surveys of the views of practitioners or stakeholders
- commissioned or undertaken by national or international agencies with responsibility for implementation of the EIA or SEA process.

Following this schema, examples of reviews of EIA and SEA systems and components are outlined in the following sections. These have been selected to illustrate dimensions of success in EIA and SEA and factors that contribute to an effective process and good practice, as well as to give some examples of macro-evaluation concepts and approaches. The discussion is divided into four components:

- enabling conditions for EIA or SEA effectiveness and performance
- approaches to comparing the effectiveness and performance of EIA or SEA systems
- selected findings of effectiveness and performance reviews of three leading EIA and SEA systems
- lessons related to improving the effectiveness and performance of EIA and SEA systems and components.

Enabling conditions for EIA or SEA effectiveness and performance

A litmus test of the effectiveness of EIA and SEA is whether and how these processes make a difference to decision-making. The application of this test involves making a distinction between *the quality of the information* delivered by the EIA or SEA process and *the degree of influence* on the choices throughout the decision-making process, culminating in formal approval and condition setting (Sadler 1996). The *influence* of EIA or SEA on decision-making is indirect, issue-specific and circumscribed by the political culture of a country or organization. By contrast, the *quality of information* provided by assessments can be linked directly back to the integrity of the process.

From this distinction, the enabling conditions of EIA and SEA effectiveness come into sharper focus. They reflect the interaction of two basic components of an EIA or SEA system:

- appropriate institutional arrangements for implementing the process, including defined procedure, guidance on its application and mechanisms for quality control and assurance
- adequate competencies for the conduct of assessment, sometimes summarized as the 'three Rs' of good practice:
  - *rigorous* analysis
  - *responsive* consultation
  - *responsible* administration.

Comparing the effectiveness and performance of EIA or SEA systems

Status reports on the main characteristics of the EIA systems of 25 countries and jurisdictions are available as part of the international effectiveness study (Sadler and Verheem, 1997). They describe the institutional framework of law, policy and regulation; the process and procedures that are applied; and the use and results of EIA in decision-making. A comparative evaluation of the performance of EIA and SEA systems was included in the final report of the effectiveness study focusing on the extent to which certain principles or criteria of effectiveness are reflected in procedure and practice and how these aspects vary from country to country (Sadler, 1996). Earlier studies include Hollick (1986), Ortolano et al (1987), Gibson (1993), Lee et al (1994) and the definitive review of leading EIA systems by Wood (1995, updated 2003), whose methodology has been replicated by others (e.g. Annandale, 2001) (Box 11.5).

Box 11.5 Comparative Review of EIA Systems

Theme and approach: The evaluative framework of Wood (1995, 1999) comprises 12 questions that are applied to analyse and compare EIA procedure and implementation. In his updated review, Wood (2003) compares the EIA systems of seven countries – Australia, Canada, The Netherlands, New Zealand, South Africa, UK and US. Each system is reviewed in terms of how well it meets the evaluation criteria and then each criterion is examined to identify how performance varies with regard to particular steps and components of the EIA process.

Evaluation framework: As paraphrased below, Wood's evaluation criteria centre on four main dimensions of EIA systems:

- basis and requirements – is the EIA system based on clear and specific legal provision? Does it apply to policies, plans and programmes as well (SEA)?

- scope of application – must the relevant environmental impacts of all significant actions be assessed and must there be consideration of alternatives?
- main steps and activities – does the EIA process meet appropriate standards of screening, scoping, report preparation, report review, decision-making, monitoring and auditing, impact mitigation and public consultation?
- monitoring and review of EIA implementation – is there mandatory provision for this type of follow-up? Are the financial and time costs acceptable to those involved and perceived as weighing less than environmental benefits?

Some findings (Wood 1999): For present purposes, these can be divided into two main types related to:

1 *The performance of individual EIA systems.* An overall rating of the EIA systems can be derived from their aggregate standing against the evaluation criteria. Several broad conclusions stand out:
   - The Netherlands and the US (to a lesser extent) rate high on almost all dimensions and form a first tier of EIA systems (the state of Western Australia also is in this category)
   - Canada, Australia and New Zealand meet more than the half of the criteria and form a second tier of EIA systems (the state of California also is in this category)
   - the UK performs worst of the countries on the basis of this rating scheme and is described 'as a fairly typical first generation EIA system'.
2 *The performance of particular steps and activities of the EIA process.* Of particular note are conclusions regarding:
   - impact monitoring and auditing – no country meets the criterion for this component, although Canada and The Netherlands do so partially (together with California and Western Australia which do so fully)
   - system monitoring – three of the countries reviewed – Canada, The Netherlands and US (together with Western Australia) – have formal arrangements that meet this criterion. For example, the Canadian Environmental Assessment Agency has a legal duty to undertake a five-year review of experience under the Act and the US Council on Environmental Quality is required under NEPA to submit an annual report to Congress.

Source: Wood, 1995, 1999, 2003.

Attributes of effectiveness identified in these macro-evaluation reviews are variously stated and some are specific to individual countries or compare EIA performance within federal states, for example, Canadian federal, provincial and territorial EIA systems (Doyle and Sadler, 1996). Others are common or generic and can be employed as criteria to screen the performance of EIA systems by asking if there is:

- *clear legal provision* with specific requirements and prescribed responsibilities?
- *appropriate scope of application* to all proposed actions likely to have potentially significant impacts on the environment?
- *specified process and procedure* in accordance with internationally accepted steps and activities?
- *authoritative guidance* on process application steps and activities?
- *explicit opportunity for public involvement* preferably tailored to the parties involved?
- *focus on decisions* and issues that matter, with a transparent linkage to formal approval and condition setting?
- *requirement for follow-up* as and when necessary including the full complement of activities as described in this book?

Similar criteria also apply to SEA systems, although certain additions and modifications need to be introduced to take account of their different characteristics compared to EIA systems. These can be drawn from various reviews of the effectiveness and performance of SEA systems. For example, the SEA component of the effectiveness study (Sadler and Verheem, 1996) has been updated by a survey of the experience of approximately 20 countries, which follows the structure of the EIA status reports described previously (IEA, 1997, 1999). This survey considers the status and practice of SEA in OECD countries and identifies emerging trends and challenges (Box 11.6).

Effectiveness and performance reviews of national and multilateral EIA and SEA systems

At the national level, relevant studies include annual reports, periodic evaluations and ad hoc studies of the operation of EIA and SEA systems by official bodies with either responsibility for their implementation or for auditing or evaluating performance. Internationally, comparable studies focus on the EIA or SEA experience of the World Bank and the implementation of the EIA Directive within the European Union (CEC, 2003). From among these formal reviews, comprehensive evaluations of national and multilateral EIA or SEA systems are of particular interest. Three examples follow that correspond to this criterion, namely reviews of experience under NEPA (US), World Bank Operational Policy, and the Canadian Environmental Assessment Act and the Cabinet Directive on SEA of Policy and programmes.

Review of NEPA experience
The US NEPA is the founding EIA legislation and remains its Magna Carta as much for the declaration of purpose and goals (s101) as for the introduction of the environmental impact statement (EIS) as an action-forcing mechanism to reform federal policy-making and administration (s102). Under Title II of the Act, the Council on Environmental Quality (CEQ) was established to oversee its implementation and was required to report annually on environmental

Box 11.6 Comparative Review of SEA Systems

Theme and approach: This study verified and updated data from an initial survey of the status and practice of SEA in OECD countries (IEA, 1997). It includes a more detailed and comparative analysis of SEA arrangements and implementation in nine jurisdictions (Canada, California, Denmark, The Netherlands, New Zealand, Sweden, UK, US and the World Bank). This analysis was based upon a questionnaire survey sent to the responsible authority for the SEA process. A similar format was followed to that used to obtain information for the status reports of the international study of EIA effectiveness (Sadler and Verheem, 1997).

Evaluation framework: This review centred on the following dimensions of SEA systems:

- form of provision for SEA – focusing on the different types of legal and administrative arrangements
- scope of application – the sectors and levels of decision-making covered and the factors and issues addressed
- process and procedure – the steps and elements of SEA including compliance and oversight responsibilities
- practice and outcomes – the number of SEA applications, time taken and impact on decision-making.

Some findings: Key findings include:

- SEA frameworks and procedure vary far more than for EIA
- there are evident differences in approach to SEA of policy and legislation as compared to plans and programmes
- so far, few countries have a comprehensive scope of SEA application covering all levels of decision-making and sectors with potentially significant environmental effects
- although difficult to establish, the quality of SEA practice and reports and their contribution to decision-making appears to be mixed at best, often falling short of good practice or failing to comply with requirements
- a paucity of factual information (as compared to rough estimates) regarding numbers, type and quality of SEA practice indicates weaknesses in monitoring and effects tracking.

Source: IEA, 1999.

trends and conditions (s201), including progress and issues related to NEPA implementation. CEQ annual reports provide an unparalleled record of EIA process development. In addition, special reports and guidance on particular issues and aspects of NEPA experience have been prepared (see *NEPANet* at www.ceq.eh.doe.gov).

Early CEQ annual reports, for example, document experience with EIS content, quality and use in decision-making; NEPA litigation; and problems related to costs and delays (CEQ, 1975). Reference was also made to the increased use of 'programme impact statements' some 25 years before the SEA Directive was finalized. Most federal departments and major agencies had applied this form of SEA by 1975, although less than 50 per cent had adopted procedures for this purpose, and they differed considerably in their approach at this level (CEQ, 1976a). Subsequently, CEQ (1977) recommended wider and more frequent use of 'broad scale statements' covering area-wide, agency policy and generic actions.

A major report on the first six years of NEPA performance provided an in-depth analysis of these and other key trends and made a series of recommendations to improve the quality of impact statements and their value for decision-making (CEQ, 1976b). For example, the review concluded that impact statements had substantially improved government decisions over the first six years of NEPA implementation but 'not as consistently or as well as they should or can'. It recommended that the EIS should be focused on the issues of chief concern and 'in a form that is clear in content and manageable in size', and called for better guidance from CEQ to help agencies draft programme level statements (CEQ,1976b).

Some 20 years later, CEQ (1997) carried out a review of NEPA effectiveness after 25 years of operation. Overall, the study found that NEPA is a success and has left an enduring legacy on government decision-making, particularly in relation to public participation. Five key elements identified as being critical to NEPA process effectiveness and efficiency were: strategic planning; public information and input; inter-agency coordination; interdisciplinary approach; and science-based, flexible environmental management by federal agencies (Box 11.7). Despite its successes, CEQ (1997) reported that NEPA implementation has not always met its goals and improvement is needed in a number of areas. These include producing extensive analysis and litigation-proof documents rather than focusing on specific ends, thereby increasing time and costs but not necessarily quality – concerns that find an echo in earlier performance reviews as exemplified previously.

Review of World Bank experience

The World Bank has carried out three reviews of EIA experience based on documentary sources and internal consultation. The third review of EIA experience at the World Bank (Green and Raphael, 2002) covers the fiscal years 1996 to 2000 and highlights the progress and innovations made since the completion of previous reviews (World Bank, 1993, 1996). Particular reference is made to EIA in relation to the Bank's new environmental strategy and its environmental and social safeguard policies. As one of ten safeguard components, EIA policy and procedure were strengthened in 1999 and a new compliance system was introduced to ensure that Bank activities met these requirements (Mercier, 2001). In this context, the establishment of a quality assurance compliance unit is presented as an important step forward. The

Box 11.7 CEQ Review of NEPA Effectiveness after 25 Years

Background: This review was undertaken for the 25th anniversary of NEPA to identify the factors critical to the success of NEPA process and practice and ways they could be streamlined and improved. It engaged 'the people who know NEPA best – who know what works and what does not'. These included some of the original framers of the Act and drafters of CEQ regulations, federal administrators and practitioners responsible for implementing NEPA, and representatives of the major constituencies. Other information was obtained through surveys of the public, business and academics.

Evaluative framework: The study sought to distinguish the strengths and weaknesses of NEPA, focusing particularly on identifying limitations to the effective and efficient implementation of the Act. Four criteria were used to identify priority areas:

- consensus among the majority of stakeholders that a problem was important
- potential for realistic solutions to the problem
- CEQ authority to address the problem
- potential for cost-effective improvement.

Main findings: The participants in the NEPA effectiveness study identified five elements that are critical to effective and efficient process implementation:

- strategic planning – the extent to which agencies integrate the NEPA framework into their decision-making at an early stage. Not yet fully realized
- public information and input – the extent to which agencies involve and take account of the views of those affected and interested in a proposal. Major innovation of NEPA but agencies should be more creative in their outreach
- inter-agency coordination – the extent to which agencies share information and integrate their responsibilities with other agencies in support of NEPA implementation. Helped to avoid duplication and improved environmental permitting but opportunities exist for further streamlining
- interdisciplinary approach – the extent to which agencies focus knowledge and values from a variety of sources on specific needs of decision-making. Good beginning but challenges remain, notably in assessing cumulative effects
- science-based, flexible management approach – the extent to which agencies modify mitigation and project implementation once proposals are approved. Increasingly successful, but monitoring and adaptive management are cited as the challenge for the future.

Source: CEQ, 1997

review includes specific evaluations of the effectiveness of EIA safeguard implementation in selected countries, and regions and sector.

Despite certain shortcomings, the third EIA review indicates definite progress by the Bank in compliance with safeguard policies, especially in the most recent assessments (Green and Raphael, 2002). Public consultation and disclosure of information, two areas that have received considerable attention in the past, were reported to have shown particular improvement. However, the review also found considerable variation among the assessments in quality of consultation. Other areas of concern include:

- inadequate assessments of projects with potentially serious impacts because they were wrongly classified at the screening stage
- insufficiencies in terms of reference and project legal documentation, which allow non-compliance
- failure to address the broader environmental and social impacts beyond the immediate project area.

Environmental supervision, including *monitoring of implementation* of environmental management plans (i.e. follow-up), also reportedly needs to be improved.

At the strategic level, the third EA review notes that sectoral environmental assessments are being carried out with increasing frequency, but regional environmental assessments still occur relatively infrequently (Green and Raphael, 2002). Both instruments must comply with safeguard requirements. So far, however, their scope of application has been relatively narrow, limited largely to investment programmes with a strong project component and not reaching the policy level (see also Kjorven and Lindhjem, 2002). Although not operating in accordance with safeguards, the use of other SEA-type instruments is increasing across a range of World Bank operations and activities. These include SEA of both sector and structural adjustment loans and the incorporation of SEA elements within new lending instruments, such as country assistance strategies and poverty reduction support credits.

Review of Canadian experience

Canada was among the first countries to follow the path laid down by NEPA. The federal environmental assessment and review process (EARP) was established by Cabinet Memorandum in 1973 and formalized by the 1984 Guidelines Order. Under increasing legal challenge, it was subject to major review beginning in 1987. A reform package, announced in 1990, had three cornerstones: EIA legislation to apply at the project level, a new SEA process to apply to policy, and programme proposals and a funding programme for public participation in panel reviews.

The *Canadian Environmental Assessment Act* came into force in 1995. Section 72(1) requires the Minister to conduct a comprehensive review of the provisions and operations of the Act after five years (Box 11.8). The review process was carried out with extensive public and stakeholder consultation.

Box 11.8 Five-year Review of the Canadian Environmental Assessment Act

Background: As mandated by the Act, the purpose of the review was to identify the issues arising from the first five years of experience in implementing the Act and to propose improvements. Based on extensive public input and completed at a cost of CAN$2 million, the scope of the review appears to have few precedents internationally.

Elements of review: Key features included:

- background papers and soundings over an 18 month period to identify problems with the Act
- preparation of discussion paper for public consultation outlining issues and options for improvement
- nationwide consultation (public meetings in 19 cities, 6 regional workshops, discussions with indigenous peoples and provincial governments, 200 written submissions)
- development of consensus recommendations by the multi-stakeholder Regulatory Advisory Committee (RAC)
- consultation 'in confidence' with provincial governments and certain stakeholders (a new departure for Canada) on the draft bill to amend the Act.

Lessons: The review process was considered to be successful by officials of the Canadian Environmental Assessment Agency. Key contributory factors cited include the preparatory ground work, extensive consultation on the paper and draft bill, use of the RAC to try and integrate views and forge a consensus, and limiting legislative only to what is necessary (Gershberg, 2001). However, the latter restriction also means that the implementation of some proposed changes, such as the introduction of regional assessment, remains open to discretion and circumstances. Time will tell.

Source: CEAA, 1999; Gershberg, 2001.

A discussion paper, prepared by the Canadian Environmental Assessment Agency (1999), identified three main challenges for EIA:

- making the process more predictable, consistent and timely
- improving the quality of assessments
- strengthening opportunities for public participation.

It also acknowledged specific deficiencies of *follow-up* programmes, including inconsistent design and application, inadequate compliance monitoring and a lack of regulations, standards and procedures for this purpose. Recently, amendments to the Act were introduced to address these issues including mandatory follow-up for larger projects to ensure that sound mitigation measures are in place.

SEA was introduced in 1990 as a non-statutory process for policy and programme initiatives of the federal government. This 'parallel' regime was the first of a 'new generation' of SEA systems to be established (Box 11.4). Now, more than a decade later, Canadian practice and experience with SEA is relatively extensive. During this period, reviews of the implementation of the federal process were conducted initially by the Canadian Environmental Assessment Agency (CEAA, 1996) and more recently by the Commissioner for Environment and Sustainable Development (CESD, 1998, 1999). All three reviews found overall performance was relatively poor and identified a number of shortcomings with SEA compliance and implementation by federal agencies (Box 11.9). Subsequently, SEA provisions and procedures were updated and new guidance issued to address these deficiencies, although progress towards better performance has been slower than was hoped (CEAA, 2003).

Box 11.9 Audit and Review of SEA Implementation within the Federal Government of Canada

Background: Established by Cabinet Directive in 1990, the process for assessing policy and programme proposals of federal government agencies applies to all environmentally significant submissions sent to Cabinet for approval (the highest level of decision-making). Several reviews of agency compliance and implementation have been conducted, including two by the Commissioner for Environment and Sustainable Development (CESD, 1998, 1999).

Audit process: The Commissioner, who is appointed to the Office of the Auditor General and reports directly to Parliament, audits the environmental performance of federal agencies on an annual basis. The 1998 audit focused on EA as a sustainability tool and addressed performance against the Act at the project level and against the Cabinet Directive at the policy and programme levels. The 1999 audit was directed at 'green' federal policies and programmes and highlighted, inter alia, continuing issues and concerns related to SEA.

Main findings and lessons: The audits found that government-wide SEA performance was poor and improved compliance by federal agencies was necessary, together with better understanding of the benefits of SEA in relation to decision-making for sustainable development. A clarification of the requirements of the 1990 Cabinet Directive and provision of better guidance on SEA practice were recommended. The Government subsequently introduced *The 1999 Cabinet Directive on the Environmental Assessment of Policy, Plan and Program Proposals* and *Guidelines for Implementing the Cabinet Directive* (CEAA, 2000). In sum, the audits resulted in a major reform of SEA arrangements although the real test lies in their implementation.

Source: CEAA, 2003.

Lessons from macro-evaluation of the effectiveness and performance of EIA and SEA systems and components

At the macro level, evaluation studies indicate the success of EIA and SEA, and reflect the context within which they operate. In that regard, some aspects of effectiveness and performance are specific to national experience and the interplay of particular EIA or SEA arrangements, methods, capacities and practices. However, certain factors of success can be abstracted that are common or apply widely across the EIA or SEA systems of different countries or jurisdictions. They include the enabling conditions and attributes of effectiveness and performance of EIA and SEA systems identified earlier and key elements of quality control and assurance that support process implementation at both a macro and micro level.

Operationally, lessons of effectiveness from macro level evaluation studies can help address what are termed 'perennial problems' or 'major shortcomings' of EIA and SEA implementation (Ortolano and Shepherd 1995; Sadler, 1996; Wood, 1999). They can be summarized in three interrelated categories:

- *Integrity of the EIA/SEA system*, which addresses the quality of the whole process, is based on prescribed legal and institutional arrangements and is dependent on their appropriate implementation (Sadler, 1997). Principles of EIA and SEA process design emphasize the relationship of the parts so that steps and activities are mutually reinforcing and effective in their overall application. The notion of integrity also encompasses *structural integration* of the EIA or SEA implementation with the process of decision-making (embedded in the larger policy or project cycle) and *operational integration* of technical analysis, public consultation and process management. Although widely recognized, these linkages remain insufficiently developed (e.g. as identified in the NEPA review).
- *Quality 'controls'* include requirements for compliance, guidance and due procedure, particularly at the stages of scoping, EIS or report review and follow-up, which comprise, respectively, early, pre-decision and final checks on operational effectiveness. In principle, the three steps determine the appropriate approach to assess a specific proposal, the adequacy of the information to be submitted to the decision-making authority, and the acceptability of the actions taken and measures implemented. In practice, they have been long acknowledged as weak links of the EIA process, and strengthening follow-up, in particular, is a major priority (e.g. as identified in the CEAA 5 year review). Guidance on SEA at these stages is being developed (Table 11.5).
- *Good practices* in carrying out the main steps and activities of EIA and SEA represent the ingredients of success for proposal-specific applications. Insights on the effective conduct of an EIA from screening to follow-up are summarized in Table 11.6. These also apply broadly to SEA of plans and programmes under EIA-derived arrangements and procedure (e.g. in accordance with European Directive 2001/41/EC). A more flexible,

Table 11.5 *Guidance on SEA Quality Control and Assurance*

Scoping: Identify the important issues/ impacts and alternatives to be examined	EIA scoping procedure can be adapted to purpose (e.g. establish the basis for an 'objectives-led' SEA by reference to environmental policy on aspects of concern). Modified EIA methods such as matrices, overlays and case comparisons can be used to scope the environmental dimensions of specific plans and programmes. Where environmental considerations are generalized and less immediate (e.g. immigration policy), appraisal methods can be used, such as environmental scanning, to clarify the implications and/or issue tracking to a stage when key impacts become clarified (e.g. immigration projections linked to housing demand, nationally or regionally)
Review of quality: Check the information is adequate for purposes of decision-making	SEA reports should be reviewed to ensure they contain the information necessary for decision-making prior to submission. Review procedures can be informal or formal; internal or external; and conducted by the competent authority, environment agency or an independent body. Provision for public comment on a SEA report, although not uniform, promotes transparency and robustness. As in EIA, review of quality takes place against terms of reference or other guidance issued for SEA preparation. But the scope of review can differ markedly with the type of proposal and policy context
Monitoring: Check to see that implementation is environmentally sound and in accordance with approvals	Monitoring the implementation of a policy, bill or plan can be a simple check to see if environmental objectives are being met or a systematic programme to measure its impact. Information tracking systems can be used to monitor issues and progress, and to focus and streamline any subsequent SEA or EIA process. Cumulative effects monitoring may be appropriate for plans and programmes that will initiate regional-scale change in environmental stock or critical natural assets. Methods and indicators for this purpose are not well developed

Source: Sadler, 2001a

Table 11.6 *Ingredients of Success in EIA – Good Practice Step by Step*

Screening	Start as early as possible; preplanning is an investment in success
Scoping	Identify priority issues and impacts to focus the EIA study
Terms of reference	Establish clear timelines and requirements for EIA
Public consultation	Match techniques of involvement to the scope of the issues and the capacities of affected parties
Impact analysis	Apply 'best practice' science, e.g. choice of methods should be consistent with the type and importance of impacts
Mitigation	Custom design measures to the problem; follow-up on the success of untried innovative techniques
Evaluation of significance	Draw judgements based on the likelihood, range and severity of residual impacts
Preparation of EIS	Write in plain language for decision-makers and other users to identify the main issues, predicted impacts and estimated consequences of a proposal and the alternative considered, and specify confidence limits in impact predictions
Review of quality of EIA report	Undertake as required, whether a quick final check (e.g. for a small scale assessment) or an independent, public or expert review (e.g. for major and controversial proposals)
Follow-up	Apply some or all of the following steps depending on the potential significance and uncertainty of estimated effects: • inspection/surveillance to check terms and conditions are implemented • effects monitoring to determine if impacts are as predicted • impact management to address unanticipated problems • evaluation of effectiveness of mitigation measures • performance review or post-project analysis of lessons of experience

Source: Sadler, 1996

minimum approach is followed at the level of SEA of policy and legislation, requiring some modification of the three quality controls described above (e.g. environmental scanning and tracking of assessed laws and policies at the scoping and follow-up stages, respectively).

Micro-evaluation of the success of EIA and SEA application

Strictly defined micro-evaluation focuses on the application of the EIA and SEA process to an individual proposal, usually as part of or linked to regulatory requirements for follow-up as described in previous chapters. These chapters describe, refer to or add to many of the follow-up studies and cases that have been conducted to date. Most of this work relates to EIA of projects and – to date – SEA follow-up has been limited, although it is identified above and in Chapter 10 as an area for further attention. This literature will be taken as read and not covered here, other than to note the evaluative components of follow-up and studies that illustrate dimensions of success of EIA and SEA at the micro level.

Evaluation as a formal component of EIA/SEA follow-up

As a formal procedure, effectiveness and performance review and post-project analysis or policy/plan analysis can be represented as a subset of EIA/SEA follow-up that is undertaken at or near the end of this process to learn from operational experience and improve future applications (Table 11.7). This approach will be appropriate when changes have been introduced to an EIA process or practice, or major proposals are complex and controversial, involve new technology or intrusion into frontier areas, or have impacts that are poorly understood (Sadler, 1990; Storey and Jones, 2003). Reviews of SEA effectiveness and performance have been undertaken as part of follow-up to particular applications by the responsible agency (Sadler, 2001c; Whitehead and Saul, 2001). Increasing attention is now given to tracking the evolution of policies or plans from initiation to finalization and implementation, recognizing the iterative role of SEA processes at this level.

Other EIA follow-up activities undertaken primarily for control purposes indicate elements of successful operation (Table 11.7). These activities also provide critical input for later effectiveness and performance review or post-project analysis. Monitoring and impact audit are particularly important for providing information on EIA outcomes and should be built into the EIA process from an early stage to establish an appropriate base-line (Davies and Sadler, 1990). When the need for such data is determined later, other approaches may be used including the 'impacts-backwards' approach described by Lee Wilson and Associates (1992). Depending on the purpose, effectiveness and performance review or post-project analysis may use inspection reports, project or planning documents and interviews or surveys of

Table 11.7 *EIA Follow-up Activities, Measures and Indications of Success*

Activity	Purpose	Characteristics and element of success indicated
Surveillance	To check the implementation of environmental terms and conditions of approval	Periodic site inspection to track progress and address outstanding issues with implementation of conditions; basic indication of EIA performance
Supervision	To ensure environmental terms and conditions are carried out as specified	Overseeing implementation in accordance with environmental management plan or mitigation schedule; basic and specific indications, respectively, of EIA performance and effectiveness
Monitoring	To measure the environmental impact(s) of project construction and operation	Repetitive measurement of environmental parameters (or, more generally, a process of systematic observation); key indication of overall EIA performance in meeting one of its main purposes (particularly when impact measured against base-line and control data)
Auditing	To verify the results of EIA activities and follow-up	Systematic examination to compare practice against standards and requirements, e.g. 'as monitored' versus 'as predicted' impacts or mitigation within acceptable thresholds; specific indication of technical aspects of EIA performance and effectiveness
Impact management	To take corrective action(s) when impacts are greater than forecast or mitigation measures do not work as expected	Response to contain or offset environmental damage as indicated by results of surveillance, supervision, monitoring or audit; key indication of overall EIA performance and satisfactory EIA follow-up
Effectiveness and performance review	To evaluate how well the EIA process worked and what it achieved	Analysis and interpretation of success of EIA implementation, either for the whole process or particular components, against defined measures and criteria with a view to improve future applications
Post-project analysis	To review EIA experience for particular types of projects	Comprehensive or 'spot' analysis of success of EIA implementation in relation to planning and design of major projects, e.g. dams, roads, energy generation and transmission

key participants in the EIA or SEA process. The latter, in particular, will be important to gain a full perspective on the success or otherwise of an EIA or SEA and the contributory factors (Box 11.1).

Towards a framework for integrating micro- and macro-evaluation into EIA/SEA follow-up studies

Evaluation has long been recognized as a key element of EIA follow-up, beginning early with a focus on the use of NEPA in federal decision-making in the US[5]. In the mid-1980s, a large body of work on Canadian and international experience with EIA follow-up was brought together comprising some 50 studies, synthesis reports, workshop conclusions and a research-and-development prospectus (Munro et al, 1986; Sadler, 1987; CEARC, 1988). The terms, concepts, methodologies and relationships, including evaluation of success, established in this phase are still current, although recently there has been much minor redefinition (which does not appear to have moved theory building on EIA follow-up very far ahead). More positively, increasing attention has been given to follow-up studies of a sample of 'typical' EIAs to test hypotheses regarding process effectiveness (Wende, 2001) and to what makes EIA follow-up itself successful, including the 'contextual' factors that influence good practice (Morrison-Saunders et al, 2003).

This focus, inter alia, reinforces the importance of effecting a closer relationship of macro- and micro-evaluation of the success of EIA. Ways and means of doing so include building on current evaluative-type approaches. For example, a thematic approach applied to a cross-section or discrete sample of EIA and SEA applications can have comparative value, particularly if it is based on extensive practical experience (Netherlands EIA Commission, 1996) or uses systematic evaluation criteria (Lawrence, 1997). Specific types of review packages are available for evaluation of the quality of EIA reports (Lee and Colley, 1990) and other documentation that is material to decision-making (Weston et al, 1997). The same approach has now been applied to SEA of plans and programmes (Bonde and Cherp, 2000). Used as a follow-up tool (as opposed to a pre-decision check), the quality of individual or aggregated EIA/SEA reports gives a primary (but not the only) indication of the value of the information for decision-making (Sadler, 1996).

Ultimately a more systematic or 'whole process' approach to EIA/SEA follow-up is required to fully unpack the dimensions of success, i.e. from the first step through approval and condition setting to implementation and environmental outcomes. Effectiveness and performance review should also be firmly related to macro-evaluation of the EIA/SEA regime under which the process is applied. A framework and review package for integrating the elements and ingredients of success is outlined in Appendix 1. It can be applied in full or in part to aggregate or project-specific EIA follow-up, used as an aide-memoire on field development, or customized to purpose in a particular context. With modifications, the framework may be applied to SEA of plans and programmes when the approach follows EIA-derived procedure and methodology.

Conclusion

The focus of this chapter has differed from that of other chapters. It is concerned with highlighting the 'dimensions of success' of EIA and SEA by reference to the levels of meta-, macro- and micro-evaluation. Cross-referencing of the results from these three scales of evaluation can help to transfer information to and from EIA and SEA follow-up, leading towards a number of benefits at all levels. For example, these benefits should include more robust policy-oriented interpretations of process effectiveness and performance that meet the 'so what?' test at the micro level and go beyond simply recycling the 'conventional wisdom' on EIA and SEA at the meta level.

At the meta level, EIA and SEA can be considered as successful policy tools and concepts when judged against tests of wide adoption, continued innovation and broadening scope of application. Both processes, to a lesser degree, also add value to decision-making and condition setting. To date, however, EIA and SEA fall short as cost-effective means of protecting environmental sources and sinks, although this also reflects the limitations of other policy and regulatory instruments. Increasing calls are being made for more integrated approaches on all levels, for example, horizontally by linking EIA and SEA with economic and social assessment and vertically by linking EIA follow-up with EMS of operating facilities. These steps are precursors of paradigmatic change leading respectively towards sustainability appraisal (all impacts of new proposals) and integrated environmental management (all sources of environmental impact).

Macro-evaluation of EIA/SEA systems traces the anatomy of success at the national level. The enabling conditions for effectiveness and successful performance may be summarized as follows:

- institutional arrangements that ensure the integrity of the EIA/SEA process and its implementation including application of quality controls at key stages (e.g. scoping, review of report quality and follow-up)
- operational capacity to carry out the main components of EIA/SEA process (e.g. conducting technical studies, consulting with affected and interested parties, preparing EIA report and other necessary documentation for decision-making)
- applying good practice for each step and activity of the EIA/SEA process from screening to follow-up (Box 11.1).

The provision that is made for follow-up in the EIA/SEA systems established by different countries or international agencies condition what can be achieved at the level of micro-evaluation of the success of individual proposals. At this level, the focus is on effectiveness and performance review and post-project analysis to distil the lessons of experience, recognizing that the control and learning functions of EIA/SEA follow-up are not clearly separable and the emphasis changes from one to the other over the course of implementation.

'End of term' evaluation focuses on outcomes and results of the EIA/SEA process or key steps (i.e. performance) and the elements and factors that contributed to success or shortfall (i.e. effectiveness). A comprehensive review, inter alia, would cover key steps and activities, institutional and methodological dimensions, and documentation and other inputs to decision-making. These aspects are incorporated within a broader framework for EIA/SEA follow-up and effectiveness and performance review at both the micro and macro level in Appendix 1; it packages many of the lessons and dimensions of success described in this chapter.

Notes

1   Other than the US, the earliest development of EIA was in Australia, Canada and New Zealand. Key legal and policy benchmarks comprise: in Canada, the Cabinet Directive on Environmental Assessment and Review Process (1973, amended 1977, 1987) replaced by *Canadian Environmental Assessment Act* 1992; in Australia, the *Environment Protection (Impact of Proposals) Act* 1974, replaced by *Environment Protection and Biodiversity Conservation Act* 1999; and in New Zealand, the *Cabinet Directive on Environmental Protection and Enhancement Procedures* 1974, still in force but largely superseded by the *Resource Management Act* 1991 (amended 1995).

2   A total of 35 countries signed the SEA Protocol to the UNECE (Espoo) Convention on EIA in a Transboundary Context at Kiev in May 2003. The protocol will enter into force only on ratification by the 16th country and is open to Parties from outside the region.

3   Data on the cost-effectiveness of EIA limited. Few agencies appear to keep a detailed record of the financial costs associated with the implementation of mitigation measures or the application of the EIA/SEA process as a whole. The costs of technical work, such as preparing studies and documentation, typically account for less than 1 per cent of total project costs according to the World Bank (1996). Although generally accepted as a rule of thumb, this does not appear to include the cost of implementation of mitigation measures. These appear to be regarded as a relatively low percentage of the total cost of project construction for projects such as hydro dams or power stations. Others might question the calculus and proponents and industry representatives may claim that a broader range of costs is associated with EIA or SEA compliance, including delays to proposals and excessive demands on a proponent's time and resources.

4   Even when approvals reflect the EIA-specified mitigation actions, the difference they make is often indirect or unclear because of changes to project implementation or incomplete knowledge of natural variability. By definition, successful mitigation is characterized by the avoidance or reduction of impacts and, as such, may not be measurable or may be identifiable only by circumstantial evidence. Often, this aspect is overlooked in EIA and SEA theory and practice and it has particular implications for follow-up activities.

5   An early review by the Council on Environmental Quality (1975) indicated that the EIS process had a 'significant influence on numerous projects', including design changes to the Trans-Alaska Pipeline, abandonment of two major radioactive waste disposal sites and the development of a long range programme for planning US forest lands. Other evaluative studies of the period to document the use of NEPA

analyses in planning and decision-making include Caldwell et al (1982). So-called 'utilization studies' of the role of technology assessment and social impact concepts in federal policy-making also began in the late 1970s (see Berg 1982), and this was a keynote theme of the First Annual IAIA Meeting in 1982.

References

Annandale, D (2001) 'Developing and evaluating environmental impact assessment systems for small developing countries', *Impact Assessment and Project Appraisal*, vol 19, pp187–193

Arts, J (1998) *EIA Follow-up – On the Role of Ex Post Evaluation in Environmental Impact Assessment*, Groningen, Geo Press

Berg, M (1982) 'Increasing the utility and utilization of assessment studies', *Impact Assessment Bulletin*, vol 1, pp41–51

Bonde, J and Cherp, A (2000) 'Quality review package for strategic environmental assessments of land-use plans', *Impact Assessment and Project Appraisal*, vol 18, pp99–110

Caldwell, L, Bartlett, D, Parker, D and Keys, D (1982) *A Study of Ways to Improve the Scientific Content and Methodology of Environmental Impact Analysis*, Advanced Studies in Science, Technology and Public Affairs, School of Public and Environmental Affairs, Bloomington, Indiana University

CEAA, Canadian Environmental Assessment Agency (1996) *Review of the Implementation of the Environmental Assessment Process for Policy and Program Proposals*, Ottawa, CEAA

CEAA, Canadian Environmental Assessment Agency (1999) *Review of the Canadian Environmental Assessment Act: A Discussion Paper for Public Consultation*, Ottawa, CEAA

CEAA, Canadian Environmental Assessment Agency (2000) *Guidelines for Implementing the Cabinet Directive*, Ottawa, CEAA

CEAA, Canadian Environmental Assessment Agency (2003) 'Strategic Environmental Assessment at the Federal Level in Canada', in Ministry of Housing, Spatial Planning and Environment (ed) *SEA Systems and Applications to Policy and Legislation*, The Hague, Ministry of Housing, Spatial Planning and Environment

CEARC, Canadian Environmental Assessment Research Council (1988) *Evaluating Environmental Impact Assessment: An Action Prospectus*, Ottawa, CEARC

CEC, Commission of the European Community (2003) *Report from the Commission to the European Parliament and the Council on the Application and Effectiveness of the EIA Directive*, Brussels, CEC

CEQ, Council on Environmental Quality (1975) *Environmental Quality*, The Sixth Annual Report of the (US) Council on Environmental Quality, Washington, DC, US Government Printing Office

CEQ, Council on Environmental Quality (1976a) *Environmental Quality*, The Seventh Annual Report of the (US) Council on Environmental Quality, Washington, DC, US Government Printing Office

CEQ, Council on Environmental Quality (1976b) *Environmental Impact Statements: An Analysis of Six Years' Experience by Seventy Federal Agencies*, Council on Environmental Quality, Washington, DC, US Government Printing Office

CEQ, Council of Environmental Quality (1977) *Environmental Quality*, The Eighth Annual Report of the (US) Council on Environmental Quality, Washington, DC, US Government Printing Office

CEQ, Council on Environmental Quality (1997) *The National Environmental Policy Act – A Study of its Effectiveness after Twenty-five Years*, Council on Environmental Quality, Washington, DC, US Government Printing Office

CESD, Commissioner for the Environment and Sustainable Development (1998) 'Environmental Assessment – A Critical Tool for Sustainable Development', in *1998 Report of the Commissioner for the Environment and Sustainable Development*, Ottawa, Government of Canada

CESD, Commissioner for the Environment and Sustainable Development (1999) 'Greening Policies and Programs – Supporting Sustainable Development Decisions', in *1999 Report of the Commissioner for Environment and Sustainable Development*, Ottawa, Government of Canada

Dalal-Clayton, B and Sadler, B (1998) 'Strategic Environmental Assessment: A Rapidly Evolving Approach', in Donnelly, A, Dalal-Clayton, B and Hughes, R (eds) *A Directory of Impact Assessment Guidelines*, International Institute for Environment and Development, Nottingham, Russell Press, pp31–42

Dalal-Clayton, B and Sadler, B (2003) *The Status and Potential of Strategic Environmental Assessment*, London, International Institute for Environment and Development

Davies, M and Sadler, B (1990) *Post Project Analysis and the Improvement of Guidelines for Environmental Monitoring and Audit*, Environment Protection Series EPS 6/FA/1, Ottawa, Beauregard Printers Ltd

Devuyst, D (1994) *Instruments for the Evaluation of Environmental Impact Assessment*, Brussels, Vrije Universiteit

Doyle, D and Sadler, B (1996) *Environmental Assessment in Canada: Frameworks, Procedures and Attributes of Effectiveness*, Ottawa, Canadian Environmental Assessment Agency

Emmelin, L (1998) 'Evaluating environmental impact assessment systems – part 1: Theoretical and methodological considerations', *Scandinavian Housing and Planning Research*, vol 15, pp129–148

Gershberg, S (2001) *Five Year Review of the Canadian Environmental Assessment Act*, presentation to intergovernmental forum, *Impact Assessment in the Urban Context, 21st Annual Meeting of the International Association for Impact Assessment*, 26 May–1 June 2001, Cartagena, Colombia

Gibson, R (1993) 'Environmental assessment design: Lessons from the Canadian experience', *The Environmental Professional*, vol 15, pp12–24

Goodland, R and Sadler, B (1996) 'The analysis of environmental sustainability: From concepts to application', *International Journal of Sustainable Development*, vol 3, pp2–21

Green, K and Raphael, A (2002) *Third Environmental Assessment Review* (FY 96-00) Environment Department, Washington DC, the World Bank

Hollick, M (1986) 'EIA: An international evaluation', *Environmental Management*, vol 10, pp157–178

IAIA, International Association for Impact Assessment (2002) *IAIA Survey of Impact Assessment Practice, Trends and Developments*, Fargo, ND, IAIA

IEA, Institute of Environmental Assessment (1997) *The Status and Practice of SEA*, Tokyo, report prepared in consultation with Japan Research Institute for Japan Environment Agency

IEA, Institute of Environmental Assessment (1999) *The Status and Practice of SEA*, unpublished report, Lincoln, UK, IEA [now Institute of Environmental Management and Assessment]

Kjorven, O and Lindhjem, H (2002) *Strategic Environmental Assessment in World Bank Operations: Experience to Date – Future Potential,* Environment Strategy Paper No. 4, Environment Department, Washington, DC, World Bank

Lawrence, D (1997) 'Quality and effectiveness of environmental impact assessments: Lessons and insights from ten assessments in Canada', *Project Appraisal* vol 12, pp219–232

Lee, N and Colley, R (1990) *Reviewing the Quality of Environmental Statements, Occasional Paper 24,* EIA Centre, Department of Planning and Landscape, Manchester, University of Manchester

Lee, N, Walsh, F and Reeder, G (1994) 'Assessing the performance of the EA process', *Project Appraisal,* vol 9, pp161–172

Lee, N and George, C (eds) (2001) *Environmental Assessment in Developing and Transitional Countries,* Chichester, John Wiley

Lee Wilson and Associates (1992) *Verification of NEPA Predictions on Environmental Assessments of Oklahoma Surface Coal Mines,* Dallas, Lee Wilson and Associates, report for US Environmental Protection Agency Region 6

Mercier, J R (2001) 'Environmental Assessment at the World Bank: New Developments and Strategic Directions,' in *Environmental Assessment Yearbook 2001,* Lincoln, UK, EIA Centre, University of Manchester and Institute of Environmental Management and Assessment, pp63–65

Morrison-Saunders, A, Baker, J and Arts, J (2003) 'Lessons from practice: Towards successful follow-up', *Impact Assessment and Project Appraisal,* vol 21, pp43–56

Munro, D, Bryant, T and Matte-Baker, A (1986) *Learning From Experience, A State-of-the-Art Review and Evaluation of Environmental Impact Assessment Audits,* Hull, Quebec, Canadian Environmental Assessment and Research Council (CEARC), Minister of Supply and Services

Netherlands Commission for Environmental Impact Assessment (1996) *Environmental Impact Assessment in The Netherlands: Experience and views presented by and to the Commission for EIA,* Utrecht

O'Riordan, T (1998) 'Interdisciplinarity in environmental science', *Environmental Assessment,* vol 6, pp28–29

Ortolano, L, Jenkins, B and Abracosa, R (1987) 'Speculations on when and why EIA is effective', *Environmental Impact Assessment Review,* vol 7, pp285–292

Ortolano, L and Shepherd, A (1995) 'Environmental Impact Assessment' in Vanclay, F and Bronstein, D A (eds) *Environmental and Social Impact Assessment,* Chichester, John Wiley, pp3–31

Petts, J (ed) (1999) *Handbook of Environmental Impact Assessment: Volume 1. Environmental Impact Assessment: Process, Methods and Potential,* Oxford, Blackwell Science

Porter, A and Fittipaldi, J (eds) (1998) *Environmental Methods Review: Retooling Impact Assessment for the New Century,* Fargo, ND, The Press Club

Sadler, B (ed) (1987) *Audit and Evaluation in Environmental Assessment and Management, Canadian and International Experience Volumes I and II. Commissioned Research,* Ottawa, Beauregard Press Ltd

Sadler, B (1988) 'Evaluation of Assessment: Post-EIS Research and Process Development' in Wathern, P (ed) *Environmental Impact Assessment, theory and practice,* London, Unwin Hyman, pp129–142

Sadler, B (1990) *An Evaluation of the Beaufort Sea Environmental Assessment Panel,* Ottawa, Federal Environmental Assessment Review Office

Sadler, B (1996) *International Study of the Effectiveness of Environmental Assessment, Final Report, Environmental Assessment in a Changing World: Evaluating Practice to Improve Performance*, Canadian Environmental Assessment Agency and the International Association for Impact Assessment, Minister of Supply and Services, Canada

Sadler, B (1997) EIA Process Strengthening – Perspectives and Priorities, in *EIA Process Strengthening Workshop*, Canberra, Environment Protection Agency

Sadler, B (1998) 'Ex Post Evaluation of the Effectiveness of Environmental Assessment' in Porter, A and Fittipaldi, J (eds) *Environmental Methods Review: Retooling Impact Assessment for the New Century*, Fargo, ND, International Association for Impact Assessment, pp30–40

Sadler, B (1999) 'A Framework for Environmental Sustainability Assessment and Assurance' in Petts J (ed), *Handbook of Environmental Impact Assessment: Volume 1. Environmental Impact Assessment: Process, Methods and Potential*, Oxford, Blackwell Science, pp12–32

Sadler, B (2001a) 'A Framework Approach to Strategic Environmental Assessment: Aims, Principles and Elements of Good Practice' in Dusik, J (ed) *Proceedings of the International Workshop on Public Participation and Health Aspects in Strategic Environmental Assessment*, Szentendre, Hungary, Regional Environment Center, pp11–24

Sadler, B (2001b) 'Strategic Environmental Assessment: An Aide Memoire to Drafting a SEA Protocol to the Espoo Convention' in Dusik, J (ed) *Proceedings of the International Workshop on Public Participation and Health Aspects in Strategic Environmental Assessment*, Szentendre, Hungary, Regional Environment Center, pp25–34

Sadler, B (2001c) 'Strategic Assessment and Planning in the UK – Thames Water Case Study', in *Environmental Assessment Yearbook 2001*, Lincoln, Institute of Environmental Management and Assessment and EIA Centre, University of Manchester, pp98–101

Sadler B (2002) 'From Environmental Assessment to Sustainability Appraisal', in *Environmental Assessment Yearbook 2002*, Lincoln, Institute of Environmental Management and Assessment and EIA Centre, University of Manchester, pp145–152

Sadler, B and Baxter, M (1998) 'Guide to environmental management', *Environmental Assessment*, vol 6, pp15–20

Sadler, B and Verheem, R (1996) *Strategic Environmental Assessment – Status, Challenges and Future Directions*, The Hague, Ministry of Housing, Spatial Planning and Environment

Sadler, B and Verheem, R (1997) *Country Status Reports on Environmental Impact Assessment*, Utrecht, Commission for Environmental Impact Assessment

Storey, K and Jones, P (2003) 'Social impact assessment, impact management and follow-up: Case study of the construction of the Hibernia offshore platform', *Impact Assessment and Project Appraisal*, vol 21, pp99–108

UNEP, United Nations Environment Programme (2001) *Reference Manual for the Integrated Assessment of Trade Related Policies*, Geneva, United Nations Environment Program

UNEP, United Nations Environment Programme (2002) *Global Environment Outlook 3 (GEO 3): Past, Present and Future Perspectives*, published in association with United Nations Environment Program, London, Earthscan

Wende, W (2001) 'Evaluation of the effectiveness and quality of environmental impact assessment in the Federal Republic of Germany', *Impact Assessment and Project Appraisal*, vol 19, pp93–100

Weston, J, Glasson, J, Therivel, R, Wilson, E and Frost, R (1997) 'Environmental statements, environmental information, environmental assessments and the UK planning process', *Project Appraisal* vol 12, pp233–242

Whitehead, L and Saul, D (2001) 'Strategic Environmental Assessment of the UK Strategic Defence Review', in *Environmental Assessment Yearbook 2001*, Lincoln, Institute of Environmental Management and Assessment and EIA Centre, University of Manchester, pp98–101

Wood, C (1995) *Environmental Impact Assessment – A Comparative Review*, 1st edition, Harlow, Longman Scientific and Technical

Wood C (1999) 'Comparative Evaluation of EIA Systems', in Petts J (ed) *Handbook of Environmental Impact Assessment: Volume 2 Environmental Impact Assessment in Practice: Impact and Limitations*, Oxford, Blackwell Science, pp10–34

Wood, C (2003) *Environmental Impact Assessment – A Comparative Review*, 2nd edition, Harlow, Pearson Education Ltd

World Commission on Dams (2000) *Dams and Development: A New Framework for Decision-Making*, London, Earthscan, Available: http://www.dams.org/report/ (19/9/03)

UNECE, United Nations Economic Commission for Europe (1990) *Post Project Analysis in Environmental Impact Assessment*, New York, United Nations

World Bank (1993) *Annual Review of Environmental Assessment 1992*, Washington, DC, Environment Department, World Bank

World Bank (1996) *The Impact of Environmental Assessment - A Review of World Bank Experience*, Environment Department Technical Paper No. 363, Washington, DC, World Bank

12

Lessons for EIA Follow-up

Jos Arts and Angus Morrison-Saunders

Introduction

Follow-up is one of the 'last frontiers' of the very successful instrument of Environmental Impact Assessment (EIA). By capturing follow-up, together with Strategic Environmental Assessment (SEA) and the inclusion of broader issues (e.g. health, social and economic considerations), EIA may become an important instrument for safeguarding sustainable development. Follow-up plays a vital role in a living and efficacious EIA. It fills the implementation gap by providing the missing link between plan and project preparation and subsequent operation. It thus ensures that EIA is not reduced to being just paper-based 'sweetheart statements'. EIA follow-up is the complement of pre-decision EIA. Both are necessary to deal adequately with uncertainty intrinsic to project planning and decision-making. Follow-up is a key mechanism for putting in place (adaptive) management measures to protect the environment and to enable learning from experience.

Although long identified in the literature as an area of importance, EIA follow-up remains a relatively new field with respect to practical application. This book has sought to capture the state of play in EIA follow-up theory and practice at the start of the 21st century, based largely on case studies from follow-up professionals around the world. The learning from experience evident from these case studies is drawn together in this chapter and presented in terms of the contextual factors that influence EIA follow-up. These factors should be taken into account when using the generic EIA follow-up framework (presented in Chapter 3) in specific situations. Subsequently, key guiding principles that underpin effective EIA follow-up are identified. It is hoped that these will assist practitioners in future development of the field. The chapter concludes with some reflections on future directions for the practice of EIA follow-up.

Best practice EIA follow-up

Like EIA itself, EIA follow-up will always have to be tailored to specific project circumstances; thus screening and scoping is essential. There is no single 'recipe' for success. What constitutes best practice EIA follow-up will vary according to the specific context in which EIA occurs. The contextual factors for EIA follow-up (Chapter 1) are addressed in turn with respect to the examples showcased in Chapters 4–10 and from the EIA literature. The discussion is based largely upon Morrison-Saunders et al (2003).

Regulations and institutional arrangements

The past decade has seen a slow but steady growth in development of formal regulations and institutional arrangements for EIA follow-up. Previous chapters have summarized institutional arrangements in The Netherlands, US, UK, Hong Kong, Western Australia and Canada, as well as the European Commission Directive on strategic proposals. Morrison-Saunders et al (2003) note that EIA follow-up legislation also exists in Portugal, Malaysia, Nigeria and elsewhere and that there appears to be an upsurge in legal requirements for EIA follow-up. The legislative approaches range from prescriptive command and control requirements (e.g. Hong Kong and to a lesser extent Canada) to more open interpretive arrangements (e.g. UK and Western Australia).

Having prescriptive EIA follow-up requirements clearly establishes the 'rules' for all stakeholders. However, these need to be combined with a scoping mechanism since not all impacts or projects will warrant follow-up. A prescriptive system applied in a blanket fashion could be costly in both financial and staff resource terms for proponents and regulators alike. Consequently, some EIA systems contain steps for follow-up screening and scoping. If these are not formalized, it can be undertaken in the EIS and consent decision-making stages.

While it is generally agreed in the literature that having EIA legislation in place is an essential precursor to effective practice (e.g. Sadler, 1996; Wood, 2003), a legal requirement for EIA follow-up is not sufficient on its own to guarantee that action actually occurs in practice, as examples from The Netherlands demonstrate (Chapter 4). Here, follow-up only occurred for some 60 projects of almost 400 EIA projects that had been implemented since compulsory EIA follow-up regulations were put in place. Other similar cases are also reported in Morrison-Saunders et al (2003). A clear commitment from regulators is needed for ensuring that regulations for follow-up translate into effective action in practice.

The regulatory framework extends beyond legislation alone to include voluntarism and industry self-regulation. Activities outside the formal EIA framework – such as permit and area-wide monitoring as well as industry-led initiatives such as environmental management systems (EMS) (Chapters 4 and 6) – may achieve similar follow-up outcomes. These activities may fill gaps in government regulation for follow-up.

The public play an important role here too in providing the motivation for industry to participate in self-regulation and other environmentally responsible initiatives. Public pressure also heightens the political priority of follow-up within government. An innovative example of proactive public participation in EIA follow-up is that of the Independent Environmental Monitoring Agency (Chapter 8) and a similar approach has been used in South Africa (Hulett and Diab, 2002). The public are important in a reactive capacity too, when unacceptable environmental impacts in the community precipitate corrective action by proponents and regulators (e.g. Ross et al, 2001).

Incentives and disincentives may be applied to encourage proponent involvement in EIA follow-up and bolster environmental performance such as a bonus–penalty system, the use of environmental performance bonds (refundable upon successful implementation of mitigation) or contractual agreements which establish binding responsibilities. The construction sector often adopts similar approaches (Chapter 9).

Irrespective of the driving force within a particular setting, it is important that an appropriate quality control mechanism is in place to ensure that all aspects of follow-up (monitoring, evaluation, management and communication) are undertaken to the best practicable standard. Quality control might be achieved: by checking compliance by the regulator; by an independent party (Chapters 8 and 9); by an accredited body operating under a formal system as ISO 14000; or by public pressure and accountability ensuring that follow-up programmes are carried out appropriately.

Various regulatory and institutional arrangements for EIA follow-up are summarized in Table 12.1. While having clear and strong legislation may not be sufficient to guarantee successful EIA follow-up outcomes, this is not to say that EIA regulations are not important. Apart from their legal role, they increase transparency and outline expectations for stakeholders as well as establishing structured and systematic procedures. However, the commitment of the regulators themselves, the proponent (self-regulation) and public pressure cannot be provided for in legislation, but these are also important drivers in achieving constructive outcomes (Figure 1.3). Some best practice suggestions appear in Box 12.1.

Approaches and techniques

EIA follow-up approaches and techniques can vary tremendously from formal scientific and technical approaches to relatively uncomplicated and pragmatic approaches utilizing simple monitoring techniques and existing processes. The key to appropriate technique selection lies in the scoping stage when an initial assessment of follow-up needs should be made bearing in mind regulatory requirements, follow-up objectives and resource capacity.

Recognizing resource constraints as well as political sensitivities, a pragmatic approach has been advocated in The Netherlands to take advantage of existing environmental regulations and monitoring systems that exist

Table 12.1 *Regulatory and Institutional Arrangements for EIA Follow-up*

Aspect of EIA follow-up	Regulatory setting		
	Command and control	**Self-regulation**	**Public pressure**
Who? *main driving force*	Regulator	Proponent	Community
How? *instruments*	Formal EIA regulations	Industry-based self-regulation instruments (e.g. EMS)	Public concern, media
What? *output*	Compliance with law, insight in environmental and EIA system performance	Third party accreditation, compliance with industry standards, management of the activity, green profile	Transparency and accountability of management of activity, information about project, enhancement of local environmental knowledge, public participation

Source: after Morrison-Saunders et al, 2003

independently of the EIA process (Chapter 4). In contrast, follow-up in Hong Kong revolves around permits and contracts specially designed for this purpose, along with the provision of independent verification bodies (Chapter 9). Examples from the UK (Chapter 6) and Western Australia (Chapter 7)

Box 12.1 Best Practice EIA Follow-up: Regulations and Institutional Arrangements

- Formal requirement for follow-up in the EIA system outlining stakeholder roles and responsibilities, performance standards and timing of events.
- Strong commitment by EIA regulators to undertake EIA follow-up.
- Harness industry self-regulation tools in a pragmatic way to achieve EIA follow-up goals where practicable.
- Encourage (reward) proponent voluntarism.
- Public pressure is an effective driver for both proponent- and regulator-led follow-up programmes.
- Improve quality control through establishment of external (independent) bodies responsible for reviewing follow-up programmes and results.

show how environmental management plans and other EMS-like mechanisms can be used as bridging tools between EIS proposals and post-decision project implementation. In such an adaptive approach to follow-up, the responsibility is explicitly laid with the proponent in accordance with the 'polluter pays' principle.

The use of rigorous scientific monitoring programmes can be useful to test impact predictions and determine environmental outcomes of cumulative developments on ecosystems, as the Colombia River Basin case in the US demonstrates (Chapter 5). Scientific monitoring is also used in the Canadian Ekati diamond mine project (Chapter 8), but equally effective use is made of traditional aboriginal knowledge. Such use of expert knowledge is consistent with rational scientific expectations of EIA, but may be less demanding on resources than classic ecological monitoring programmes.

Social impacts can often be detected by simple (but suitably rigorous) techniques such as the detection of odours by the human nose during site inspections (Morrison-Saunders et al, 2001). A risk here is that it may be reactive to actual impacts and based on responding to complaints. A proactive approach such as stack emission testing could detect a rise in concentration of emission components known to cause odour and alert managers prior to an offensive odour event. To advocates of EIA as a rational-scientific process, it is desirable that scientifically rigorous and defensible systems are put in place. Where this is not feasible (e.g. as a result of time, capacity or resource constraints), the use of simple but suitably rigorous approaches may suffice for an adequate (adaptive) management of environmental performance. Ultimately it is important that some system of follow-up is put in place for significant issues in order to enable them to be controlled or managed.

To avoid causality problems, EIA follow-up should focus on issues that are easily measured and can unambiguously be appraised against clear criteria (Chapter 4). Measurements early in the chain of causality (e.g. emissions or performance of protective facilities) may be combined with measurements of the changes in the state of the environment (e.g. area-wide monitoring or complaint registration) – a sort of *two-track monitoring strategy*. If important environmental changes are observed, this may warrant in-depth monitoring and evaluation of the specific issue(s) in order to determine whether the impacts are caused by the project at hand (i.e. a form of *ongoing scoping*).

EIA follow-up results can be benchmarked against EIS expectations, consent decision specifications and legal standards. As project planning and development takes place in a dynamic context, a flexible and adaptive follow-up approach is useful to allow for adequate action in response to issues arising from monitoring and evaluation. Early warning (performance) indicators and pre-determined contingency plans for accommodating unwanted environmental outcomes have been successfully employed in Western Australia (Chapter 7) and Hong Kong (Chapter 9) and can be linked to formal standards or criteria.

The diversity in approaches to EIA follow-up in different jurisdictions highlights different cultural approaches to EIA. For example, practice in Hong

Kong is based upon a strict command and control approach but maximizes proponent accountability through open Web-based reporting. The system in Western Australia is focused more on meeting environmental protection objectives, but with a similar expectation that proponents are responsible for the environmental management of their projects. This has promoted an adaptive approach. In contrast, the examples of UK industry (Chapter 6) highlight how the culture of an individual proponent can significantly influence EIA follow-up outcomes in a setting where legislative requirements are not so strictly enforced. The notion of having EIA follow-up championed by a body independent of both government and the proponent (Chapter 8) is entirely different again. There is no evidence to suggest that any of these approaches is any more effective than the others. What will work in a given setting will be dependent upon cultural norms and expectations operating in that particular jurisdiction (Morrison-Saunders et al, 2003). It is perhaps most useful to adopt an open-minded approach during EIA follow-up scoping (i.e. 'anything goes'), resulting in a creative mixed application of approaches and techniques.

A typology of EIA follow-up related to the effort needed

An important consideration when choosing EIA follow-up approaches and techniques is the effort required (e.g. for monitoring and evaluating a particular issue) compared with the functions and objectives of follow-up. For a practicable EIA follow-up, insight into the amount of effort is vital and two basic components emerge here:

- *content dimension* – the comprehensiveness of EIA follow-up in a specific case (e.g. does the EIA follow-up aim at providing a general overall picture or at providing detailed insight into selected issues?)
- *process dimension* – the extent to which the EIA follow-up is an autonomous action or how much it ties in with other evaluative actions, and consequently whether it requires more or less effort.

When these two dimensions are cross-tabulated, four categories of follow-up emerge (Table 12.2):

1 *'Stand-alone', overall EIA follow-up*: oriented at giving a comprehensive overview of the environmental performance of a project in which there are few links with existing monitoring and evaluative activities. Consequently, a relatively large effort may be needed.
2 *EIA follow-up of specific issues*: investigations that are carried out if there is special interest in particular issues or impacts (e.g. because of gaps in knowledge or identified uncertainties). This may require considerable effort, especially when there is need to investigate issues in a rigorous (scientific) manner.
3 *Complementary, integrated EIA follow-up*: the results of existing monitoring and evaluation activities are supplemented by some specific investigations

Table 12.2 *A Typology of EIA Follow-up Approaches Related to the Effort Needed*

		Content	
		Extensive/comprehensive	**Selective/specific**
Process	Autonomous/ separate action	1 Stand alone, overall follow-up	2 Follow-up of issues
	Supplementary/ linked-up action	3 Complementary, integrated follow-up	4 Quick scan of issues

Source: after Arts, 1998

to fill any gaps. This approach may provide an integrated picture of project performance with relatively little effort required.

4 '*Quick scan*' of the major issues: a few selected issues are quickly studied. This will usually require the least effort since it is closely linked with existing information and considers only selected issues.

These four types of EIA follow-up are not mutually exclusive. For example, a 'tiered' approach may be useful in which a quick scan (type 4) might be followed by a type-2 follow-up if the former reveals a need for in-depth monitoring and evaluation of a specific issue. The quick scan functions as an early warning device in looking for situations that require a widening of the scope of EIA follow-up (Chapter 2). It is also consistent with an adaptive approach to follow-up that is subject to ongoing scoping. Best practice suggestions are provided in Box 12.2.

Resources and capacity

The provision of adequate resources (finance and capacity) is essential to make EIA follow-up a reality (Arts et al, 2001). However, follow-up need not place an onerous burden on proponents and regulators, as examples using pragmatic approaches and utilizing existing feedback mechanisms independent of the EIA system have demonstrated (Chapter 4). Having limited resources does not preclude the implementation of effective follow-up but the sorts of activities pursued may be different for high- and low-resource capacity programmes (Table 12.3).

The resources required for follow-up will depend on the programme that is put in place and the administrative procedures that need to be addressed. For example, a sophisticated ecological monitoring programme such as that implemented in the Colombia River Basin (Chapter 5) will clearly cost considerably more in both financial and capacity resource terms than the community-based air quality monitoring programme reported by Ross et al

Box 12.2 Best Practice EIA Follow-up: Approaches and Techniques

- Conduct screening and scoping to identify significant projects and adverse environmental impacts requiring follow-up. Not all pre-decision EIA matters need to be investigated. To be cost-effective, follow-up should be 'objective-led' and screening and scoping should start early (preferably during EIS preparation). Ongoing scoping during the various stages of a project's life-cycle is valuable.
- Use existing data and monitoring activities for EIA follow-up where available both as information sources and for benchmarking performance.
- Sometimes issues may require rigorous scientific monitoring approaches; however, simple monitoring techniques (e.g. sensory inspections) may be all that is needed.
- A two-track strategy in which activity performance (e.g. emissions) and changes in the environment are measured may be necessary to get a grip on causality and cumulative and synergistic environmental impacts.
- Where many environmental issues are at stake, a mixed scanning approach of an initial quick scan (functioning as an early warning device) may assist the scoping process in determining which issues warrant in-depth study.
- EIA follow-up approaches need to be in accordance with the local 'EIA culture'.

(2001) for an industrial estate in Thailand. Here, the detection of volatile organic compounds, known to have been causing adverse health impacts in the vicinity of the estate previously, was undertaken by a small group of community representatives during site inspections simply by using their noses. Remedial action could then be undertaken by the industry proponents.

Although it seems inevitable that EIA follow-up will require some additional financial resources by proponents and regulators, there is also the potential to save money. By monitoring performance and enabling adaptive management to occur, follow-up enables adverse effects either to be avoided outright or to be addressed before a significant problem emerges. The benefits of industry-led audit programmes such as EMS in terms of cost savings arising from environmental improvements in an organization's operations have previously been well documented (e.g. Sullivan and Wyndham, 2001; Annandale et al, 2004). Several EIA follow-up case studies similarly reporting cost saving benefits are given in Morrison-Saunders et al (2003); however, no empirical studies have been undertaken to date which quantify the financial benefits of EIA follow-up.

Other resource considerations for the implementation of successful EIA follow-up include:

Table 12.3 *Consequences of Resources and Capacity Available for EIA Follow-up*

Aspect of EIA	Follow-up activities	
	Limited resources and capacity	**Adequate resources and capacity**
Comprehensiveness	Focus on specific issues, pragmatic approach using other existing feedback mechanisms	Custom made, comprehensive monitoring and audit programmes (yet still focused)
Number of parties	One/two parties only (e.g. self-assessment/audit)	Multi-party involvement (external scrutiny)
Finance	No specific budgets, no funding for public involvement	Specific budgets allocated, may fund e.g. public involvement
Methods, techniques	Inspections, early warning devices, low-frequency monitoring, utilize existing data sources	Rigorous scientific methods, long-term and high-frequency monitoring
Instruments	Permit monitoring and surveillance, volunteer community involvement	External inspection teams, independent committees
Reporting	Follow-up report (once, periodic)	Frequent reports (possibly continuous Internet-based monitoring and reporting)
Safeguard, accountability	Mainly regulator surveillance	Proponent surveillance, public accountability and certification by independent auditors in addition to regulator surveillance

Source: after Morrison-Saunders et al, 2003

- *technological capability* – the ability of equipment to detect environmental impacts at critical thresholds may be a limiting factor as a result of technological, resource or infrastructure limitations (e.g. not all countries could expect to implement the Web-based follow-up and communication system utilized in Hong Kong (Chapter 9) as the computer technology and supporting infrastructure may not be readily available to stakeholders)

- *practitioner expertise* – e.g. for designing and undertaking rigorous monitoring programmes that can accurately measure environmental change
- *community resources* – e.g. the use of the local knowledge and/or people in monitoring and other follow-up activities can only occur if the community have appropriate skills and knowledge.

In all cases, capacity building may be required to enable such expertise to be developed. Best practice suggestions are provided in Box 12.3.

Box 12.3 Best Practice EIA Follow-up: Resources and Capacity

- EIA regulators require staffing capacity and budgets to implement follow-up programmes (but relatively simple and pragmatic approaches can harness existing resources to achieve follow-up outcomes).
- Proponents must be committed to carrying out follow-up. Responsibilities can be incorporated into contractor agreements and employee job functions.
- Public involvement can be a resource in its own right. Local community knowledge and feedback on project implementation plays an important role in ongoing project decision-making and in ensuring follow-up success. The public will welcome becoming involved provided that they are genuinely consulted and know they have a say in outcomes of follow-up programmes.
- Having sufficient resources to communicate EIA follow-up findings to stakeholders is essential for success. Internet-based reporting (where available) may increase public participation and provide 'real time' feedback compared to traditional print-based media.
- Staff continuity in proponent and EIA regulator organizations from project planning through to operation improves learning from experience and avoids disruptions to follow-up activities which may adversely affect the utility of results.
- Education, training and capacity building support for follow-up is needed. Apart from enhancing expertise and skills it is important to develop 'institutional memory' and knowledge brokering (e.g. by universities and research institutes) from micro level EIA follow-up of individual projects through to macro level and meta level follow-up of EIA systems and generic concepts underlying EIA.

Project type

The project type will often be closely related to resources and capacity in terms of the types of EIA follow-up approaches adopted. For example, there may be room (and often also a need) for more sophisticated forms of EIA follow-up for projects with large capital investment. The case studies presented in Chapters 4–9 essentially fall into this category. It is especially noteworthy that the scale of the Hong Kong Airport Core Programme (Chapter 9) was such that it was instrumental in driving the development of the Hong Kong follow-up system in the first place. However, money and size is not a precursor for success. Case studies of effective follow-up for small projects and where limited amounts of money were invested are well documented (Arts et al, 2001; Morrison-Saunders et al, 2001, 2003).

Project type may be important in terms of the spatial extent of impacts and the timeframe in which a project operates (i.e. large projects operating over longer time frames may warrant additional follow-up attention). Furthermore, some activities will be more strategic than others. These will not only require different approaches to follow-up (Chapters 9 and 10) but may also lead to future decisions and projects that will also require follow-up attention. The focus of SEA follow-up is more on tracking subsequent decision-making (i.e. tiering) about locations and/or operational projects as well as the cumulative impacts and sustainability questions that transcend individual projects and less on detailed, specific environmental changes associated with project level follow-up.

The profile of the proponent organization may also affect the nature of EIA follow-up. For example, a government agency may be expected to behave differently to a private company, especially given that a government proponent would presumably be developing public resources. For private proponents, EIA follow-up undertaken by a large multinational corporation could generally be expected to be more sophisticated relative to a small company involved in a single-site operation, owing to their experience and staff and finance capacity.

The main differences between major and minor projects and proponents that may influence EIA follow-up practices are summarized in Table 12.4. It is important to realize that some small projects may cause significant environmental impacts that would require comprehensive and sophisticated follow-up approaches. Additionally, major companies often also operate small projects with only minor environmental issues that may not always warrant EIA follow-up.

For best practice EIA follow-up, it is important to take into account project type with respect to investment size, time frame, spatial extent and whether it is strategic or operational in nature (Box 12.4).

Parties/stakeholders

Ideally all three stakeholder groups (regulator, proponent and public) should be involved in EIA follow-up. This will be determined by the contextual factors operating for a particular project and the cultural context in which EIA occurs (e.g. not all EIA systems are equally transparent or engage the public). Each stakeholder group can play an important role in determining the nature and outcomes of EIA follow-up programmes as previous chapters demonstrate. In

Table 12.4 *Project Type Characteristics and Approaches to EIA Follow-up*

Aspect of EIA Follow-up	Project characteristics	
	Major Projects	**Minor Projects**
Amount of investment, time frame and spatial extent	Large investment, long-term, multiple projects over time in same area, larger areas, line infrastructure or networks	Small investment, short- to medium-term, once-only activity, smaller area, single site
Planning level	Strategic projects	Operational projects
Proponent	Large companies, multinationals, government	Often small, single operation companies (may also be large companies, multinationals or government)
Involvement of other parties	Government, public	Limited involvement of government (often local government)
Objectives	Controlling (checking compliance, contingency planning), learning for future application, informing	Controlling (mainly checking compliance)
Nature of follow-up	Elaborate, sophisticated, comprehensive, scientific studies	Simple check, straightforward methods

Source: after Morrison-Saunders et al, 2003

Box 12.4 Best Practice EIA Follow-up: Project Type

- During EIA follow-up screening and scoping, the project type should be considered such as:
  1. large/small capital investment
  2. long-term/short-term
  3. private/government development
  4. spatial extent
  5. strategic/operational nature.
- Controlling functions are relevant to all projects; informing and learning may also be useful for more complex projects.
- SEA follow-up will be different from project-related EIA follow-up (e.g. focus on subsequent tiers of decision-making and less directly on tracking detailed, specific environmental changes).

Hong Kong (Chapter 9), it is evident that follow-up has been mainly driven by the regulator, although public accountability plays an important role. The example of ScottishPower (Chapter 6) demonstrates how the proponent may take the lead in circumstances where the regulator does not require EIA follow-up. The role of the public in the Independent Environmental Monitoring Agency example in Canada (Chapter 8) ensures public accountability of both the proponent and government agencies responsible.

The relevance of the EIA follow-up objectives may vary for different stakeholders as they will bring different values to the EIA process (Chapter 4). For instance, controlling compliance of the project may be relevant for the EIA regulator, while the proponent wants to use follow-up for maintaining decision-making flexibility and enabling adaptive management. The community may stress the relevance of providing information about issues of public concern (e.g. health, safety and nuisance). Even though the various stakeholder groups may be seeking different outcomes from EIA follow-up, each can be a driver for the process in their own right (Figure 1.3). Suggestions for best practice stakeholder involvement in EIA follow-up are provided in Box 12.5.

Box 12.5 Best Practice EIA Follow-up: Involvement of Stakeholders

- Regulators should ensure that EIA follow-up is carried out in accordance with the regulations.
- Proponents should be made aware that EIA follow-up can be a useful project management instrument and may realize cost savings.
- At the very least, the public should be informed of outcomes, but direct public involvement in EIA follow-up programmes is desirable and beneficial for all stakeholders.
- Proponent, regulator and public stakeholder interests are often intertwined and their singular or combined interest (pressure) may initiate EIA follow-up programmes.
- Open screening and scoping for EIA follow-up may promote a well-balanced programme (preventing a distorted or too narrow scope), active stakeholder participation and improve utility of the results.
- Roles and responsibilities of all parties in follow-up should be specified in clear and accountable commitments.

Principles for effective EIA follow-up

From the lessons learnt from EIA follow-up case studies, common themes emerge from which core values as well as principles for effective follow-up can be derived. These are outlined here along with emerging needs for furthering EIA follow-up practice (see also Marshall et al, 2005).

Box 12.6 presents suggested core values that should underpin EIA follow-up. As might be expected, many of these are related to the basic principles of EIA (IAIA and IEA, 1999). Most issues affecting these core values have been discussed previously; others (e.g. scale of follow-up) are addressed later.

Box 12.6 Core Values for EIA Follow-up

Need for follow-up

- Follow-up is essential to determine EIA outcomes; it can and should occur in any EIA system to prevent EIA being just a pro-forma exercise.
- EIA follow-up addresses uncertainties and deficiencies which are intrinsic to planning and decision-making processes – thereby it rationalizes these processes.
- Follow-up bridges the implementation gap between pre-decision EIA and activity implementation.

Scale of follow-up

- Follow-up can be applied from the micro level (individual activities) to the macro level (EIA system) and meta levels (EIA concept).
- Follow-up can be applied to strategic policies, plans and programmes and to operational projects.
- Follow-up can be applied to singular or multiple projects/plans and undertaken at a local or regional scale.

Application of EIA follow-up

- Follow-up should be appropriate for the EIA culture and societal context in which it operates.
- EIA follow-up should dovetail with existing planning, decision-making and project management activities and utilize clearly defined steps to provide a structured process.
- To deal with cumulative impacts and sustainability issues above the individual project level, follow-up application at higher levels is needed (e.g. strategic level or area-oriented approaches).

EIA follow-up outcomes

- EIA follow-up should be efficacious, proactive, adaptive and action oriented.
- Follow-up should minimize adverse environmental effects and maximize positive outcomes.
- EIA follow-up should contribute to sustainable development.

Participation and transparency

- Transparency and openness are paramount: all stakeholders have a right to receive feedback on the EIA process and environmental outcomes of the project, and they should have opportunities for genuine involvement in follow-up processes.
- Credibility is essential: a clear and accountable commitment to undertake follow-up is needed and all parties must be committed to meet their responsibilities in full; follow-up should enhance participation and build trust between all stakeholders.
- It should be recognized that different stakeholders have different needs or expectations of follow-up as a function of their role in the process, their values and past experience with EIA and follow-up activities.

Communication and learning

- Good follow-up requires good communication.
- Follow-up should facilitate informed discussion among stakeholders.
- EIA follow-up should promote continuous learning from experience to improve future practice.

Note: 'EIA' is used generically here and also includes SEA applications.

Further to the best practice suggestions derived for each of the contextual factors previously mentioned, Box 12.7 identifies general principles that should guide EIA follow-up practice. These are grouped according to:

- the *content* of EIA follow-up – i.e. the focus and what is included in follow-up
- *procedural* considerations – i.e. steps to be undertaken during a follow-up programme
- *process*-related elements – i.e. the manner or ways in which a follow-up programme should be carried out.

The core values and principles in Boxes 12.6 and 12.7 provide a theoretical standpoint for EIA follow-up. To become reality they have to be implemented in practice whereby some needs arise (Figure 12.1; Chapter 2). There is a primary role here for EIA practitioners to develop the field, to learn from experience and to form networks that will help promote best practice follow-up and to embed the values and principles into regulations and EIA practice worldwide.

Box 12.7 Principles for EIA Follow-up Practice

Content of EIA follow-up

- Ensure EIA follow-up is objective led and goal oriented.
- Tailor EIA follow-up to the proposed activity; consider its stage as well as its (dynamic) context.
- Link up with existing monitoring and evaluation activities and stakeholder knowledge where possible.
- Identify realistic actions that can be implemented in a reasonable time frame on the basis of follow-up results.
- Keep EIA follow-up practicable and feasible – focus on the 'art of the possible'.

Process of EIA follow-up

- Start EIA follow-up early (prior to the consent decision) and sustain follow-up action over the entire life of the activity.
- Maintain a focused follow-up programme – engage in ongoing scoping.
- Adopt a multi-disciplinary and multiple-perspective approach to EIA follow-up.
- Make EIA follow-up cost-effective, efficient and pragmatic and reserve adequate budgets, time and capacity in advance.
- Carry EIA follow-up out in a well-structured and transparent process of clearly defined steps with stakeholder involvement and a clear division of roles, tasks and responsibilities.

Procedural steps for EIA follow-up

- Undertake screening and scoping to ensure that follow-up is conducted for relevant projects and that it focuses on significant issues; record results in a clear follow-up programme.
- Monitor rigorously and evaluate against accepted benchmarks (e.g. clear predictions, established standards or performance indicators).
- Evaluate results (e.g. monitoring data) in light of the follow-up objectives and link up with logical evaluative moments in the project life cycle.
- Manage projects and impacts in an adaptive and flexible manner in which decisions are made and appropriate action is taken in response to issues that emerge.
- Openly communicate the results, decisions and management outcomes of EIA follow-up to all stakeholders in the process.

Note: 'EIA' is used generically here and also includes SEA applications.

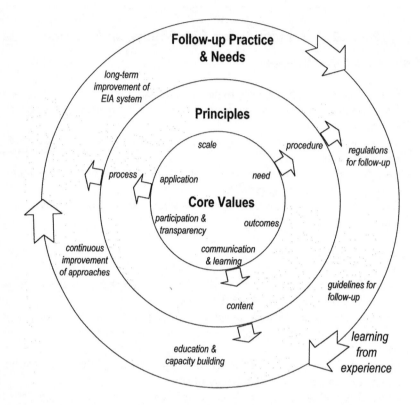

Figure 12.1 *Core Values, Principles, Practice and Needs for EIA Follow-up*

Some further *needs for improving and enhancing EIA follow-up* practice that such networks might address include:

- *Development of formal procedures for follow-up* in EIA regulations where either no system is in place or reliance is made on informal arrangements.
- *Development of guidelines* to promote EIA follow-up practice. Just as EIA guidance within a particular jurisdiction is generally tailor-made for the unique culture and context in which it occurs, there is equal need for specialized guidance on follow-up expectations, procedures and practice. These should offer practicable methods and techniques, process and organizational arrangements, provide best practice cases, and be developed for their regulatory and practical context.
- *Education and capacity building* for follow-up at a range of levels. This includes both generic practice internationally and practice within individual jurisdictions as well as strategic and project level follow-up applications
- An orientation towards *continuous improvement, openness to and development of new approaches and innovations*. It is hoped that best practice guidelines for EIA follow-up will emerge as a first step towards achieving this as the field matures

- Determination of more *structural, longer-term action for improving EIA practice and systems* on the basis of EIA follow-up. There is an important role here for increasing and enhanced feedback of micro level evaluations into macro level and meta level improvements in EIA practice.

In short, the key to advancement of EIA follow-up is to enhance learning from experience at all levels of application and practice. This is indicated in the outer circle of follow-up practice and needs in Figure 12.1. Just as follow-up is needed to ensure the efficacy of EIA, so too feedback from follow-up activities needs to be used for field development of EIA follow-up itself. Learning can be enhanced by establishing a network of practitioners for exchanging experiences and information about follow-up (Arts et al, 2001). The next section elaborates on the core values, principles and needs for EIA follow-up identified here to discuss future directions for improving follow-up practice.

Future directions for EIA follow-up

This book has showcased successful examples of EIA follow-up mainly at the project level. This is because the development of follow-up expertise has largely mimicked the development of EIA itself, with initial focus at the individual project level. However, EIA follow-up at the project level is not a panacea for everything and does not operate in isolation from other factors. Just as EIA practice has progressively broadened, the field of follow-up needs to similarly evolve. Project-oriented EIA follow-up has some spatial, time and organizational limitations which all pose challenges for the future development of follow-up.

Moving beyond project-oriented follow-up

One limitation of project-based EIA (and follow-up) is the narrow focus on single developments in isolation from other activities in the vicinity (both existing and in the future). Multiple projects and events in an area can have synergistic interactions and can contribute to cumulative environmental impacts. Moreover, this context is often highly dynamic over time and numerous parties may be involved in the process. With too restrictive a focus on individual projects, one may ignore these combined effects which clearly may have implications for sustainability assurance (Chapter 11).

Once a project has commenced, its impacts should preferably be considered from the perspective of the area as a whole, including all ongoing and planned activities as well as changing environmental values and priorities. The situation before and after the consent decision may be different. In most jurisdictions the pre-decision stages of EIA are often narrowly focused on the individual proposal of the initiating party and its immediate surrounds and this is the subject of consent conditions. For post-decision monitoring and evaluation, the scope of consent decisions for projects or plans may be less suitable in many cases as interest in environmental performance will often extend beyond individual project activities and boundaries. This gives rise to several potential problems including:

- determination of *causality* – where multiple projects are operating in close proximity it will be difficult to link environmental changes observed in follow-up programmes with a discrete activity
- determination of *liability* – as an extension of the causality issue, it may be difficult to determine who should be responsible for mitigating environmental impacts where multiple projects are involved (following the polluter pays principle)
- limited ability to account for *cumulative and synergistic effects*. It has always been a challenge for EIA adequately to address the cumulative impacts of multiple projects that affect a particular area and this applies equally to follow-up (Ross et al, 2001).

Solutions to these problems of the spatial, time and organizational limitations of project-related EIA follow-up include (e.g. Arts, 1998):

- area-oriented follow-up
- strategic level follow-up
- environmental management as 'follow-up of follow-up'
- sector-oriented follow-up
- multiple party follow-up
- sustainability assurance approach to follow-up.

As will become clear hereafter, these approaches (Figure 12.2) are more or less related to each other.

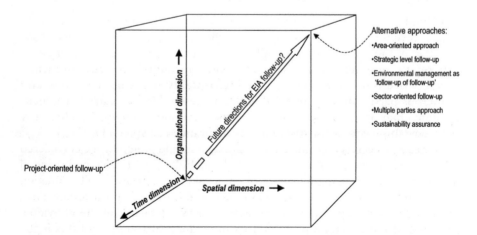

Figure 12.2 *Future Directions for EIA Follow-up: Relevance of Spatial, Time and Organizational Dimensions for Moving Beyond Project-oriented Follow-up*

Area-oriented follow-up

One way to overcome project-based follow-up limitations is to take an area-oriented approach involving focus at the regional scale and on multiple projects. Existing examples include Hong Kong's Environmental Project Office (Chapter 9) and state of the environment reporting. An area-oriented approach enables linkage to existing area-wide monitoring schemes and allows other developments to be taken into account; thus causality problems may be avoided. It enables the total impact of activities in an area to be monitored and evaluated, thereby addressing cumulative and synergistic effects that characterize many environmental problems. This paves the way for concerted action and more integrated measures on the regional scale such as formulating regional plans, local land-use plans or policies for regional environmental management. The approach relates to various environmental planning instruments (e.g. bubble concept, the carrying capacity concept, ambient quality standards, and tradeable emission rights; Arts, 1998). Region-wide approaches are usually better connected with the scale of ecosystems than intervention on the scale of individual activities. Consequently, area-oriented EIA follow-up offers potential added value relative to that of single projects.

Strategic level follow-up

SEA follow-up similarly lends itself towards area-oriented evaluations and other higher order evaluation. SEA provides ways to deal with cumulative impacts and sustainability questions that transcend individual projects (IAIA, 2002). Environmental considerations can be incorporated into planning and decision-making at an early stage to overcome fragmentation and the foreclosure of options and opportunities. Likewise SEA follow-up may provide ways to deal with:

- aggregate effects of decision-making on giving consent to individual projects as well as policies
- long-term and large-scale effects of strategic decisions at plan or policy level that set the objectives and conditions for decision-making for operational projects
- effects of this after-linked decision-making at the operational level to implement plans or policies that have been subject to SEA
- the dynamic and cyclic nature of planning and decision-making at the strategic level. By ending a planning cycle and starting a new round, strategic level follow-up may be considered less ex post and more ex ante in nature
- effects on the ecosystem as a whole.

The trend towards SEA has been underway for many years now and there is a need to extend follow-up capability in this direction (Chapter 10). SEA follow-up requires identification and management of multi-direction and multi-sectoral impacts that can be expected at the various decision-making tiers. It will involve long time frames, be less site specific, and conformance with the original plan (or policy or programme) will be of less relevance than for project follow-up. It will be more useful to focus SEA follow-up on uncertainties, adaptive actions in response to these, and performance of the plan in subsequent decision-making as well as on the environmental benchmarks and expected deliveries indicated in the original SEA (Arts, 1998). Additionally, state of the environment reporting will be useful to SEA follow-up for evaluating regional environmental pressures.

By carrying out follow-up on an area-wide basis and/or at a strategic level, the need to conduct EIA follow-up for individual projects may diminish. A system of *tiering* could be applied for moving from SEA to project level follow-up (Chapter 10). Where such 'higher order' evaluations are carried out, only limited EIA follow-up studies dealing with project-specific issues on a 'needs only' basis may be warranted (Table 12.2). This reiterates two key principles for EIA follow-up presented in Box 12.7; that the objectives of a follow-up programme be clearly defined and that screening and scoping be undertaken to establish the need for (and scale of) follow-up.

Area-oriented and SEA follow-up will not solve all problems that arise when relating the impacts of individual EIA projects to regional environmental management. Conflicts of interest may emerge when remedial measures are needed that affect individual proponents. Furthermore, as these approaches transcend the jurisdiction of individual proponents, they will likely become the responsibility of government. There is a resourcing issue at stake here as well as a philosophical one (e.g. extension of the polluter pays principle suggests that proponents should be responsible for EIA follow-up).

Environmental management as the follow-up of follow-up

The relevance of the original EIS and consent decision in project-oriented EIA follow-up diminishes over time and follow-up programmes tied to these may eventually become outdated. A combination of a changing physical and social context and emerging new knowledge, environmental management techniques and project modifications gradually invalidate pre-decision assumptions. Additionally, the tendency for projects and their management to become routine after a while may reduce the need for project-related EIA follow-up over time. EIA is triggered because of the likely risk of significant impact occurring from proposal implementation. Most of the process, including the consent decision and subsequent follow-up focuses on minimizing this risk. New developments naturally attract attention as impacts start to occur and are responded to by project managers. Hence the construction phase and early years of project operation usually command the greatest attention. However, the introduction of new operational patterns of work slowly become more static as the organization learns from experience and the activity settles down into organized patterns of behaviour (Chapter 6). At this point, it can be useful to blend the project-specific follow-up activities into the regular monitoring for maintenance and management activities of the proponent. Thus attention gradually moves away from evaluation relating to the original EIA consent decision and aspects described in EIS documents (e.g. impact predictions) onto organization-wide matters (e.g. EMS, meeting legal requirements or internal policy objectives etc.). In this way, EIA follow-up may become subsumed into broader environmental management practices.

Notwithstanding the potential finite nature of EIA follow-up and the tendency towards organized management behaviour, the dynamic nature of the environment demands that a flexible and adaptive approach to management is permitted. In Western Australian EIA practice, for example, consent decision conditions are tied to environmental objectives rather than fixed management strategies and there is an expectation that project management and associated follow-up programmes adapt with changing environmental parameters (Chapter 7). This again highlights the role of ongoing scoping in EIA follow-up. To some extent EIA, as well as EIA follow-up, might be considered as an exercise to clarify which environmental issues have to be dealt with during the environmental management of a proponent's activity. In a sense, by keeping follow-up programmes dynamic in this manner, even while blending them into broader proponent environmental management practices, a kind of 'follow-up of follow-up' will eventuate. Hence there will be ongoing evaluation of environmental performance, even if the EIA follow-up programme envisaged at the consent decision point is finite in practice.

Sector-oriented follow-up

With respect to the organizational dimension of follow-up, other avenues for improving future practice can be identified. Where multiple projects of the same type occur, a sector-oriented follow-up approach may be valuable (equivalent to the 'category-oriented' approach of Arts, 1998). There are already guides for undertaking EIA for particular sector types (Petts, 1999) and a similar approach to EIA follow-up could be undertaken. Projects of the same type or class could be subjected to a specific follow-up programme. This could be particularly beneficial when multiple small-scale projects occur near each other (e.g. a programme of projects), which would not on their own warrant individual follow-up. Sector-oriented follow-up offers efficiency savings as well as better learning opportunities which could guide future policy making for those sectors. To implement a sector-oriented follow-up programme will clearly require cooperation between multiple proponents and may require additional input from EIA regulators compared to traditional project-based approaches. Perhaps the example of the Environmental Project Office utilized in Hong Kong for multiple projects (but not necessarily of the same type) provides a useful role model of how such a system might be conducted in practice.

A variation on sectoral evaluation is the notion of *thematic follow-up* in which a number of specific themes relevant to the category as a whole may be targeted. This may promote learning for future projects and EIAs (e.g. better scoped EISs, cause–effect/intervention–impact relations, standardization of approaches, improving EIA efficiency for the sector etc.), as well as provide information for future policy-making and insight on the value of EIA for certain sectors. Consequently thematic and sectoral EIA follow-up may serve as input for the macro level analysis of EIA practice within a jurisdiction.

Multiple parties in follow-up

Project-oriented EIA follow-up will be limited from an organizational perspective if it is (mainly) confined to just one party. Most examples of EIA follow-up presented in this book have been principally driven by a single stakeholder in the process (i.e. proponent, regulator or public). This is a potentially limiting situation, especially given that project development and management operates in networks of parties with different stakes but each with some power to take or obstruct action (Chapter 2). Different stakeholders will have their own particular wants and needs as well as different expectations for a given follow-up programme (e.g. the public may have little interest in the performance of an individual project but be keenly interested in the cumulative performance of all industries in an area on health). Ideally all three stakeholders would have a full stake – i.e. of equal status and fully engaged to the extent of their role in the process – in the initiation and ongoing operation of a follow-up programme and in the resulting management actions.

A multiple parties approach to follow-up has various *advantages* not only in better addressing the general environmental interest but also for the different stakeholders themselves, including:

- adequately addressing issues specific to all stakeholders, thereby ensuring that follow-up is comprehensive and avoiding a too narrow or distorted scope and enhancing its responsiveness (feedback, early warning)
- using information from all stakeholders as well as skills and techniques available among them – a multiperspective and multidisciplinary approach to corroborate results – and thereby maximizing cost saving potential (for all stakeholders)
- 'enlightened self-interest' of a proponent which seems to be especially relevant if proponents have to deal frequently with the other parties because of (new) development proposals (Chapter 6)
- maximizing proponent accountability, transparency of governmental decision-making and public involvement to achieve a careful system of checks and balances during the whole process of decision-making and project development
- facilitating ongoing open communication and informed discussion among stakeholder networks about adaptive management actions that may affect (positively or negatively) the stakes of the various parties
- promoting learning from experience among all parties.

Notwithstanding these advantages, several *potential barriers* to operationalizing this ideal can be identified. First, the regulatory framework will largely determine the extent to which stakeholder groups can be involved (e.g. does the EIA system provide for public consultation or third party appeal rights?). Transparency of EIA procedures and availability of guidance materials for stakeholders are also important. Second, legally providing for a participative follow-up process does not guarantee that effective stakeholder involvement will eventuate (e.g. where there is lack of trust or cooperation between stakeholders, especially when they perceive that they have conflicting interests). As with EIA processes generally, there is a role for facilitation and mediation in follow-up activities. Finally, resource availability may limit the ability for participative and interactive follow-up processes. For proponents and regulators it may be costly (in both time and money terms) to fully open a follow-up system to the public (e.g. not all jurisdictions could hope to implement the Web-based continuous public involvement approach operating in Hong Kong). As follow-up may reveal that previous decisions and actions have to be revised, proponents and regulators may also view such an open follow-up process as threatening (e.g. opening up 'Pandora's Box', Chapter 2). For the public, involvement in follow-up is something that will usually occur in people's (often limited) spare time. Ideally, people would freely engage in the process in a proactive manner. However, after a consent decision has been made, the public may shift their attention to new project proposals still in the pre-decision stages. In reality many people may only get involved when (new) problems arise or when they are concerned about one specific issue, leading to reactive or 'knee-jerk response' involvement which will often manifest itself in a NIMBY response.

These barriers to stakeholder participation have to be satisfactorily addressed in future follow-up applications (see good practice examples given in Chapters 6, 8 and 9) in order to realize some of the core values and principles for EIA follow-up.

Follow-up for sustainability assurance

There is increasing interest in sustainability assessment, which represents a 'fourth generation' of impact assessment evolution for many jurisdictions (IAIA, 2002; Chapter 11), along with emerging trends such as the assessment of trade and funding-related activity initiatives. With its emphasis on outcomes, follow-up is essential for sustainability assurance.

Project-oriented follow-up poses some serious challenges with respect to sustainability assurance. First, application of sustainability approaches will increasingly require assessment and follow-up of social (e.g. well-being, health, poverty, quality of life etc.) and economic (e.g. employment, wealth, economic growth, efficiency etc.) issues, but so far most EIA follow-up activity has focused on environmental issues only. As with cumulative environmental effects, social and economic considerations may extend beyond the immediate responsibility of proponents and thereby require additional input from government. Nevertheless the core values and principles of EIA follow-up outlined in this chapter should not be affected by this broadening of the scope of follow-up activity.

Second, the demands of sustainability assessment are related to all *three dimensions of space, time and organization* distinguished in Figure 12.2:

- space – 'here versus there' (e.g. regional or area-oriented and strategic considerations)
- time – 'now versus then' (e.g. the concept of inter-generational equity requires consideration of the needs of future generations)

- organization, parties – 'us versus them' (e.g. the concept of intra-generational equity requires striking a balance between various individuals and groups within society).

Hence, for sustainable assurance purposes, a shift in EIA follow-up focus, range and undertakings is required.

The ability of project-oriented EIA follow-up to provide sustainability assurance is limited, in part, by the nature of the project or plan being evaluated. Since EIA follow-up cannot turn an environmentally unacceptable project into an acceptable one, sustainability assessment clearly needs to start before follow-up does. Even where an environmentally sound project has been designed and implemented, project-based follow-up programmes may only be able to provide sustainability assurance if consideration is given to the broader context in which a particular development occurs (i.e. area-oriented and strategic considerations discussed previously).

The bottom line for EIA follow-up is environmental protection. Follow-up success ultimately will be judged by looking backward to check whether sustainable outcomes were achieved. The nature of sustainability is that it is a moving target owing to the dynamic nature of the environment and society. It is not really possible to know whether sustainability has been attained at any one point in concrete terms. However, through evaluative mechanisms such as follow-up it is possible to be aware of past mistakes and areas for improvement. In the context of being a tool for sustainability assurance – while EIA follow-up itself seeks to be evaluative in a proactive and adaptive manner – ultimately it can only be judged as successful or not in hindsight. An important challenge is therefore to tie EIA follow-up (and sustainability assessment more generally) to clear sustainability performance indicators and criteria.

The meta level analysis in Chapter 11 indicates that EIA and SEA practice to date has fallen short of being an effective means of achieving environmental protection. Nevertheless, it is argued that they are useful tools, and without them, trends in resource depletion and environmental degradation would be far worse. To evaluate the attainment of sustainability objectives requires feedback at the various stages of the planning process. This can be facilitated by building in follow-up in EIA and SEA at both the macro and micro levels. The emerging and strengthening field of SEA follow-up also offers some future directions for field development in this area. More generally, the notion of ongoing learning (about performance) through follow-up can be seen as important for sustainable development. Feedback builds in an indispensable 'flexing' element as a complement to the 'hedging' strategy in the planning process (the limits to development posed by the sustainability concept, e.g. by application of the precautionary principle). This might be seen as the *process element* that follow-up provides after pre-decision impact assessment (i.e. *content* of EIS). Such process flexibility is needed in order to cope with the dynamic and uncertain nature of sustainability issues and our still limited understanding of this complex phenomenon. Follow-up above the micro level will play an important role in determining the extent to which sustainability goals have been reached. An important future challenge for EIA practitioners is to integrate follow-up at different levels to provide for sustainability assurance.

Integrating follow-up at different levels

In this book, the focus has been especially on micro level analysis of EIA follow-up (individual activities). In light of strategic and sustainability considerations, movement to macro level and meta level evaluation is needed.

At the *meta level* it can be concluded that EIA (and SEA) is a highly successful policy tool in light of its wide adoption of use, its continued innovation and improvement, and its broadening scope (Chapter 11). This success is especially true for the procedural dimension of EIA. However, the rate of success is less clear for the substantive dimension (e.g. added value to decision-making and condition setting) as well as the transitive dimension (e.g. cost-effectiveness and equity). To date EIA and SEA fall short as effective and efficient means of achieving their objectives – that is, to support informed decision-making and achieve their ultimate aim of environmental protection. They have this in common with other instruments used for this purpose. In future applications, there is need for better integration of (IAIA 2002):

- social, economic and environmental aspects (i.e. sustainability assurance)
- the various environmental management tools currently in employ (permit monitoring and enforcement, EMS, area-wide monitoring etc.)
- the various stages in the planning process (from the strategic to the implementation stages).

The picture at the meta level is corroborated by evaluations of EIA/SEA systems at the *macro level*. On the basis of collective learning from experience, some main ingredients for success in EIA (and SEA) can be distinguished. Important elements are system monitoring and evaluation at the macro level as well as micro level evaluations of individual activities (i.e. what has been termed 'EIA follow-up' throughout the book). Macro level evaluation should promote changes in EIA systems (e.g. regulations and practices) in order to adapt the instrument of EIA to new developments and needs in society.

At the *micro level*, the control and learning functions are not clearly separable in EIA follow-up. Moreover, the evaluations at all three levels are closely related. The meta-evaluation underlines the need for macro level and micro level evaluation. And the results of these evaluations provide useful information that can be used at the meta level.

No hard and fast line can be drawn for differentiating evaluation based on follow-up of individual projects and those based on more generalized studies at the macro level and meta level. There exists both 'single loop' and 'double loop' learning cycles between them (Chapter 2) in that:

- the evaluation at either the micro, macro or meta level may result in some form of adaptive action on that same level (single loop learning)
- the evaluation of project implementation and EIA practice at the micro level may lead to learning for EIA systems, while both micro level and macro level evaluations may lead to feedback relevant to our insights about the EIA concept and its efficacy (double loop or 'deep learning'); and the other way around
- evaluation at the meta level and macro level may lead to improvements at the lower levels of abstraction through 'feeding forward' of, for example, good principles that will guide future practice (Box 12.7).

Figure 12.3 depicts these learning cycles and the feedback and feed-forward relationships between the various levels. The final outcome of the three levels of follow-up is hopefully input to good principles of environmental management which contribute to meeting environmental sustainability goals (the ultimate aim of the EIA concept).

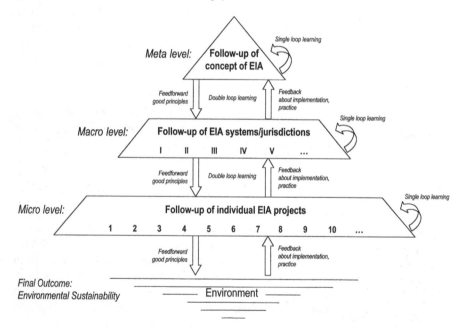

Figure 12.3 *EIA Follow-up at Different Levels and their Relationships*

Conclusions

After more than 30 years of EIA practice, emphasis is increasingly being placed on the outcomes of the process. There is a growing trend to include EIA follow-up procedures in regulations to ensure accountability for EIA decision-making and environmental performance. Consequently, there is increasing need for practical guidance on how to undertake EIA follow-up effectively and to showcase innovative and successful approaches. This book has attempted to do this. It is hoped that the case studies presented here, along with the theoretical framework for EIA follow-up, will help to stimulate a wider application of best practice follow-up and the principles of follow-up more generally.

It could be argued that the whole idea of the need for follow-up in EIA has an implicit negative message on first sight – namely, that EIA is somehow deficient or inadequate. However, distinction needs to be made between an EIS (which always will suffer from limitations intrinsic to project planning and decision-making) and the EIA process (that can and should include follow-up as a response to such deficiencies). By including follow-up, feedback loops are built in EIA, thereby strengthening it as an instrument for decision-making and adaptive environmental management. Follow-up is an essential element of EIA to demonstrate that the process works to achieve its objectives. It is about coping with uncertainties and learning by doing. Not only can it offer cost savings to proponents and regulators, but it provides accountability to all EIA stakeholders and the opportunity to make project developments and strategic initiatives more environmentally sustainable. In this way follow-up ensures that EIA (and/or SEA) practice delivers on its promised outcomes. It is both a driver of best practice environmental management as well as a provider of safeguards and checks on performance. Whether undertaken at the micro, macro or meta level, follow-up provides proof of the efficacy of EIA and SEA at achieving intended outcomes of environmental sustainability.

EIA follow-up, although being finite in itself (especially when project based), is part of an ongoing, cyclic process of planning and management. As an ex-post evaluation, it is essential to rationalize pre-decision EIA, but having an ex-ante element of proactive action is also crucial. Being the final stage of one project, it may also be the start of another. When monitoring and evaluating the impacts of a project through follow-up, new problems may be identified. This can lead to new studies, new solutions, new project development, new decision-making and again, new follow-up. Hence it is an ongoing process responding to a dynamic context in which EIA follow-up is itself followed up, or can be ended only with the words: to be continued...

References

Annandale, D, Morrison-Saunders, A and Bouma, G (2004) 'The impact of voluntary environmental protection instruments on company environmental performance', *Business Strategy and the Environment*, vol 13, pp1–12

Arts, J (1998) *EIA Follow-Up – On the Role of Ex Post Evaluation in Environmental Impact Assessment*, Groningen, Geo Press

Arts, J, Caldwell, P and Morrison-Saunders, A (2001) 'EIA follow-up: Good practice and future directions: Findings from a workshop at the IAIA 2000 Conference', *Impact Assessment and Project Appraisal*, vol 19, pp175–185

Hulett, J and Diab, R (2002) 'EIA follow-up in South-Africa: Current status and recommendations', *Journal of Environmental Assessment Policy and Management*, vol 4, pp297–309

IAIA and IEA, International Association for Impact Assessment and Institute of Environmental Assessment, UK (1999) 'Principles of Environmental Impact Assessment Best Practice,' available at: www.iaia.org/publications.htm

IAIA, International Association for Impact Assessment (2002) *The Linkages between Impact Assessment and the Sustainable Development Agenda, and Recommendations for Agenda*, Statements and Policy Briefing for the World Summit on Sustainable Developments in Johannesburg August 2002, Fargo, ND, IAIA International Headquarters

Marshall, R, Arts, J and Morrison-Saunders, A (2005) 'International principles for best practice EIA follow-up', *Impact Assessment and Project Appraisal*, vol 23, pp175–181

Morrison-Saunders, A, Arts, J, Baker, J and Caldwell, P (2001) 'Roles and stakes in environmental impact assessment follow-up', *Impact Assessment and Project Appraisal*, vol 19, pp289–296

Morrison-Saunders, A, Baker, J and Arts, J (2003) 'Lessons from practice: Towards successful follow-up', *Impact Assessment and Project Appraisal*, vol 21, pp43–56

Petts, J (ed) (1999) *Handbook of Environmental Impact Assessment, Volume 2. Environmental Impact Assessment in Practice: Impact and Limitations*, Oxford, Blackwell Science

Ross, W, Green, J and Croal, P (2001) 'Follow-up Studies in Cumulative Effects: Management Implications in Developing Nations', presented at *Impact Assessment in the Urban Context, 21st Annual Meeting of the International Association for Impact Assessment*, 26 May–1 June 2001, Cartagena, Colombia, published on CD ROM: *IA Follow-up Workshop*, Hull, Quebec, Environment Canada

Sadler, B (1996) *International Study of the Effectiveness of Environmental Assessment, Final Report, Environmental Assessment in a Changing World: Evaluating Practice to Improve Performance*, Canadian Environmental Assessment Agency and the International Association for Impact Assessment, Minister of Supply and Services, Canada

Sullivan, R and Wyndham, H (2001) *Effective Environmental Management: Principles and Case Studies*, Crows Nest, New South Wales, Australia, Allen and Unwin

Wood, C (2003) *Environmental Impact Assessment – A Comparative Review*, 2nd edition, Harlow, Pearson Education Ltd

Appendix 1

Framework for EIA follow-up and effectiveness and performance review

This package is a framework and checklist for EIA effectiveness and performance review. It is adapted from Sadler, 1996. Depending on requirements, this review package can be applied in full or in part or used as an aide memoire for field development or to develop a project-specific or system-wide (aggregated) approach to follow-up. It is organized into five parts:

- preliminary audit of the adequacy of institutional arrangements
- step-by-step review of EIA implementation and operational performance
- review of the technical, consultative and administrative components of the EIA process
- review of the contribution of the EIA process for decision-making
- review of overall EIA effectiveness and performance.

Each part incorporates an evaluation checklist that can be completed as a separate exercise or as part of a comprehensive review of EIA process implementation from start to finish or to compare the effectiveness and performance of one or more elements across a number of EIAs. Some questions may not be relevant and others may need to be added for an in-depth, on-the-ground review. In most cases, some adaptation to purpose and circumstances will be needed. While aimed at EIA practice, it could apply also to the evaluation of SEA of plans and programmes, particularly when the SEA process is derived from EIA procedure.

Part 1: Preliminary audit of institutional arrangements

This section is based in part on Wood (1995). The following rating scale may be used to answer the following questions in detail:

A excellent (comprehensive and sufficient)
B good (minor gaps and inadequacies)
C satisfactory (some gaps and inadequacies)

D   poor (significant gaps and inadequacies)
E   very poor (fundamental flaws and weaknesses)
F   no opinion (insufficient basis/experience on which to judge).

I Is the EIA process based on, or does it include:	**Yes/ No**	**Rating/ Comments**
(a) Clear legal provision with prescribed application?		
(i) Specifies type and scope of actions or decisions subject to EIA?		
(ii) Specifies powers and responsibilities of government agencies in implementation?		
(b) Explicit requirement to assess all environmentally significant proposals?		
(i) Projects only?		
(ii) Plans and programmes?		
(iii) Policy and legislation?		
(c) A defined environment and/or impacts to be taken into account?		
(i) Includes cumulative effects?		
(ii) Includes global or transboundary impacts		
(iii) Includes social, health, cultural or economic impacts?		
(d) Formal process and procedure in accordance with internationally accepted steps and activities (also e, f, h, j, k)?		
(i) Beginning with screening?		
(ii) Requirement for scoping?		
(ii) Consideration of alternatives to proposed action?		
(iv) Identification of potentially significant impact(s)?		
(v) Identification of mitigation measures?		
(e) Defined opportunities for public involvement?		
(i) At the scoping stage?		
(ii) Review and comment on EIA report?		
(iii) At other stages or throughout the process?		
(f) Requirement to prepare EIA report?		
(i) Based on specific terms of reference?		
(ii) Contents are described in law or guidance?		
(g) Guidance on application of process and procedure?		

(h)   *Requirement to review EIA report?*
(i)   *Externally by independent commission or panel?*
(ii)   Internally by inter-agency committee or equivalent
        body?

(i)   *Transparent linkage to decision-making?*
(i)   Approval based on submission of EIA report?
(ii)   Specification of terms and conditions of project
        implementation?

(j)   *Obligations placed on decision-makers?*
(i)   To take account of the information contained in EIA
        report?
(ii)   To consider the results of public consultation?
(iii)   To provide written reasons for decision?

(k)   *Requirement for monitoring and follow-up?*
(i)   All proposals subject to EIA?
(ii)   As and when considered necessary?

Part 2: Step-by-step review of EIA implementation and operational performance

The following rating scale may be used to answer the following questions in detail:

A   excellent (thoroughly and competently performed)
B   good (minor omissions and deficiencies)
C   satisfactory (some omissions and deficiencies)
D   poor (significant omissions and deficiencies)
E   very poor (fundamental flaws and weaknesses)
F   no opinion (insufficient basis/experience on which to judge).

2 *Were the following activities completed fully and successfully?*	*Yes/ No*	*Rating/ Comments*
(a) *Screening – proposal classified correctly as to level and requirement for assessment?*		
(b) *Scoping – process completed and resulted in closure on:*		
(i) Priority issues and relevant impacts identified?		
(ii) Key stakeholders to be involved?		
(iii) Alternatives to be considered?		
(iv) Terms of reference/study guidelines prepared?		

(c)   *Impact analysis – process completed in scope and depth necessary, including:*

(i)   Affected environment (base-line) conditions described?

(ii) Estimation and prediction of main impact categories, including:
- indirect and cumulative effects?
- other relevant factors?

(iii) Suitable database and methodologies used?

(d)   *Mitigation – appropriate measures identified (or environmental management plan completed) including:*

(i)   Follow-up and monitoring arrangements if strategies are untried or impacts uncertain?

(ii) Specification of contingency plans or non-standardized operating responses?

(e)   *Significance – residual effects evaluated as to potential severity, including:*

(i)   Scope, duration and irreversibility?

(ii) Relative importance to dependent communities or ecological functions?

(iii) Possible compensation or offset mechanisms (also 2d)?

(f)   *EIS/ EIA report – information included is consistent with the process followed and:*

(i)   Complete – informed decision can be made?

(ii) Suitable – right type of information included?

(iii) Understandable – easily apprehended by decision-maker?

(iv) Reliable – meets established professional and disciplinary standards?

(v)   Defensible – risks and impact are qualified as to proposal uncertainties?

(vi) Actionable – provides clear basis for choice and condition setting?

(g)   *Review of quality – undertaken to the degree and the level necessary including:*

(i)   Use of suitable methodology?

(ii) Subject to public review and expert comment?

(h)   *Follow-up – carried out appropriately:*

(i)   As provided for by a consent decision?

(ii) Consistent with the potential significance or degree of uncertainty of impacts predicted for the project?

(iii)   As warranted by the information from follow-up
        study (monitoring and evaluation) or activities
        undertaken during project implementation and
        environmental management?
(iv)   Results of the follow-up study were communicated
        to external parties?

Part 3: Review of EIA implementation and operational performance of major components

Note: this analysis may be completed for the process as a whole or included as part of a step-by-step examination of Part 2 previously and uses the same rating scale.

3 Were the following components undertaken fully and successfully?	Yes/ No	Rating/ Comments
(a) *Technical studies:*		
(i) Rigorously conducted, consistent with the nature and complexity of the issues?		
• at all stages?		
• at some stages?		
(ii) Work conformed to prevailing standards of good science and EIA practice?		
• at all stages?		
• at some stages?		
(iii) Resulted in the preparation of high calibre, defensible basis for assessment?		
• at all stages?		
• at some stages?		
(b) *Public involvement:*		
(i) Proponents and decision-makers were responsive to the people involved having regard to:		
• likely extent of environmental impact and social dislocation?		
• degree of public concern/conflict that was evident?		
• the traditions of the affected population?		
(ii) Approaches and techniques used were relevant to issues and constituencies involved?		
• in all cases?		
• in some cases?		

(iii)   Resulted in views and concerns of affected and
interested parties being clearly identified and
incorporated?
  * into all key documentation?
  * into final EIS report only?

(c)   *Process administration:*
(i)   Applied in accordance with established principles and
basis provisions?
  * at all stages?
  * at some stages?
(ii)   Process managed efficiently, i.e. without undue delay
or cost to proponents and others?
  * time lines and schedules negotiated up front?
  * completion in accordance with these?
(iii)   Oversight of activities was consistent and impartial?
  * fair to minority and other groups?
  * without bias to proponent etc.

Part 4: Evaluation of the contribution of EIA to decision-making

Note: the analysis in this section should be based on documentation such as
the EIA report, reasons for decision, terms and conditions of approval and/or
interviews with a cross-section of participants.

This is a key test of the effectiveness of the EIA process. It may be applied
using the following rating scale for the contribution to decision-making:

A   High influence
B   Moderate influence
C   Low influence
D   No influence

4 What was the contribution of EIA to decision-making?	Yes/ No	Rating/ Comments
(a) At the pre-approval stage – proposal was modified or changed for the better environmentally on the basis of the EIA process, e.g. by:		
(i) Alteration of the initial concept?		
(ii) Selection of alternative approach?		
* technological		
* locational		
* redesign		

(iii) Other pre-submission decisions by the proponent?
e.g. to
- provide offsets, such as setting aside natural areas?
- negotiate impact compensation package with affected communities?
- other?

(b) At the formal approval stage – information contained in the EIS/ EIA report was incorporated into approval and condition setting, e.g.:

(i) Reasons for decision?

(ii) Terms and conditions for project implementation and environmental management?

(iii) Requirements for EIA follow-up?
- supervision or surveillance of compliance?
- effects monitoring?
- impact audit?
- post-project analysis or other studies?

(c) At the implementation stage – terms and conditions, including follow-up requirements, were carried out?

(i) Fully?

(ii) Partly?

(iii) Inadequately or not at all?

(d) Reasons for non-compliance – if terms and conditions were not fully implemented, what were the reasons, e.g.:

(i) Unforeseen impacts and/or ineffectiveness of mitigation measures necessitated changes?

(ii) Other events and circumstances intervened?

(iii) Institutional or technical limitations?

(e) Reasons for non-contribution to decision-making – if the EIA process had a limited influence on approval and condition setting, what were the reasons, e.g.:

(i) Due to process or information deficiencies? (specify)

(ii) Due to intrusion of other factors and circumstances? (specify)

Note: What is the evidence for the interpretation:

(i) As described by the analysis completed in Parts 2 and 3?

(ii) Comparison of EIS report content with record of decision?

(iii) Interviews with participants?

Part 5: End of term review of overall EIA effectiveness and performance

Note: for many judgements in this section, reviewers will need to have information from Parts 2, 3 and 4 and, preferably, factual data from monitoring, auditing and other sources relevant to the actual results of the EIA process. Judgements about effectiveness and performance should be made with regard to the context and circumstances, for example, to reflect the degree of scientific or policy uncertainty.

5 Review of overall EIA effectiveness and performance	Yes/ No	Rating/ Comments
(a) *Impacts were as predicted or forecast?*		
(i) In most cases (>66%) with only minor inaccuracies?		
(ii) In the remaining cases without major problems or controversy?		
(iii) In all cases within legal or policy thresholds of environmental acceptability?		
(b) *Mitigation measures or management plans worked as intended?*		
(i) In most cases (>66%) with little or no variance?		
(ii) In the remaining cases without major problems or controversy?		
(iii) In all cases within legal or policy thresholds of environmental acceptability?		
(c) *Environmental objectives, criteria or standards were met by the project as implemented?*		
(i) In most cases (>66%) with little or no exception?		
(ii) In the remaining cases without major difficulties or controversy?		
(d) *The implementation of the project did not result in significant environmental damage (a) during construction or (b) in the initial start up or operation phase?*		
(i) In most cases (>66%) impacts were classified as minor or moderate?		
(ii) In the remaining cases major impacts were manageable or could be offset?		
(iii) In all cases the total or cumulative effect was justifiable in the circumstances?		

(e) *Other environmental and community benefits were realised as described?*
(i) In most cases (>66%) in full or with minor variances?
(ii) In the remaining cases without major problems or controversy?

(f) *The EIA process was within the usual 1 per cent cost range in relation to the overall capital investment in proposal development? (If not specify why)*

(g) *On balance, the EIA process was effective when judged against three basic yardsticks:*
(i) Substantive – terms of reference and basic objectives were achieved?
   • as documented by inputs to decision-making?
   • as demonstrated by environmental and community benefits (impact avoidance)?
(ii) Procedural – the process conformed to established or accepted principles, provisions and procedures?
   • as shown by appropriate institutional arrangements?
   • as evidenced by successful completion of main stages and components?
   • as indicated by terms and conditions being carried out?
(iii) Transactive – results and environmental gains were achieved cost-effectively, e.g.:
   • at least cost as shown by appropriate methodology?
   • at reasonable cost as estimated by informed judgement?

References

Sadler, B (1996) *International Study of the Effectiveness of Environmental Assessment, Final Report, Environmental Assessment in a Changing World: Evaluating Practice to Improve Performance*, Canadian Environmental Assessment Agency and the International Association for Impact Assessment, Minister of Supply and Services, Canada

Wood, C (1995) *Environmental Impact Assessment – A Comparative Review*, 1st edition, Harlow, Longman Scientific and Technical

Index